JOHN R]

STUDIES

IN THE

ARTHURIAN LEGEND

The Arthurian Legend

London

HENRY FROWDE

Oxford University Press Warehouse

Amen Corner, E.C.

STUDIES

IN THE

ARTHURIAN LEGEND

BY

JOHN RHŶS, M.A.

FELLOW OF JESUS COLLEGE
PROFESSOR OF CELTIC IN THE UNIVERSITY OF OXFORD

Ne sont que trois matieres a nul home entendant,
De France et de Bretaigne et de Rome la grant.

Oxford

AT THE CLARENDON PRESS

M DCCC XCI

𝕺𝖝𝖋𝖔𝖗𝖉

PRINTED AT THE CLARENDON PRESS

BY HORACE HART, PRINTER TO THE UNIVERSITY

PREFACE.

My chief object in the following pages is to make Welsh literature help to shed light on the Arthurian Legend; and that term is here construed loosely, so as to include other legends more or less closely associated with Arthur. Most of the following chapters arose out of my Hibbert Lectures on Celtic Heathendom, which were delivered in the year 1886. In consequence of that origin they take for granted the same views, in the main, as to Aryan mythology.

It is hoped, however, that the reader who disapproves of those views, will not regard me as now perpetrating a fresh offence, though I have been obliged to continue the use of some of the terms of the Solar Myth Theory. They are so convenient; and whatever may eventually happen to that theory, nothing has yet been found exactly to take its place. Nevertheless, we are possibly on the eve of a revolution in respect of mythological questions, as Mr. Frazer's *Golden Bough* seems to indicate.

The publication has been much delayed owing to the pressure of other work, but the delay has not been profitless, as I have had the advantage of reading for my last chapter two remarkable articles by Prof. Zimmer in this year's *Göttingische gelehrte Anzeigen.* Had they appeared sooner, several things in this volume would have been handled otherwise than they have been.

Finality is not, in any case, to be dreamed of in a field of research where so much remains to be learned. I shall feel, therefore, only too gratified if this book should be found to contain any contribution, however trifling, to the fund of knowledge already acquired concerning Arthur and his Knights, the Table Round and the Holy Grail.

J. RHŶS.

Oxford : *Dec.* 31, 1890.

CONTENTS.

—••—

CHAPTER I.

ARTHUR, HISTORICAL AND MYTHICAL.

THE system as a whole, of which Arthur forms the central figure, is later as we know it than any represented by the other cycles of Welsh sagas, such as those, for example, in which Gwydion appears, or Pwyll, or Pryderi. The comparative lateness of the Arthurian cycle, as contrasted with them, may readily be seen from the fact that they are contained in the Mabinogion, which is the case with no story concerning Arthur. This requires to be explained; for, since the publication of Lady Charlotte Guest's edition of the Mabinogion, the idea seems to prevail that any Welsh tale of respectable antiquity may be called a *mabinogi*, plural *mabinogion*; but there is no warrant for so extending the use of the word; and of the eleven stories contained in Lady Charlotte Guest's collection, only four are entitled to be called *mabinogion*. More strictly speaking, they are not *mabinogion* so much perhaps as the 'four branches of the *mabinogi*[1].' We allude to those entitled Pwyll Prince of Dyved, Branwen daughter of Llŷr, Manawydan son of Llŷr, and Math son of Mathonwy. What then is the meaning of the word *mabinogi*, and why was it applied to some of the Welsh tales and not to others? The word *mabinogi* is derived from *mabinog*, and that

[1] *The Text of the Mabinogion and other Welsh Tales from the Red Book of Hergest*, ed. by Rhŷs and Evans (Oxford, 1887).

was a term belonging to the bardic system, meaning
a sort of a literary apprentice or young man who was
receiving instruction from a qualified bard; and the
lowest description of *mabinog* was one who had not
acquired the art of making verse [1]. The inference to be
drawn is that *mabinogi* meant the collection of things
which formed the *mabinog's* literary training and stock
in trade, so to say [2]. He was probably allowed to relate the tales forming 'the four branches of the Mabinogi' at a fixed price established by law or custom.
If he wanted to rise in the hierarchy of letters, he must
acquire the poetic art; but he was usually a young man,
not a child in the nursery; and it is utterly wrong
to suppose the Mabinogion to be nursery tales, as any
one will admit who will take the trouble to read them.

The original machinery, so to say, of Welsh tales was
magic and the supernatural, in which respect the four
Mabinogion do not differ from the old stories of the
Irish. This was also probably the case with the stories
about Arthur, as they came from the mouths of
Brythonic Celts; but the Normans, having made their
conquests in South Wales, became familiar with them,
and handled them freely so as to adapt some of them to
their own tastes. The result was that in some cases the
second-hand versions would seem to have been brought
back to the Welsh, and to have in some instances modi-

---

[1] See the *Iolo MSS.* pp. 626-7; the original, pp. 211-2, has the older
spelling *mebinog* and *mebinogion.*

[2] This would be the technical meaning of the word *mabinogi,* the reference
being to the youthfulness of the narrators of the stories so called; but it
might be to the youthfulness of the hero of the story, as when one of the
Apocryphal gospels is called *Mabinogi Iesu Grist,* or the *Infantia Jesu Christi.*
Stephens, in his *Literature of the Kymry,* p. 417, gives the so-called History
of Taliessin the title Mabinogi. Lastly, the words here in question are
accented Mabínog, Mabinógi, and Mabinógion, all being pronounced with the
g of the English words *get* and *give.*

fied the originals or even replaced them. Take, for
example, the allusions in the story of Peredur to the
fortress of *Ysbidinongyl*. Now *Ysbidinongyl* is clearly
the Welsh reproduction of some form of the name of
a knight called Epynogrys by Malory, and by some of
the Grail romancers Espinogre; nor is it less certain
that the French forms themselves were derived from the
Welsh *Yspydaden Pencawr* [1], or *Yspydaden Gawr*—that
is to say, Yspydaden the Giant. Thus *Ysbidinongyl*
proves that the story was derived in the first instance
from a Brythonic source, at the same time that it also
proves it to have been brought into the Peredur, not
from Welsh, but from French [2]. The five Arthurian
stories still extant in Welsh, without counting Geoffrey's
quasi-history and the Welsh versions of the Quest of the
Holy Grail, fall into two groups : the first consists of the
story of Kulhwch and Olwen, and the Dream of Rhonabwy, neither of which seems to have been taken up
by the Normans ; so both have remained Welsh
stories with plenty of the supernatural and hardly anything of knight-errantry. The other group embraces
the stories of Owein and Lunet, of Peredur son of
Evrawc, and of Gereint and Enid, most of the materials of which are also to be found in some form or
other in the French and English versions of the Arthurian romances, or the stories relating to the Holy
Grail ; and the three Welsh stories bear unmistakable
marks of the influence of the non-Welsh versions.
Nay, it is quite possible that in the form in which we
have them, some portions of some of them may be

---

[1] See the author's Hibbert Lectures (for 1886) on Celtic Heathendom,
p. 487 : we shall refer to them as *Hib. Lec.*

[2] See the *R. B. Mab.* pp. 240, 242 ; Guest, i. 366, 369; Malory's *Morte
Darthur* (ed. by Sommer and publ. by Nutt, in 1889), vii. 26, x. 55, 65, 82,
xviii. 10, xix. 11 ; also Nutt's *Holy Grail*, p. 20.

merely free translations or adaptations by the Welsh of versions popular among their neighbours. For the re-action on the native stories does not appear to have been much hindered by the fact, which the proper names place beyond reasonable doubt, that the materials were purely Brythonic. It follows, that if one wished to make a comprehensive collection of the sagas about Arthur, one would have to take all the romances into account, since things even of mythological interest have been lost in Welsh, and are now only to be found in the Anglo-Norman versions and those based on them: in-stances will offer themselves as we go on. The four Mabinogion contain no allusion to Arthur and his Knights, which is a fact that makes for their earlier date, and is corroborated by the very loose way, compara-tively speaking, in which the Normanized Welsh tales have been put together. The men of letters of the Welsh formed a very exclusive and conservative class, so that this kind of literature remained to some extent the luxuriant growth of an imagination delighting in knight-errantry and other Norman ideas, both lay and ecclesiastical: literary Welshmen showed no hurry to train or prune it. But even the purely Welsh tales about Arthur are also relatively later than the Mabin-ogion, as may readily be seen by glancing at the Mabinogi of Branwen, where we learn that the head of Brân son of ꟷLŷr, the chief character in it, was by his command buried in the White Hill in London, with its face looking towards France; and, so long as it re-mained undisturbed, this island would have nothing to fear from foreign invasion [1]; but we learn from a triad, that in a subsequent age Arthur uncovered the head, as he thought it undignified to hold the island otherwise

---

[1] *R. B. Mab.* pp. 40, 42; Guest, iii. 124-5, 128.

than by valour: this was known afterwards as one of
the Three wicked Uncoverings [1]. Had we here to deal
with history one would expect to find that the Arthurian
stories did not treat the characters of the Mabinogion as
Arthur's contemporaries; but that of Kulhwch and
Olwen looks as if the story-teller had set himself the
task of swelling Arthur's train by introducing into it all
kinds of possible and impossible persons and personifi-
cations he could think of. Several of them are only
interesting as supplying us with the titles of sagas
which have been irretrievably lost. But the way in
which, generally speaking, the romance writers en-
deavour to form a court for Arthur, reminds one of the
collecting of Irish heroes round Conchobar mac Nessa,
and especially of the Norse literature of the Wicking
period organizing a great Valhalla for Woden by bringing the scattered Anses to live together. Such materials
were, however, in some instances very difficult to deal
with in such a way as to make them court ornaments.
The result in the case, for example, of Thor was, that he
was usually kept away killing giants when there were
festive proceedings going on around Woden, where his
presence would have been found somewhat awkward.
To judge from the list in the Kulhwch story, it must
have been much the same with Arthur's train. The
gentleman, for instance, whose only recorded acquire-
ment was the power of standing all day on one foot [2],
however interesting mythologically, was hardly calculated to grace a court; nor can the society of another
have been really delectable, who never smiled except
when his stomach was full, and of whom it is said that,

---

[1] Triads, i. 45, iii. 53, where the numerals refer to the three versions of
the Triads as published in the *Myvyrian Archaiology of Wales*, vol. ii.
pp. 1–22, 57–80.

[2] *R. B. Mab.* p. 110; Guest, ii. 209.

having once on a time acquired the right of demanding a boon of his king, he asked for a good meal : the catering for that meal proved one of the Three great Plagues of Cornwall[1]. Other equally queer or untractable members of the service might be mentioned, and the existence of the institution of the Round Table must have depended in no small degree on their being usually away on leave of absence. The desire to make a great court and a numerous following for Arthur probably coexisted with the tendency to develop the original myth about him into long-winded romances : we presume that both were late, comparatively speaking, and traces of the spread of Arthur's popularity are to be found even in the Triads, as, for example, in the one which has Arthur superadded, as a fourth person of celebrity, in sheer despite of the triadic limitation[2] : otherwise the Triads give us the oldest account of Arthur, and this now and then in a form which the story-tellers and the romance-writers found thoroughly untractable and best ignored. When, however, it is suggested that the full development of the Arthurian legend was the work of a comparatively late period, no such remark is meant to apply to the materials of it. They must have always been there from time immemorial, wherever there was a Celt who spoke a Brythonic language, whether in Great Britain or in the Lesser Britain on the other side of the Channel.

Thus far nothing has been suggested that could be said to bear essentially on the difficult question, whether there was a historical Arthur or not ; so a word or two

---

[1] *R. B. Mab.* p. 111 ; Guest, ii. 266.

[2] See *Hib. Lec.* p. 249; but the triads there mentioned, i. 50, ii. 7, and ii. 49, as compared with iii. 61, which has remained a triad, are not the only ones in point: witness ii. 24 as compared with i. 25 and iii. 31, where Lleu Llawgyffes would appear to have been omitted to make room for Arthur.

must now be devoted to it; and here one has to notice
in the first place that Welsh literature never calls Arthur
a *gwledig* or prince but emperor, and it may be inferred that his historical position, in case he had such a
position, was that of one filling, after the departure of
the Romans, the office which under them was that of
the *Comes Britanniæ* or Count of Britain.   The officer
so called had a roving commission to defend the Province wherever his presence might be called for.   The
other military captains here were the *Dux Britan-
niarum*, who had charge of the forces in the north and
especially on the Wall, and the *Comes Littoris Saxonici*,
who was entrusted with the defence of the south-eastern
coast of the island.   The successors of both these
captains seem to have been called in Welsh *gwledigs*
or princes [1].   So Arthur's suggested position as *Comes
Britanniæ* would be in a sense superior to theirs, which
harmonizes with his being called emperor and not
gwledig.   The Welsh have borrowed the Latin title
of *imperator* 'emperor' and made it into *amherawdyr*
later *amherawdwr*, so it is not impossible, that, when the
Roman *imperator* ceased to have anything more to say
to this country, the title was given to the highest officer
in the island, namely the *Comes Britanniæ*, and that in the
words *Yr Amherawdyr Arthur* 'the Emperor Arthur'
we have a remnant of our insular history.   If this view
be correct, it might be regarded as something more
than an accident that Arthur's position relatively to that
of the other Brythonic princes of his time is exactly
given by Nennius, or whoever it was that wrote the
Historia Brittonum ascribed to him: there Arthur is
represented fighting in company with the kings of the
Brythons in defence of their common country, he being

---

[1] See Rhŷs's *Celtic Britain*, pp. 135-8.

their leader in war[1]. If, as has sometimes been argued[2], the uncle of Maglocunus or Maelgwn, whom the latter is accused by Gildas of having slain and superseded, was no other than Arthur, it would supply one reason why that writer called Maelgwn *insularis draco*[3] 'the dragon or war-captain of the island,' and why the latter and his successors after him were called by the Welsh not *gwledigs* but kings, though their great ancestor Cuneda was only a *gwledig*. On the other hand the way in which Gildas alludes to the uncle of Maelgwn without even giving his name, would seem to suggest that in his estimation at least he was no more illustrious than his predecessors in the position which he held, whatever that may have been. How then did Arthur become famous above them, and how came he to be the subject of so much story and romance? The answer, in short, which one has to give to this hard question must be to the effect, that besides a historic Arthur there was a Brythonic divinity named Arthur, after whom the man may have been called, or with whose name his, in case it was of a different origin, may have become identical in sound owing to an accident of speech; for both explanations are possible, as we shall attempt to show later.

Leaving aside for a while the man Arthur, and assuming the existence of a god of that name, let us see what could be made of him. Mythologically speaking he would probably have to be regarded as a Culture Hero; for, a model king and the institutor of the Knighthood of the Round Table, he is represented as the leader of

---

[1] San-Marte's *Nennius et Gildas* (Berlin, 1844), p. 68 :—*Tunc Arthur pugnabat contra illos in illis diebus cum regibus Brittonum, sed ipse dux erat bellorum.*

[2] Prof. Sayce in the *Academy* for 1884, vol. xxvi. p. 139.

[3] Haddan and Stubbs, *Councils*, i. 52.

expeditions to the isles of Hades, and as one who stood
in somewhat the same kind of relation to Gwalchmei as
Gwydion did to Ꮮeu.   It is needless here to dwell on
the character usually given to Arthur as a ruler: he
with his knights around him may be compared to
Conchobar[1], in the midst of the Champions of Emain
Macha, or Woden among the Anses at Valhalla, while
Arthur's knights are called those of the Round Table,
around which they are described sitting ; and it would be
interesting to understand the signification of the term
Round Table.   On the whole it is the table, probably,
and not its roundness that is the fact to which to call
attention, as it possibly means that Arthur's court was the
first early court where those present sat at a table at all
in Britain.   No such a thing as a common table figures
at Conchobar's court or any other described in the old
legends of Ireland, and the same applies, we believe,
to those of the old Norsemen.   The attribution to
Arthur of the first use of a common table would fit in
well with the character of a Culture Hero which we have
ventured to ascribe to him, and it derives countenance from the pretended history of the Round Table ;
for the Arthurian legend traces it back to Arthur's
father, Uthr Bendragon[2], in whom we have under one
of his many names the king of Hades, the realm
whence all culture was fabled to have been derived.
In a wider sense the Round Table possibly signified
plenty or abundance, and might be compared with the
Table of the Ethiopians, at which Zeus and the other

---

[1] Contrary to the view advocated in the *Hib. Lec.* p. 136, the author
would now prefer to treat Conchobar as a Culture Hero.   The similarity
of attributes between the Culture Hero and the Celtic Zeus is probably to
be accounted for in part by the more or less complete assumption of the
rôle of the latter by the former.

[2] Sommer's Malory's *Morte Darthur*, iii. 1.

gods of Greek mythology used to feast from time to time.

Arthur's mythic visit to Hades had for one of its chief objects, as appears from the poem in which Taliessin [1] describes himself one of the party, the bringing away of the cauldron of the Head of Hades. The same story in a more detailed form served probably as the basis of one which occurs in the account of Kulhwch and Olwen. This represents Arthur and his men sailing, not on a voyage to Hades which had become unintelligible, but to Erinn, to obtain possession of the cauldron of a certain Diwrnach. This forms a sort of pendant to the Irish story of Cairbre's visits from Ireland to Hades, described as made to Britain [2]. Arthur and his warriors are represented killing Diwrnach and routing his men, whereupon they return to Dyved with the cauldron full of the money of Ireland [3]. In the hands of Geoffrey of Monmouth this myth became the quasi-history of a great invasion of Ireland by Arthur, resulting in the annexation of that country to his empire. The same was probably the nature of Arthur's march as far as the Caledonian Forest, when he made Arawn [4] king of Scotland. For the Welsh knew only one Arawn, and he was king of Hades, and for the matter of that the substitution of Scotland for Hades will not be deemed very surprising by any one who will call to mind the ancient idea of the region beyond the Wall as described by Procopius, to the effect that no man could live there for half an hour on account of the

---

[1] Skene's *Four Anc. Bks. of Wales*, ii. 181.   See also the *Hib. Lec.* p. 248.

[2] *Hib. Lec.* p. 246.

[3] *R. B. Mab.* pp. 135–6; Guest, ii. 307–8.

[4] This is from the Welsh versions published in the *Text of the Bruts from the Red Book of Hergest*, ed. by Rhŷs and Evans (Oxford, 1890), pp. 194, 208 : we shall refer to this as *R. B. Bruts* : the Latin text has instead of Arawn the name *Auguselus*, see San-Marte's ed. (Halle, 1854), ix. 9.

unwholesomeness of the air, and that it was infested with vipers and all kinds of noxious beasts[1]. But it is possible that Geoffrey confounded Ireland, the old home of the Scotti, with the north of Britain to which they carried their name, nor does it much matter so far as we are concerned. Similarly Arthur's conquest of Scandinavia was probably founded on a change in the meaning of the word Ꝉychlyn, which at first meant the fabulous land beneath the lakes or the waves of the sea, but got in the time of the Norsemen's ravages to mean the land of the Fiords or Norway, as did Lochlann in Irish. Arthur, be it noticed, when he conquered Ꝉychlyn, made Loth king of it. Loth, though he is also associated with Loudonesia or Lodoneis[2], whereby Lothian was meant, a district of which he may be regarded as the eponymus, his correct name being some form of that which is in Welsh Ꝉûḋ. A different account of the relations between Arthur and Loth is to be met with in some of the romances ; nor is it at all clear what authority Geoffrey had for making Arthur interfere on behalf of Loth. But, be that as it may, when he had thus represented Arthur in a manner conquering Scotland, Ireland, and Scandinavia, nothing could have been more natural for him than to extend his conquests east and south to the Alps or even to Rome, as some versions of the story do. It appears on the whole, then, that Arthur's subjugation of the west of Europe was directly or indirectly founded on the mythic invasion of Hades by him in the character of Culture Hero.

At the risk of seeming to make the proverbial step from the sublime to the ridiculous, we must here men-

---

[1] Procopius, *De Bello Gothico* (ed. Dindorf, Bonn, 1833), vol. ii. p. 566.

[2] *Geoffrey*, viii. 21 ; *R. B. Bruts*, p. 194. The Welsh versions of Geoffrey give Loth or Lot the name Ꝉew in the story of Arthur.

tion another phase of Arthur's contest with the powers below. The story need not be here repeated how Gwydion went to Pryderi and by fraud induced him to present him with some of the swine of the Head of Hades[1]. Strange to say one of the Triads[2] represents Arthur and his Knights trying by all means in their power to do the same with the swine of March son of Meirchion, the King Mark of the romances, and according to legends, both Brythonic and Irish, an unmistakable prince of darkness. March married the fair Essyĺt, and he had as his champion or general a famous knight called Drystan or Trystan. March's general, who was also his nephew, is called in the Triads one of the Three War-captains of Britain[3], and he was enamoured of Essyĺt. One day Drystan sent March's swineherd on a message—so goes the s ory—to that lady, to ask her to appoint a meeting with him ; and in the swineherd's absence Drystan himself undertook to watch March's swine. But just in that interval Arthur arrived to seek some of the swine, and one would have expected from the Gwydion parallel that he should succeed. The Triad, however, as it stands, states that by no means, fair or foul, could he obtain as much as one little porker from Drystan. But the Triad has attained its form by gradual expansion : the three swineherds were Pryderi son of Pwyĺĺ, Drystan son of Taĺĺwch, and Coĺĺ son of Coĺĺvrewi, and they are styled the Three Stout Swineherds of Britain, a description which some later writer glossed into a statement that they were so called because no one could by force or fraud get any of their swine ; and that is here applied to Pryderi as though the tale had never been told, which described how

---

[1] *Hib. Lec.* pp. 242-3.   [2] i. 30; ii. 56; iii. 101.
          [3] Triads, i. 24 ; ii. 36; iii. 32.

Gwydion successfully cheated him in the matter of his charge.   Possibly the myth about Arthur made him equally successful, but no story to that effect is extant ; and the Triad as we have it only serves to prove that there once was one, which described him trying to secure some of the swine of March without any scruple whatever as to the means employed, and gave Arthur the unscrupulous character in which Gwydion appears as a bard at Pryderi's court.

The third point to be noticed is Arthur's relation to a hero called Gwalchmei.   The latter was of the same class as Ꮮeu and Cúchulainn, and he had a brother called Gwalchaved, whose name has yielded the Grail romances the more famous name of Galahad.   Now Gwalchmei is usually represented as the son of Arthur's sister, who was married to the King Loth already alluded to, and his name, which in Geoffrey's Latin becomes Walganus, appears in French as Gauvain, English Gawayne : we have it also in the Scotch Gavin.   The Welsh form seems to analyse itself into *gwalch*, 'a hawk or falcon [1],' and *Mei*, 'the month of May:' so the whole would seem to have meant the hawk or falcon of May.   But the explanation is still to be sought why he should be so called, and all that one can say is that the reference to the month of May suits the Solar Hero well enough as the summer sun, if one may venture to treat him as such.   Now among Arthur's knights Gwalchmei enjoyed the reputation of

---

[1] Of course it may be that *gwalch* in this name is quite another word, but we have an ancient form exactly corresponding to it in point of phonology, in that of the various Gaulish tribes that called themselves *Volcæ*.   This national appellation is one of great interest, as that which in Teutonic mouths yielded such forms as *Walh* and *Wealh*, whence *Wales*, *Welsh* or *Welch*, and their congeners in the various Teutonic languages, as to which see the word *welsch* in the fourth edition of Kluge's *Etym. Wörterbuch der deutschen Sprache*.

being Arthur's favourite. His character, studied from the point of view of morals and intellect, will come under our notice later; so we shall at this point only mention two or three things concerning him as a warrior. He was an intrepid knight; he had the solar peculiarity, that when engaged in battle his strength grew apace till mid-day, when it would begin to wane as rapidly[1]; and his horse is likened to the gleam of the sun. Nor does Welsh romance mention his rider at any time vanquished out and out in combat till the day of his death. And Geoffrey assigns Gwalchmei an illustrious part in Arthur's wars on the Continent. Thus it was when the news reached the king that Gwalchmei's brother Medrawt, or Medrod—called in English Modred, or even Mordred—had in his absence taken possession of the queen and the crown, Gwalchmei hurried back with Arthur, and fell fighting on the strand, where Medrod vigorously resisted their landing. Gwalchmei, foremost in the conflict, was slain by his brother's own hand. And this is a myth which has many parallels, by means of which one is enabled to see its interpretation. The Solar Hero has not infrequently a brother by whose hand he falls, as in the case of the Irish Diarmait and the Norse Balder; and the conflict between Gwalchmei and Medrod is that between light and darkness. Medrod represents the latter; and in Geoffrey's quasi-historical strain his allies consist of Saxons, Picts, and Scots; so the mythic war becomes one of treachery against the Brython. But to continue the story. Arthur succeeded at length in landing, when

---

[1] Malory, xviii. 3, where he is described as 'a passyng hote knyght of nature,' and iv. 18, xx, 21, where the growth of his strength is represented going on 'from vnderne tyll hyhe none.' This peculiarity is also ascribed to a Red Knight, vii. 15, 17.

he routed Medrod and his forces, driving them further and further westwards, until a great engagement took place between them, known in Welsh as the Battle of Camlan, and in English as that of Camelot. The result was that Medrod was left dead on the field and Arthur was carried away mortally wounded.

That is Geoffrey's account; for, having lightly taken Arthur away to the Continent, he makes him land at a point on the south-east coast in Kent, and drive Medrod before him into the peninsula south of the Severn Sea. The substance of this story is also to be found in the Welsh Triads[1]; but as they lay no claim to much consistency they contain brief statements which go to form a different account of the disagreement between Arthur and Medrod: they do not all require Arthur's absence in the neighbourhood of the Alps nor lay any stress on Medrod's supposed treachery. The hostility between the two is traced to a blow given by Arthur to Medrod and another by a certain Gwenhwyvach, otherwise unknown, to Gwenhwyvar or Guinevere[2]. Among other things they speak also of two great raids made by Arthur and Medrod on one another's courts. The one occurred when Medrod went to Arthur's court at Kelli Wic in Cornwall, where he left neither food nor drink unconsumed, as much as would support a fly, and where he dragged the queen from her throne and outraged her. The other took place when Arthur went to Medrod's court doing likewise with the provisions he found there, and leaving alive neither man nor beast[3]. The final battle is represented as brought about by the treachery of one of

---

[1] Triads, i. 91; iii. 21, 100.

[2] Ib. i. 87; ii. 13; iii. 49; but i. 51 treats the second blow as dealt by Gwenhwyvar to Gwenhwyvach, which is probably the result of an error.

[3] Ib. i. 46; iii. 52.

Arthur's men called Iďawc Corď Prydein, who meets Medrod in Nanhwynain, now sometimes called Nant Gwynant, between Pen y Gwryd and Bêď Gelert in the neighbourhood of Snowdon. He betrayed Arthur's secrets to Medrod[1] and subsequently falsified Arthur's messages to him just before the battle of Camlan, when Arthur had appealed to him as his uncle. All this and more Iďawc is represented confessing, in the story called the Dream of Rhonabwy[2], to have done from the love of war, and he is there made to add that he escaped from the field of slaughter three nights before it was over to undergo a seven years' penance[3] and to obtain forgiveness of his sins. As regards the protracted conflict itself, it is ranked in one of the Triads[4] with Gwydion's battle of Goďeu as one of the Three frivolous Battles of Britain, a name countenanced by another triad which represents Arthur sharing his men with his antagonist Medrod three times during the fighting. This proceeding, the idea of which is borrowed from a tournament and not from war, is styled one of the Three criminal Resolutions taken in Britain[5]. Lastly, only three warriors escaped from Camlan alive, namely Morvran, whose hideousness made all flee before him, believing him to be a demon from Hell, Sanďe, whose good looks inspired the notion that he was an auxiliary angel from Heaven, so that no one had a wish to strike him, and Glewlwyd Gavaelvawr, whose strength and stature, as suggested by his name,

---

[1] Triads, iii. 20, 22.

[2] *R. B. Mab.* p. 47; Guest, ii. 398.

[3] The place he went to is called *y Ilech Las ym Prydein*, 'the Grey Stone (or the Blue Slate) in Pictland;' some place beyond the Forth was meant, but where?

[4] i. 47; iii. 50.

[5] i. 48; ii. 22; iii. 51.

that signified Brave-grey Great-grasp, were such that
no one could resist him [1].

It has been thought necessary to go into these details
as corrective of the historical colouring given to the battle
of Camlan by Geoffrey and those who have followed in
his footsteps. After the battle of Camlan Geoffrey makes
Arthur's power pass successively through the hands
of Constantine, Aurelius Conan, Vortiporius, and
Malgo, in whom one at once recognizes the Brythonic
princes contemporary with Gildas, who rated and rebuked them in this very order in his *Increpation of
the Kings of Britain* [2], with the exception that he
omitted Cuneglasus, of whom he could probably make
no more than modern historians can [3]. All that Geoffrey
seems to have thought needful was to place the kings
contemporary with Gildas in possession of Arthur's
power one after another. To return to his account of
the war with Medrod, even that has a touch of history
about it. The conquest of the Solar Hero by the powers
of darkness is just what one might expect, and the death
of Gwalchmei at the hands of his brother Medrod might
be regarded as the close of the incident; but when
the Culture Hero, the protector and guardian of the
Solar Hero, survives to conquer the representative of
darkness and is himself taken off the scene mortally
wounded, such is not the proper ending of the myth,
and the Solar Hero should have been brought back in
some form or other, as may be seen from the return of

---

[1] i. 85 ; iii. 83.

[2] The Latin title is *Increpatio in Reges Britannicos* : it forms a part of the
Epistola Gildæ, printed in Haddan and Stubbs' first volume of *Councils*, and
begins at p. 48 : see Geoffrey xi. 3–7.

[3] The author has ventured to surmise in his *Celtic Britain*, p. 123, that Cuneglasus was connected with Glamorgan, but the correctness of this view may
be questioned.

Lleu effected by Gwydion's wand. So here one seems
to detect the disturbing influence of a historical fact and
to be entitled to regard the death of the Culture Hero in
a mythic war with his nephew as suggested by the real
death of a man Arthur, at the hands of a real nephew
in some such person as that of Maelgwn as already
suggested (p. 8). This is to be taken for what it may
be worth as a possible explanation of the unmythlike
ending of the myth. The popular mind, however, pursued the myth to its normal conclusion without allowing
any difficulty originating in history to be placed in its
way. Arthur, according to the popular fancy, did not
die: he was merely borne away to the Isle of Avallach
or Avallon to be healed of his wounds; that done, he
was to return to reign again. The story slightly modified has lived down to modern times in places far apart:
sometimes it represents Arthur and his men dozing
away, surrounded by their treasures, in a cave in Snowdon, till the bell of destiny rings the hour for their
sallying forth to victory over the Saxon foe; sometimes
they allow themselves to be seen of a simple shepherd,
whiling away their time at chess in the cavities of Cad-
bury; and sometimes they are described lying beneath
the Eildon Hills buried in an enchanted sleep to be
broken at length by one

> 'That bids the charmèd sleep of ages fly,
>   Rolls the long sound through Eildon's caverns vast,
>   While each dark warrior rouses at the blast,
>   His horn, his falchion, grasps with mighty hand,
>   And peals proud Arthur's march from Fairyland[1].'

We have a trace of this sort of story even in the

---

[1] *The Poetical Works of John Leyden* (Edinburgh, 1875), p. 36. See
also Sir Walter Scott, Appendix to General Preface to Waverley, Edinburgh
edition, pp. 22–3, and Stuart Glennie's *Arthurian Localities* (Edinburgh,
1869), pp. 61, 62.

narrative of Geoffrey, who though he speaks of Arthur mortally wounded, could not help adding that he was carried away to the Isle of Avallon to be healed of his wounds. The same idea is also to be detected in the twelfth century manuscript called the Black Book of Carmarthen, where the poet after alluding to the graves of a considerable number of heroes, both historical and mythical, uses the following words when he comes to Arthur :—

> Bet ẏ march. bet ẏ guẏthur.
> bet ẏ gugaun cletẏfrut.
> anoeth bid bet ẏ arthur [1].

> *A grave for March, a grave for Gwythur,*
> *A grave for Gwgawn of the ruddy Sword,*
> *Not wise (the thought) a grave for Arthur.*

We may safely accept the dictum of the anonymous Welsh poet and now discard the story of Arthur's death, together with all that appertained to the historical man, in order to devote our attention to the greater Arthur.

It will doubtless have occurred to the reader that we have not shown how Arthur could have stood in the same relation to Gwalchmei as Gwydion to Ỻeu, as both Gwalchmei and Medrod are usually called the king's nephews, the sons of his sister and her husband Loth. The relative lateness of the story, in the form we have it, would be enough to account for its not placing Arthur in too close a relation to his nephews, just as it does not refer to his having besides his wife

---

[1] Evans's Autotype Facsimile of the *Black Book of Carmarthen* (Oxford, 1888), p. 34 a. The above triplet, together with poem xxx. in the *Book of Taliessin* (Skene, ii. 181, 2), supplies an answer to Stephens' statement in his *Lit. of the Kymry*, p. 416, respecting Arthur, that 'there is no trace of the hero in the early poetry of Wales,' and that 'the earlier bards make no distinction between Arthur and the other warriors of his day.'

no less than three mistresses[1]. In fact his character
and his history have most probably and naturally undergone repeated improvement at the hands of story-tellers
and poets, until they have attained a perfection of which
those most ardently devoted to his cult in old times
can have had no notion. The English laureate is the
last who has seriously contributed to the glorification
of Arthur, accompanied, however, with the blackening
of Gwenhwyvar's character as contrasted with that of
her husband: take, for example, the passage in the
course of which Arthur says to his distracted wife—

> 'For I was ever virgin save for thee;'

or the soliloquy full of remorse in which she is represented uttering the following words in reference to 'the
faultless king':—

> 'Ah great and gentle lord,
> Who wast, as is the conscience of a saint
> Among his warring senses, to thy knights—
> To whom my false voluptuous pride, that took
> Full easily all impressions from below,
> Would not look up, or half-despised the height
> To which I would not or I could not climb—
> I thought I could not breathe in that fine air,
> That pure severity of perfect light.'

But let us turn from the falsetto preachments of the
modern muse and the grave narrative of Geoffrey to
the more gossiping pages of Malory, and there we at
once recognize the distinctive feature of the Gwydion
myth: Chapter XIX opens as follows[2]:—

'Thenne after the departyng of kyng Ban and of kyng Bors
kynge Arthur rode vnto Carlyon/And thyder cam to hym kyng Lots
wyf of Orkeney in maner of a message/but she was sente thyder to
aspye the Courte of kynge Arthur/and she cam rychely bisene

---

[1] Triads, i. 59; ii. 16; iii. 109; i. 60; ii. 17; iii. 110.
[2] Sommer's *Malory*, vol. i. pp. 64, 5.

with her four sones/gawayn Gaherys/Agrauaynes/and Gareth
with many other knyghtes and ladyes/for she was a passynge fayr
lady/wherfore the kynge cast grete loue vnto her/and desyred to
lye by her/so they were agreed/and he begate vpon her Mordred/
and she was his syster on the moder syde Igrayne/So ther she
rested her a moneth and at the last departed/Thenne the kyng
dremed a merueillous dreme wherof he was sore adrad/But al
this tyme kyng Arthur knewe not that kyng Lots wyf was his
syster.'

The succeeding chapter represents Merlin disguised
as a child telling Arthur whose son the latter was, and
Arthur, ignorant of his own descent, contesting his
statement, until the magician cast off his disguise, when
Malory introduces the following dialogue [1] :—

' Yes said the old man/the child told yow trouthe/and more wold
he haue tolde yow and ye wolde haue suffred hym/But ye haue
done a thynge late that god is displeasyd with yow/for ye haue layne
by your syster/and on her ye haue goten a chyld/that shalle de-
stroye yow and all the knyghtes of your realme What are ye said
Arthur that telle me these tydynges/I am Merlyn/and I was he
in the childes lykenes/A sayd kyng Arthur ye are a merueillous
man/but I merueylle moche/of thy wordes that I mote dye in
bataille/Merueylle not said Merlyn/for it is gods wyll youre body
to be punysshed for your fowle dedes/but I may wel be sory said
Merlyn/for I shalle dye a shameful deth/to be put in the erthe
quyck/and ye shall dye a worshipful deth.'

Here [2] the crime is minimized by making Arthur
ignorant of the fact that the lady was his sister, and
by further representing her as his sister only on the
mother's side [3]. But the stories which ignore the
incest altogether usually treat Gwalchmei and Medrod
(Gawayne and Modred) as if full brothers, and it

---

[1] Sommer's *Malory*, vol. i. pp. 66, 7.

[2] See also the *Seynt Graal*, ed. by Furnivall for the Roxburghe Club (London, 1863), ii. 339, and the whole story in a MS. of *Merlin* and Lonelich's
translation, in the appendix to the same volume, pp. 393-6.

[3] The Welsh versions of Geoffrey make her Arthur's full sister : see
R. B. Bruts, pp. 180, 1.

may be supposed that one form of the original myth represented both the one and the other as the son of Arthur and the wife of King Loth. The process, in that case, of cleansing the Arthurian legend of this blot may be presumed to have been completed by degrees. The first step was to free the good and illustrious Gwalchmei from the suspicion of a shameful origin; it might attach longer to the traitorous Medrod, as in Malory's version. But the stain still remained on the father's character, so the crime was represented as committed in ignorance on his part: even this was at length found inconsistent with the ideas entertained of Arthur, so the two brothers came at length to be commonly regarded merely as his nephews by most of the romancers, including the Welsh ones. For this mythic scandal is one of those things which have completely dropped out of Welsh literature, and not even the Triads refer to it. It is inconceivable, however, that it should håve been invented by any one of the romance writers, and we are forced to regard it as from of old a part of the myth, even if the study of other myths had not prepared one to look out for it; and the importance of it as a proof of the parallelism between Arthur and Gwydion or Cairbre must be our apology for alluding to it at all. In all these cases the incest is probably to be explained as owing to the Culture Hero having been thrust forward into the position of an older personage, that is, of him who, as the Zeus of Greek mythology, marries his sister Here.

Geoffrey calls Loth's wife Anna, but she is probably to be identified with Arthur's sister, called Morgan le Fay in the romances, where *Morgan* is, doubtless, to be taken to stand for a Welsh *Morgen*, 'sea-born,' and identified in point of etymology with the Irish *Muirgen*, one of the names of the aquatic lady Liban[1]. In case we are right in reducing these two sisters to one, the feud between him and Morgan, never very intelligible in the romances[2], might be regarded as an obscure version of that between Gwydion and Arianrhod[3]; nay, the parallel might be extended to their sons, more especially to the contrast between Gwalchmei and Medrod, and that between ILeu and Dylan. This contrast is a feature of the myth, which has sometimes been obliterated. The romancers, failing clearly to seize it, have fallen into the error, as we think, of making Gwalchmei's character too like that of Medrod. This applies especially to the Tristram stories; and they were followed to a considerable extent by Malory: so Gwalchmei is made in them to play the part of a cunning and treacherous knight who led Arthur unsuspecting into the greatest misfortunes. It is possible that we have a trace of the converse error, to the advantage of Medrod, in one of the Triads[4], which makes the latter one of the three kingly knights of Arthur's court: they were so called, we are told, because of their being so meek, so gentle, and so fair of speech that no one ever found it easy to say them 'nay.' Lastly, the relation in which Merlin stands to Arthur may be said to be much the same as that of Mâth to Gwydion.

We have here ventured to treat Arthur as a Culture Hero; it is quite possible that this is mythologically wrong, and that he should in fact rather be treated, let us say, as a Celtic Zeus. In such a case the whole

---

[1] *Hib. Lec.* pp. 342, 460-3, 641.
[2] Malory, iv. 6-14.
[3] *Hib. Lec.* pp. 236-9.
[4] i. 83; iii. 118.

setting of the theory advocated in these pages would
require to be altered, and arguments might be found
for so altering it; but on the whole they seem to us to
carry less weight than those which favour the treatment
of the mythic Arthur as a Culture Hero.

CHAPTER II.

ARTHUR AND AIREM.

IRISH mythic history derives the Goidelic people of Ireland from two brothers called Emer and Airem or Erem respectively: they were the sons of Golam or Mil, whose name means a warrior or soldier, and the parallel between their story and that of Remus and Romulus, sons of Mars, deserves notice in passing. Now Emer, whose name was pronounced *Ever*[1], was the elder brother and the eponymus in all probability of the Ivernians or the non-Celtic inhabitants of the island. He was killed by his younger brother Airem[2], who is more commonly called Echaid Airem, and is to be regarded as the ancestor of the conquering Celts, who invaded the ancient race. His name Echaid Airem, which would be understood to mean Echaid (the) Ploughman or (the) Farmer, seems to bring him into close contact with agriculture, and to mark an important distinction between the Aryan invaders and the aborigines of the island; but the reader must not make too much of this evidence, which we shall have in some degree to qualify as we go on.

The monarch of Erinn was wont to hold a periodical feast at Tara, his capital, and this was reckoned an

---

[1] So it is written indifferently Emer or Eber, both *m* and *b* between vowels being softened into *v*: see also the *Hib. Lec.* pp. 526-7.

[2] See Fiacc's Hymn in Stokes's *Goidelica*, pp. 127, 131, where the genitive has the form *Erimon*, implying a nom. *Erem*.

institution[1]; so Echaid Airem in due time sent out invitations to the nobles of his realm to appear at the feast; but they replied with one accord that they would not attend, because he had no queen. The king therefore sent his messengers forth to search for a fitting woman to be his wife and queen, and as he was not easy to please they were away some time. At last they found one whom they thought suitable, at a place called *Inber Cichmuini*[2], on the east coast of Ulster. Her name was Etáin, and she was so lovely and so beautiful that she became the standard of comparison, so that 'fair as Etáin,' and 'as lovely as Etáin' became common sayings. The king hastened to fetch her to Tara as his queen; and when he asked her who she was, she described herself as the daughter of Étar, king of Echraidi in Faery, adding that she had refused all offers of marriage made to her in her own country, because of her love for him on account of his fame.

Some time afterwards a great king of the Fairies, called Mider of Bri Léith[3], found her out and introduced himself to her in the form of Airem's brother Ailell, who was in love with her. Mider met her three times and cured the king's brother of his embarrassing passion; but his wish was to induce Etáin to elope with him. She

---

[1] For the story of Echaid Airem see the fragments in the *Book of the Dun*, occupying folios 129ᵃ–130ᵇ, 131ᵇ, 132ᵃ; also 99ᵃ. Most of the former have been published in Windisch's *Irische Texte*, pp. 117–133, with another version from the British Museum MS. Egerton 1782; see also O'Curry's *Manners*, &c., ii. 192; iii. 190.

[2] O'Curry, in his *Manners*, iii. 188, calls it a bay: the name means the *inver*, mouth or confluence, of a water called after a Cichmuine, who was possibly a water goddess. Her name is hardly to be severed from that of Cigva, wife of Pryderi (*R. B. Mab.* p. 25; Guest, iii. 71), and a related masculine form occurs in a genitive written in Ogam *Ccicamini*.

[3] This is said by O'Curry, *Manners*, ii. 193, where the story is briefly given, to have been a fairy settlement in a hill to the west of Ardagh, in the present county of Longford.

replied that she would not forsake the king of Erinn for
one whose origin and history were unknown to her.
Then he reminded her that in a previous stage of existence when she was Etáin, daughter of another father than
Étar, he, Mider, was her husband; but as she did not seem
to understand this, she asked, if such was the fact, how it
was that they had been separated. He replied that it
was brought about by the jealousy of another woman and
the spells of a druid who aided her[1]. He repeated his
request that she should elope with him, and he explained
to her that it was he who had saved her from committing
the crime to which her brother-in-law was about to lead
her, but he could not prevail on her to go with him; so
he waited, according to one account, till Airem held a
great fair, and the queen came with the ladies of the
court to look at the races. Thither Mider also came
unobserved and carried away Etáin, together with her
handmaid, disappearing with them in a way which
nobody could comprehend. According to another
account Mider did not execute his purpose quite so
hurriedly, as he is represented asking Etáin whether she
would come away with him in case her husband gave
her permission, to which she replied in the affirmative.

His next step was to labour to get the king's word;
and in order to do so, he suddenly appeared one day
before Airem within the royal *ráth* of Tara. After
introducing himself, Mider asked the king to play chess
with him; but he would have been no nearer his object,
except by playing for stakes to be fixed by the winner
at the end of the game. This was right royally agreed
to, and Mider was beaten; the king named as the price
of his victory that Mider and his fairies should, besides
making a considerable payment, do four things for him,

---

[1] *Hib. Lec.* p. 145.

which were, to construct a causeway across *Móin Lám-raide* or Lámraid's Bog, to clear Meath of stones, to cover the district of Tethba with rushes, and that of Darbre*ch* with trees[1]. By observing the fairies at their laborious work of making the causeway, Airem learned to yoke his oxen at the neck and shoulder; for hitherto the men of Erinn had been in the habit of making their cattle draw by their heads and foreheads. This, we are told, was the reason why the king received the surname of *Airem*.

When Mider and his men had performed their tasks, the former suddenly presented himself before Airem, who was surprised no less by his unexpected appearance than by his wretched look: Mider complained to the king of his hard treatment by him, and induced him to play again. This time the king lost, and Mider said he could have beaten him long before, if he had chosen. Then came the question what Mider asked as the price of victory. Mider replied that all he wanted was to be allowed to put his arms round the queen in the middle of the court and to kiss her. Airem was amazed, and told him to come in a month's time, when his request would be granted him. When the appointed day came the king took care to have his court stoutly guarded within and without; and that evening he and the queen sat surrounded by the best champions of Erinn in the midst of the palace. But all of a sudden, about midnight, the king beholds Mider standing before him. He looked more comely that night than they had ever seen him before, and he said that he had come for what was due to him. The king excused himself, saying that he had not thought over it; but Mider was not

[1] See the *Bk. of the Dun*, 132ᵃ, but compare the *Bk. of Leinster*, 163ᵇ: in both instances we refer to the Royal Irish Academy's facsimiles.

to be put off. He said that Airem had in effect staked
his possession of the queen, whom he ought now to allow
to depart with him. The queen blushed to hear this,
whereupon Mider told her not to blush, since he had
been seeking her for a whole year with the best and
rarest of treasures, but had not taken her away till he
had Airem's leave. The queen admitted having told
Mider that she would not comply unless her husband
gave her away, and that, in case the latter made up
his mind to permit it, she would consent to go. The
king said that he would not give her away but
only allow Mider to put his arms round her in the
midst of the palace. So Mider, grasping his weapons
with his left hand, placed the other round the queen, and
hurried out with her before anybody could stir; so
when the host at length rushed to rescue the queen,
they could see naught save two swans making the circuit
of Tara. Mider took Etáin to a fairy habitation called
Sith Arfemun and the Mound of the Fair Women.
According to one account, Airem was for a whole year
unable to find whither Etáin had been taken; but at last
Dalán, his druid, took four rods of yew and wrote
ogams on them; so that by means of his ogams and
his keys of seership he discovered that Etáin was with
Mider in the fairy abode of Bri Léith. Then the king at
the head of the men of Erinn went there, and dug into
the fairy mound with such determination that Mider
was obliged to surrender Etáin.

The story of Etáin's previous existence is very fragmentary, but we find her first in the possession of
Mider, king of the fairies and the other world. From
him she was separated by a rival of hers, and we find
her next in the Mac Óc's glass bower as the consort of
that divinity, from whom she was severed by the wiles

of the same rival. She was now blown, in the form of
a fly, hither and thither over Erinn for the space of
seven years in great misery and wretchedness, until at
length she alighted on a beam in the roof of a house in
Ulster where there happened to be an ale banquet going
on. She fell at last into the golden goblet that stood
by the wife of Étar, and she was swallowed unawares
with the drink. In due time she was born the daughter
of Étar's queen, and they called her Etáin daughter of
Étar, by whom she was brought up in great state and
surrounded with fifty maidens of her own age, the
daughters of princes, as her companions. Somewhere
near the water where, years later, Airem's messengers
found her dressing her golden hair, she and her youthful companions happened one day to be bathing together,
when they beheld a man of the most distinguished
appearance riding over the plain towards them. When
he arrived he sat him down on the bank, and sang a lay
alluding to the scenes through which Etáin had already
passed, and ominously referring to the wars with which
Erinn was to be cursed on this fair Helen's account.
His words, somewhat freely rendered, so far as they
are to the point, run thus :—

> Etain indiu sund amne
> oc sid banfind iar n-albai
> eter maccaib beccaib di
> for bru inbir cichmuini.
>
> Is hí rohíc súil ind rig
> a topor locha dá líg

1. *So is Etáin here to-day*
   At the Fair Wives' Mound behind Alba;
   Among little children is her lot
   On the bank of Cichmuine's Inver.

2. *It is she that healed the monarch's eye*
   From the well of Loch dá Líg;

is hi asibed sin dig
la mnái nétair hi tromdig.

Is tría ág dossib in ri
inna héonu di Theththí[1]
ocus baidfid a dá ech
illind locha dá airbrech.

Bíat imda coicthe ili
tría tág for echaig midi
bíaid togal for sídib
ocus cath for ilmilib.

It is she was gulped in the drink
By Étar's wife in a heavy draught.

3. *For her sake the king will chase*
   The birds away from Tethba[1]
   And will drown his chargers twain
   In Loch da Airbrech's waters.

4. *Many great battles will chance*
   For thy sake to Echaid of Meath;
   Ruin will fall on Faery
   And war on myriads of men.

When he had done, the stranger vanished, nobody
knew whither; but as to the wars of which he prophesied Etáin about to be the cause, one of them was
that which led Airem to destroy Mider's stronghold, an
act which the fairies never forgave; so there was to be
another famous war, namely one brought about by them
to avenge the defeat of Mider; but it did not happen
till the time of Airem's great-grandson. For Airem and
Etáin had no son, but they had a daughter, called after
her mother, Etáin, who in turn had a daughter called
Messbúachallo[2], mother of Conaire the Great, monarch
of Erinn, who fell the innocent victim of the long smoul-
dering wrath of the fairies[3]. The remoteness of the

---

[1] The allusions are obscure; but chasing the birds from Tethba may be
another account of covering it with rushes.

[2] *Bk. of the Dun*, 99 a.

[3] *Hib. Lec.* p. 135.

fairies' vengeance is remarkable, but it has a parallel in
a Welsh tale, in which a remote descendant of a farmer
is punished on account of the latter having ploughed up
a field, where they were wont to dance and hold their
nightly merrymakings[1].

What, it may be asked, can be the meaning or origin
of such a story as that of Etáin, which, as the reader
ought to have been told, places more than a millennium
between her second birth as the daughter of Étar, and
her first birth as that of a father called Ailill? Some
aid to answer this difficult question is to be got from
another case of re-births in Irish legend, namely, that of
Cúchulainn, in whom we have, as has been shown elsewhere[2], an avatar or a son of Lug the sun-god. This
is readily intelligible, for, as the sun rises every day,
the sun-god may well have been represented as
repeatedly re-born, either once a day or once in a
longer period; and we get nearer the answer to
the question, what the goddess was that was similarly
liable to be born anew. In fact, it is found on looking
carefully at the story, that no interpretation suits it so
well as that which makes Etáin a personification of the
dawn. Not only does the dawn admit of being regarded as born afresh as often as popular fancy may
suggest, but the rising of the dawn from the darkness
of night, her travelling over the sky, and her finally disappearing as the gloaming into the darkness of night
once more, explains the mythic contest about her
between her husband above ground, Airem, and her
husband under ground, Mider: her society must necessarily be divided between them, and in fact all

---

[1] *Cymmrodor*, v. 127–141. The story forms the groundwork of Lewis
Morris's 'Curse of Pantannas,' *Songs of Britain*, pp. 102–125.

[2] *Hib. Lec.* pp. 431–5.

goddesses involving this nature 'myth are liable to appear in the character of unfaithful wives. It is worth while observing, that we have not only Etáin daughter of Étar, who was an avatar of a previous Etáin, but a third Etáin, represented not as an Etáin re-born, but as a daughter, of Echaid and his wife Etáin, in the ordinary course of nature. The same mixing of the two ideas occurs in the case of Cúchulainn, who is sometimes regarded as an avatar of Lug and sometimes as his son. When Lug is to be re-born he also has to assume the form of a fly, as was the case with Etáin, and to be swallowed with her drink by the lady whom he has selected to be his mother. Lastly, the interpretation of Etáin as originally the dawn, derives some confirmation from her name Etáin or Étáin[1], which probably means 'the shining one': she was otherwise called *Be Find*, more correctly *Bebind*[2], the 'White or Fair Woman.'

Airem had a brother called Ailill, who has been alluded to as having fallen in love with Etáin. The stories sometimes give him another brother called Echaid Fedlech, which, however, they sometimes make to be another name of Echaid Airem[3]: which is the more correct view to take, we cannot say. With regard to the latter, *Airem* makes in the genitive

[1] It is also found written Etaoin and Eadaoin, as to which see O'Curry's ed. of the *Battle of Magh Leana*, pp. 38, 52, where it assonates with *eagcaoin* and *aoibh*. Irish itself seems to suggest no explanation of its meaning or etymology, but it would appear to be a word of the same origin as the following Brythonic vocables—Breton *étéó* or *éteo*, 'tison de feu,' Welsh *etewyn* or *ytewyn*, and *tewyn*, ' a brand or live coal,' *tywynnu*, 'to shine,' also *echdywynnu* and *echdywynygu* of the same meaning.

[2] The Four Masters in their *Annals of the Kingdom of Ireland* give it as a historical name, A. D. 1363, and the editor, Dr. O'Donovan, Anglicizes it into *Bevin*.

[3] See Windisch, p. 123, and O'Curry, *Manners*, iii. 190, where a MS. at Trinity College, Dublin, is quoted.

D

Airemon, which is also written *Erimon* or *Eremon*, and
Airem is not only called *Echaid Airem*, that is to say,
provisionally, Echaid the Ploughman, but also *Echaid
Airemon* [1], which would mean either Echaid (son) of
Airem, which Irish literature does not corroborate, since
his father's name is given as Finn; or else Echaid of
(the) Ploughmen, in reference to the fairies compelled
to work for him, but in this case the definite article
is wanting in the Irish, contrary to what one might
expect. On the whole, then, it seems more probable
that Echaid Airemon is due to a declensional change,
which was ultimately stereotyped by treating *Eremon*
as nominative and providing it with a genitive *Eremoin*.
This in its turn probably helped Irish mythographers to
split Echaid Airem into two kings, reigning respectively
as Eremon, A. M. 3501, and Echaid Airem, A.M. 5070 [2]: it
is to the former that Emer was reckoned brother, while
the latter's brothers are Ailill and Echaid Fedlech.

Now though *Airem* is usually explained to mean
a ploughman, it will be seen to fail to fit the story
about the origin of the proper name. For it is not
said that ploughing was learned in his time from the
fairies, nor does any ploughing appear included in the
labours imposed on them by Airem. What the story
relates is, that he saw how the fairies yoked their cattle,
and that he followed their example in a way which was,
till then, unknown to the men of Erinn. So the inference
is, that, by applying to him on that account the epithet
Airem, it was not so much intended to call him a
ploughman as one who yokes or harnesses his teams:
in other words, the later and attested meaning of *Airem*

---

[1] This occurs in the *Bk. of the Dun*, 129[b], where it is written eochaid
hæremon. The genitive is also written *Aireman* : see the *Bk. of Leinster*, 163.
[2] See the *Four Masters* under those years respectively.

as that of ploughman is too narrow for the require-
ments of the story, and we may accordingly distinguish
two meanings of the word, (1) the later and narrower
one of ploughman, and (2) the earlier meaning of har-
nesser or binder, which probably included the other
more restricted signification. Nay, it is possible that
the original meaning was still wider, but we need not
now discuss it any further.

Returning to the Arthurian legend, the reader need
scarcely be told that the story of Arthur's queen
seized by Medrod, or eloping with Melwas after he had
lain in wait for her a whole year, has its parallel in that
of Mider searching for a year for Airem's queen Etáin,
and finally carrying her away to his own abode. Provided due allowance is made for the difference between
the social settings of the respective stories, the similarity becomes more unmistakable the more it is
scanned. For even the avatars of Etáin have something which can be set over against them in the Welsh
Triads, a something which can only be understood by
means of them. We allude more especially to the fact
that one of the Triads[1] speaks of Arthur as the husband
not of one wife called Gwenhwyvar, but of three wives
bearing each that one and the same name. This has
sometimes been regarded as too absurd to deserve
serious consideration ; but in the light of Etáin's story
it is readily seen to have had a meaning. The three
Gwenhwyvars are the Welsh equivalents of the three
Etáins, and the article in the Triads must be admitted
to bear the stamp of great antiquity; for no Arthurian
story-teller, whether Welsh or Norman, ever avails
himself of the three Gwenhwyvars. The reason is
evident: the three would have spoiled his plot and

_____
[1] i. 59; ii. 16; iii. 109.

reduced the human interest in it far more than three-fold, at any rate in the state of society in which the Arthurian myth developed itself into romance. So we are forced to refer the basis of the Triad to a far earlier age.

The Gwenhwyvars are described respectively as the daughters of Gwryd Gwent [1], Gwythur son of Greidiawl, and Ogrvan the Giant. The first name reminds one of some of the Culture God's names, and the bearer of it as father of Gwenhwyvar may, perhaps, be regarded as holding, in the Triad, the place assigned in the Irish story to Airem as father of the third Etáin. Ogrvan, or Ogyrven, the Giant is known as one of the terrene powers [2], who may be therefore placed over against the father of the first Etáin, whose name Ailill seems cognate with the Welsh ellyll 'an elf or demon.' Then we have left Gwythur son of Greidiawl, who contests with Gwyn son of Nûd, the love of Creidylad or Cordelia, daughter of Ỻûd of the Silver Hand. His attributes may be regarded as the opposite of those of Gwyn, the god of death and darkness, and he was probably a form of the sun-god, the summer sun: it remains that he should here match Étar, the father of the second Étáin. But whether that be so or not, the dawn as the subject of a myth is readily represented as a daughter either of the sun, from whom she derives her light, and before whose face she hurries forth every day, or of darkness

---

[1] *Hib. Lec.* pp. 267-9, 274-5.

[2] This is found also written *Gawryd* (or *Gawrwyd*) *Ceint*, to be corrected probably into *Gwryd Ceint*, which would mean the Valour of Kent, as the other *Gwryd Gwent* literally means the Valour of Gwent. The person so called is otherwise unknown, but his name sounds decidedly more human than that of the other two, and so far as its evidence goes, it tends to identify him with the Culture Hero, among whose names one seems to find *Gweir* and *Gwron* (*Hib. Lec.* pp. 249-54, 282) of the same origin as *Gwryd*, 'manliness in the sense of valour or courage, *virtus*.'

from which she emerges in the morning and which she
hies away to meet in the gloaming. That the dawn
should also have been considered the daughter of the
Culture Hero is no more surprising than that the Solar
Hero should have been regarded as his son, and the
introduction of that third origin would have been calculated agreeably to meet the Celtic fondness for Triads ;
but this attempt to equate the fathers of the Gwenhwyvars individually with those of the Etáins is a mere
guess, and the point of importance is the virtual equiva-
lence of the three Gwenhwyvars with the three Etáins.

It is, moreover, worth while to note briefly that
the former three did not stand alone on Brythonic
ground: witness the Arthurian tales that speak of more
than one Essyllt. The name is better known in them as
Iseult, Isold, Isoud or Isoude, and the first lady they
mention of that name was, according to Malory, the wife
of King Mark of Cornwall, to whom allusion has already
been made at page 12. Now Tristram, the story of
whose birth somewhat resembles that of Kulhwch,
always contested the love of Isoud with Mark, and
sometimes successfully; so that lady is described in the
Triads as Essyllt Vyngwen or 'Essyllt with the white
Tresses,' mistress of Drystan son of Tallwch, and one
of the Three unchaste Ladies of Britain[1]. But on one
occasion King Mark, recovering possession of Isoud,
compelled Tristram to flee, when he found another
Isoud, with whom he went through the ceremony of
marriage. The first of the two is called La beale Isoud,
and the second is distinguished as Isoud la blaunche
Maynys, or Isoud with the white Hands ; but the story
of Tristram and the Isouds does not occur in Welsh,

[1] The Triad referring to that happy time of wholesale morality is i. 56; iii. 105.

being probably derived from Cornwall or Brittany. Be that as it may, it describes the two ladies as equally beautiful and equally famous for their skill in the medical art, by means of which they severally heal Tristram of dangerous wounds. They are referred to in the story of Kulhwch[1], where they have the epithets Vinwen, 'of the white Visage,' and Vingul, 'of the narrow Visage,' respectively. The key to the enigma of the double Isoud is, doubtless, the same as to the triple Gwenhwyvar, that supplied by the story of the Irish Airem and the three Etáins.

A word or two must now be said with regard to the name Gwenhwyvar: it analyses itself into *gwenn* or *gwèn*, 'white,' and *hwyvar*, a word which, while it has no explanation in Welsh, is doubtless cognate with the Irish *siabur*, 'a ghost or phantom,' and *siabræ*, 'a ghost, spectre, or goblin.' So there can be little doubt that Gwenhwyvar originally meant the white phantom or white apparition, which reminds one of the Irish Be Find as a name of one of the Etáins, and of the conjectured signification of the latter name itself.

Another name to be noticed here is that of Medrawt or Medrod, made in English into Modred and Mordred: this would seem to be of the same origin as the Welsh verb *medr-u*, 'to hit with a missile, also metaphorically with the intellect in the sense of knowing or understanding;' Irish *midiur*, 'I judge.' But the proper name is synonymous with, and derived from, a simpler one Medr, written Medyr in the story of Kulhwch, where it is given to a wonderful marksman, who, from Kelli Wic in Cornwall, could shoot a wren on Esgair Oervel in Ireland through both its legs evenly[2]. We

---

[1] *R. B. Mab.* p. 113; Guest, ii. 269.
[2] Ib. p. 112; Guest, ii. 268.

read of Ḷeu's foe, Goronwy Pevr[1], both making a spear
and hurling it with fatal accuracy and force. It is even
more to the point to notice that Airem's rival's name
was closely related to that of Medrod and identical with
that of *Medr*: we allude to *Mider*, genitive *Midir*.

It might, perhaps, be thought that the similarity of
meaning between the vocable Gwenhwyvar and Etáin
or Be Find is merely accidental, and that the kinship of
those of Medrod and Mider is only apparent, if one
were to stop short of bringing together the more
weighty ones of Arthur and Airem. Now it may be
shown that *Airem*, genitive *Aireman* or *Erimon*, represents, that is, the latter, an early genitive *Arịomanos* or
Arịomonos, and that *Erimon*, genitive *Erimoin*, was in
Gaulish a man's name, *Ariomanus*[2], as written in its
Latin form, the stem being *arịo-*, which in Irish yields
airim, ' I plough,' and Welsh *arḍu*, ' to plough,' of the
same conjugation as English *ear*, 'to plough,' which
was in A.-Saxon *erian* and in Gothic *arjan* of the same
meaning. The Welsh word *âr*, 'plough-land,' involves
a simpler base, with which are connected Welsh *aredig*,
'to plough,' and *aradr*, Irish *arathar*, 'a plough,' neither
of which is, as sometimes supposed, the Latin *arâtrum*,
'a plough,' borrowed, which could only yield in Welsh
arawdr and *arodr*: rather are the Celtic words for a
plough native ones, and parallel to the Greek form
ἄροτρον connected with the verb ἀρόω, Latin *aro*,
' I plough.'

It is deserving of notice that all these verbs, Greek,
Latin, Teutonic and Celtic, are derivative ones; but if
Latin, for instance, had instead of *arāre* a strong verb

---

[1] *R. B. Mab.* pp. 76–7; Guest, iii. 243–5.
[2] Gruter, 670, 3: *Ariomanus Iliati f (ilius) Boịus)* : it is quoted also in
the *Gram. Celtica*, p. 773.

arĕre, a ploughman would in that case have been not *arātor* but *artor*, and that is just what we have in the name *Arthur*, as representing an early Celtic equivalent *artor*, genitive *artôros*, which in the later stages of the language could not avoid being reduced to *Arthur*. There is no phonologic difficulty; but was there ever such a word as *artor* of this origin? There certainly was in the Litu-Slavic languages, as its exact equivalent appears in Lithuanian in the form *artójis*, 'a ploughman,' Old Prussian *artoys*, 'a husbandman,' Old Bulgarian *rataj*, Bohemian *ratey*, of the same meaning. With these words are connected Lith. *arklýs*, 'a horse,' *àrklas*, 'a plough,' which is closely related to Bohemian *rádlo*, 'a plough,' Old Bulg. *ralo* and *oralo*, likewise 'a plough,' Old Norse *arðr*, gen. *arðrs*, 'a plough.' Add to this the O. H. German *arl*, 'a ploughshare,' as closely akin. In all these last words, together with Lith. *árti*, 'to plough,' and *arta-s*, 'ploughed[1],' the root *ar* is found with the terminations affixed without an intervening vowel; but no Celtic word is included, though such an instance is not altogether wanting—we allude to the Gaulish goddess called Artio[2], whom one may compare, at least in name, with the English *Earth* and the old Germanic *Ertha*[3]. Still more to the point is the Gaulish epithet of the god called in Latin *Mercurius Artaius*, who may perhaps be more intelligibly described in Latin as *Mercurius Cultor*, mentioned in

---

[1] See Johannes Schmidt in Kuhn's *Zeitschrift*, xxv. 27-9; and Schmidt's *Vocalismus*, ii. 145; see also Brugmann's *Grundriss der vergl. Grammatik*, ii. 115, 201, on the formation of the words *rádlo, ralo*, &c.

[2] *Hib. Lec.* p. 73.

[3] There is some difficulty about the reading of the passage in the Germania of Tacitus, c. 40. Bekker prints 'nisi quod in commune Herthum, id est terram matrem, colunt,' while Ritter differs in giving the proper name the form Ertham; but Holder ventures to print thus—'nisi quod Mammun Ertham, id est Terram Matrem, colunt,' the italicized *a* is Holder's.

an inscription from Heilbronn[1]. This is something more than a mere matter of etymology, for it is a Mercury and Culture Hero that we have all along taken the mythological Arthur to have been; at the same time it raises the question as to the exact meaning of the name Arthur. On the whole, we should probably not be far wrong in regarding it as coinciding in this respect with the Irish *Airem*, taken in its wider sense of one who binds or harnesses. But in what way, it may be asked, can Arthur have been connected with agriculture? It is hardly to be expected that a great monarch would be described engaging himself in the common-place operations of farming; one will, however, remember how the Irish story of Echaid describes the latter acquiring the surname Airem. He is not represented doing any agricultural work himself, but only compelling the fairies to undertake work for him, and learning from them how to yoke his oxen in a way never till then practised by the Men of Erinn. The Welsh counterpart is to be found in the story of Kulhwch, who asks a boon of Arthur, which involves the latter's having to see to the execution of the labours insisted on by Yspyđaden[2] before he lets his daughter Olwen become Kulhwch's wife. One of the labours was to find the prison of the sun-god Mabon, and release him to take part in the fabulous hunt of the boar called Twrch Trwyth: but precedence over it is given to another labour, which in fact takes the position of importance at the head of the list, and it is of an agricultural nature, as will be seen from the following extracts:—

"Seest thou that vast hill yonder? said Yspyđaden to Kulhwch . . . .

---

[1] Brambach's *Corpus Insc. Rhenanarum*, No. 1591.
[2] *Hib. Lec.* pp. 486–492. .

"I must have it rooted up from the ground, and the grubbings burned for manure on the face of the land: I must have it ploughed and sown in one day, and have it ripen in the space of one day. Of that wheat it is that I must have food and liquor duly made for the wedding of thee and my daughter . . . .

"No husbandman can till or dress that land on account of its tangled state except Amaethon son of Dôn: he will not follow thee of his free will, and thou canst not force him. . . .

"Though thou wert to get that, there is yet that which thou wilt not get, and that is Govannon son of Dôn to attend at the furrows' ends to rid the iron: he only works of his own free will for a rightful king, and thou canst not force him. . . .

"Though thou shouldst get that, there is that which thou wilt not get, namely the two oxen of Gwlwlyd Wineu as fellow-feeders, to plough that rugged land there well: he will not give them of his free will, and thou canst not force him. . . . .

"The Yellow Ox of Spring and the Brindled Ox I must have as fellow-feeders. . . . .

"Though thou wert to get them, there is yet that which thou wilt not get, namely, the Bannawc Oxen, of which the one is on the further side of Bannawc Mountain and the other on this side, to be yoked together to the same plough. They are, to wit, Nynniaw and Peibiaw, whom God made into oxen on account of their sins[1]."

Kulhwch acting, like Jason, on the advice of her he loves, undertakes to have all the difficulties laid in his way duly removed; but in harmony with the usual Celtic treatment, the Celtic Jason performs his tasks by

---

[1] *R. B. Mab.* pp. 120-2 ; Guest, ii. 280-2.

deputy, and that deputy is chiefly his uncle Arthur. So to each of Yspyḍaden's demands Kulhwch replies that he will readily meet it, and the whole plot depends on Arthur getting for him, by force or friendship, all that Yspyḍaden specifies, involving, besides the plough- ing in question, other processes of husbandry, such as harvesting a crop of flax under peculiar circumstances, making incomparable bragget for the wedding, and procuring proper vessels to hold it uninjured. It would be tedious to describe these matters severally: suffice it to say that, as compared with the Irish tale about Airem, Arthur's connection with agriculture is more abundantly set forth in this story, excepting only that the story-teller does not pause to say, 'and therefore was he called Arthur.'

It is impossible to say whether the name *Arthur* can have been narrowed like *Airem* to mean a ploughman : it is enough for our purpose that it may have, like *Airem*, meant one who harnesses or binds; but the original meaning of both names may have, as already suggested, transcended this limitation and conveyed no special allusion to employing any domestic animal for work by hunter or husbandman. For two possibilities suggest themselves : the names Airem and Arthur may have all along had a wider meaning, and in the next place that meaning may have been influenced and modified by association with that of other words shewing a similarity of origin. Take for example the Irish word *ara*, 'charioteer,' which suggests a way of harmonizing the name Airem with the story of its bearer ; take also the Welsh stem *ar*, whence *Arawn* as name of the king of Hades [1], *arawd*, 'speech, eloquence,' and *araith*, 'speech, an oration,' Irish *airecht*, 'a public assembly.' These

---

[1] *Hib. Lec.* pp. 244, 276.

last, pointing as they do in the direction of eloquence
and oratory, remind us of that side of the character of
the Culture Hero, which is delineated with so much
quaintness by Lucian in his account of the Gaulish
Ogmios[1]. In this connection it may be worth the while
to mention that in Welsh literature Arthur, like Gwydion,
is more than once ascribed the rôle of poet or bard[2].

The question, however, of the original meaning
of the names Arthur and Airem would not be much
advanced by further examining etymology, as it only
refers us to a root *ar* (or to several roots of that form)
of widely divergent meanings[3]. In fact, the names
here in question might so far as any help could be
derived from this source be said to have meant one who
joins, holds, or puts together, also one who thereby con-
trols or directs the movements of others. These senses
might diverge indefinitely according to the sphere of
action contemplated, and according as one referred,
let us say, to yoking oxen or harnessing horses for
work, to bringing friends together, to uniting man
and wife in matrimony, to putting words together in a
discourse, and so on, or else to managing, guiding, or
directing others in the right course, as in speaking of
chariot-horses or of a plough-team. So we are not
much the wiser from knowing that *Airem, Erimon,* has
its equivalent, letter for letter, in the Sanskrit word
aryaman. This last as an appellative is said to mean
one's bosom friend, playmate, or comrade ; and it occurs
in the sense of a bridegroom's best man[4]; but as a

---

[1] *Hib. Lec.* pp. 14-16.

[2] *R. B. Mab.* pp. 133, 308 ; Guest, ii. 304 ; the Triads, i. 23 ; iii. 29 ; i. 18 ;
ii. 9 ; iii. 123.

[3] See Fick's *Vergleichendes Wörterbuch*[3], i. 19-22, 493-6.

[4] See B. and Roth's *Dic.* s.v., where the word is defined thus : 'Busen-
freund, Gespiele, Gefährte, Camerad, sodalis . . . Gebräuchlich ist es insbes.

proper name it was borne by a god Aryaman, who
usually appears as one of a triad of divinities and
without any attributes of his own, or any attributes of
so distinctive a nature as to help one in arriving at
any certainty respecting his origin and individuality.
But whatever else might be said of these and the
kindred words, they bring together in a manner the far
extremes of our family of nations; for, while the Persian
King of Kings was committing his pedigree to everlasting cuneiform in the East, and proudly posing as Aryan
of the Aryans, his distant kindred were asserting with the
sword the right of the stronger to dominion over the
Ivernian Isle of the Atlantic. This they did as *Meicc
Erimon*, or sons of the Aryaman of the West[1].

The length, at which we have been obliged to spin out
the comparison between Arthur and Airem, may perhaps
create the impression that the similarity between them
is only to be seen through the glasses of an etymologist;
but, so far from that being really the fact, it is possible
to produce a case where the popular fancy seems to
have unreservedly given the Arthurian names to the
dramatis personæ of the Airem story: this we believe
to have been the case with the group of supposed
Arthurian legends prevalent on the borders of the
counties of Perth and Forfar, north of the Sidlaw
Hills, in Scotland. Besides a stone called the Stone of
Arthur, in the parish of Cupar Angus, and such names
as Arthurstone, Arthur's Fold, and Arthur's Seat

von demjenigen *Gefährten* eines Bräutigams (παρανύμφιος), welcher bei der
Hochzeit als *Brautwerber* und *Ehestifter* thätig ist.'

[1] See Zimmer's article on *Arisch* in Bezzenberger's *Beiträge*, iii. 137-151,
and more especially p. 150; but we are unable to follow our learned friend
when he interprets the name of Erinn to mean an 'Aryan' land; for we are
disposed to think that the early form of the nominative was *Iverjo*, which
makes a nearer approach, perhaps, to an 'Iberian' land.

scattered over a considerable area, 'a confused tradition
prevails of a great battle having been fought on the
East Mains of Dunichen [in Forfarshire], between
Lothus king of the Picts, or his son Modred, and
Arthur king of the Britons, in which that hero of
romance was slain[1].' Further, on a height called
Barry Hill, formerly Dunbarre, not far from Alyth,
are the remains of a fortification in which the Pictish
king Modred is said to have kept Gwenhwyvar or
Wanor, called Wander in that neighbourhood, as his
mistress, after defeating her husband in a great battle.
The story goes on to say that Arthur, on recovering possession of his wife, was so enraged at her
conduct, that he had her put to death in a most bar-
barous manner, and that a well-known sculptured stone
at the neighbouring kirk of Meigle marks her burial
place[2]. It was visited by the poet Gray on the 11th
of September, 1765, as he states in a letter to Dr.
Wharton dated three days later at Glamis Castle: some
women at Meigle spoke to him of the tomb of 'Queen
Wanders that was riven to dethe by staned horses for
nae gude that she did;' and one reads in Bellenden's
Boece that 'all wemen abhorris to strampe on that
sepulture[3].'

To proceed no further in this direction, the district indicated may be said to abound in legends involving Arthur's name; and the question is, how they
came there, especially as it is doubtful whether any
Brythonic people ever had its home so far north in
this island, and as nothing Arthurian seems to be known
in the tract of country between Perth and Stirling.

---

[1] *New Statistical Account of Scotland*, xi. 146.

[2] Stuart Glennie's *Arthurian Localities*, pp. 36-7.

[3] *The History and Chronicles of Scotland*, ii. 87.

The most satisfactory answer that can be suggested is, that some form of the story about Airem had long been familiar in the non-Brythonic parts of Scotland, which, generally speaking, agree far more closely in the matter of folklore and legend with Ireland than with Wales; and that among other appropriate spots Barry Hill had been fixed on as the scene of a part of the story. So, when literary Scotchmen or Norman adventurers had made the people of the Low-lands familiar with the Arthurian romances, the sub-stitution of the names of Arthur, Wanor, and Modred for the less generally known ones, handed down by the descendants of the Goidelic conquerors of the district above-mentioned, would follow probably pretty much as a matter of course. And when we are told [1], in reference to the Barry Hill legends, that the people have a tradition which makes Queen Wander, not only into a badly behaved wife but a malignant giantess, that seems the echo of the legends respecting an Etáin, rather than of any of the more widely known romances about Gwenhwyvar. The substitution of names could not be more readily accounted for than on the supposition of the mutual resemblance, evident to all, of the tales in question about Arthur and Airem respectively. The result for us is the singular appearance of an Arthurian oasis, so to say, in the midst of a non-Arthurian land.

To sum up these remarks, it may be granted that there was a historical Arthur, who may have held the office, which under the Roman administration was known as that of the *Comes Britanniæ*; that he may, like Aurelius Ambrosius, have been partly of Roman descent; that Maelgwn was his nephew, whom Gildas accuses of slaying his uncle; that his name *Arthur*

---

[1] *New Statistical Account of Scotland*, x. 1118.

was either the Latin *Artorius*, or else a Celtic name
belonging in the first instance to a god Arthur; for
the Latin *Artôrius* and the god's name, which we
have treated as early Brythonic *Artor*, genitive *Artôros*, would equally yield in Welsh the familiar form
Arthur. In either case, the name would have to be
regarded as an important factor in the identification
or confusion of the man with the divinity. The latter,
called Arthur by the Brythons, was called Airem by the
Goidels [1], and he was probably the Artæan Mercury of
the Allobroges of ancient Gaul. His rôle was that of
Culture Hero, and his name allows one to suppose
that he was once associated, in some special manner,
with agriculture over the entire Celtic world of antiquity. On the one hand we have the man Arthur,
whose position we have tried to define, and on the
other a greater Arthur, a more colossal figure, of which
we have, so to speak, but a *torso* rescued from the wreck
of the Celtic pantheon.

---

[1] The name Artur occurs but sparingly in Irish literature, and usually in
connection only with Britain, but Keating (Dublin, 1880), p. 84, mentions an
Artur, son of Nemed, fighting with the Fomori: this, if genuine, is a remarkable exception.

CHAPTER III.

Gwenhwyvar and her Captors.

Arthur has chiefly occupied us up to this point, but something must now be said of his wife. Her name in Welsh was Gwenhwyvar or Gwenhwyfar, which in the Anglo-Norman romances becomes Guenièvre; and the English metrical romances have the still shorter forms Wannour or Wannore, also Gwenore and even Gonore, Ganor or Gaynore. This last has been introduced to North Wales, where it is by no means an uncommon name for a woman; but it is not associated with the name of Arthur's queen, which is rarely to be met with in Welsh history; for, in some parts of the Principality, to call a girl a Gwenhwyvar is as much as to suggest that she is no better than she should be. The unpopularity of the name is in no small degree perpetuated by an old rhyme to the following effect :—

'Gwenhwyfar, ferch Ogrfan Gawr,
Drwg yn fechan, gwaeth yn fawr.'

Guinevere Giant Ogurvan's daughter,
Naughty young, more naughty later.

The character of the queen had probably been established, such as we find it in the rhyme, from time immemorial. We seem to find it implied in a 14th century copy of the Welsh Laws after the manner of Gwent: take for example a clause which runs thus:

E

'When the queen shall will a song in the chamber, let the bard sing a song respecting Camlan, and that not loud, lest the hall be disturbed[1].' The song is not known, but the subject is indicated clearly enough by the title; it was the infidelity of Gwenhwyvar and the catastrophe to which it led, culminating with the battle of Camlan: she was the dreadful example, by contemplating which the queen was to be helped to walk in the path of virtue. But how did Gwenhwyvar acquire her notoriety? The question is not so easy to answer as it might at first sight seem to be. It is true that the Latin version of Geoffrey charges her with wickedly marrying Modred in violation of her marriage to Arthur; but the words carry little weight, as nothing is said which would go to shew that she was a free agent in the matter. She is described in other stories as carried away by Melwas, of whom more anon; and the Anglo-Norman romances add one or two more similar incidents, but it is not stated that the queen was a consenting party. In the literature of the Welsh, her guilt is rather assumed than proved; but it is quite possible that popular tales dwelling on her levity have been lost. Be that as it may, no attempt to discuss Gwenhwyvar's reputation from the Welsh point of view could take the burden of Lancelot du Lac's story into account, as the passion for her ascribed to him is unknown to Welsh literature; nor had it probably any foundation in the myth which served as the ground-work of the Arthurian legend.

Several allusions have been made to the queen being seized by Arthur's foes. From the mythological point of view, these last may be said to reduce themselves

---

[1] *Ancient Laws and Institutes of Wales* (Record Office ed. of 1841), the Gwentian Code, Bk. I. chap. xxxvii. 7 (vol. i. 679).

to various expressions of the one idea of a god of darkness and death carrying away the goddess of the dawn and the gloaming: this was, however, only a part of his doings, for he was also represented as killing the sun-god, but we have now to deal with the former alone. First and foremost must be mentioned Medrod, but the story has more variety of detail in connection with another name, that of Melwas or Maelwas. The latter form is not the one usual in Welsh, but it is established by the spelling *Maheloas* in Chrétien de Troyes' poem about Erec and Enide: in fact, Melwas must have been the Cornish form for a Welsh Maelwas which it replaced. This last would have been written in the 12th century Maelgwas or Mailguas, from which the romancers made a variety of others, the most distorted of which were perhaps Malory's *Mellyagraunce* and Heinrich von dem Türlin's *Milianz*, the one to which M. Gaston Paris gives the preference being *Meleaguant*[1], nominative *Meleaguanz*[2]. *Maelgwas*, which six centuries earlier would have been *Maglouassos*, readily analyses itself into *mael* and *gwas*, the latter of which means a youth or young man, also a servant. *Mael* seems to have meant a lord or prince, and has its equivalent in the Irish *mál*, a hero or prince; so the full name Maelwas would appear to have meant a prince-youth, a princely youth, or a prince who was a youth, and that corresponds to the description given in Irish story of Mider, who, though represented as at least over a thousand years old, looked comely and youthful. On the whole, then, it is not improbable that *Melwas* or *Maelwas* described the bearer of the name as one who was fancied to be ever young.

[1] *Romania*, xii. 474.
[2] Ib. xii. 467; *Le Conte de la Charrette*, line 637.

The first version to be noticed of the capture of the queen by Melwas is composed in the historical style : it occurs in the *Vita Gildæ*[1] usually ascribed to Caradoc of ILancarvan, who lived in the 12th century. There Melwas is represented as the king reigning over the realm, which the writer terms *Æstiva Regio*, by which he must have meant the reader to understand Somerset. Melwas is said to have been looking out for a whole year, *per unius anni circulum*, for an opportunity to take the queen. Having at last espied a suitable time— whether with or without her connivance we are not told—he carried her away *violatam et raptam*, to a place of great strength on account of the waters and marshes around it : that was Glastonbury, or as the writer Latinizes it, Glastonia, to which he adds the explanation that the name meant *Urbs Vitrea*. In due time, Arthur, whom he styles *tyrannus*[2], marched with the armies of Cornwall and Devon to lay siege to Glastonbury ; but at the instance of Gildas and the abbot peace was made, and the queen was restored to her husband. It is very doubtful that the Life was written by Caradoc, but it is certain that the story is ancient, for Chrétien de Troyes in his Erec speaks of Maheloas[3] as the lord of the Glass Island—' Li sire de l'isle de voirre,' and Malory gives a romantic

---

[1] Giles's *Original Lives*, &c. (London, 1854), p. 313 ; also *Romania*, x. 491, where M. G. Paris has published a different text of the incident here in question.

[2] The choice of this term may be regarded as a touch of history, in so far as the writer avoids calling Arthur a *rex*, while that title, as applied to Melwas, belongs undoubtedly to mythology, as does the story as a whole, in spite of Gildas and the abbot introduced into it. *Tyrannus* here, presumably, marks the same distinction which is kept up in Welsh by calling Arthur emperor.

[3] Chrétien had the forms *Maheloas* and *Meleaguanz* from different sources and was not aware that they meant the same person : see *Romania*, x. p. 491, xii. p. 511.

version, in which he places Arthur's court at Westminster and the castle of Melwas not more than seven
miles away: his words are[1]—'Soo it befelle in the
moneth of May/quene Gueneuer called vnto her knyȝtes
of the table round/and she gafe them warnynge that
erly vpon the morowe she wold ryde on mayeng in to
woodes & feldes besyde westmynstre/& I warne yow
that there be none of yow but that he be wel horsed/
and that ye alle be clothed in grene outher in sylke/
outher in clothe and I shalle brynge with me ten ladyes/
and euery knyght shalle haue a lady behynde hym/and
euery knyghte shal haue a squyer and two yomen/and
I wyll that ye alle be wel horsed/Soo they made hem
redy in the fresshest maner.'

While the queen and her party were engaged a-
maying, Mellyagraunce (Melwas) came and attacked them
with such a following that they were obliged to surrender, whereupon the victor carried the queen and her
followers away to his castle. Now we are told that the
knight 'that hyghte Mellyagraunce . . . was sone vnto
kynge Bagdemagus/and this knyghte had at that tyme a
castel of the yefte of kyng arthur within seuen myle of
westmynstre/And this knyghte sir Mellyagraunce loued
passynge wel Quene Gueneuer/and soo had he done
longe and many yeres/And the book sayth he had layne
in a wayte for to stele away the quene/but euermore he
forbare for by cause of sir launcelot/for in no wyse he
wold medle with the quene/and sir Launcelot were in
her company/outher els and he were nere hand her.'

That day Lancelot was not with the queen; but no
sooner did that knight hear the news of the queen's
capture than he set out on his horse, who swam
the Thames at Lambeth; he had not proceeded far,

[1] Malory, xix 1.

however, ere the faithful beast was attacked by archers
sent by Melwas to lie in wait for him. Then Lancelot,
compelled to go on foot, met a cart belonging to Melwas
and mounted into it, compelling the carter to drive
to his master's castle. Melwas is forced to surrender
the queen and her followers, and the rambling story
is brought to a close by a duel between Melwas and
Lancelot about the queen's reputation: Melwas had
his skull cloven by a mighty stroke of Lancelot's sword.
Chrétien de Troyes' metrical romance, *Le Conte de la
Charrette*, is a long and laborious version of the story;
and it adds some very important items to our information as to the nature of the realm of which Melwas
was lord: it was, among other things, the land from
whose bourne no traveller returns, for once he is there,
he must there for ever abide in bondage and exile. In
his own words it was a country[1]—

> 'Dont nul estranges ne retorne:
> Mès par force el païs séjorne
> En servitute et en essil.'

Here we have an unmistakable allusion to the world
of darkness and death, and M. Paris dwells[2] on the
striking similarity between the capture of Gwenhwyvar,
whilst out maying in the woods, with the rape of
Proserpine by Pluto, while she was collecting flowers in
the fields. Nor did[3] it escape him how the recovery of
the queen by Arthur or Lancelot forms a knightly
counterpart to the peaceful story of Orpheus trying
to bring his beloved Eurydice back. That the realm
of Melwas, whatever name it might have, was the
abode of the dead, is further proved by Chrétien's

---

[1] *Chevalier de la Charrette* (ed. by Tarbé), p. 22; *Romania*, xii. 467, 515.

[2] *Romania*, xii. 508.

[3] Ib. xii. 512.

description in the same poem of the accesses to it. These consisted, he says, of two bridges, one called *li Ponz Evages* or the Water Bridge, because it was a narrow passage a foot and a half wide and as many in height, with water above and below it as well as on both sides. This was reckoned less perilous than the other, and was chosen by Gauvain (Gwalchmei), who had set forth with Lancelot to the queen's rescue. The other, which Lancelot crossed with infinite pain, was called *li Ponz de l'Espée* or the Sword Bridge, because it consisted of the edge of a sword two lances in length[1]. The Water Passage attempted by Gauvain, but without success[2], would seem to have been the way to some subaqueous country, while the Sword Bridge reminds one of the Bridge of the Souls in the Vision of Adamnán, of that in the *Visio Tnugdali*, and of that in the Purgatory of St. Patrick. This notion of a narrow bridge leading to the realm of the dead has been familiar to many nations[3], and whether the romance writers got it from the Celtic tales at their service or from another source, it was a picture which it was natural that they should elaborate in other ways and other connections. Thus Walewein (Gwalchmei) in the Dutch romance of Walewein[4], is described in one of his adventures, arriving at a bridge more sharp than a blade of steel and forming the only means of passing a river of clear and fresh water that burned like fire. The Welsh version[5] of an adventure of the same Gwalchmei describes another

---

[1] *Romania*, xii. 467-8, 473-4.

[2] Ib. pp. 468, 477-9.

[3] Ib. xii. 508-10, where M. G. Paris gives a number of instances and valuable references.

[4] *Roman van Walewein*, edited by Jonckbloet (Leyden, 1846-8), lines 4939, &c., referred to by M. G. Paris, *Romania*, xii. 509.

[5] Williams' *Saint Greal* (London, 1876), part II. pp. 241-2, 593-4.

kind of bridge: the court of King Peleur, which was
his destination, was surrounded by a great water,
crossed by three bridges. One of them was an arrow
shot in length but only a foot wide, and it was called
the Bridge of the Eel. The other two bridges seemed
to be of ice and weak at the foundations, while a mighty
current struck underneath them. Gwalchmei came on
his horse to the Bridge of the Eel and hesitated, when
he was warned by a person standing on the other side,
that he had better venture the bridge at once. He did
so, and no sooner had the horse stepped on it than it
became wide enough for two cartwains to cross side by
side: in this respect it resembled much more closely
the Bridge of the Souls in the Irish visions alluded to.
But the Bridge of the Eel was the bridge over the Eel,
the Snake, or Rainbow River, to which Taliessin refers
as a stream of venom flowing round the world[1].

The description of the realm of Melwas, as the land
whence nobody returns, deserves notice as one of
the things which come exclusively from Chrétien's
poem, there being, so far as we know, no such trace
of the original myth left in the Welsh versions of the
story; but with the aid of Chrétien's hints and the
account of the Eel Bridge it is possible to identify an
allusion to Arthur proceeding in person to rescue the
queen from her captor: we refer to a curious dialogue,
the meaning of which has hitherto been a puzzle. In
the Myvyrian it is headed, 'A conversation between
Arthur and his second wife Gwenhwyvar: this was the
maid carried away by Melwas, a prince from Alban.'
It runs thus[2]:—

---

[1] Skene's *Four Ancient Books of Wales*, ii. 159.

[2] See the *Myv. Arch.* i. 175, where we are told that the text was copied
from the Green Book, a manuscript about which the author knows nothing,

ARTHUR.

Du yw fy march a da dana',
Ac er dwr nid arswyda,
A rhag ungwr ni chilia.

Black is my steed and brave beneath me,
No water will make him fear,
And no man will make him swerve.

GWENHWYVAR.

Glas yw fy march o liw dail,
Llwyr dirmygid mefl mawrair[1]:
Nid gwr ond a gywiro ei air.

Green is my steed of the tint of the leaves
No disgrace like his who boasts and fails:
He is no man who fulfills not his word.

The next triplet which should have been spoken by
Arthur has been lost, together with the first half of
Gwenhwyvar's answer; that is, if the lacuna is not to
be regarded as still more extensive.

. . . . . ymlaen y drin
Ni deil gwr ond Cai hir ab Sefin.

. . . . . in the forefront of the fray
No man holds out but Kei the Tall, son of Sevin.

ARTHUR.

Myfi a ferchyg ac a sai',
Ac a gerdda yn drwm gan lan trai:
Myfi yw'r gwr a ddaliai Gai.

It is I that will ride and will stand,
And walk heavily on the brink of the ebb:
I am the man to hold out against Kei.

except that a dialogue between Arthur and the eagle that had been his
nephew, Eliwlod son of Madog (*Myv. Arch.* i. 176), is also said to have been
taken from it.   But he has recently found a copy of the dialogue in the text—
somewhat more imperfect than the one in the *Myv. Arch.*—in a paper book
(113 D. 4, no. 160) of Welsh poetry in the library of Lord Macclesfield.
The handwriting of the copy would seem to belong to the latter part of the
17th century.   The text here given is that of the *Myvyrian*, checked by
means of the transcript.

[1] The rhyme *dail* and *mawrair* would seem to argue some antiquity; but it
is right to say that *mawrair* occurs in a part of the line which the Shirburn
scribe was unable to read: at any rate he has left it blank. The text as a
whole is modern.

GWENHWYVAR.

Dyd was, rhyfed yw dy glywed:
Onid wyd amgen no'th weled
Ni dalid di Gai ar dy ganfed.

Pshaw, young man, it is strange to hear thee!
Unless thou be other than thou lookest,
Thou wouldst not, one of a hundred, hold against Kei.

ARTHUR.

Gwenhwyfar olwg eirian
Na difrawd fi cyd bwy' bychan
Mi a daliwn gant fy hunan.

Gwenhwyvar of the bright face,
Do not insult me small though I be:
I would hold against a hundred myself.

GWENHWYVAR.

Dyd was o du a melyn,
Wrth hir edrych dy dremyn
Tybiais dy weled cyn hyn.

Pshaw, young man of black and yellow!
After scanning long thy looks
Methought I had seen thee before.

ARTHUR.

Gwenhwyfar olwg wrthroch,
Doedwch i mi, os gwydoch,
Y'mha le cyn hyn i'm gwelsoch.

Gwenhwyvar of the —— face,
Tell me, if you know it,
Where you saw me before.

GWENHWYVAR.

Mi a welais wr gradol o faint
Ar fwrd hir Arthur yn Dyfnaint
Yn rhannu gwin i'w geraint.

I have seen a man of moderate size
At Arthur's long table in Devon,
Dealing out wine to his friends.

ARTHUR.

Gwenhwyfar barabl digri',
Gnawd o ben gwraig air gwegi:
Yno y gwelaist di fi.

Gwenhwyvar of facetious speech,
It is woman's nature to banter:
There it is thou didst me see.

Such is the gist of this curious dialogue, and the question is what the scene was, and what the occasion to which it refers. It is unfortunate that the text is imperfect; but clearly it represents a meeting of Arthur with Gwenhwyvar after she had left his court in Devon; and the strange colour of her horse recalls the story of her going forth with her attendants, all clad in green, when she was taken from them. Further, the reference to the water, to the fearlessness of Arthur's horse and to his own confidence that he should ride without falling off, if one be right in interpreting it so, seem to point to some such a feat as crossing the Eel Bridge and performing some deed like Lancelot's rescue of the queen from Melwas. But how different from the story as told by the romancers! Here, if we are not mistaken, we have Gwenhwyvar challenging Arthur to cross, and even pretending not to know him; but he is fearless and rides a fearless horse, wherein he contrasts with Lancelot, who, having lost his horse, had to ride in a cart. But the most remarkable thing about the dialogue is the praise Gwenhwyvar lavishes on Kei, by whose side Arthur would appear to have been of insignificant stature. Nay, one cannot help suspecting that the implied story made the ravisher of the queen no other person than Kei, whom she does not appear to have been in any hurry to leave. This agrees with the stories which represent Kei first slaying Arthur's son, ILacheu, then making war on Arthur, and finally withdrawing to a castle beyond the sea[1]. That this view of Kei is mythologically admissible is proved by his murdering ILacheu.

We may premise that ILacheu was the son of Arthur

[1] Williams' *Seint Greal*, part II. pp. 304-5, 340-1, 373-4, 379, 635, 658-9, 680-1, 684.

and Gwenhwyvar[1], so that Tennyson is mythologically wrong, when, pursuing his relentless treatment of Gwenhwyvar's character, he makes Arthur address her in the words:—

> 'Well is it that no child is born of thee.
> The children born of thee are sword and fire,
> Red ruin, and the breaking up of laws,
> The craft of kindred and the Godless hosts
> Of heathen swarming o'er the Northern Sea;
> Whom I, while yet Sir Lancelot, my right arm
> The mightiest of my knights, abode with me,
> Have everywhere about this land of Christ
> In twelve great battles ruining overthrown.'

On the whole very little is to be read about Ilacheu, but that little is very significant. His death is alluded to in the Black Book[2] in the following terms put into Gwyn ab Nûd's mouth:—

> ' Mi awum lle llas llachev
> mab arthur uthir ig certev[3].
> ban ryreint brein ar crev.'

> *I was there where Ilacheu fell,*
> *Arthur's son renowned in song,*
> *When ravens flocked on the gore.*

We may next mention that he is credited in the Triads[4] with a thorough insight into the nature of material things: he is accordingly classified with Gwalchmei and Rhiwalton[5].

These references to Ilacheu agree in making him a man of a most accomplished character; but the story

---

[1] *Seint Greal*, pp. 341, 358, 372 (659, 671, 680). Other sons of Arthur bore the names Amhar and Gwydre: see the *R. B. Mab.* pp. 246, 138; Guest, ii. 70, 311.

[2] Evans's Autotype Facsimile, 50 a; Skene, ii. 55.

[3] This line admits, however, of being explained as 'Arthur's son wonderful with regard to his skill in song,' not to mention that *certev* is a plural and may possibly mean the *arts* of the time.

[4] i. 10; ii. 21[b]; iii. 70.

[5] *Hib. Lec.* p. 423.

of his death, as given in the second part of the Welsh version of the Grail[1], makes him hardly human at all: the contrast is remarkable:—He left his father's court to seek adventure, and hearing of a terrible giant called Logrin, who had proved himself one of Arthur's most cruel foes and allowed nobody to live in the same country with him, he fought him and prevailed. Now Ilacheu, whenever he killed a pest of the kind, had a habit of sleeping on the dead body: so he did in this instance, but Kei happening to be attracted by the dying howl of the giant, came by, and finding Ilacheu asleep on the body, he cut off the sleeping hero's head and hid it. Then he cut off Logrin's head and took it to Arthur's court to shew that he had killed the giant. Kei was there made much of on account of his supposed achievement; but it was not long ere Kei's treachery became accurately known to Arthur and the queen: the hostility with Kei arising therefrom ended with his retiring to fortify himself in a castle in Little Britain beyond the sea. To return to Ilacheu, he is said to have worn a circle of gold to distinguish him as a king's son. This, taken together with his marvellous knowledge of all material things and the meaning of his name, points undoubtedly to Ilacheu's nature as a solar person; for *Ilacheu* cannot but be cognate with the Welsh adjective *llachar*, ' gleaming, flashing,' and *llacheu* as a common noun is interpreted to mean gleams or flashes. Then as to Ilacheu's strange habit of sleeping on the body of his fallen foe, that is a curious nature myth, the meaning of which is transparent. Ilacheu's antagonist is the giant of darkness who fills the world with his ravages ; but when he is vanquished and slain his carcase is identical with the vast body of the ocean,

[1] *Seint Greal,* pp. 278, 304, 341, 617, 634, 658, 671.

in which darkness, according to the Celtic notion, takes refuge, and on which the sun is seen setting. The Frenchman, retaining a touch of mythology in his every-day language, describes this action by saying that the sun goes to sleep—*le soleil va se coucher.* In its turn, darkness becomes again victorious and the sun-god is killed; his slayer in the Ilacheu story is made to be the treacherous Kei.

This passing insight into the character of Kei will help us to understand, why the romances represent Kei as being present when the queen is carried away by Melwas. M. Paris[1] has carefully analysed Chrétien's poem, and we need only give a brief summary of his words:—Arthur was holding his court with due magnificence one Ascension Day, when a strange knight arrived, boasting that he held in captivity many of the king's subjects, both knights and ladies, who could never return except on the condition that Arthur would let a single knight accompany the queen to a neighbouring forest and there fight with him for her with success. The court was much troubled, and Ké (Kei) came to the king and queen pretending that he was about to quit the service; so he was allowed to have a boon of them. But when the boon came to be specified it proved, to their consternation, to be a demand that he, Ké, should be entrusted to take the queen out and to fight for her with the challenging knight. The king was obliged to acquiesce and the queen went much against her will: Gauvain (Gwalchmei) followed at a distance to find out the issue and Lancelot came on the scene after Ké had been sorely wounded. Lancelot obtaining a horse from Gauvain pursued, giving battle to Melwas, for he was the strange knight.

---

[1] *Romania,* xii. 464-485.

Lancelot lost his horse, and that without succeeding in preventing both the queen and Ké from being carried away towards the realm of Goire, whence nobody was wont to return. Gauvain overtook Lancelot and they fell in with a dwarf driving a cart: they asked him to tell them if he had seen the queen passing, but he would not answer unless they stepped into his cart. After a momentary hesitation, Lancelot did so and Gauvain rode behind. The next day Lancelot got a horse and he and Gauvain continued the pursuit for some time, but before night they separated, Gauvain to go to the Water Passage and Lancelot to the Sword Bridge, which he reached and crossed, as already mentioned, after travelling several more days and meeting fresh adventures. By fighting with Melwas and through the intervention of Melwas's father, King Bademagu, who was a just man, Lancelot procured the release of the queen, and the captives in Goire were now at liberty to return to their country. But when Lancelot came to speak to the queen she was indignant with him, and, instead of thanking him, she declined to converse with him : Ké also was indignant at Lancelot's accomplishing with honour the adventure he had commenced with disgrace. Afterwards Ké was charged by Melwas with having visited the queen's chamber during one of the nights they spent in his castle. Ké denied it, and rightly according to Chrétien's narrative, which makes Lancelot the guilty visitor, after the queen had ceased to be angry with him. In due time she reached Arthur's court, as did also Gauvain, but Lancelot was missing; for he had been entrapped on the way by Melwas, who confined him in one of his dens, but Lancelot was released thence by Melwas' sister just in time to fight with him in defence of the queen's reputation: it was then that Lancelot clove the skull of Melwas and left him dead in the field.

Looking at Chrétien's romance in the light of the Welsh dialogue between Arthur and Gwenhwyvar and of the Irish story of Mider, we are induced to think that the materials which the French romancer had to work upon consisted of two distinct versions of the myth. The queen in the romance frowns at her deliverer, just as in the dialogue she makes a pretence of not knowing him or of not considering him comparable to Kei; and when one has accounted for the rôle of Melwas, there still remain Kei's disgust with Lancelot's success, the charge laid against Kei of over intimacy with the queen, and the fact of that lady having been brought away from her husband's court with her husband's consent, the same unwilling consent which Echaid could not help giving to Mider previous to his carrying away Echaid's queen, Etáin, in the presence of the Irish court. Mider had played with Echaid for a stake unnamed; he had beaten the king, and when Mider chose his prize the king was astounded to find that it was the queen; but there was no escape. Similarly Arthur having allowed Kei to ask a boon of him, discovered that it was a demand that Kei should lead Gwenhwyvar to the forest to meet the strange knight who was to fight with him for her: the king and all felt that they were undone, but there was no help for it. The Irish tale would lead one to suppose that the strange knight was a confederate of Kei's, and that the latter had not to fight at all till Arthur reached his stronghold and forced him to surrender the queen, though she did not appear to have been eager to quit her captor; but Chrétien's poem rather suggests that his story is a jumble of two versions of one and the same mythic incident.

To return to Melwas, he cannot be dismissed without
a brief notice of the allusions to him by the 14th century
poet D. ab Gwilym. The first of them describes the
bard standing in a forlorn condition one cold night at
his leman's window thus [1]—

> ' Erchais gusan gwedlanach
> I'r fun, drwy'r ffenestr derw fach ;
> Gem adwyn, oedd gam idi,
> Gomedod ; ni fynnod fi !
> Astrus fu'r ffenestr oesdraul,
> Ile rhoed i dwyn lleufer haul :
> Na bwy' hen ! a bu o hud
> Ffenestr a hon unffunud,
> Dieithr hwyl da uthr helynt,
> Yr hon o Gaerlleon gynt,
> Y doe Felwas o draserch
> Drwydi, heb arswydi serch,
> Cur trymhaint cariad tramawr,
> Gynt ger ty ferch Gogfran Gawr.
> Cyd cawn fod, ped fai'n odi,
> Hwyl am y ffenestr a hi,
> Ni chefais elw fal Melwas.'

I demanded a kiss in sweeter wise
Of the lady through the little oak window ;
Gentle gem—it was wrong of her—
She declined me, would none of me.
Troublesome has been the life-wasting window
Where it was placed to let the sunlight in.
May I die ! if it was not of magic make
A window of this the very counterpart—
Except the course of the wondrous adventure—
That was the one at Caerleon of yore,
Which entrance gave of old to Melwas—
Driven by over-love without love's fears,
The dire plague and pain of mighty passion—
At the house of Giant Ogurvan's daughter.
As for me, though left, when falls the snow,
A while with the window between us twain,
No reward have I had like that of Melwas.

---

[1] D. ab Gwilym's Poetry (London, 1789), poem CLXI. (pp. 326 7).

Here the poet attributes, it would seem, some such an adventure to Melwas at Caerleon as that associated by Chrétien with Lancelot during his last night in Melwas' castle, and it suggests the question whether we have not to do with an instance of Chrétien's dealing with Lancelot's name in a way not warranted by the story in its Celtic form. But perhaps the more correct view to take of the foregoing verses is, that Ab Gwilym's version of the Melwas legend was, that he had not lain in wait for the queen but entered her chamber by the window, and carried her away from Arthur's palace itself. Ab Gwilym makes another allusion to Melwas when he describes a pleasant dream he had : among other things he compares it to—

'Hun Melwas dan y glas glog,'
The sleep of Melwas beneath the green cloak;

or, according to another reading [1],

'Hun Melwas yn y glas glog,'
The sleep of Melwas in the green cloak.

This last might naturally be explained to mean, that Melwas had clothed himself in green ; and it would fit in well with Malory's story to suppose, that, as the queen and her followers had gone forth in green, Melwas had donned a dress of the same colour the better to escape observation by them. Some Welsh writers [2] accept this view; but we must confess that we prefer following the other reading, and that the green cloak (*y glas glog*) related to a bower or some sort of half-covered place to which Melwas took his fair captive. This is favoured

---

[1] D. ab Gwilym's Poetry, poem CXI. line 44 (p. 220).
[2] For instance, in the last century Lewis Morris in his *Celtic Remains* (London, 1878), p. 220 (s. v. *Gwenhwyfor*), and in this century William Owen (better known as W. Owen Pughe, and Dr. Pughe) in the *Cambrian Biography* (London, 1813), p. 248 (s. v. *Melwas*).

by a passage in a poem which has also been usually
attributed to Ab Gwilym, though it is more probably
the work of another Welsh poet, D. ab Edmwnt, who
flourished in the 15th century.   He describes himself,
in the lines to be quoted, in much the same forlorn condition as Ab Gwilym in the first verses cited : the night
is cold, but the fair one will not open for the poet, and
the following is his pitiful complaint [1] :—

> 'Och ! nad gwiw ochenaid gwas,
> I mi alw am grefft Melwas ;
> Y lleidr, drwy hud a lledryd,
> Aeth a bun i eitha' byd :
> I'r coed lr ai'r hocedyd,
> I furiau cainc o frig gwyd—
> A dringo heno, fal hwn,
> Yn uchel a chwenychwn.'

> *Alas that a bachelor's sigh avails not*
> *For me to invoke the art of Melwas!*
> *The thief, that, by magic and illusion*
> *Took a fair one to the world's end :*
> *To the green wood that juggler went*
> *To the leafy rampart of a bough—*
> *And to climb to-night aloft like him,*
> *That is what I could wish to do.*

Here the poet would at first sight seem to place the
bower of Melwas high above the ground, among the
branches of a tall tree ; but his words do not necessarily
mean that, as he may have only meant to picture
Melwas ascending to the top of a wood-clad hill such as
Glastonbury Tor may have been ; and in one of the
next versions to be noticed of Gwenhwyvar's story the
queen is discovered by her deliverer sitting with her
captor under a tall tree.

Thus we have found the queen's captors bearing the
names Medrod, Melwas, and Kei ; but some of the

---

[1] D. ab Gwilym's Poetry, poem LV. (p. 106).

romances give other names such as Brun de Morois in
that of *Durmart le Galois*, Valerin in Ulrich's *Lanzelet*,
and Gasozein in Heinrich von dem Türlin's *Crone*. These
two last names have not yet been identified with any
Celtic names; but Valerin, whose name is also given as
Falerin, is described coming to Arthur's court to take
possession of Ginover (Gwenhwyvar), who, he will
have it, was promised to him before Arthur married
her: the matter was to be decided by single combat, but
nobody would undertake it until Lanzelet (Lancelot)
came forward and conquered Falerin. He did not,
however, give up his claim, and one day some time
afterwards during a hunt, Falerin carried the queen
away to his castle, which was surrounded by an impenetrable wilderness teeming with monsters, serpents,
and the like. Great difficulties attended the delivery of
the queen from the stronghold of Falerin, who had cast
her into a magic sleep: Lancelot took a leading part in
her rescue and Falerin was slain, but in bringing about
the release of the queen, Walwein (Gwalchmei) and Erec
(Gereint) had fallen into the hands of a mortal enemy of
theirs called Malduc, an enchanter, whom Lancelot and
his friends killed, setting Gwalchmei and his companion
at liberty[1]. The story of the capture of the queen by
Brun de Morois resembles that by Falerin: the queen
had gone out accompanied by Ydier li fiz Nu (Edern
son of Nûđ) to look one day at the chase, when Brun
came and carried the queen away in spite of Edern,
who was unarmed. Brun was powerful and rich: he had
been in love with the queen more than seven years, and
now he seized her and placed her in front of him and
galloped away with her to Morois, where he had a castle

---

[1] *Romania*, x, 475.

which was rendered impregnable by the nature of its situation [1]—

> 'Quar de mares et de croliere
> Estoit fermes en tel maniere,
> Que nus nel pooit assaillir.'

He cannot be dismissed without taking some notice of his name, Brun de Morois, representing as it does the Welsh *Du Moroed*, which occurs in the Triads, i. 93, where it is the name of a fabulous horse said to have belonged to Elidyr Mwynvawr: the great feat of that beast was his carrying $7\frac{1}{2}$ men from Penłłech Elidyr in the North to Penłłech Elidyr in Anglesey [2]. Du Moroed would mean the Black (Horse) of (the) Seas, but this form of the name is probably an attempt to give a meaning to an older one, *Du March Moro*, 'Black, the Horse of Moro.' It is the steed ridden by Gwyn ab Nûd, king of the other world, in the story of Kulhwch. It may be thought strange that we should introduce a horse, but in the romance known as the *Queste del St. Graal* we read of Perceval (Peredur), wearied and distressed for the want of a horse, accepting from a lady a very fine steed, of the hue of the blackberry, according to the Welsh translation [3]. Peredur mounted, and the beast soon brought him several days' journey out of a deep forest into the bright light of the moon; then he speedily traversed a broad valley and made straight for a vast and formidable river. Peredur pulled him up and made the sign of the cross, whereupon the horse fell down, left his rider on the bank, and plunged with a hideous cry into the flood, which he seemed to set all ablaze [4]. Of course the

---

[1] *Li Romans de Durmart le Galois*, ed. by Stengel (Bibliotek des litterarischen Vereins in Stuttgart, CXVI.), Tübingen, 1873, lines 4185-4340.

[2] *Hib. Lec.* pp. 370-1, 608.

[3] Williams' *Seint Greal*, pp. 60-1, 474-5.

[4] The *Queste del Saint Graal*, ed. for the Roxburghe Club by Furnivall, London, 1854, pp. 80-1. See also Nutt's *Legend of the Holy Grail*, p. 44.

romancer explains that the horse was the devil, and the devil in the form of a jet black steed is a familiar picture to the fancy of the Welsh: at any rate it was when the author was a child. Further, one of the chief names of the Celtic Pluto was Morc or Marc[1] in Irish, and March ab Meirchion in Welsh, which might be rendered into English by Steed son of Steeding or the like: he was also the Cornish king Mark of the romances, who contested the love of the Fair Isoud with Tristram (pp. 12, 37). His name referred to his having horse's ears[2], in spite of which he is represented sometimes as a king, and sometimes as the captain of a great fleet. So there cannot have been any insuperable difficulty to prevent the anthropomorphic treatment of the Black Steed of Moro: in all probability he was variously pictured as a horse, as a man, and as a monster sharing the features of both, and all that previous to the acquaintance of the romancers with his story. For the allusion, in *Durmart*, to a garden full of groves, roses, and lilies, where Brun de Morois, under the shelter of a mighty tree, sat by the queen on a cloth of silk and beaten gold, is not of the romancer's own invention so much as an echo of the Aryan myth regarding the King of the Other World.

[1] The Irish name is more usually Morc, but it also occurs as Margg and Marg in the *Book of Leinster*, 160ᵃ, where he is called steward of the king of Fomori. The name in the form *Marc* is borne by one of the foes killed by Cúchulainn on the Táin : see the *Book of the Dun*, 70ᵇ.

[2] The Midas-like story how they were detected will be found in the *Cymmrodor*, vi. 181-3. The Breton version is briefly mentioned in the *Rev. Celtique*, ii. 507-8, where instead of *March* one reads of '*le Roi de Portzmarch*.' A Cornish version is postulated by Malory's reference, x. 27, to 'the laye that sire Dynadan made kynge Marke/the whiche was the werste lay that euer harper sange with harp or with ony other Instrumentys.'

CHAPTER IV.

Peredur and Owein.

One of the chief heroes of Arthur's court is called in Welsh Peredur Paladr-hir or Peredur of the Long Shaft: he is also addressed more than once as Peredur the Fair, in the Welsh story bearing his name. There he is represented as the youngest son of Evrawc, Earl of the North, a connection in which possibly the term north is to be regarded as pregnant with the ancient meaning given it by an age, when the whole northern portion of Britain was supposed to be an accursed land given up to the ghosts of the departed, and the desolation described by the belated Greek author Procopius. It is not impossible that the mythic figure of Evrawc gave its ancient name of *Eboracum* to York, called in Welsh Caer Evrawg or Evrawc's Castle; but something like the contrary is also conceivable. Be that as it may, there was another Peredur, or, better perhaps and more correctly speaking, the same Peredur had several pedigrees; for according to the Triads a certain Eliver Gosgorđvawr, or E. of the large Retinue, had to wife a lady called Eurđyl, who gave birth at one time to three children, whose names were Gwrgi, Peredur, and Ceindrech [1].

Welsh literature treats this Peredur as distinct from

---

[1] Triads, i. 52.

the son of Evrawc so named, but that is probably to be accounted for as a difference in the version of the story of Peredur.　Now Ceindrech has the remarkable epithet of Pennasgett or wing-headed; add to this the fact that Gwrgi's name appears to have meant a man-dog, and we seem to have before us a highly mythic family: for a sun-hero to have a winged dawn-goddess to sister cannot be considered surprising, and his having a monster for a brother recalls Diarmait with his brother the Boar of Benn Gulbain, and the story of Morann's birth, together with others needless to enumerate[1].　Suffice it to mention the distinction between Gwalchmei and Medrod, and how its being overlooked led to the two dissimilar brothers becoming extolled together or depreciated together (p. 23); so in the case of Gwrgi and Peredur, when they are named together, we fail to seize on any definite characteristics of the one as distinguished from the other.　Thus in the Triad of the Horseloads of Britain[2], we find them riding on their horse Cornan to see the funeral pile of Gwendoleu at Arderydd[3].　Another Triad speaks of Gwrgi and Peredur at a place called Caer Greu, about to engage in battle, when they were deserted by their men, who thus left them to be killed by Eda Glinvawr or E. Big-knee, Nennius' Aetan or Eata Glinmaur[4] of Deira, the introduction of whose name would seem to give the story a touch of history, which has found its

---

[1] *Hib. Lec.* pp. 310, 507-8.

[2] Triads, i. 93; ii. 11 : compare also *Hib. Lec.* pp. 370-2.

[3] This should be part of a scene like the Norse description of the Anses riding or driving to Balder's bale-fire : see Vigfusson and Powell's *Corpus,* ii. 23.

[4] Triads, i. 35; ii. 42; iii. 81; Nennius, p. 72.　The Triad here referred to is that of the disloyal Retinues, one of which consisted of Goronwy's men deserting him when Ileu was to have his revenge on him : see the *Hib. Lec.* pp. 239-40.

way into the Welsh Chronicle[1]. The association of
Gwrgi's name with that of Peredur may be regarded
as accounting for the former occurring in later times as
a man's name[2]; but when the mythic Gwrgi is mentioned alone, it is never pretended that he was in any
way related to Peredur; and one would seem to be
warranted in assuming a second Gwrgi, who is described as Gwrgi Garwlwyd or G. the Rough and
Grey, the killing of whom by a certain Diffeidell of
Deira ranks as one of the Three commendable Slaughters
of Britain; for Gwrgi, who had become an ally of
Æthelfrith and married his sister, had contracted a
liking for human flesh at Æthelfrith's court, so that he
used to have a Welshman killed for him every day of
the week except Saturday, when he had two in order
to avoid breaking the Sabbath[3]. This is otherwise
alluded to as the catering for the Bald Man[4], which
probably means that there was, besides the name as-
cribing to him a dog's head, a story which treated him as
cropped and earless, in a word as a monster of a type
not unusual in the case of the sun-hero's brother[5].

---

[1] We refer to the entry under the year 580 : ' Guurci et Peretur moritur.'
See the *Cymmrodor,* ix. 155, also the *Annales Cambriae,* p. 5, where manuscript B is said to style Gwrgi and Peredur sons of Elifer.

[2] For instance, in late letters on a stone found at Ilangors, near Brecon :
see Hübner's *Inscript. Brit. Christianæ,* no. 41.

[3] See Triads, i. 37; iii. 45, 46; also Stephens' *Gododin* (London, 1888), pp.
148-51. The last-mentioned triad ascribes the like or worse cannibalism to
Æthelfrith himself. The allusion to the keeping of the Sabbath need not be
supposed to prove the triad modern : see the Tract on Sunday-keeping published from a Welsh MS. of the year 1346, known as *Ilyvyr Agkyr Ilan-
dewivrevi* (published in the *Anecdota Oxoniensia*), pp. 157-9.

[4] Triad, i. 79; iii. 82. The term used is *Anrheg y Gwr Moel,* ' the Dish or
the Meal of the Cropped Man,' but it has not been recognized as referring to
Gwrgi, because *anrheg* has been taken to mean simply a gift, whereas it has
here the well-established meaning of a dish or mess of food.

[5] See the stories of Corc and Morann, in the *Hib. Lec.* pp. 308, 311, and
compare pp. 391, 546.

The Triads concerning the feeding of the Bald Man, his alliance with Æthelfrith, and his leadership of renegade Brythons, will serve admirably to shew how the traditions about the struggles between the Welsh and the English could be drawn into the vortex of mythology.

Peredur is sometimes given a brother Elidyr, called Elidurus in the Latin text of Geoffrey, who makes Owein also brother to Peredur[1]. So far as we know, Geoffrey stands alone in treating the two latter warriors as brothers, but it cannot be regarded as an accidental slip on his part, as he represents them taking violent possession of the kingdom of their elder brother Elidyr, who was reigning then for the second time. They divided the island so that Owein took as his share all the country on this side of the Humber and Peredur all beyond the Humber, including the whole of Alban. In the course of years both died, and Elidyr[2] became king for the third time, an alternation not impossibly derived from the nature-myth picture of the never-ending struggle between the powers of light and those of darkness. But if there ever was a historical Peredur

---

[1] *Hist. Regum. Brit.*, ed. by San-Marte, iii. 17-18; *R. B. Bruts*, p. 81, *Myv. Arch.* ii. 162-4. But in the list of names in ix. 12 San-Marte prints Peredur son of 'Eridur,' where we have Eridur instead of Elidurus ; the Welsh makes Elidyr the name of Peredur's father in the same list (*R. B. Bruts*, p. 200).

[2] This is probably the same name, which in Giraldus Cambrensis' *Itin. Kambriæ*, i. 8, is given as Eliodorus to a priest, who, according to his own account, had spent a portion of his youth underground among the Fairies of Dyved. *Eliodorus* looks as though it should be the Greek Ἡλιόδωρος, but it is much more likely to be the Welsh Elidyr, that is to say, if it should not rather be regarded as a fairy name, for Eliodorus found the Fairies talking a language which resembled, according to the specimens he gave, Welsh with a touch of Irish and Greek. The Welsh Elidyr is probably to be regarded as of the same origin and formation as the Irish word *ailither*, 'pilgrim or *peregrinus*.'

he must have been one of the leaders of his race in the struggles with the Angles of Deira[1].

The Welsh story of Peredur, to which allusion has already been made, is so important that we now proceed to give the reader an abstract, and to compare it as we go on with the story of Owein. It consists of two parts, of which the second professes to busy itself about Peredur and Gwalchmei. The first[2] opens with the statement that Peredur had six brothers, who, together with his father, Evrawc, Lord of the Earldom of the North, are represented as having perished in wars and tournaments when Peredur was a child. So his mother, who was a prudent woman, retired with her young son and her household to a desert place far from the haunts of men, and her son was not to see or hear anything calculated to give him any hint about arms or knighthood. He was in fact reared in such innocent simplicity, that, noticing one day two does near his mother's goats, he concluded they must have lost their horns from long running wild in the woods: so by his swiftness of foot and much exertion he forced them with the goats into an outhouse used for the latter, and told his mother of the two goats that had run wild until they had lost their horns. The further news, that he had driven them in with the goats, brought the whole household out to look at them, and to judge for themselves of the truth of that statement. This curious incident, which looks at first sight like a mere embellishment of the story, is probably an ancient and integral part of it, as it has a kind of counterpart in the

---

[1] For the legend which connects Peredur with the Yorkshire town of Pickering, see Stow's *Annales or general Chronicle of England* (London, 1615), i. 12.

[2] *R. B. Mab.* pp. 193-232 ; Guest, i. 297-353.

story of Cúchulainn's early achievements[1] and his bringing the wild animals of Slieve Fuait home to Emain at
the bidding of Conchobar, who thought that such a task
would serve to make him forget a matter that was
causing him irritation [2]. Peredur, however, was not
destined to be always kept out of the world, for one
day three of the knights of Arthur's court passed near
his mother's abode. Peredur asked her what they were,
and she replied that they were angels, whereupon he
insisted that he would become an angel like them. He
procured the strongest of his mother's horses, and
imitated in a rustic fashion the equipment of the
knights ; his mother fell into a swoon when she
heard of it, and not long after she died broken-hearted
at his departure. But, before he went, she gave him
advice characteristic of the ideas of the Middle Ages,
and directed him to make for Arthur's court.

After journeying two days and nights in a wilderness
of woods and forests, he came to a clear spot, where he
saw a tent. It belonged to a knight, called in Welsh
Syberw y Llannerch, or the Proud one of the Glade,
and in French the Orgellous de la Lande ; he was away,
and his lady was alone in the tent. She bade Peredur
welcome, and he partook of the provisions he saw there.
Having conducted himself strangely, but honourably,
towards his hostess, he went his way, and reached
Arthur's court just when it had been the scene of a very
remarkable occurrence : a strange knight had entered

---

[1] *Hib. Lec.* p. 436.

[2] This was on the day he had brought his bride home, and the question of
the *jus primæ noctis* had made him furious : the difficulty was solved (*Bk. of
the Dun*, p. 127[a], and the Stowe MS. 84[c]), by an arrangement somewhat like
that adopted at Arthur's court when Gereint brought his bride Enid there :
the bed, in the latter case, was made in Arthur's chamber by the side of his
and the queen's: see the *R. B. Mab.* p. 263 ; Guest, ii. 94.

and insulted Gwenhwyvar the queen by seizing the
golden goblet from which she was being served, and
by throwing the wine over her, challenging any one
of the knights present to come forth to avenge the insult
by a duel with him. They all clave to their seats, since
they believed that he who would dare such a deed, must
be in some way invincible. Peredur, arriving when
they felt so uncomfortable, occasioned a temporary di-
version of their attention by the rusticity of his equipment; and he caused no little merriment by explaining
how he had come to see Arthur in order to be knighted.
In the meantime a dwarf, who had been at Arthur's
court for a whole year without saying a word to anybody, entered, and on seeing Peredur, greeted him,
saying: 'The welcome of Heaven to thee, fair Peredur,
son of Evrawc, chief of warriors, and flower of knighthood!' This, from one who had been like a mute all
the year, though he had had his choice of associates,
was too much for Kei the butler, so he dealt him a box
on the ear which felled him on the floor. Thereupon
the dwarf's companion enters, and she hails Peredur in
almost the same terms, and is kicked by Kei, so that
she fell on the floor as if dead. The dwarfs had been
in the service of Peredur's parents—that is hòw they
recognized him. Peredur observed their treatment by
Kei, and asked him where Arthur was. Kei told him
to hold his peace, and bade him go after the insolent
knight and recover the gold goblet. Peredur took the
hint; but the knight could not at first be made to understand the coming of such a rustic stripling, whom he
wished to treat lightly; he was, however, soon rid of
his uncertainty, and paid for his levity with his life.
Owein found fault with Kei for sending such a fellow
after the strange knight, so he followed in order to see

the issue, and was surprised to find the knight already
dead, with Peredur trying to strip him. Peredur now
took for his own use the fallen knight's horse and his
arms ; but, as nothing would induce him to return to
the court, he asked Owein to take the goblet to the
queen, and to tell Arthur that he would always be his
man, though he would not come back till he had avenged
himself on the tall fellow at his court : this was Kei the
butler.

Peredur had not journeyed long ere he was challenged by an enemy of Arthur's : he vanquished
him, but granted him his life on the condition of his
going to offer Arthur his submission, and to tell him
that he was sent by Peredur, who would not return till
he had avenged himself on Kei. In the course of
the week this was repeated no less than sixteen times,
and as each vanquished knight delivered the threat
directed at Kei, that officer of the court began to feel
uneasy. Peredur, wandering on, came to a wild wood,
by the side of which he beheld a lake, and beyond the
lake a fair castle. Peredur made his way thither, and
was received by the owner of the castle, who was seated
on a satin cushion on the shore, watching his men fishing on the lake ; he was himself lame and grey-haired.
He welcomed Peredur, and told him that he was his
mother's brother, and that he, Peredur, was to be
educated now for a while at his castle. So in the course
of the evening he made him go through a sword exercise, whereupon the uncle remarked that Peredur would
eventually excel everybody in the use of that kind of
weapon. Peredur was moreover to learn there the
manners of polite society, and to rid himself of the
homely speech of his mother, and his uncle was to dub
him a knight. There was one special rule which he

was to observe, and it was this: whatever marvel he
saw, he was not to ask questions, for the old man
explained that it would be his fault as his teacher, if he
was not duly informed.

To all this Peredur appears to agree; nevertheless
he takes leave of his uncle the next morning, and
arrives in the evening at the house of another brother
of his mother, where his skill in the use of the sword
was submitted to a test, at the end of which his
uncle declared that he was already the best swordsman in the kingdom, but that he had as yet only
acquired two-thirds of his martial excellence; when the
remaining third had been added, it would be useless,
he said, for anybody to contend with him. In the
course of the evening, while Peredur and his uncle are
conversing together, two young men appear, bringing
a lance of extraordinary length in, with three streams of
blood seen to trickle from it to the floor. At this sight
the whole household set up a great cry of wailing and
lamentation; but neither did the uncle break the course
of his conversation in order to explain to Peredur, nor
did the latter ask any questions. When this disturbance had ceased, they beheld two damsels coming in,
bearing a large charger with a man's head in it surrounded with much blood. The same scene of wailing
and lamentation occurs again, and the same apparent
unconcern as before is displayed by Peredur and
his host. These incidents, whatever they may have
meant, served here to test how far Peredur had learned
the lesson given him by his first uncle, just as the
ordeal with the sword was intended to test his progress
from a martial point of view.

Peredur, on leaving his uncle, met with his own foster-
sister, who bitterly reproached him with having caused

his mother's death. The sister's husband had a short time previously been slain by a knight, whom Peredur now overcame and compelled to take the widowed lady to wife. He was then to go to Arthur's court to relate his story and tell the emperor, that Peredur would never return till he had found Kei and taken vengeance on him for his insolence to him at the court. Peredur then wandered in quest of more adventure, and met with a knight whom he vanquished, and sent to Arthur's court with orders to repeat the threat against Kei. He then reached the castle of a young lady who was supported by her foster-brothers against the attacks of a neighbouring earl, who had deprived her of all her lands because she would not be his wife. Peredur found the castle running short of provisions and expecting to be besieged the next morning by the forces of the hostile earl; but he was most generously entertained by his hostess and in due time led to his chamber. Her foster-brothers now forced their sister to go and offer herself to Peredur as wife or mistress, just as he might choose, on condition of his aiding them in their extremity against the earl. She very naturally declined, and her sobbing waked Peredur, who asked her the cause of it. She told him the whole story, and he bade her go to rest, assured that he would do his best. In a few days this promise was redeemed beyond all expectation; for by his prowess he so vanquished the earl and his chief knights as to enable his hostess to recover her domain and obtain indemnity for the losses and the wrongs she had suffered.

Peredur having tarried there three weeks to settle matters, again betook himself to his wanderings, and the first thing recorded of him is his meeting the Proud Knight of the Glade, who was so enraged at Peredur

having visited his tent in his absence, that he had been
all this time in pursuit of him. It was of no avail to
his lady to declare that Peredur had offered her no
violence: he forced her to follow him in great wretchedness in quest of the man whom he charged with
insulting her. The result was that this knight was
speedily worsted and bound over to publish the fact,
that the lady had been found innocent, and that,
as an indemnity to her, he had been vanquished by
Peredur. The latter went his way and arrived at a
castle on a mountain, where he was hospitably entertained by the lady whom he found living there; but
he was advised by her to go elsewhere to sleep, as the
place was subject at night to grievous attacks from the
Nine Witches of Caer Loyw or Gloucester. Of course,
he insisted on staying to give his aid; so about the
break of day he was waked by a noise, and he rushed
out half dressed, sword in hand, just in time to rescue
a sentinel who was being assailed by one of the
witches. Peredur dealt her a stroke of his sword on
her head with such force that her helmet was flattened
like a dish; and the witch entreated Peredur by name
to spare her life. 'Hag,' said he, 'how knowest thou
that I am Peredur?' 'It is destiny and revelation,' she
replied, 'for us to have trouble from thee, and for thee
to have arms and a horse from me; and with me shalt
thou learn to ride and to handle thy weapons.' So,
on condition that the witches would no more injure
his hostess, the lady of the castle, Peredur went with the
witches to the Witches' Court; and when he had been
there three weeks and finished his training, he chose
his horse and his arms and took leave of the witches.
This latter part of Peredur's education corresponds to
that of Cúchulainn at the court of Scáthach, who would

G

not teach him till he had threatened her life, as did Peredur with the lady principal of the witches.

Peredur, on his way from the witches' abode, found lodgings the first evening in a hermit's cell, and the next morning, as he was setting out to continue his journey, his fancy was arrested by seeing in the snow that had fallen during the night the blood of a duck killed by a hawk. At the tramp of Peredur's horse the hawk flew away, leaving a raven in possession of the duck; the knight stopping short, sat stock still on his horse and leaned pensively on his long spear, comparing in his mind the fairness of his lady-love's complexion to the whiteness of the snow, the blackness of her locks to the sable plumage of the raven, and the brightness of the red in her cheeks to the drops of blood in the virgin snow[1]. While thus lost in his reverie he was espied by Arthur and his men in quest of Peredur, whose absence from the court was no longer to be endured; and Arthur asked, 'Who is the knight with the long lance, that stands above us yonder in the valley?' One of Arthur's men was despatched to enquire; and as he could get no answer, he struck Peredur, who then turned and thrust him off his horse without paying any further attention to him. The same thing happened in the case of twenty-four other men, who came to him one after the other. Lastly came Kei, who behaved very roughly to Peredur, which brought upon him the latter's anger. Kei fell in a swoon severely hurt, while his horse returned to the camp; men were then sent to fetch Kei, whose life was

---

[1] This passage is to be found in some form or other in most of the Perceval romances, and Prof. Zimmer, who calls attention to a more original form of it in the Irish story of the Children of Usnech (Windisch's *Irische Texte*, p. 71; *Bk. of Leinster*, 260ᵃ) makes some instructive remarks on it in his *Keltische Studien*, ii. 201–208.

thought to be in great peril. In spite of the fuss made
about the fallen butler, Peredur budged not until
Gwalchmei came, the knight of the golden tongue, who
soon elicited a gentle answer from the love-lorn warrior,
and commended the poetic nature of the generous
fancy occupying his thoughts. He further discovered
that it was Peredur, and told him his own name, whereupon a lasting friendship began between them, and
Gwalchmei brought Peredur to the camp, rejoicing to
learn that the knight he had so terribly punished was
no other than Kei, the one who had insulted him.

Arthur and Gwenhwyvar hardly knew how to make
enough of Peredur, but in the course of his first evening
at Caerleon he met a lady named Yngharad of the
golden Hand, whom he passionately loved and to
whom he declared it. She, however, said that she did
not love him or wish to have anything to say to him
as long as he lived; so he rashly swore that he would
not speak to any Christian on earth, till she had declared her love for him above all others. Accordingly
he departed the next morning from the haunts of his
fellow-men, and wandered in an unknown land till he
came to a spot called the Round Valley, the entrance to
which was guarded by a lion, whose habits were illustrated by the many human bones that filled a sort of
dungeon near where he was chained. Peredur killed
the lion and led his horse along a difficult path into the
Round Valley, where he found a fair castle which belonged to a big grey man. The latter offered the knight
hospitality, at the same time that he cursed his porter in
an aside, which taught Peredur that the lion was meant.
At their meal the Grey Man's daughter, in pity for her
father's guest, let the latter know that he would be
murdered in the morning, and at his request she readily

undertook to see that his horse and arms should be within his reach. So, when the Grey Man and his henchmen proceeded in the morning to carry out their purpose, they found themselves so far mistaken that many of them fell at Peredur's hands, and the Grey Man's own life was only spared by Peredur on the condition of his going to offer his submission to Arthur, and receiving baptism at his court. Peredur, finding that they of the Round Valley were heathens, rejoiced that he had not broken his oath.

Peredur's next adventure was his contest with a terrible serpent, that lay on a gold ring and kept the country waste for seven miles round; the struggle was a hard one, but Peredur succeeded and carried away the ring.

Now Peredur wandered so long without associating with any Christian, and longed so grievously for his comrades and the lady he loved, that his bloom and vigour departed from him. He resolved at last to return to Arthur's court as a dumb knight; but, before reaching there, he met Arthur's household going on an expedition under the leadership of Kei, who accosted Peredur, and, as he could get no answer, wounded him severely in the thigh; but Peredur would not retaliate, and Owein took the wounded knight to the queen to be healed, complaining bitterly of Kei's cruel conduct towards a youth who could not speak. It happened, however, before Arthur's men returned from their expedition, that a knight arrived demanding a man to fight with him. Peredur accepted the challenge, and vanquished the stranger: this occurred daily for a week, until Arthur at last resolved to accept the challenge himself; but Peredur, meeting the grooms as they were bringing the emperor his horse, took it away from them and rode to the meadow. As soon as this was known, spectators hurried to place themselves in advantageous positions to look on, and when everything was ready Peredur, the dumb knight, motioned with his hand to his antagonist to begin. He did so, but without being able to make Peredur budge. The latter now taking the offensive, lifted the challenging knight clean out of his saddle, and threw him a long cast from him. This done, he left the horse to the grooms, and walked back admired by all, and especially by Yngharad of the golden Hand, who said she was sorry that he could not speak. She went so far as to add, that, had he not been dumb, she could love him above all other men, and that, even as he was, she did so already. The dumb knight, delighted with these words and released from his oath, remained no longer dumb, but spoke to reciprocate Yngharad's love. It was not found out till then that it was Peredur. He now tarried at Arthur's court, and cultivated the society of Owein and Gwalchmei.

At this point in the story the scribe of the *Red Book* has suggested a break, and taking the hint we may for a moment pause to note, that the whole incident of Peredur's returning wasted and disabled to Gwenhwyvar to be healed, his being brought by Yngharad of the golden Hand to make use of speech again, and his upholding the honour of the court, in the absence of Arthur's men, against the challenging knights, has its counterpart in the story of Owein. It is that part of it [1] which relates how, after Owein had been living with wild beasts, he came in extreme weakness to the park of a widow lady, who took compassion on him, and sent her handmaid to anoint him with a precious ointment. This, as the narrative proceeds to tell, began to restore him his senses

---

[1] See the *R. B. Mab.* pp. 183-6 ; Guest, i. 70-5.

and his vigour; and he remained three months in the
widow's castle until he had, under her handmaid's care,
fully recovered his former strength. Then a neighbouring earl, who had appropriated all the widow's domains
except the castle in which she was living, came to besiege
her in that her last refuge, whereupon Owein rode forth
to meet him in the middle of his host, and succeeded in
dragging him out of his saddle and galloping away with
him to make him a present to the widow in her castle;
so that the earl was forced to restore to her all that
was hers and to make her ample amends. Here, in the
Peredur, the two ladies are represented as Gwenhwyvar,
Arthur's wife, and Yngharad of the golden Hand, one of
the ladies of the court; but we hear no more of either
in connection with Peredur.

The story[1] recommences with Peredur engaged in the
chase with Arthur's household, when his hound in
pursuit of a stag led him away to a desert place. There
Peredur came to the castle of one called the Arrogant
Black Fellow, a one-eyed robber not unlike a Perverse
Black Man slain by Owein[2], and the issue of Peredur's
adventure also resembles that of Owein's. Peredur, by
killing the robber-knight, gave their freedom to the
young men and women in his stronghold; but when it
was suggested to him that the immense wealth of the
Black Fellow belonged to him and his choice of the fair
maidens there, he declined both, and set out for the court
of the King of Suffering, of which the Arrogant Black
Knight had been forced to tell him. He was hospitably
received there, but he had not been there long when he
saw a horse entering with a dead knight on his back.
One of the women, who did all the service in the castle,

---

[1] *R. B. Mab.* pp. 220-232; Guest, ii. 269-282.
[2] *Hib. Lec.* pp. 352-4.

arose and bathed the corpse near the door; she then
applied a precious ointment to it, when it became alive,
and the man proceeded to welcome Peredur and converse with him. Two more dead knights arrived in due
time and underwent the same treatment with the same
result: it was explained to Peredur that they were slain
daily by the Avanc of a lake in the neighbourhood.

Next morning, however, they would not allow Peredur
to accompany them to the monster, since the knight, if
killed, could not, they said, be restored to life; but
Peredur resolved to find the Avanc for himself; so he
set out in quest of the Avanc's cave, when he was
stopped on his journey by a wondrously fair damsel
seated on a mound near his path. The story makes her
tell him, that she both knew whither he was going, and
how the Avanc would kill him by craft and not by
valour; for he abode, she said, in a cave whence he saw
everybody that came, whilst he was himself seen of no
one, so that he used to cast at every comer a poisoned
spear from behind a pillar that stood at the mouth of the
cave. She would, however, give Peredur a precious
stone which would render him invisible at will, but it
was on the condition that he would love her above all
other women. Peredur pledged his honour that he did
so, even from the moment he beheld her; and he
enquired where he should find her, to which she
replied that he was to seek her in the direction of
India.

She then vanished, and Peredur arrived in a land
of wonders, consisting of a valley with level meadows.
On one side he saw a flock of white sheep, and on
the other a flock of black ones; he observed that
when one of the white sheep bleated a black sheep
would cross the river and become white with the white

sheep, and vice versa[1]. Other strange things he saw
there, such as a tree with its one half burning and the
other covered with green leaves, while a little above he
perceived a man in the prime of life sitting on a mound
with a greyhound lying on either side of him. From
the wood in front of him he heard the barking of dogs
starting the deer and driving them into the open.
Peredur asked the man on the mound his way, and was
told whither the roads led which branched off there.
He thanked him, and took the narrower way, which
led to the Avanc's cave. When he reached the cave, he
took the stone of invisibility in his left hand and his
spear in his right. He found the Avanc and killed him ;
then he cut off his head and gave it to the three brothers,
whom he met on his way back as they were hastening
to their daily death. They thanked him, and added that
it had been prophesied that the pest was to be slain by
Peredur; they then offered him to wife whichever of
their sisters he might choose. Peredur replied, as was
his wont, that he had not come to their country to marry.

The mythological meaning of the incident cannot, we
think, be mistaken : the three men daily slain represent
the divisions of the daylight portion of the twenty-four
hours[2] into morning, noon, and afternoon or evening,
which daily pass away to come again. The Lake
Avanc with his poisonous spear stands for darkness ;
and the death of the monster at Peredur's hands means
the victory of the sun over night and its cold blasts.
This is less readily perceptible in the corresponding
incident in the story of Owein and Lunet, namely
where it makes the former slay the Black Knight of

---

[1] This also forms one of the wonders in the Irish story of Maildun's Coracle :
see Joyce's *Old Celtic Romances*, p. 134, and the *Bk. of the Dun*, 23[b].

[2] *Hib. Lec.* p. 494.

the Fountain without being himself, thanks to the
Gygean ring given him by Lunet, made to suffer death
as the reward of his bravery. On the other hand,
another part of Owein's story is more explicit in that
it represents the twenty-four hours of the day as so
many matrons whom he releases from captivity in the
castle of a robber called the Perverse Black Man[1].
In the corresponding account in the story of Peredur, the captives form a vague number of either sex,
released with all their wealth by Peredur's killing the
Black Fellow that held them in his power. In any
case, the comparison between the two stories throws
light on both ; and here may be mentioned the stone of
invisibility given to Peredur by the lady on the mound
as being matched in the story of Owein by the Gygean
ring given him by Lunet. The ring is probably to
be regarded as a form of the wheel symbol which
M. Gaidoz has shown to be solar[2]: it refers in a word
to the disk of the sun with its light overpowering the
strength of human vision and concealing the body of
that luminary from the unaided eye of man. In another
story it becomes the magic armour that makes Cas-
wallon invisible, all except the sword with which he
cut down all opposition to his rule[3].

We left Peredur benefited by the good-will of the
woman he met on the mound; and we have now to
relate the sequel. As he was journeying away from
the court of the King of Suffering he was overtaken
by one who offered to be his man: it was a knight
in red armour and mounted on a red charger. He
said his name was Edlym of the red Sword, from

---

[1] *R. B. Mab.* p. 191 ; Guest, i. 82.

[2] See his *Études de Mythologie gauloise*, pp. 8, 19.

[3] *R. B. Mab.* p. 41 ; Guest, iii. 126.

the region of the East. His offer was accepted, and
the two knights travelled towards the court of the
Lady of the Feats, who was so called because she had
three hundred knights, and was to be the wife of him
who could vanquish them in feats of arms. Peredur
did so and sat then by right next to her at her table,
whereupon she remarked that she was very happy to
have such a husband, as she had not had the man she
loved best. Peredur, on asking to whom she alluded,
was told that it was one she had never seen, namely,
Edlym of the red Sword; and Peredur was delighted
to introduce that knight to her as his friend, and to give
her to him to wife that very day. This princess seems
to be the one called in some of the romances the queen
of Pluris, and Peredur giving his own bride away to his
friend, the red knight, has a parallel in the story of
Cúchulainn delivering the daughter of the King of
the Isles to his friend Lugaid of the red Stripes to be
his wife, though he was himself entitled to marry her
as having rescued her from the Fomori [1].

Peredur now journeyed towards the Mound of Mourning, where there was in a cairn a dragon with a stone in
its tail of such virtues, that whoever held it in one hand,
would have as much gold as he could wish in the other.
Around the mound he found 300 kings and princes
encamped, and bent each on securing the precious
stone for himself. So Peredur first vanquished them
and then proceeded to assail the dragon, which he did
successfully. He took possession of the precious stone
and paid the kings the expense of their war on the
monster, on the condition of their declaring themselves
his men. He next paid Edlym for his services by
presenting him with the precious stone; he then bade

[1] *Hib. Lec.* pp. 465, 479.

him farewell and left him to return to his wife, the
Queen of the Feats.

Peredur now went his way and chanced on a spot
where a great tournament was to be held by a lady
called the Empress of Constantinople the Great, who
would have to husband no other man than the bravest
in the world. Peredur did not recognize her, but he
was so charmed with her beauty that after inertly
gazing at her for two days, he entered the lists to fight
for her hand. The result was that he distinguished
himself above all the other knights, but when the
Empress sent for him, he maltreated her men. At last,
however, he was prevailed upon to come to her presence; but his manner was not all that she could wish.
So at a second interview she addressed him thus:
'Fair Peredur, remember thy troth thou gavest me
when I gave thee the stone, what time thou slewest
the Avanc.' 'Lady,' said he, 'thou speakest truly,
and now do I remember it.' On this part of the story,
which adds that Peredur reigned with the Empress no
less than fourteen years, let it suffice that the question
will be raised, in a later chapter, as to the identity of
the Empress with the damsel who gave Peredur the
stone alluded to by the Empress.

Single incidents in the Peredur have been identified
with single incidents in the story of Owein, and it
now remains to be shown that we were warranted in
so doing, by further showing that the principal sequence
in the one corresponds to that in the other. This
applies to the story of Peredur from his setting out for
the Avanc's cave to his reigning with the Empress;
but to make the parallelism clear, it will be necessary
to give here an abstract of the passages in question in
the Owein story. The latter hero, then, after wandering

on desert mountains in the furthermost parts of the
earth, comes to a valley where he finds a castle, in
which he is hospitably received for the night. He
asks how he should find the Black Knight of the
Fountain, whom he desires to encounter. His host,
pitying him, is reluctant to answer his question, but
consents to do so in the morning; so Owein, put on
the right way and informed where to make further
enquiries, journeys through a wood until he comes
to a large open field with a mound in the middle of
it. On the mound sits a black giant whose peculiarity
is his having only one foot to walk with, and only
one eye in the middle of his forehead. Around him
a thousand wild beasts graze ; he is their shepherd,
and they obey him through the medium of a stag who
plays the part, so to say, of bell-wether among them.

The black giant told Owein the way to take and how
to challenge the Knight of the Fountain ; he directed
him to a spacious valley in the middle of which stood
a remarkable tree, beneath which there was a well.
By the well he would find a marble slab with a silver
tankard attached to it : he was to fill the tankard with
water and to throw it on the slab. This would bring
on a fearful thunder followed by a destructive hailstorm,
which would be followed by a marvellous warbling of
birds ; and then at last the Knight of the Fountain,
arrayed in black satin, and with a black flag streaming
from his spear, would himself arrive on a black horse,
charging at full speed. Owein did as he was told,
and fought with the sable knight, until the latter, feeling
that he had been mortally wounded, took to flight.
Owein pursued so hotly that he followed him into
his city, when the portcullis was so let down that it
cut off the part of his horse behind his saddle, while

the inner door was shut in front of him: thus was he left in a perilous position.

He could see the street through a crack; and presently a young lady in yellow satin and with a diadem of gold on her head, which was adorned with yellow curly hair, came to the gate and asked him to open. He replied that he could not; she expressed her sorrow at his plight and complimented him on his gallantry and merits with regard to her sex, though the story gives no hint how she knew of his coming or who he was[1]. However, what she could she would do for him, so she gave him a ring with a stone in it, which, when turned inwards so as to be concealed in his hand, had the virtue of concealing his entire person from the knight's men, who would come soon to fetch him for execution. Lunet, for that was her name, would also come, and Owein was to put his hand on her shoulder to show her that he was there; she would then lead the way for him. This was in due time done, and Owein found himself at last in an upper chamber large and gorgeous. Lunet attended to his comforts; she not only brought him food and drink, but she also shaved his beard and washed his head for him. In the night the death-wail of the Black Knight was heard, and in the course of the next day they saw his funeral pass, where a lady, distinguished by the intensity of her grief, attracted Owein's attention, who declared to Lunet that he loved that lady above all others. She replied that it was her mistress, whose husband he had slain the day before, and added that he might be sure that her mistress had no love for him. Nevertheless she

[1] The omission may be said to be supplied, after a fashion, by Malory's story of Beaumayns and Lynet.

undertook to woo her for him, but her mistress reproached
her with having kept away from her throughout her
trouble.   She was well-nigh inconsolable, and when
Lunet hinted that she had best bethink her how she
might win the victorious knight, her indignation was
boundless.   After a stormy scene, Lunet urged her to
consider that her earldom could only be maintained by
one who could hold his own at the well, by overcoming
all those who chose to challenge him.   Such a one,
she added, could only be found at Arthur's court,
whither she would go on this errand, and she expressed
her confidence that she would not fail in her object.

This she pretended to do, and when time enough
had lapsed, she prepared Owein to visit the castle, by
shaving his beard and washing his head.   When,
however, they arrived at the castle as though coming
from Arthur's court, the widow Lady of the Fountain
did not fail to see through the ruse ; but it was urged
by Lunet that, unless Owein were the more valiant
knight, he could not have overcome the other ; and
after some delay, when the chief men of her earldom
were consulted, she consented to become Owein's wife.
He lived three years with her before Arthur and his
men could discover what had become of him.

Here one will have noticed the following points
of agreement between the romances of Peredur and
Owein :—

1. The sons of the King of Suffering, at whose court
Peredur was hospitably entertained, refused to lead their
guest to the Avanc's cave, as they did not wish to see
him killed by that monster.

The lord of the castle where Owein past the night on
his way to find the Knight of the Fountain would not
at first give him the information he wanted, because he

did not wish to have any hand in bringing him into trouble.

2. Peredur, setting out alone for the Avanc's cave, comes into a land of wonders, and is put on the right way by a comely youth sitting on a mound watching wild animals hunted.

Owein, after journeying through a wood, comes to a mound with a kind of Cyclops sitting on it surrounded by wild animals: he pointed out to him the way he was to take.

3. Peredur finds the Avanc and kills him, his own safety being insured by the stone of invisibility given him for that purpose by a lady on the way.

Owein inflicts a mortal wound on the Black Knight, and his own life is saved by the invisibility thrown over him by the stone in the ring, given him by Lunet to ensure his escape from his perilous position.

4. The lady who gave Peredur the precious stone would have no husband but him who proved the most valiant in the tournament which she instituted to help her choice.

The Lady of the Fountain could only have as husband a knight who overcame all those who chose to challenge him at the Well.

5. Peredur, proving victorious in the Empress' tournament, reigns with her fourteen years.

Owein having slain the Black Knight is the only eligible husband for his widow, so he upholds her power and lives with her for three years.

6. The Avanc of the Lake is so far of the human form that he is represented using a spear.

Owein's antagonist is called the Knight of the Fountain, who rides like other knights and fights with spear and sword.

One of the chief differences between the two stories
is that no Lunet appears in the Peredur, and that while
the wooing is done by her for Owein, the Empress
in the Peredur has to do it herself, the hero being
treated as too proud to acknowledge how profoundly
smitten he was with her charms. Add to this that
the Lady of the Fountain, appearing first as the Black
Knight's consort and then as Owein's, places herself
beyond doubt among the goddesses who at one time
consort with dark beings and at another with light
ones. On the other hand, nothing is said as to any
previous husband of the Empress ; but that is not
a difference between them so much as a lack of data
to warrant any inference.

The correspondences indicated will serve as our jus-
tification for identifying single incidents in the one story
with single incidents in the other. To these we would
now add one which was disposed of in few words as
leading up to no consequences in the Peredur. Its
importance is easily overlooked among the incidents in
which precious stones and rings so commonly figure.
Peredur, it will be remembered, is represented, among
his many exploits, killing a serpent which lay on a gold
ring and kept the country waste for seven miles round.
He took the ring away, and we read nothing more about
it. We seem, however, to detect the incident in the
story of Owein, where it is pregnant with results [1] :—

Owein journeying in a wood came near a large knoll
with a grey rock in the side of the knoll. The rock
had a cleft in it, where there was a serpent, and near
the serpent stood a pure-white lion trying to get away ;
but when the lion moved, the serpent would dart at him.
It was the howling of the lion that had attracted Owein

[1] *R. B. Mab.* pp. 186-191 ; also *Hib. Lec.* p. 402.

in that direction, and when he saw the cause of it he drew his sword, and as the serpent came out of the cleft he cut it in two. Thereupon the lion followed him like a greyhound wherever he went, and fought his antagonists for him. Here we have the serpent in both incidents, but a seemingly impassable gulf is fixed between the ideas of a ring and a lion. The necessary means, however, for bridging it over is supplied by a confusion of speech based on the similarity between the Welsh words ȴeu, 'light,' and ȴew, 'lion [1].'

The ring is probably to be regarded as a solar symbol : referred to its original in mythology, it meant the disk of the sun. So the gold ring on which the serpent of darkness lay stands here for the sun and his light; but the Welsh word for *light*, treated mythologically, was *ȴeu*, which therefore appears as the proper name of ȴeu, the most remarkable of Welsh sun-heroes. In Irish the name was Lug, and we have it also in the Lugus of *Lugudunum* in southern Gaul : in fact, the worship of this divinity of light, known to us by the names ȴeu and Lug, was one of the most widely spread, and his feast one of the most celebrated among the Celts of antiquity [2]. But in Welsh the meaning of his name ȴeu being forgotten, it was, perhaps, the more readily confounded with ȴew, the Welsh for *lion*. In any case, ȴew came to be preferred to ȴeu as his name. At what date and by whom the confusion was first made is not known; but the contrast between the incident in question, as given in the stories of Peredur and Owein respectively, marks the point of a new departure which may be studied on a larger scale in Chrétien de Troyes' poem entitled the *Chevalier au Lion*.

[1] *Hib. Lec.* pp. 398 409.   [2] Ib. p. 420.

CHAPTER V.

PEREDUR AND THE EMPRESS.

THE second portion of Peredur's story is one purporting to be also about Gwalchmei [1]. Arthur was
holding his court one Easter at Caerleon, and there
were there together Owein son of Urien, Gwalchmei
son of Gwyar, Howel son of Emyr Llydaw, and Peredur
of the Long Lance, when they saw entering on a mule
a black maiden of hideous form and uncanny appearance. She greeted all except Peredur, to whom she
said: ' Peredur, I will not greet thee, for thou dost not
deserve it. Blind was Destiny when thou wert granted
genius and renown. When thou camest to the court
of the Lame King, and when thou sawest there the page
bringing in the ground-spear with the blood running
from its point, blood that flowed in a stream down on
the page's fist, together with other wonders there
beheld by thee, thou didst not ask their meaning or
their cause; whereas, if thou hadst but asked, the king
would have health and his dominions peace. As it
is, he has battles and conflicts and loss of knights, and
wives widowed and ladies without dowry; and all that
on thy account.' Then she said to Arthur: 'With thy
leave, my lord, far hence is my home in a proud castle,

---

[1] *R. B. Mab.* pp. 232–243, Guest, i. 354-370, as to which it is to be
noticed, that most of what is here related of Peredur is said of Gwalchmei
in the second part of the *Seint Greal*: see Williams' edition, pp. 190-246.

of which, may be, thou hast not heard.   In it are six knights and three score and five hundred, all knights of rank, each with the lady he loves best.   Whoever wishes to earn fame by arms and combat and battle, may find it there if he undertake it; but whoever wishes for the highest fame and honour, I know where he might find it: there stands on a conspicuous mountain a castle in which there is a maiden, and it is undergoing siege: whoever could free it, would have the highest fame in the world.'   Thereupon she went her way, and Gwalchmei said that he could not enjoy sleep till he delivered the besieged maiden, and others gave expression to similar sentiments.   As for Peredur, he said that he could not rest till he discovered the meaning of the story of the Black Maiden.   While the knights were preparing to go forth on their errands, there entered a strange knight, who was distinguished by the azure colour of his arms: he greeted all present except Gwalchmei, whom he accused of having slain his master.   Gwalchmei denied the charge, and undertook to follow the knight to prove his innocence.   Gwalchmei and Peredur, on account of their friendship, set out together; but we soon find them severed.

Gwalchmei, after an adventure of no sequence in the story, disappears till we approach the close of it; but Peredur wandered about the island for a whole year, associating so little with his fellow-creatures that he lost his reckoning of time.   So, at the last, he falls in with a knight arrayed in the habit of religion, and he asks him for his blessing; but the reply to his request was, 'Alas, thou wretched man! thou dost not deserve it, nor will it profit thee, because of thy bearing arms on such a day as this.'   'What day is it, then?' asked Peredur.   'To-day is Good Friday,' answered the

other knight. 'Do not rebuke me,' replied Peredur,
' I did not know it : it is twelve months to this day since
I set out from my country.' Peredur then alighted and
led his horse ; for some distance he kept to the high
road, but on finding a by-way he followed it through
a wood, at the further side of which he descried a tower-
less castle. As it showed signs of habitation he drew
near, and found at the gate the man of religion who had
a short while previously refused him his blessing. On
his repeating his request he granted it, remarking that
Peredur was now journeying in a fashion more becoming the day. He was then invited to stay there that
night ; and in fact he was not allowed to depart till the
fourth day, but then his host gave him information
which was to bring him nearer to the Castle of Wonders,
where a later passage in the story places the home of
his consort, the Empress. Now the Black Maiden,
when causing Peredur to roam far away from the
haunts of men until he had lost his reckoning of the
days, has her unmistakable parallel in the more gorgeous
maiden who, similarly entering Arthur's hall, uttered
bitter words to Owein, which resulted in making him
for a time a madman and the companion of the wild
beasts of the forest. But the part of the widow lady
and her handmaid, who brought Owein to his senses
and so enabled him to proceed with the search for his
forgotten spouse, is here assigned to a religious knight,
who recalls Peredur to a sense of the obligations of
religion which he had forgotten, and puts him on the
way to find the Castle of Wonders.

Peredur, according to his host's directions, was to
cross a mountain pointed out to him, and make his way
down into a valley, where he was to find a king's court ;
there, if anywhere, he was to learn how to reach his

destination.   On his way towards the court, Peredur
met the king in question going out to hunt; and he
gave Peredur his choice, whether he should join in the
hunt or be led by one of his attendants to the court,
where the king's daughter would give him food.   Peredur chose the latter, but the king's attendant who led
Peredur to the princess thought it necessary, on his
rejoining the hunt, to tell the king that the princess was
not to be trusted with the knight: so suspicious, to his
thinking, was the levity she showed in her manner of
welcoming the knight and of conversing with him.
The result was that the king sent men to put Peredur
under arrest; but the princess came to entertain him,
and when it was night she had his permission to have
her bed made near Peredur, so as to be able to converse
with him.   The next morning there was a combat to
take place between the king's hosts and those of a
neighbouring earl, who contested the king's power.
Peredur begged to be allowed to go to look on, a request which the princess granted on condition of his
returning to his prison.   She provided him with horse
and arms, and he wore a red robe over his armour and
carried a yellow shield.   He came back in the evening,
and the princess learned from her father, that the man on
his side who had distinguished himself above all others,
was one with a red robe and a yellow shield: so she
knew it was the captive knight.   This went on for three
days, and on the fourth the red-robed knight slew the
earl opposed to the king, whereby he enabled the latter
to add the former's earldoms to his own kingdom.   At
last the king was told by his daughter who the red
knight was, and he now knew not how to show him
honour enough, except by offering him his daughter's
hand and the fallen earl's lands.   Peredur replying, as

was his wont, that it was not to marry he had come,
was asked what he was in quest of: he said it was the
Castle of Wonders. 'The prince's mind,' said the
princess to the king, 'is set on greater things than we are
asking.' She then told Peredur that she loved him more
than any other man, and giving him guides to lead him
out of her father's territory, she provided that his journey should be free of expense to him. 'Go,' she said,
'over that mountain facing us, and thou wilt see a lake
with a castle within the lake: that is the Castle of Wonders, but we know nothing about it, except that it is
called so.' The same incident happens to Lancelot in
Chrétien's poem of the *Charrette*: M. Paris summarizes
it as follows [1]:—' Le chevalier de la charette rencontre
ensuite, à la tombée de la nuit, une demoiselle qui lui
offre l'hospitalité, mais à une condition, c'est qu'il cou-
chera avec elle. Il y consent, bien que fort peu volon-
tiers. Il livre chez elle un combat terrible, qu'elle
semble avoir fait naître pour l'éprouver, et, pour accom-
plir sa promesse, partage son lit, mais sans la toucher.
Elle a pitié de lui et se retire seule dans sa chambre ; là
elle réfléchit à cette aventure, et se dit que ce chevalier,
auquel ne se compare aucun de ceux qu'elle a connus,
a certainement en tête quelque entreprise bien haute et
bien périlleuse ; elle souhaite qu'il y réussisse.' The
knight escorts her on a journey in the morning, and
they reach a meadow where another knight would offer
violence to the lady and fight with her protector.

Now the Welsh version presents a difficulty of its
own ; for why should the levity of the king's daughter
make the former imprison Peredur and then allow the
princess absolute power over his movements ? Probably the original made the lady independent of, or

---

[1] *Romania*, xii. 468.

unconnected with, the man called in the story the king ;
at any rate, there can scarcely be any doubt as to their
not appearing originally as father and daughter. This
is seen very clearly from a comparison of the second
part of the Peredur with the second part of the Owein.
The latter is in short this : Owein had left his wife, the
Lady of the Fountain, to go to spend three months at
Arthur's court; but he had forgotten her and been
away as many years, when a damsel in gorgeous array
rode into the hall and upbraided Owein in bitter terms.
He in consequence became mad, as already related, and
avoided the haunts of men ; at last he was restored to
his senses and his strength by the care of a widow lady
and her handmaid, whom he requited by delivering
them from the neighbouring earl who oppressed and
wronged them. He next met with the adventure which
resulted in giving him the lion as his ally and servant [1].
This brings us to the incident here in point ; for the
first evening the lion was with him the animal procured
venison for his master, who was engaged in cooking it
when he heard a groan. It was repeated, and on examination he found that it issued from a stone prison hard
by : it proved to be the voice of Lunet, the handmaid
of the Lady of the Fountain. Without finding out who
Owein was, she told him her story to the following
effect :—'I am imprisoned because of a knight who
came from Arthur's court to obtain the Lady of the
Fountain to be his wife. He remained a while with
her, and went to sojourn at Arthur's court and has
never returned. He was to me the companion I loved
most of all in the world. Now, two of the Lady of the
Fountain's chamberlains spoke ill of him and called him
a deceiver. I said their two persons could not contend

[1] *Hib. Lec.* pp. 402-4.

with his alone. Therefore am I incarcerated in this stone receptacle and told that my life will not be left me, unless he come to defend me within a certain time, and that is no further off than the day after to-morrow. But I have nobody to seek him, and he is no other than Owein, son of Urien.' On being asked if she thought Owein would come if he knew the plight she was in, she expressed her belief most positively that he would. Owein, without disclosing his identity, divided his meal with her and spent the night hard by her, conversing with her till it was daylight.

In the course of the day, Owein, following Lunet's directions, went to a neighbouring castle whose lord was famous for his hospitality. He was well received there, but he observed that everybody was sad there and mournful in the last degree, and on enquiry he found that the reason of it was, that the day before a man-eating giant had caught his host's two sons on the mountain, and was to come on the morrow and kill them before their father's face, unless his only daughter should be given up to him. When, however, the morning came and the cannibal arrived, Owein and the Lion fought with him, and the latter despatched him. So were the sons of his host rescued by Owein, who then hastened back to the meadow where he had left Lunet. He appeared on the spot just in time to prevent her being burnt alive : he had to fight with the two chamberlains, who were both killed by Owein, aided by the Lion. Then Lunet takes Owein to her mistress, the Lady of the Fountain, who remained his wife as long as she lived.

Here, it is needless to point out, there is nobody who could be set over against the father of the princess in the Peredur incident. Another difference between the

incident in the Peredur and in the Owein is, that while
Peredur himself is the prisoner, and the princess his
consoler who makes her bed near him, Owein is free
and finds Lunet a prisoner, whom he entertains with his
conversation till daybreak.   In this matter the Peredur
may be supposed, as will be seen later, to be the more
original, while the unusual nature of the rôle assigned
the woman may be regarded as supplying the motive for
the exchange of the parts played by Owein and Lunet
respectively in their story.   Lastly, Lunet, after the
death of those who would burn her, took Owein to his
wife, her mistress; but the daughter of the king in the
Peredur only makes herself responsible for the expenses
of Peredur's journey out of her dominion, and shows
him the way to the Castle of Wonders, where his consort lived.   The former story does not tell us what
passed between Owein and his wife on his return, or
how she received him after his inexcusable absence,
whereas the other story throws in Peredur's way a
number of labours, which he has to accomplish before
he is permitted to see his wife's face.

Following the directions given him, Peredur arrived
at the gate of the Castle of Wonders, which he found
open; so he entered and espied a game of chess being
played by the pieces themselves.   He ventured to give
his assistance, but the side he aided always lost.   This
so irritated him that he threw the board and all into the
lake, whereupon the Black Maiden appeared on the
scene and began to scold him, and to emphasize the
loss he had caused the Empress, who valued her chess-
board more than half her empire.   Peredur asked if he
could in any way make amends for it, when he was told
that he could, namely, if he went to the Castle of
Ysbidinongyl (p. 3), and slew the Black Man there, who

was laying waste a part of the Empress's territory; if
he did that, he would find the chess-board restored to its
place. He did so and vanquished the Black Man, but
spared his life on condition of his placing the chess-
board where it was first seen by Peredur. The Black
Maiden intervenes again, and curses Peredur for
leaving the pest alive: so he goes and kills the Black
Man. Having done so, he comes to the Castle of
Wonders and asks for the Empress, but the Black
Maiden replies: 'Thou wilt not see her now, unless thou kill a pest there is in that forest yonder.'
She referred to a one-horned stag that roved about in
a neighbouring forest. He went and succeeded in his
undertaking, but, just as he had cut off the stag's head,
a lady came riding up to him and began angrily to
rebuke him for having destroyed the finest gem in her
dominion. He replied that he had been ordered to do
so, and he asked if there was any way in which he
might win the lady's good-will: she replied there was,
namely, if he went to a mountain she indicated to him,
on the side of which he would find a grove with a stone
slab underneath it: there he was to ask thrice for a
man to fight with him. He did as he was told, and
there emerged from beneath the stone a black man on
a bony horse, with rusty armour on him and his beast.
They fought, but no sooner was the Black Man un-
horsed than he mounted again; so Peredur thought it
expedient to dismount and draw his sword, but as soon
as he did so the Black Man vanished into his own
place with both horses. Peredur now wandered on
the mountain till he espied a castle in a valley, for
which he made. On arriving, he found the gates open:
he entered and beheld a lame, grey-haired man sitting
there with his friend Gwalchmei at his side; and his

horse that he had lost was feeding at the same manger
as that of his friend. Peredur met with a joyous reception, and he sat on the other side of the lame lord
of the castle, who proved to be his uncle.

He was, however, not yet at the end of his labours;
for a yellow-haired youth came and knelt before Peredur, and begged him to grant him his good-will. 'My
lord,' said he, 'it was I that came to Arthur's court
in the form of the Black Maiden; it was I also when
thou threwest the chess-board, when thou slewest the
Black Man from Ysbidinongyl, when thou killedst the
stag, and when thou foughtest with the Man from under
the Stone. It is I likewise that brought in the head all
bleeding on the charger, and the spear with the blood
streaming down the shaft from the tip to the but; the
head was a cousin's of thine, whom the Witches of
Gloucester had killed; it was they that have lamed thy
uncle; I am cousin to thee; and it is foretold that
thou art to avenge us.' Peredur and Gwalchmei took
counsel together, and resolved to invite Arthur and his
men to come and make an attack on the witches. This
was done, and the fighting began with one of the witches
killing a man of Arthur's close to Peredur, in spite of
the latter's forbidding it: the same thing was done by her
a second and a third time, when Peredur, enraged,
drew his sword and struck the witch such a blow on
her head that he split her helmet, her headgear, and her
head itself in two. She had time, however, to scream
to the other witches to flee, for this was Peredur, she
said, that had been their pupil, who was destined to kill
them. Then Arthur and his men dashed among the
witches, slaughtering them with such despatch that not
a single witch escaped alive.

The explanation offered by Peredur's cousin, while

presenting difficulties of its own, helps to remove certain others. Thus, we are not told how Peredur's horse was brought to the Lame King's Castle; but as the cousin asserts that he was present when Peredur was deprived of his horse, we may presume that the cousin had something to do with bringing the horse away. Further, the words ascribed to the cousin, at the beginning and at the close of the second part of Peredur's story, erroneously reduce Peredur's two uncles to one; namely, that one whom Peredur, on the occasion of his making his acquaintance, found engaged in watching his men fishing on the lake near his castle : he is in fact the Fisher King and the Rich Fisher of the Grail romances, which give him a brother variously called Goon and Gonemans or Gornumant. The two are sometimes called Pelles and Peleur or Pellam; but their various names need not detain us now, as they are to come under special notice later.

A word must next be devoted to the strange things seen of Peredur at the Lame King's Castle. The Black Maiden asserts, when she appears at Arthur's court, that, if Peredur had asked the meaning of them, the Lame King would have been healed and his realm delivered from war and misfortune; but the fault thus found with Peredur stands in contradiction to the teaching of the Lame King himself in the first part of the story; nor does the Black Damsel, after throwing off her disguise, make any allusion to such a result of Peredur's action. It is, probably, one of the things which the scribe has clumsily incorporated from the Grail stories; at any rate, we feel convinced that the whole incident of the bleeding head and the spear, together with the asking of questions about them, Welsh as they may have been, in point of origin, and as we shall try to show later, formed no part of this story. As it stands, however, the wonders of the Lame King's Castle are made to lead up to the grand finale [1], the annihilation of the amazons termed the Witches of Gloucester.

Nevertheless, this cannot have been the original ending: what that was we learn from the parallel story of Owein, and from comparisons to be mentioned presently: it was the reconciliation of the hero with his wife the Empress. Nay, the Peredur itself requires this supplement to give it meaning and consistency. For when the hero returns to the chess-board Castle of Wonders from slaying the Black Fellow of Ysbidinongyl, he asks to see the Empress; but the Black Damsel told him that he should not see her then. Her words seem to imply that there were certain labours remaining for him to perform, and that, when they had been successfully disposed of, he should be admitted to the presence of the Empress. The difference between the two stories is, that in the second part of the Owein the labours are shortened and the hero is brought back without much delay to the wife he had forgotten; whereas, in the corresponding part of the Peredur, the labours fill a great place and the scribe has forgotten the reconciliation of the hero with his wife the Empress, although he had prepared his readers for a scene of that nature.

These explanations and qualifications leave the story of Peredur full of strange things, and foremost among them one may mention the name and position of the hero's wife. In the second part she is called simply

---

[1] Mr. Nutt, pp. 138-9, 144, 181, invests Peredur with the rôle of avenger of blood, so that the sight of the head in the charger is to rouse him to the discharge of his duty to his kinsmen. Mythologically speaking, no objection can be raised to the idea of Peredur acting as the avenger of his kinsmen: compare Conall avenging Cúchulainn.

the Empress, which implies that she was a well-known
personage. Arthur is called Emperor in Welsh literature, but it is not the habit to call his wife Empress,
which is a fact of historical interest: she is usually
spoken of as Gwenhwyvar, Arthur's wife. But from
a careless reading of the second part of Peredur's story
one might rise with the notion that the Empress, whom
that hero was in quest of, was no other than Gwenhwyvar; we mention this as it is virtually the error into
which Chrétien has fallen in one of his most widely
influential poems, as will be seen later. There is, it is
needless to say, no real reason to take the Empress to
have been Gwenhwyvar; for the former is the same
person who is described in the first part of the narrative
as *Amherodres Cristinobyl Uawr*, or the Empress of
Constantinople the Great. Her name is not given, but
this strange description suffices to fix it with almost
absolute certainty as Elen. This, besides being a name
famous in Welsh mythology, happens to coincide with
the form which the classical Helena takes in Welsh;
thus the latter lady becomes in a Welsh translation
of Dares Phrygius 'Elen Fanawc,' or Elen with the
Love-spot. But the Helen who led to the description
of Peredur's wife as Empress of Constantinople the
Great, was doubtless Helen the mother of Constantine
the Great and wife of Constantius. The Welsh Elen,
as the heroine of another story, namely Maxen's Dream,
is called Elen Lüyđog or Elen of the Hosts, and she is
described as becoming Empress of Rome by marrying
Maxim or Maxen, emperor of Rome. It is the name
Elen, probably, and the title of Empress, that led Welsh
stories to connect her with Rome and the New Rome,
or Constantinople; and we have elsewhere[1] hinted

[1] *Hib. Lec.* pp. 165-6.

that the Welsh Elen was the consort of no foreign potentate, but of the Zeus of the Celts in one of his native forms. She is treated in the Peredur as the Empress *par excellence*, and this would suit her mythological position as the consort of the god, who was once the chief of the Celtic pantheon. In *Maxen's Dream* she is the wife of an emperor, while in the Peredur she is empress without reference to an emperor; and she becomes the wife of Peredur, who is no emperor or king, nor cares to be the lord of a single castle or an acre of ground: she chooses him as the knight who surpasses all others in prowess and valour. This is probably to be understood as an instance of the younger sun-hero taking the place of the older sun-god, the Zeus or Jupiter of the system: the latter is forgotten, while his consort so far retains her pristine position as to be called the Empress; and we are enabled to fix on her counterpart in Irish mythology, namely, in the person of the Mórrígu, whose name probably meant the Great Queen.

The parallel between the Mórrígu and the Empress does not end here. For the Mórrígu was wife of Néit[1], the Irish Zeus, in his character chiefly of a god of war; but the Great Queen is in Irish tales as little associated with a Great King as the Empress is with an Emperor in the story of Peredur. In the story of Cúchulainn on the Táin, the Mórrígu suddenly introduces herself to the hero[2]: she is in love with him on account of his martial renown, and she offers to be of assistance to him at a time when he has great dangers before him, just as the Empress offers to aid Peredur when he would have been slain by the Lake Avanc.

---

[1] *Rev. Celt.* i. 36, and *Hib. Lec.* p. 215.

[2] A summary of the Mórrígu story is given in the *Hib. Lec.* pp. 468-71.

Peredur accepts the lady's aid, but Cúchulainn treats the Mórrígu's proffered help with such contempt that she becomes hostile to him for a time. So what we have to compare with this in the story of Peredur, is his leaving his wife and forgetting her; nor is the sequel very different. The Mórrígu comes in various forms against Cúchulainn just when he is engaged in a duel with a formidable foe: she is wounded in her attempts, and cannot be healed without Cúchulainn himself interfering; so she disguises herself again, and succeeds in getting him to heal her. Later she appears as a friend to the hero, and tries by all means in her power to avert his death. Similarly the Empress, after having been left by Peredur, moves him, through the instrumentality of the Black Damsel, to go through a variety of hardships and conflicts before he is allowed to see her face again.

There is one remarkable difference : the Mórrígu is never represented as Cúchulainn's wife or mistress, while the Welsh story of Peredur goes so far as to make the Empress his wife, whereby it departs further from the mythological original, in that it not only drops the Celtic Zeus out of account, but even gives his place as husband to the younger sun-hero [1]. The modification has had one very obvious effect on the Welsh story of Peredur : it has caused the hero's first love, Yngharad of the golden Hand, to disappear wholly, and otherwise unaccountably, from the later portions of the story. The story of Owein belongs to the same stratum, mythologically speaking, but the reader's curiosity as to Owein's attachments before he married the Lady of the Fountain is not roused by any direct allusion to them. In this respect the editing may be presumed to have been more thorough than in the case of the Peredur story.

[1] *Hib. Lec.* pp. 575-6.

Now that Cúchulainn has been brought into the comparison, the subject ought to be followed further; but it would be tedious to enumerate all the possible similarities. So let us see how the martial training of the one corresponds to that of the other [1]. Cúchulainn went one day to woo Emer, the beautiful daughter of Forgall the Trickster, a dark fellow, who, as a formidable magician, shifted his shape at will. Forgall came to know of Cúchulainn's visit to his daughter, and he resolved to prevent his having her to wife. So he went in disguise to the court of Conchobar, king of Ulster, at Emain Macha. There he reviewed the drilling of the young heroes of Ulster, and paid particular attention to Cúchulainn, whom he commended above his fellows; but he remarked that if Cúchulainn wished to become really skilful in his feats, he must go to Alban or Britain, to be instructed by a certain famous person called Domnall; and that if he wished to excel all the other warriors of Europe, he must proceed to be trained by Scáthach in her island beyond Alban. Forgall even succeeded in making Cúchulainn bind himself by a solemn oath to go to Domnall and Scáthach, who were both of Forgall's kindred. His object was to bring about Cúchulainn's death, for he thought young Cúchulainn would never come back alive. Cúchulainn set out to Domnall in Alban, and soon learned all he had to teach him; and Domnall advised him, if he wished really to excel, to travel much further and seek the abode of Scáthach, which Cúchulainn resolved to do. But let us pause for a moment to point out that the review of Cúchulainn's drill at Emain by Forgall is the Irish equivalent to the testing of Peredur's skill as

---

[1] The story of Cúchulainn's education is summarized in the *Hib. Lec.* pp. 449 et seq.

swordsman by his lame uncle, while Domnall teaching
Cúchulainn and sending him further, in order to attain
perfection in his feats, is matched by the testing of
Peredur by the second uncle, who told him that he
had acquired two-thirds of his martial excellence, and
that, when the remaining third had been added, it would
be useless for anybody to contend with him.

In the last chapter it was related, among other things,
how Peredur first fell in with the Witches of Gloucester,
and how he went with them to their court to finish his
training as a warrior; but the journey with the witches
to their home is not described. In the story of Cúchulainn, however, the journey has considerable importance; for when Cúchulainn left Domnall he met with
all kinds of difficulties and perils, placed in his way by
Forgall. But when the hero's weariness and despair
had reached their climax, a wild beast resembling a lion
carries him on its back for four days; and after overcoming various difficulties, he arrives at Scáthach's court;
but she would not teach him till he found an opportunity to threaten her life, which he did with his foot on
her body and his sword pointed to her heart. So was she
forced to undertake his training, and there his military
education was finished. On the other hand the Black
Damsel, after throwing off her disguise, compels Peredur,
as an avenger of blood, to proceed at the head of Arthur's
men to make a war of extermination on the Witches.
But Cúchulainn is not represented as fighting with his
hag tutor and her hosts, which is probably due to the
fact that he had become her foster-son, and that for
a foster-son to turn on his foster-parents was reckoned
a greater crime in ancient Erinn than if they had been
his father and mother. Nevertheless, the incident is to
be detected in the story of Cúchulainn, but cleared of

the difficulty arising from the laws of fosterage : we allude to him at the head of the Men of Ulster routing and pursuing the hosts of the West, who had invaded Ulster while its king and his warriors were in their couvade. The invaders were led by Ailill and Medb, king and queen of Connaught, together with their eight sons, originally nine, in whom we have the counterparts of Peredur's victims curiously described as the Nine Witches of Gloucester together with their father and mother. We have elsewhere [1] tried to show that the number nine, in these instances, refers to the nine-night week of the ancients.

The next point of comparison might seem to lie between the tricksy Forgall and Peredur's cousin, who takes the form of the hideous Black Damsel ; her counterpart in the story of Owein is, however, all gorgeous in satin and gold, though engaged on the same sort of errand as the blacker person in that of Peredur. On Irish ground, Forgall is of the same uncanny kindred as Domnall and Scáthach, Cúchulainn's warlike foster-mother and teacher in arms. On the other hand, the Welsh story makes Peredur himself nearly related to those who try him in his sword exercises, and to the Black Damsel who left him no peace, whereas Cúchulainn is not represented as in any way related by descent to Domnall or Forgall. In other words, the story has been simplified in Irish by leaving out all reference to the mythological pedigree of the hero, while in Welsh it has led to serious modifications of the original, in so far as it may be said to be based on mythology. Thus Peredur is the son of Evrawc, earl of the North, in that sense probably in which ' the North ' was an alias for Hades ; and his mother is one of the amphibious

---

[1] *Hib. Lec.* p. 367.

divinities associated at one time with light beings and at another with dark ones. Her brothers, who try Peredur in his exercises, are of the latter description. The greyness, for example, of the Lame King may possibly be taken as significant in this respect; and so undoubtedly may his lameness, namely, as a part of the characteristics which went to form a corpse-god like Uthr Bendragon [1], or like the Evalach to be mentioned later. In fact, not only is Peredur's uncle to be equated with Domnall, but the Cúchulainn parallel might perhaps be carried further, as Domnall has a daughter Dornolla, who is more black and hideous than even the Black Damsel in the Peredur; and she tries to compass Cúchulainn's death as soon as he leaves her father's house for Scáthach's court. Other forms, however, of the story make the hostile agency to have been no other than Forgall himself. Here, then, we have variants which put together would seem to give us something very like the counterpart of Peredur's cousin haunting him in the form of the Black Damsel; in other words, the cousin who disguises himself as the Black Damsel might be regarded as a sort of compound character, resulting from confusing two persons corresponding to Forgall and Dornolla. This might be accépted as explaining in a way the cousin's change of sex, but it fails to account for the fact, that the Welsh version gives no ground for regarding the Black Damsel as downright hostile to Peredur.

The Grail romances enable us to give a better analysis of the Black Damsel; namely, as a fusion of a character corresponding to that of the wizard Forgall with that of a damsel of the lake-lady type, who helps Peredur in the difficult exploit of entering the Turning Castle, to be mentioned in another chapter. She might also be said to

[1] *Hib. Lec.* p. 567.

be the person who appears, free of the Forgall element, in the gorgeously arrayed lady who enters Arthur's court in order to reproach Owein. The blackness of the Peredur maiden and her shape-shifting may, therefore, be removed from her in order to be predicated of Peredur's uncle, who thereby becomes our Forgall. Here we are aided by the prologue to Chrétien's *Conte du Graal,* a composition which cannot help striking a student of Welsh literature and mythology, as one of the oldest in point of tone and allusion within the whole cycle of Grail romance: this is what it says of Peredur's uncle, under the name of the Rich Fisher, who, after the manner of a consummate wizard as he was, had made his court all but impossible to find[1]: 'Arthur's knights resolved to seek the court of the Rich Fisher—much knew he of black art, more than an hundred times changed he his semblance, that no man seeing him again recognized him. Gauvain found it, and had great joy therefrom; but before him a young knight, small of age, but none bolder of courage—Percevaus li Galois was he.'

There is a still more important point, in the treatment of which the Peredur story as we have it must be regarded as departing from the original: when the Black Damsel ascribes the laming of the Fisher King, Peredur's uncle, to the Witches, this, unless we are mistaken, can have had no foundation in mythology; for the King and the Witches should belong to the same side in the conflicts in question. In fact, it is highly probable that the story of Peredur in its original form represented the Fisher King and his brother as hostile to Peredur; and

---

[1] See Nutt, p. 8; and for a special instance of the disappearance of the Fisher's Court and Castle see pp. 11, 31. Compare also a passage in the Bodley MS., Laud 610, f. 95ᵇ¹, which speaks of the *ráth* of Ailill to be seen afar, but not to be found on the spot.

the deviation may be supposed due, in part at least, to the mythic pedigree making them brothers to his mother. Nay, one might go so far, perhaps, as to say that the hostility in question survives to a certain extent in the Grail romance, which gives Peredur's mother two good brothers, Peles and Peleur, as they are called in a Welsh version [1], and one wicked one, the King of the Dead Castle, who is their enemy. This last is resolutely assailed more than once by Peredur [2], and originally he was presumably either Peles or Peleur. So when, in the same romance, Peredur is described storming Peleur's castle, the expedient has to be adopted of representing Peleur as dead and his stronghold as held by the King of the Dead Castle, who had converted Peleur's subjects from Christianity to paganism.

We have also a description of the hostility that should have raged between Peredur and his uncles, together with a very different account of the disabling of the Lame King, in the story of Balyn, of which we now submit a summary. According to Malory's narrative (ii. 14–19), in which Peleur is called Pellam (and Pelles [3]), the latter had a fiendish brother called Garlon, who had a dark face except when he chose to be visible; for it was his custom to go about mostly unseen, so as the more safely to murder with his spear the knights with whom he chanced to meet. In this guise, he had slain two knights who belonged to Balyn. He had also wounded the son of a knight who gave Balyn hospitality. Balyn's host's son could not be healed without some of the blood of Garlon, so Balyn slew the latter at a feast made by Pellam in his own castle; and, while Balyn invited his friend to take some of the blood to heal his son, Pellam

---

[1] Williams' *Seint Greal, passim.*   [2] Ib. pp. 276, 616.
[3] Malory, xiii. 5 ; xvii. 5.

proceeded to avenge his brother's death by an attack on Balyn, in which the latter's sword broke. Balyn, now defenceless, fled from room to room in the castle until he chanced on a gorgeous chamber, in which lay on a bed the body of Joseph of Arimathea. There he found the spear of Longinus, and with it he faced Pellam, wounding him so sorely that he fell in a swoon, which was followed by the instant collapse of the castle itself. Some days afterwards both knights were extricated alive from the ruins by Merlin, but ' Kynge Pellam lay so many yeres sore wounded/and myght neuer be hole tyl Galahad/the haute prynce heled hym in the quest of the Sangraille.'

One may compare Garlon with Echaid Glas in the story of Cúchulainn in quest of the sons of Dóel Dermait, and notice a similar use made of Echaid's blood by his released victims[1].

To return to Balyn, Malory makes him die in a duel with his brother Balan, which they fought without recognizing one another until it was too late. Lastly, Merlin is said to find Balyn's sword, which is thenceforth preserved for Galahad the *haute prynce*[2]. Now, in Balyn one readily recognizes Geoffrey's Belinus[3], whose name represents the Celtic divinity described in Latin as Apollo Belenus or Belinus[4]. With this key

---

[1] *Hib. Lec.* p. 344. [2] Malory, ii. 19 ; xiii. 5.

[3] *Hist. Reg. Brit.* iii. 1, 3, 5-6, 8, 10 ; but the Welsh versions of Geoffrey call Belinus and Brennius respectively Beli and Bran (*R. B. Bruts*, pp. 71-8). The former should have been *Belin*, as *Beli* was the name of a very different personage, and as Geoffrey derives from the name of his Belinus that of *Belinesgata* or Billingsgate, where his ashes were supposed to be preserved in a golden vessel in a tower of wonderful dimensions built by Belinus himself.

[4] It is also given as Βέλενος and Βήληνος. For the inscriptions referring to the divinity of this name see the Berlin *Corpus*, iii. 4774 ; v. 732-753, 1829, 2143-6, 8212; xii. 401 (and add.), 5693[12], 5958. See also the references to Belenus by Ausonius (ed. by Peiper, Leipsic, 1886), pp. 52, 59.

one at once comprehends how it was, that, according to Geoffrey, he had a brother Brennius, that is to say Brân, King of Britain from the Humber to Caithness. The latter is represented as being at war with Belinus and driven by him into exile, which gave Geoffrey a welcome opportunity of identifying his mythic Brân with the Gaulish leader Brennus. Thus it is seen that Belinus or Balyn was, mythologically speaking, the natural enemy of the dark divinity Brân or Balan, and so he was of Peleur or Pellam.

If one substitute Peredur for Balyn, in the story of the Dolorous Stroke, one obtains a fair notion as to the relations possible between the younger hero and his uncles; and it may be shown that the substitution here suggested is not as arbitrary as it may at first sight appear. In the first place, Peredur and Balyn are clearly to be regarded as belonging to one and the same class; and in the next, the view here advocated derives confirmation from a passage in Manessier's continuation of Chrétien's *Conte du Graal*[1]. He speaks of the Fisher King as having a brother, Goon of the Desert, living in Quiquagrant. Goon was slain by a knight called Partinal; who, in order to approach Goon, donned the armour of one of the latter's men, but Partinal's sword broke when the traitorous blow was struck. In this, as in some other instances, the Fisher King seems to change places with his brother; but the allusion to the broken sword shows that we have here to do with a version of the story of the Dolorous Stroke. Nay, we may go further: the name Partinal suggests Partiual, Parzival and Perceval, nor can there be any grave doubt that it is but a form of one of the names of Peredur. This, of course, did not dawn

---

[1] See the abstract in Nutt's *Studies*, p. 20.

on Manessier's mind ; so, by combining different versions
of the story, he has, in the sequel, achieved the feat of
making Perceval slay Partinal in revenge for the death of
his uncle Goon[1]. The name of this last, we need hardly
say, means Gwyn ab Nûd, while Garlon is probably to
be identified with the Gwrgi *Garwlwyd*, already mentioned (p. 73) as a cannibal held up to detestation in the
Triads. Lastly, Garlon's black face is the counterpart
of that of Forgall[2] in the story of Cúchulainn, and it is
also probably the key to the complexion of the Black
Damsel, who, to a certain extent, acts the part of a
Copreus in the Peredur.

Gerbert, another of the continuators of Chrétien,
favours the same conclusion as to the original hostility
between Peredur and his uncles : thus Peredur (Perceval) overcame a hag who by means of a potion used to
bring the slaughtered enemies of his uncle Gornumant
to life again ; and in so doing she was working in obe-
dience to the King of the Waste City, who hated all
Christians. She was forced to acknowledge Perceval
as her conqueror, but so long as she lived he was to
know nothing about the Holy Grail[3]. This would
seem to imply a second encounter, ending with the hag's
death at Perceval's hands, while the whole forms another account of Peredur's two encounters with the
Witches of Gloucester. Moreover, the King of the
Waste City may be said, by virtue of that designation, to
challenge classification with Goon of the Desert, another
form of whose name we have in Gonemans[4] ; and one

---

[1] Nutt, p. 21.   [2] *Hib. Lec.* p. 448.   [3] See Nutt, p. 23.

[4] *Goon* stands for the Welsh *Gwyn*, while *Gonemans* stands for *Gwynwas*,
or Gwyn's full name; for a nominative ending in *ans* sounded more like
French ; but once one had a stem ending in *an*, it was also natural to a
Frenchman to add a *t*, so as to make of it a sort of participial formation. The
next step was for a stem like *Gornumant* to yield a nominative *Gornumants*,

is tempted to identify the Waste City with Caer Loyw, and its king with the father of the Witches of Caer Loyw (p. 81), who accompanies his daughters when Peredur first attacks them. On the other hand, one can hardly help regarding the King of the Waste City as originally the same personage as the King of the Terre Gastee or Waste Country; but that, as will be mentioned later, was one of the designations of Perceval's uncle, the Lame or Maimed King.

Now that we have called attention to the question of the influence of the non-native versions on the Welsh story of Peredur, there is one bit of criticism which we wish to add, and it is this: the Welsh narrator appears to have had no difficulty in identifying such stock personages as Arthur, Gwenhwyvar, Peredur, Owein, and Gwalchmei under the various forms given to their names in the romance at his disposal; nor does he ever allow himself, under its influence, to depart from the fixed notions, which he, as a Welshman, had formed as to the character of those figures respectively. On the other hand, he omits giving the less-known figures their proper names, either because he failed to recognize the Welsh originals underlying the French forms of them, or else because he did not find the names in the French version used by him, the author of it having himself done without them, in despair of successfully manipulating their Welsh forms. At any rate, we offer this as one explanation of the comparative poverty of proper names in the Peredur, a poverty which is far less marked in the Owein, and unmistakably points to the

written *Gornumanz*: so we have *Maelguas* or Melguas yielding Meleaguant, nominative *Meleaguanz*, and Malory's Mellyagraunce. In both cases the Welsh stems in *guas* were treated as French nominatives, and this seems to be the key to the French forms.

indebtedness of the Peredur story-teller to a second-hand version. It is needless to say that this is not to be blindly urged in every case: it would not be fair, for example, to measure the original of a story with a second-hand version of it which has brought into existence a bogus name, so to say, such as Herzeloyde[1], given by Wolfram von Eschenbach to the mother of Parzival, as he calls Peredur. Now *Herzeloyde*[2] is clearly nothing but the Welsh word arglόydes, 'lady, *domina*,' applied to her in the Welsh original, drawn upon by some one of Wolfram's French predecessors in the treatment of the story. But even when such considerations as this are duly allowed for, the fact remains that the Peredur is strikingly poor in proper names, whether of persons or of places, as compared, for example, with a purely Welsh story like the Mabinogi of Branwen.

On the other hand, certain of the criticisms[3] intended to emphasize the indebtedness of the Peredur to other versions are not so sound as to be entitled to pass without a challenge. Take first the counsels which Peredur's mother gives to her son when he is on the point of leaving her. They run as follows: Go thy way to Arthur's court, where the men are the best, the most generous and the most valiant. When thou seest a church, sing thy paternoster by it. If thou see food and drink and thou have need of them, and if one lack the manners and goodness to offer thee of them, partake of them unbidden. If thou hear an outcry, and above all the outcry of a woman, go towards it. If thou see a jewel,

---

[1] Nutt, p. 25.

[2] The final *s* of arglόydes does not appear in the German, for the probable reason that it was treated as the mark of a French nominative, and, therefore, not to be transported into another language.

[3] They will be found conveniently summarized by Mr. Nutt, pp. 134, 150.

take it and give it to another : thereby shalt thou obtain praise. If thou see a fair woman, woo her, though she will have none of thee : thou wilt be a better man for it and more distinguished. As to these counsels, it has been maintained that the words 'woo her, though she will have none of thee,' owe their form to a misunderstanding of one of the counsels, as given in Chrétien's version, which Mr. Nutt renders as follows :—'Aid dames and damsels, for he who honoureth them not, his honour is dead ; serve them likewise ; displease them not in aught ; one has much from kissing a maid if she will to lie with you, but if she forbid, leave it alone ; if she have ring, or wristband, and for love or at your prayer give it, 'tis well you take it,' &c. We are not quite convinced of the soundness of this view ; but even granting that the Welsh scribe has blundered, his error does not cover the whole case, as Peredur is found to act up to the counsels, as given in the Welsh, namely, in his conduct towards Yngharad of the golden Hand : he wooes her and is rudely repulsed, but he persists until the lady yields. Should it be objected that the scribe, having misunderstood the advice in question, wished to be consistent by making his hero act accordingly ; it must suffice to answer, that the scribe's character for consistency will bear no such stress, and that in all probability he never thought of the two things together, to wit, the mother's counsel and the behaviour of her son in love with the Damsel of the golden Hand.

Let us next recall to the reader's mind the incident of the dwarfs hailing Peredur as the chief of warriors and the flower of chivalry (p. 77). Chrétien gives a different version : Perceval (Peredur) is laughingly told by a damsel that he should become the best knight in the world, and she had not laughed for ten years, as a fool had been wont to declare[1]. This has been regarded as an earlier form of the incident and closer to the original folk-tale account; but fully to understand it we are asked to read the words in the light of a passage like the following, in an Irish tale: 'Now, the King's daughter was so melancholy that she didn't laugh for seven years, but when she saw Tom of the Goat-skin knock over all her father's best champions, then she let a great sweet laugh out of her[1].' But the dwarf's words are regarded as a prophecy in the Welsh story, as we learn afterwards when Arthur, on eventually finding Peredur, addresses him in the following words: 'Welcome to thee! and with me shalt thou abide, and thou wouldst not have gone from me when thou didst, had I known thy increase about to be what it has been; this, however, was predicted thee by the dwarf and she-dwarf ill-treated by Kei[2].' Prophecy and prediction are appealed to on sundry occasions in the Peredur, as for example when the hero goes to be trained in arms by the Witches, when he slays the Avanc of the Lake, and when he finally destroys the Witches. The laughter incident in the folk-tale is more humorous than the prediction in the Peredur, but does it therefore belong to an earlier form of the story? It may be doubted.

Lastly, when Peredur first sees the three knights from Arthur's court going by (p. 76), he asks his mother what they might be, and she replies, 'They are angels, my son.' This, according to the authority of Birch-Hirschfeld, can only be a distorted reminiscence of the exclamation made by Perceval (Peredur) himself, that they were angels[3]:

> '. . . . . Ha! sire Dex, Merchi!
> Ce sont angle que je voi ci!'

---

[1] Nutt, p. 134.   [2] *R. B. Mab.* p. 215; Guest, i. 329.   [3] Nutt, p. 134.

For, according to that scholar, the mother would have been the last person so to describe knights, of whose existence she had endeavoured to keep her son in complete ignorance: she would have rather called them devils. But this very grave criticism is aimed in vain at a passage, the light playfulness of which wholly eludes the heavy hand of one unskilled in the language of the original. When Peredur's mother called the three knights *engylion*, that is to say 'angels,' she, as she doubtless knew, conveyed no information to her son's mind, and the narrator indicates this by the form of Peredur's response: 'By my faith, I will be an *engyl* with them.' This is rendered by Lady Charlotte Guest[1]: 'By my faith, I will go and become an angel with them,' for she does not appear to have been informed that *engyl* is angels, not angel. The real nature of the conversation is best explained by giving it a sort of English parallel, somewhat as follows: 'What are those, mother? They are *children*, my son. By my faith, I will be a *childer* with them.' The point missed by the serious eye of the critic is, that Peredur had so little understood what the word *engylion* meant, that, like a child, he at once provided it with an unheard-of singular. Here, at any rate, the Welsh story-teller, so far from copying, has given his narrative a seemingly artless touch of originality.

---

[1] Guest's *Mabinogion*, i. 299.

CHAPTER VI.

Peredur and Lancelot.

Several allusions have already been made to Lance-lot; but one of the earliest accounts we have of him is to be found in a German poem by Ulrich von Zatzik-hoven, who, according to M. Paris, translated it during the last years of the 12th century [1] from a French ori-ginal which has been lost. According to the analysis given of it by M. Paris, Lancelot or Lanzelet, as Ulrich calls him, was the son of a king Pant of Genewis, by Clarine his wife. Pant was hated by his subjects, and his castle was taken from him by storm. The king and queen fled with their son, who was only a year old; but the king, mortally wounded, expired after drinking a draught of water drawn for him from a neighbouring spring, and, just before the queen was taken captive, a fairy rose in a cloud of mist and carried away the infant Lancelot from where he had been left under a tree. She took him to her own land, consisting of an isle surrounded by impassable walls in the middle of the sea, whence the fairy derived her name of *la Dame du Lac*, or the Lady of the Lake, and her foster-son that of Lancelot du Lac, while her kingdom was called *Meide*

---

[1] See the *Romania*, x. 471, where M. Paris gives the details on which he bases that opinion.

lant, or the Land of Maidens. In all this we recognize the familiar figure of the heroine of many a Celtic tale: she steals babies and she belongs to a community of the fair sex, such as that of the immortal maidens to whom Conla the Red, son of the king of Erinn, was carried away by a damsel in a glass boat, which disappeared towards a western horizon ablaze with the ruddy glories of a departing sun [1].

The Lady of the Lake had a very distinct object in view in appropriating the child Lancelot: it was to bring him up to be the deliverer of a son of hers named Mabuz, who was oppressed by a giant called Iweret of Dodone. As Lancelot grew up he wished to know whose son he was, but he was only to be informed after vanquishing Iweret. At the age of fifteen the Lady of the Lake sent Lancelot forth from her isle to the world, where he fell in with a certain knight called Johfrit of Liez, who taught him all that was necessary for him to know. His first exploit was to kill one Galagandreiz, who wished to slay him on account of his daughter, who afterwards became Lancelot's wife. She disappears, however, from the story, and Lancelot enters a city called Limors, where he is thrown into prison. He is saved from death by Ade, niece of Linier, the lord of that city, but only to be subjected to most severe trials of his valour: he is forced to fight with a giant, with two lions, and with Linier, who was a still more formidable antagonist. He is victorious in all these contests, and Linier falls, whereupon Ade becomes Lancelot's wife. They go to a tournament held by Arthur, and Lancelot unrecognized beats all the knights who venture to oppose him. On his way back to Limors, he enters a castle, called by Ulrich *Schâtel le Mort*, where

---

[1] Windisch's *Irische Grammatik*, p. 91.

he is subjected to an enchantment which makes him for the time a coward, and his wife leaves him in disgust, never to reappear in the story. The castle belonged to Mabuz, but when Lancelot came out of it his valour returned to him. He is now induced to challenge Iweret, which is done by going to a well in the forest of Behforet that surrounded Dodone, and striking three times a cymbal suspended there from a lime-tree, with a hammer provided for the purpose, whereupon Iweret would hasten on the scene fully armed for battle. The result of the contest which Lancelot thus provoked was, that the giant was slain, and that Lancelot, forgetting all his former loves, married Iweret's daughter Iblis, and took possession of all Iweret's domain. Lancelot now receives rich presents from the Lady of the Lake, and learns from her the story of his origin. In due time, he takes Iblis his wife to Arthur's court at Caradigan, where the Mantle of Chastity is awarded her by the consent of all. Her name is treated as Evilieu[1] in the Welsh Triads. They style her one of the Three Chaste Women of the Isle of Britain, and call her the wife of Gwydyr Drwm[2] or G. the Heavy, of whom we have nothing

---

[1] Triad i. 55 gives the spelling *Efilieu*, and iii. 104 *Efiliau*, while ii. 47 has *Eneilyan*, but the reading of the original is here *eneilian* (see *R. B. Mab.* p. 306), and Mr. Phillimore has read *eueilian* in Hengwrt MS. 202 : see the *Cymmrodor*, vii. 130. In some of its forms this name reminds one of that of a lady known to Irish legend as *Ebliu* (genitive *Eblenn*), who could, however, not have figured to advantage in the competition for the Mantle of Chastity. But it would be hardly right to urge that consideration, as Ebliu belonged to a much more primitive and less civilized state of society. For her story see the *Bk. of the Dun*, 39 [a], and the *Bk. of Leinster*, 152 [b] ; the legend is sometimes known as that of the Overflowing of Lough Neagh, and it has been published by J. O'Beirne Crowe in the *Kilkenny Journal* for 1870-1, pp. 94-112. See also a version of it in Joyce's *Old Celtic Romances*, and especially p. 97.

[2] In a pedigree of the Welsh Saints a man called *Gwydrdrwm* is more frequently called *Gwrydr Drwm*, with the first part of the name written *Gwrydyr* or *Gwrydr*, *Gwrhydyr* or *Gwrhydr*, and *Guorhitir*, *Gurhitir* or *Gurhytyr* : see the

to say except that he ought, perhaps, to be the same person as Ulrich's Iweret.

This last name can, at any rate, be identified in a poem about Gwyn ab Nûð in the *Black Book of Carmarthen*[1]. There Gwyn is made to represent himself as present in the battle where Brân fell, but he does not, as usual, call Brân the son of ILyr, but son of Ywerit; nor are we warranted in supposing Ywerit to be another name for ILyr: rather must we assume that Ywerit was ILyr's wife and mother of Brân, and that Ulrich or his original had confounded Ywerit with her husband. We are led to this conclusion by the fact that *ywerit* is the 12th century spelling of a name which would be written later *Iweryd*, and in modern Welsh orthography *Iweryð*. But *Iweryð* is the nominative corresponding to *Iwerðon*, as representative of the oblique cases of an original Iụeriịu, genitive Iụeriọnos. These are in Irish *Ériu*, gen. *Érenn*, and denote Ireland; also the goddess eponymous of the country, of whom the mythographers now and then speak, making her, among other things, wife of the sun-god Lug.

The Welsh having long since given up distinguishing cases, in the grammatical sense of the word, employ Iwerðon alone as the name of Ireland, while Iweryð appears to have been left to mythology, and in that sphere the name is postulated by one of the epithets of ILyr. For he is sometimes called ILyr ILediaith, which means the 'ILyr of the Dialect, or the foreign Accent.' *ILyr* is supposed to mean the sea, and the personage so called was probably identified or confounded with

Myv. Arch. ii. 40, *Iolo MSS.* p. 131, also *Liber Landavensis*, pp. 140, 168, 182, 221. The name seems to have meant bold, daring, arrogant.

[1] Evans' Autotype Facsimile, p. 50a, and Skene i. 295, where, however, *Ywerit* is made into *Gweryd*.

the sea, and his marriage with Erinn, or the goddess
eponymous of Ireland, would explain why he was sometimes regarded as a foreigner.   It is further remarkable
that the name Iweryđ is found borne by a historical
person, the sister of Bleđyn son of Kynvyn[1], a Welsh
prince who flourished about the time of the Norman
Conquest. The inference to be drawn seems to be
this : the story of which Ulrich gives us a confused
echo spoke of Iweret or Iweryđ as a woman, placed
her in a favourable light, and so far associated her with
Peredur that her name came to a certain extent into
vogue in the Principality.   With regard to Ỻyr, it is
right to say that we are not to regard him as a god of
the sea alone, but to recall the Celtic habit of mythologically identifying or confounding the world of waters
with that of darkness.   So Ỻyr was a great deal more
than a god of the sea ; he was, apparently, a form of
the Celtic Dis, and assimilated under the régime of the
Romans with their Janus.   For we have the echo of
something of this kind in a remarkable passage in
Geoffrey of Monmouth, where he says that Ỻyr was
buried at Caer Lyr, in English Leir-Cestre, now Leicester, in an earth house beneath the river Soar.   That
building, he goes on to explain, was a temple of the god
Janus Bifrons ; and as his festival annually came round
all the artisans of that town and of the surrounding
country came there to pay their respects, and there they
began every work they undertook during the year until
the same day came round again[2].   This seems to mean
that Ỻyr as a Celtic Dis was a god of beginnings, and
that he had, like the Dis of the Gauls, more than one
face, which naturally led him to be identified with the

---

[1] See *R. B. Bruts*, p. 303.
[2] San-Marte's *Geoffrey*, Bk. ii. 14; *R. B. Bruts*, p. 69.

Roman Janus. The town of Leicester seems to have been a great centre of this cult, and only one thing is wanting ; but it is a very important thing, namely, the discovery on the spot of some relic of antiquity inscribed with some such words as *Deo Jano Liro Sacrum.*

It is needless now to say that we do not know what precisely the Celtic story was from which Ulrich's original was more or less inaccurately drawn. This applies not only to his Iweret but also to his Iblis, for the Welsh Triads differ from Ulrich in making her counterpart Evilieu, not the daughter of Gwydyr Drwm, but his wife. Here, however, Ulrich is perhaps to be followed, as we have such analogies as that of Kulhwch marrying Olwen and Cúchulainn marrying Emer, which was only possible after the respective brides' fathers, Yspyđaden and Forgall, had been tragically removed. Mabuz also deserves to be noticed, for one cannot help remembering here the hero called Mabon son of Modron, his father's name being, as in the case of Mabuz, seldom if ever mentioned ; but in Ulrich's poem Mabon's character has undergone a strange and incomprehensible change for the worse, if the identification here suggested is to be received. Another point to be noticed in Ulrich's poem is that it places Arthur's court not at Carleon, or any one of the usual spots, but at a place called Caradigan[1].

[1] At first sight one would have said that Caradigan was the town of Cardigan ; but this name is a form of Keredigion, 'Cardiganshire,' and we have not been able to ascertain how early Cardigan became the name of the town, called in Welsh *Aber Teivi,* which literally means the ' Teivi's Mouth.' On the other hand we are assured by Mr. Phillimore that Caradigan, standing probably for Caradignan, must have meant Cardinham near Bodmin in Cornwall, where the remains of a great fort are well known. The name Cardinham is a disguised Celtic one which is still accented Car-dín-am, consisting, as it does, of the word *caer,* 'a fortress,' and *Dinam,* a name which is not uncommon in Wales : witness Llan-Đinam in Montgomeryshire and two or three places called Dinam in Anglesey.

These references to Caradigan, Iblis, Iweret, and Mabuz suffice to show that romances in which such names occur were based on Brythonic stories; but what, it may be asked, is to be made of Lancelot's own name? Ulrich wrote Lanzelet, but the name is not known in any form to Welsh literature, except as an importation from English or French: it reminds one of that of Peredur. This last is derived from *pâr*, a spear or lance, and it meant a spearsman or one who could handle a lance; it may be added that the Welsh knight of that name was described in full as Peredur Paladr-hir or P. of the long Shaft. This is not all; not only does the name of Peredur seem to recall that of Lancelot, but the characters were originally the same, though their respective developments eventually deviated very widely. It is no objection that Peredur is admitted to be practically identical with Perceval le Gallois, or P. the Welshman. For there were probably more than one native Welsh version of the story of Peredur: we are forced to distinguish at least two. One of them is represented by the Welsh story known as that of Peredur and the French and English ones associated with the name of Perceval. The other is remarkable as involving such names as Caradigan, Iblis, Iweret, and Mabuz—we are otherwise in ignorance as to its contents. But the spelling of such names as *Iblis* and *Iweret* warrants us in supposing the Welsh sources used to have been drawn upon in an earlier form, than can have been the case with those used for the Perceval romance in its various versions.

Perhaps the best way to show the original identity of the story of Lancelot with that of Peredur is to show how some of the differences between them arose. The most salient of these is the fact that Lancelot is usually

represented as passionately in love with Arthur's queen.
Here again we have M. Paris as our guide; according
to him, no reference to Lancelot's love for the queen is
found in the earliest romances, which describe him
acting simply as a dutiful knight in hurrying to rescue
the queen from captivity in the castle of Melwas. The
first, he thinks[1], to whom the idea occurred of attributing a different motive to Lancelot was Chrétien de
Troyes, who was thereby enabled to describe the hero
of his poem of the *Charrette*, in situations which have
been held to form the principal interest of the romance[2].
Chrétien would seem to have made Lancelot love the
queen as a sort of corollary to his having rescued her, a
view which would shift the question to another point,
namely, why he did not make Arthur rescue her himself. In answer to this, it is found to have been in
conformity with a settled tendency of the romancers to
place Arthur in the background, with others thrust
forward to act for him[3]. The question is once more
shifted, and we now ask why the substitute for Arthur
in rescuing the queen should have been Lancelot rather
than any other famous knight of his court, such for
example as Gwalchmei (Gauvain). The fact, however,
is that Lancelot is not the only one of Arthur's knights
who delivers the queen from captivity: thus Gauvain
rescues her from Gasozein in the *Crone* of Heinrich von
dem Türlin, and Durmart in Chrétien's poem called after
that knight acts a similar part, when she had been
carried away by Brun de Morois[4]. Here then we get
no help to understand why Lancelot should have been
more deeply in love with the queen, than the other
knights who had been similarly engaged in releasing

---

[1] *Romania*, x. 492-3, xii. 516.　　　[2] Ib. x. 488, xii. 507, 516.
[3] Ib. xii. 513.　　　[4] Ib. xii. 507.

her from her captors. The Welsh versions of the
story of the queen offer us no help, since it is her
husband himself and no subordinate of his that they
engage in the work, as we have seen both when
Arthur was preparing to take her from Kei, and when
he marched at the head of an army to recover her from
Melwas at Glastonbury.

It would not be impossible, perhaps, to find reasons
which would make in favour of Lancelot; but we cannot
regard them as supplying a satisfactory explanation, nor
can we regard Lancelot's love for the queen as invented
by Chrétien, except in a very restricted sense of that
word; for we take it that Lancelot's passion for the
queen was not so much the result of invention on the
part of Chrétien as of blundering of his own or of those
who gave him his materials. Such, however, was his
genius, and such was the atmosphere in which he lived,
that the very blundering made, in a sense, the fortune
of his poem.

In the light of the Peredur it is not hard to lay one's
finger on the point at which Chrétien or his authorities
went wrong; he or they took the princess of whom
Peredur was in quest for Arthur's queen. In the Welsh
the former is called the Empress, while Arthur's wife is
never so styled; but once Peredur's consort was confounded with Gwenhwyvar, it followed very naturally
that Peredur in his search should have been represented
as trying to rescue her from some one who had carried
her away by force. The story chosen was that of
Melwas capturing the queen and her followers. Now,
one of the most remarkable things in Chrétien's poem
is, that, when Lancelot had gone through many perils to
reach the fortress where the queen was prisoner, and
after he had fought with Melwas forcing him to agree

to release her, she would neither look at Lancelot nor speak to him, when he was introduced to her by Melwas' father, Bademagu, who wished to treat the knight with justice and kindness. The queen is made to give her reason later for acting so ungratefully, but her explanation is an ingenious expedient of Chrétien's own invention. The real account of the matter is, that the conduct of the queen in this respect is to be regarded as a part of the story of the Peredur describing how the Empress would not allow him to see her face, until he had performed more feats of valour and braved more perils. The sequel also is parallel to that which should have closed the Peredur story: Lancelot departs in a very desponding mood after his repulse by the queen and undergoes more dangers, when he is brought back to Bademagu's fortress and a reconciliation takes place between him and the queen; and then they passed a night together[1].

Further, it might here naturally be asked why the queen was still with her captor at his head-quarters, now that she was at liberty to depart. Chrétien invents the answer that she was waiting for the coming of Gwalchmei (Gauvain), who had set out with Lancelot to rescue her; and he goes so far as to send Lancelot and others to look for Gwalchmei. The party return, having found Gwalchmei but having lost Lancelot, who had disappeared entrapped by Melwas. This traitorous knight also had a lying letter written to the queen, informing her that Lancelot was already safe at Arthur's court; so she now set out with Gwalchmei escorting her. The real reason why she did not go sooner, however, is, that she, being not Arthur's queen but Peredur's empress, was at home, or at any rate near

[1] *Romania,* xii. 478.

her home there, where she was in the fortress of Melwas.
It would, perhaps, be less misleading to call it that of
Bademagu, his father, as to whom a word must now be
said, especially with regard to his conduct in Chrétien's
poem. Among other difficulties offered by that work, this
is noticed by M. Paris in the following terms :—' Le per-
sonnage de Bademagu n'est pas clair non plus : comment
ce roi débonnaire retient-il prisonniers tous ceux que
Lancelot finit par délivrer? comment, ennemi des in-
justes prétentions de son fils, se borne-t-il à les com-
battre en paroles au lieu de les réduire à néant[1]?'

This becomes clearer if one take Lancelot to be a name
of Peredur's ; for as soon as one places the story of the
one alongside that of the other, one perceives that Bademagu in Chrétien's poem is Peredur's uncle, the Lame
King in Peredur's story, and that Melwas (Meleaguant)
taking possession of the queen and hurrying her away
from the pursuing Lancelot is Peredur's cousin refusing
to let Peredur see the Empress, his wife, till he has performed several more feats of valour. Bademagu is
friendly to Lancelot just as the Lame King is to Peredur, and the difficulty in the Lancelot arises from
attributing to Bademagu's son a rôle which is both
that of Peredur's cousin and of the robber knight that
takes Arthur's wife captive. As both Peredur and
Gwalchmei end their wanderings at the Lame King's
court, so the abode of Bademagu is Lancelot and
Gauvain's destination, though the exigencies of Chrétien's poem do not permit them to be present there
simultaneously. To return to the point from which we
set out, the home of Peredur's wife was the Castle of
Wonders, where he found the chessboard, not far from
that of Peredur's uncle. This, applied to the case of

---

[1] *Romania*, xii. 484.

Bademagu and the queen in Chrétien's poem, suggests
that the lady's home was not far distant from Bademagu's city, and that we have here the reason, at least
in part, why she is not represented as setting forth at
once for Arthur's court.

Chrétien makes the releasing of the queen bring with
it the liberation of all subjects of Arthur, who were captives at the time in the Land of Goire.   But this linking
together of the two things can hardly be of the poet's own
invention.   We have the same incident in the Peredur,
when the hero goes and slays the Arrogant Black Fellow,
and still more clearly in the story of Owein, where it
occurs as the liberation of the twenty-four matrons immediately after Owein had found his deserted wife, the
Lady of the Fountain.   Owein is represented taking his
wife with him to Arthur's court; but just before doing
so, he effects the release of the matrons.   So, even here,
the return of the hero with his wife and the liberation
of the prisoners of the Perverse Black Robber come
closely together (p. 86).   With the vanquished robber,
Chrétien leaves us nobody to equate but Melwas himself.
It may be mentioned, as a point of similarity which is
hardly due to accident, that Owein and Peredur, when
they come to the neighbourhood of the black villain
of either story, are bewailed by those who meet them
there, as about to endure the same fate which they
themselves had to undergo.   So also Lancelot, on his
way in the Land of Goire, is bewailed by a hospitable
man as going to be a prisoner in that land, just as he
was himself and the other captives from the realm of
Logres [1].

Another feature of the Lancelot story, according to
Chrétien, has light shed on it by comparison with the

---

[1] *Romania*, xii. 471.

Peredur: thus Lancelot is made to pursue the queen's
captor for five or six days in the captor's own country;
and in the early part of this pursuit, which could not
strictly speaking be a pursuit, Lancelot walks at one
time near enough to the queen for her to see that
he hesitates for a moment to step into the Dwarf's
cart, which Chrétien cleverly puts into the queen's
mouth as her reason for refusing to see him, when he
had fought with Melwas in order to secure her freedom.
But the journey which Lancelot made in the cart
brought him ahead of the queen and her captor; for as
Lancelot, after mass on the morrow, looked out at a
window of the castle to which the Dwarf had brought
him and in which he had passed the night, he was
shown the queen, led captive by Melwas, passing near
the castle. He at once procured a horse and set out
in pursuit, but we do not read of his overtaking Melwas
and his men. We do, however, read of his coming one
morning to a well, where, on the stone hard by, he found
a lady's comb with a certain quantity of her hair in it,
bright and shining. He examines it, and is told that it
belongs to the queen; extracting the hair from the
comb, he treasures it as the most precious of relics, and
altogether he goes through the antics usually ascribed
by the romancers to love-lorn knights when their reason
happens to be eclipsed by crazy sentiment. Then later,
when he approaches the abode of Bademagu, he is
allowed to make his way over the terrible river surrounding the spot. He had to cross by wriggling on
his hands and his knees along the Sword Bridge with
great pain and loss of blood; but he was not opposed
by Melwas or his men. In fact, the whole journey cannot properly be regarded simply as a pursuit, either
from the point of view of the pursuer or the pursued;

but it becomes more intelligible when it is placed alongside of the wanderings of Peredur from one peril to another on his way to his uncle's castle. Moreover, the lady, of whom he catches a glimpse one morning, and of whom he finds traces at the well the next day, the lady from whom he cannot get a grateful word later in the story, is not so like Arthur's wife as the flitting beauty whom Peredur finds sitting on a lonely mound and some time afterwards holding a tournament in a retired valley. The whole string of incidents making up the pursuit is an enumeration of the labours through which the hero has to go, and among them occurs that of slaying the Black Man of Yspidinongyl, which is such a favourite feat that it is served up twice[1].

Considerable portions of Chrétien's poem have now been very briefly noticed: there remains to be mentioned an incident or two. Towards the evening of the second day of Lancelot's journey after the queen and her captors, he met a damsel who offered him hospitality at her castle on the condition that he was to share her bed, which he reluctantly accepted. Before the day was over, Lancelot saw violence offered to his hostess by a knight of extraordinary strength. He delivered her from his hands after a terrible struggle, and when it was time, Lancelot was shown her bed. He slept without touching her, and in the course of the night she withdrew to another chamber, reflecting that it was a knight bent on some very noble and perilous undertaking: she wished him success. She is the counterpart of the princess who makes her bed near Peredur in her father's prison, as was pointed out in the last chapter (p. 102), when we took the opportunity of remarking on one of the differences between the two incidents.

---

[1] See p. 3 above ; also *Rom.* xii. 468, 473.

There is, however, another difference, which, though
of minor importance, deserves notice here: in the story
of Peredur, the princess has that knight escorted at her
own expense to the boundary of her dominions in the
direction of the Castle of Wonders, which was his
destination; while, in Chrétien's poem, the parts are
reversed and the damsel asks Lancelot to be her escort.
It comes, however, to much the same thing, as she leads
him all day in the direction he wished to take, namely,
towards the head-quarters of Bademagu, and it was in
so doing that he was brought to the well where he
found the comb, to which allusion has already been
made. It was not long ere Lancelot and the damsel in his charge met a knight who would fight with
him for her. The challenging knight was, however,
prevented from fighting by his father, who treated
Lancelot with respect. Father and son then followed
Lancelot, in order to find out whether he was the person the former surmised him to be. So they came
after him to a monastery, where there was a burial-place
with tombs destined for the best knights then living, and
bearing their names inscribed in them. In the midst
of them was one finer than the others, and covered with
a slab which it would have taken seven strong men to
lift. Lancelot nevertheless lifted it with ease, when it
was seen, by its inscription, that he was the knight who
was to liberate the captives in Goire. The father and
the son then returned home, the former satisfied that
his surmise had proved true, and the latter regretting
that he had challenged such a knight. The tomb test
is one of the favourite devices of French romance, but
the incident is to be found in the Peredur with a different
test applied. We allude to Peredur's second uncle
trying him to put together a broken sword, whereupon

he recognized in Peredur the son of his own sister, and declared that he had already acquired two-thirds of his excellence as a knight.

Lastly, Chrétien's poem was called after the *Chevalier de la Charrette*, or the Knight of the Cart, whereby he meant Lancelot, for the latter, when he had lost his horse, stepped into the Dwarf's cart, as already related. Why, you will naturally ask, does he make so much of the cart, and to what does it correspond in the stories of Peredur and Owein respectively? Chrétien says of towns where there were many carts in his time, that they had but one each in the time of his hero, and that it was used to carry malefactors through the streets previous to their being executed. Thus, to be seen in a cart was then much the same as to be pilloried in later times; and it was, according to him, unlucky even to meet a cart. Accordingly Lancelot is represented in the poem as hooted wherever he came by both men and women, as the knight who had so far lost his self-respect as to allow himself to be seen in a cart. The queen, how- ever, is made at the last to declare that it was because he had for an instant hesitated to mount the cart that she was offended with him. How far the incident of the cart is to be regarded as the poet's invention, it is diffi- cult to say; for what corresponds to the Dwarf's cart in the Peredur is the ring he takes to himself, when he slays the serpent that lay on it. It has already been shown (p. 97), how this, with the aid of a little phonetic sleight of hand, comes to be Owein's Lion. The form of the myth, however, which best compares with the incident of the dwarf and his cart is the passage in the story of Cúchulainn relating how a youth, called Echaid Bairche, gave Cúchulainn a wheel which, in a way not clearly explained, enabled him to traverse a part of the

Dolorous Plain. He had also from him an apple, which, rolling along the ground before the hero, served the same purpose as regards his journey across the rest of the same plain[1]. The wheel comes nearer to the idea of a cart, but in any case the essential point of the nature myth was, perhaps, to have a round object rolling along the ground as a representation of the daily course of the sun across the heavens.

Here we may for a moment dwell on one of the differences between the romances and the stories in their Welsh form, as illustrated by Chrétien's poem contrasted with the versions extant in Welsh. While Lancelot, disconcerted by his unexpected repulse by the queen, was wandering in the land of Goire, he was taken prisoner by the inhabitants, and the rumour reached the queen that he had been killed : she refuses to eat or drink for two days, and reproaches herself with being the cause of his death. Lancelot, on the other hand, hears that the queen is dead in the meantime, and he tries to hang himself at once but is prevented. The double scene of inconsolable grief on the part of the frantic lovers is probably of Chrétien's own elaborating. It is in fact this devotion to the subjective on the Frenchman's part, and his effort to portray the passion of love and the working of the inner man, that distinguish his work most conspicuously from the native stories of the Welsh. The latter give us the events as they follow one another; and from them we are usually left to gather what passes through the minds of those engaged in the action of the story. The story-teller tells us most meagrely, if at all, what his characters feel: he rapidly lays before us what they do. This, we take it, arises from no inherent tendency of the Celtic mind ; rather

[1] *Hib. Lec.* p. 450.

may it be said to mark a stage in the history of our Welsh stories, a stage, that is to say, when they had not been completely disengaged from the nature myths out of which they grew: when, at any rate, they had not been very far removed from the mythological stage with the natural phenomena to be explained, crowding to fill the foreground.

CHAPTER VII.

Lancelot and Elayne.

When Chrétien's poem had set the example of the *amour courtois* between Lancelot and Arthur's wife, other writers incorporated the idea, which they sometimes did at the risk of making their narrative appear inconsistent. They had recourse, therefore, to expedients, more or less artificial and clumsy, to carry them through their difficulties. One of these is in point here: the Grail romances represent Lancelot as the father of the Grail hero, Galahad. Guinevere (Gwenhwyvar), however, is not treated as the mother, but a lady called Elayne. The question then arises how Elayne came to be loved by Lancelot, who was otherwise regarded as entirely devoted to Guinevere. So somebody introduced the services of a sorceress called Brysen, who is represented as investing Elayne with the outward appearance of the queen, in order to entice Lancelot to visit her. One went even the length of making Lancelot restrain himself with difficulty from slaying Elayne, when he discovered in the morning that it was not the queen. It is needless to say, that, according to the view here advocated of the original identity of Lancelot with Peredur, Elayne was Lancelot's rightful consort, as one recognizes in her name that of Elen, the Empress, whom the story of Peredur gives that hero to wife. Malory's account is to the effect that Lancelot, seeking adventures, one day crossed the Bridge of Corbyn to a fair city, which he rid from many scourges and troubles.

The lord of that place was Pelles, king of the Foreign Country, who made Lancelot welcome: the sequel is best given in Malory's own words[1]: 'And fayne wold kynge Pelles haue fond the meane to haue hadde syre Launcelot to haue layne by his doughter fayre Elayne/And for this entent the kyng knewe wel that syr launcelot shold gete a chyld vpon his doughter/the whiche shold be named sir Galahalt the good knyghte/by whome alle the forayn countrey shold be broughte oute of daunger/and by hym the holy graale shold be encheued/ Thenne came forth a lady that hyghte Dame Brysen/and she said vnto the Kynge/Syr wete ye wel/syre Launcelot loueth no lady in the world but all only Quene Gueneuer/and therfore wyrche ye by counceylle and I shalle make hym to lye with your doughter/& he shall not wete but that he lyeth with Quene Gueneuer.' The enchantress Brysen goes to work, and the narrative proceeds to tell us that 'she maade one to come to syr launcelot that he knewe wel/And this man brouȝt hym a rynge from Quene Gueneuer lyke as hit hadde come from her/and suche one as she was wonte for the moost parte to were/& when sir laūcelot sawe that tokē wete ye wel he was neuer soo fayne/where is my lady said syr launcelot/in the castel of Case said the messager but fyue myle thens/Thenne sir launcelot thoughte to be there the same nyghte/And thenne this Brysen by the commaundement of kynge Pelles lete sende Elayne to this castel with xxv knyghtes vnto the castel of Case.' In due time Sir Lancelot arriving at the castle was brought a cup full of wine by dame Brysen, 'and anone

---

[1] Malory, xi. 2.

as he had dronken that wyn/he was soo assoted and
madde that he myghte make no delay/but withouten
ony lette he wente to bedde/and he wende that mayden
Elayne had ben Quene Gueneuer/wete yow wel that sir
launcelot was glad and soo was that lady Elayne/that
she had geten sir launcelot in her armes/For well she
knewe that same nyght shold be goten vpon her Galahalt that shold preue the best knyghte of the world.'
This remarkable expectation of the advent of Galahad
reminds one of the birth of the Irish hero Lug, who
is called the Child of Victory [1].

Some time after the birth of Elayne's son Galahad,
she made her appearance at Arthur's court at a great
festival, and her friend Dame Brysen practised her arts
on Lancelot with such success, that Guinevere became
so jealous of Elayne that she drove her away from the
court, and that Lancelot became distraught. His madness lasted several years, until at last he chanced to come
again to Corbyn, where he was recognized by Elayne
and Dame Brysen. They had him bound and placed by
the vessel of the Holy Grail, which restored him his
senses. Afterwards he instructed Elayne to ask her
father, King Pelles, to assign them a place where they
might live together. The king gave them 'the Castel of
Blyaunt' in 'the Joyous Yle,' described as enclosed in
iron, with a fair water deep and large [2]. The hero insisted on being known there as ' Le Chevaler Malfet,' so
that a nephew of King Pelles, who would call him
Lancelot, found that he had so offended him by mentioning his name, that he thought it expedient to fall on
his knees before Lancelot to ask his pardon, like Peredur's nephew after throwing off his disguise. Lancelot
lived with Elayne in the Joyous Island till certain of

---

[1] *Hib. Lec.* p. 570.   [2] Malory, xii. 5, 6.

Arthur's knights came to just with him. They recognized him and persuaded him to go with them to
Arthur's court, where he was hailed with great joy.

Without going into details, or dwelling on minor
differences, we at once perceive that we have here the
incidents of the stories respectively of Owein and Peredur. Thus Lancelot visiting Elayne at the Castle of
Case is the counterpart of Peredur abiding with the
Empress after the tournament she had instituted for the
choice of a husband, and Owein marrying the Lady of
the Fountain after the death of her previous husband.
Dame Brysen, in Malory's narrative, discharges the
same functions in part as the Black Damsel in the story
of Peredur, and as her more gorgeous counterpart in
that of Owein: both undertake to force the forgetful
husbands to think once more of their wives and to
seek them. Pelles in the romance takes the place of
Peleur in the Welsh version of the Grail legend, which
makes Peleur the father of Elen. Add to this that the
nearness of the Castle of Wonders to that of Peredur's
uncle is matched by the nearness of the Castle of Case
to that of Pelles : the distance is given as five miles, to
which attention has already been called in effect, when
the delay of the queen at the court of Bademagu was
mentioned.

Malory is not satisfied with associating Lancelot with
one Elayne : he does so with a second Elayne, called the
Fair Maid of Astolat. According to his narrative, she
should be another ; but it is needless to say, that there is
no reason to regard her as other than the same Elayne
introduced from a different version of the story. Lancelot, on his way to a tournament at Camelot, lodges at
the house of a baron called Bernard, who had a daughter
Elayne and two sons. One of the latter, called Lavayne,

was so attracted by Lancelot's manners and courtesy
that he resolved to become Lancelot's companion and
attendant, while his sister fell deeply in love with the
knight and persuaded him to wear a token of hers on
his helmet: it was a sleeve of scarlet, embroidered with
pearls[1]. This was a thing Lancelot had never done
before, for any woman's love ; and at the tournament he
was wounded well-nigh unto death by a kinsman of his
named Bors, who was exceedingly sorry when he found
out, some time afterwards, that his antagonist was no
other than Lancelot. But Bors' grief was not so great
as that of the Fair Maid of Astolat, who rested not till
she had found out the wounded knight. She thenceforth attended most tenderly upon him, till he was once
more able to ride. Then came his departure, which she
did not long survive : she declared that she must be
Lancelot's wife or die of love for him, and so it proved ;
for when he was gone, she pined away and died in ten
days ; but before dying, she dictated a letter to Lancelot
to the following effect[2] :—' Moost noble knyghte sir
Launcelot/now hath dethe made vs two at debate for
your loue I was your louer that men called the fayre
mayden of Astolat/therefor vnto alle ladyes I make my
mone/yet praye for my soule & bery me atte leest/&
offre ye my masse peny/this is my last request and a
clene mayden I dyed I take god to wytnes/pray for my
soule sir launcelot as thou art pierles.' When she was
dead, her body was according to her directions placed in
a barget and covered with cloth of gold ; the letter was
placed in the right hand of the corpse, and when the
barget was rowed to Westminster, Arthur came on
board and had the letter read. The Fair Maid of Astolat
was buried as became her ; and Lancelot offered the

---

[1] Malory, xviii. 9.   [2] Ib. xviii. 20.

mass penny: he had never treated her as a lover, but he deeply mourned her sad fate.

Now, Malory's Astolat is otherwise called Escalot, a name which cannot be overlooked as identical with that of Shalott, borne by an islet moored by lilies in the river flowing down to Camelot. It figures in a poem of Tennyson's, which perhaps surpasses everything else he has written in the weird fascination it exercises over the reader's mind, at any rate if he happens to be a Celt. In that poem the fairy isle of Shalott is represented as the home of the fairy Lady of Shalott, unseen of man, though heard at times in the early morn, when the cheery strains of her song rose from the river to entrance the toiling swain:

'There she weaves by night and day
A magic web with colours gay.
She has heard a whisper say,
A curse is on her if she stay
    To look down to Camelot.

She knows not what the curse may be,
And so she weaveth steadily,
And little other care hath she,
    The Lady of Shalott.

And moving thro' a mirror clear
That hangs before her all the year,
Shadows of the world appear.
There she sees the highway near
    Winding down to Camelot:

There the river eddy whirls,
And there the surly village-churls,
And the red cloaks of market girls,
    Pass onward from Shalott.

Sometimes a troop of damsels glad,
An abbot on an ambling pad,
Sometimes a curly shepherd-lad,
Or long-hair'd page in crimson clad,
    Goes by to tower'd Camelot;

And sometimes thro' the mirror blue
The knights come riding two and two:
She hath no loyal knight and true,
    The Lady of Shalott.

But in her web she still delights
To weave the mirror's magic sights,
For often thro' the silent nights
A funeral, with plumes and lights
    And music, went to Camelot:

Or when the moon was overhead,
Came two young lovers lately wed;
"I am half sick of shadows," said
    The Lady of Shalott.'

Now passes by one whose interest to us here stands
in need of no explanation :—

'The sun came dazzling thro' the leaves,
And flamed upon the brazen greaves
    Of bold Sir Lancelot.'

The poet, after giving us a vivid picture of the great
knight, tells us how his appearance in the mirror put an
end to the lady's weaving :—

'She left the web, she left the loom,
She made three paces thro' the room,
She saw the water-lily bloom,
She saw the helmet and the plume,
    She look'd down to Camelot.

Out flew the web and floated wide;
The mirror cracked from side to side;
"The curse is come upon me," cried
    The Lady of Shalott.'

The sequel runs as follows, in sad and mournful
numbers that recall at every step the story of Malory's
Fair Maid of Astolat :—

'In the stormy east-wind straining,
The pale yellow woods were waning,
The broad stream in his banks complaining,
Heavily the low sky raining
    Over tower'd Camelot;

Down she came and found a boat
Beneath a willow left afloat,
And round about the prow she wrote
    The Lady of Shalott.

And down the river's dim expanse
Like some bold seër in a trance,
Seeing all his own mischance—
With a glassy countenance
    Did she look to Camelot.

And at the closing of the day
She loosed the chain, and down she lay;
The broad stream bore her far away,
    The Lady of Shalott.

Lying, robed in snowy white
That loosely flew to left and right—
The leaves upon her falling light—
Thro' the noises of the night
    She floated down to Camelot:

And as the boat-head wound along
The willowy hills and fields among,
They heard her singing her last song,
    The Lady of Shalott.'

She died in her song ere she reached Camelot, and when her boat arrived, the citizens, prince and burgher, knight and dame, crowding on the wharves and reading on the prow *The Lady of Shalott*, asked each other:—

'Who is this? and what is here?
And in the lighted palace near
Died the sound of royal cheer;
And they cross'd themselves for fear,
    All the knights at Camelot:

But Lancelot mused a little space;
He said, "She has a lovely face;
God in his mercy lend her grace,
    The Lady of Shalott."'

It is needless to say that the Lady of Shalott is our Fair Elayne of Astolat, nor do we care to enquire too closely into the way in which the poet produced the

picture, lest the search should tend to remove the deep
tint of mystery which he has given his work.

To the two Elaynes, already cited from the pages of
Malory, a third of the same origin may be added.   To
the name of this latter Elayne he gives, accidentally or
purposely, the form Eleyne; and he makes her the
daughter of a king Pellinore, the father also of Perceval
(Peredur) [1].   His account of her is brief: she slew herself
for pure sorrow, caused by the death of the knight who
was to wed her.   He was called Sir Myles of the
Laundes, and his slayer was a certain Lorayne le
Saueage [2].   To place the mythological relation of this
story to that of the other Elaynes, in a clear light, would
require more data than Malory supplies for judging of
the attributes of Eleyne's lover and his antagonist respectively.   Besides the suicide of the lady we have
only her father's strange character.   When wanted, he
was to be found near a certain well, and he is made to
describe himself as King of the Isles, and he devotes
himself so eagerly to his quest, that but for this he
might have saved his daughter's life.   He was always
following a strange beast, and his quest belonged exclusively to him and his next of kin.   The animal is
called the questing or barking beast, and Malory gives
the following account of it, as it came in advance of
Pellinore to the fountain near which Arthur happened
to be, when Merlin a little later explained to him, as
already mentioned (p. 21), that King Loth's wife was
Arthur's own sister :—Arthur, seated there and absorbed
in his own musings, thought 'he herd a noyse of
houndes to the somme of xxx/And with that the
kynge sawe coming toward hym the straungest best

[1] Malory, i. 24, x. 54; also the Huth *Merlin* (ed. by Paris and Ulrich), i. 261.
[2] Malory, iii. 14, 15.

that euer he sawe or herd of/so the best wente to the welle and drank/and the noyse was in the bestes bely lyke vnto the questyng of xxx coupyl houndes/but alle the whyle the beest dranke there was no noyse in the bestes bely/and therwith the best departed with a grete noyse/wherof the kyng had grete merueyll [1].'

That fountain was a favourite haunt of Pellinore, for, on taking away Arthur's horse without his leave, he told him he might find him near that well, whenever he liked to challenge him; so he reminds one of the Black Knight of the Fountain, at which he might at any time be challenged; and it was his habit to take away the horses of the knights he vanquished, as already mentioned in connection with the story of Owein. Pellinore, however, did not achieve his quest, as we read of the strange beast being followed after his death by his 'next kyn,' Palomydes of the Black Shield, who is described as a Saracen and sometimes accused of being a treacherous knight [2]. He was the rival and enemy of Tristram, a knight who is to be classed, mythologically speaking, with Lancelot. Though Pellinore was made to swear at Arthur's court 'vpon the four euuangelystes to telle the trouth of his quest [3],' we are left unaided as to the interpretation to be put on the barking beast; but like the cropped sow of Welsh superstition [4] it is probably to be associated with night, and the many barkings of the beast remind one of Cerberus with his three heads. As

---

[1] Malory, i. 19.

[2] Ib. i. 19, 20, viii. 9, ix. 12, x. 13, 19, 20, 42, 43, 76-8, 82-8. By Pellinore's next of kin is probably meant his brother, for he is not his son, but that of *Astlabor* (x. 82), a name which looks as though it came from the Welsh word *aflavar*, 'speechless or balbutient,' for besides the similarity between f and ſ, the v of the *Red Book*, for example, is often very hard to distinguish from b. With the use of *aflavar* as a name or epithet, compare that of Ilyr Ilediaith, p. 130.

[3] Ib. iii. 15.　　　　　　　　　　[4] *Hib. Lec.* p. 516.

the animal barked like thirty hounds[1], one is tempted
to think that the original story treated it not as Pellinore's game but as his hound, and that a hound,
perhaps, with three heads described barking each as
loudly as ten ordinary hounds. A three-headed dog of
the kind is associated, on a Gaulish altar from Ober-
Seebach near Strasburg[2], with a god who appears to
have been Esus. On Welsh ground we should recognize
Pellinore and his monster as another version of Gwyn
ab Nûd, king of the other world, hunting with his
fierce hound. What Gwyn hunts are the souls of those
who are dying; but Christianity has greatly narrowed
his hunting ground, as his quarry can now only be the
souls of notoriously wicked men: at any rate, this is a
qualification which the author has heard in Cardiganshire a few years ago. We have alluded to Gwyn's
hound, but that only meant the most formidable of his
hounds, of which he would seem to have had an in-
definite number. Some lines in point occur in the
Black Book of Carmarthen, a manuscript of the 12th
century, and they run thus[3]:

> ' Gwyn :
> Ẏstec vẏ ki ac istrun.
> Ac ẏssew. orev or cvn.
> Dorma ch oet hunnv afv ẏ maelgun.
> *Fair is my hound and . . . .*
> *And of the hounds he is the best,*
> *Dormarth, that was Maelgwn's*[4].

[1] Malory gives it first as 'a noyse of houndes to the somme of xxx,'
but afterwards, as already cited, he speaks of it as a noise ' in the bestes
bely lyke vnto the questyng of xxx coupyl houndes ; ' so also at ix. 12, where
he gives a still more strange account of the monster.

[2] *Hib. Lec.* p. 66.

[3] Evans's Autotype, p. 50 a.

[4] The introduction of Maelgwn's name into a context of this kind is hard
to understand, except on some such a supposition as that it was in the first
instance borne by a mythic personage : could it be regarded as a synonym
of Maelwas or Melwas ?

GwyÐno :

Dorma ch truinrut ba ssillit
arnaw canissamgiffredit.
dẏ gruidir ar wibir winit.'

Dormarth red-nosed, ground-gazing—
On him we perceived the speed
Of thy wandering on Cloud Mount[1].

The proper name is in both instances written in the same way, with a letter erased or left uncopied, and the explanation is that the name lay before the scribe as Dormarch, involving apparently the word *march*, 'horse,' which struck him, or the reviser of his work, as wholly inapplicable to a dog : hence the gap. For by reducing the name to Dormach, he avoided the difficulty, as Dormach probably connoted nothing to him any more than it does to us. What he should, however, have done was to read Dormarch into Dormarth[2], a compound made up of *dôr*, 'door,' and *marth*, a word which occurs also in the *Book of Taliessin*, a manuscript of the 13th century, namely in the following curious passage[3] :

'Gẘeleis ymlad taer yn nant ffrangcon.
Duẘ sul[4] pryt pylgeint rẘg ẘytheint agẘydyon.
Dyf ieu yn geugant yd aethant von.

---

[1] The author does not pretend to understand these last lines ; but what he has rendered Cloud Mount was probably a place-name. The word *wibir*, in modern Welsh *wybr*, *gwybr* means sky, but it is the Latin *vapor* borrowed, and it formerly meant a cloud. 'Sky Mountain' might also do, as Gwyn's favourite haunt in the day-time was the cloud-clad tops of the hills, and one of the names for his dogs is *Cwn Wybyr*, or Sky Hounds.

[2] Further, to have been in the scribe's own orthography, the name should have been written Dorwarth (pronounced Dorvarth), and the retention of the *m* shows that he was copying from a manuscript in the orthography of the Old Welsh of the glosses of the 9th century.

[3] See the Taliessin poem, No. 16, in Skene, ii. p. 159; but the reading here given has been revised with the help of the original in Mr. Wynne of Peniarth's collection.

[4] The words *Duẘ sul*, 'on Sunday,' spoil the metre, and very possibly did not belong to the original.

y geissaᏮ yscut ahudolyon.
Aranrot drem clot tra gᏮaᏮr hinon.
MᏮyhaf gᏮarth ymarth o parth brython.
Dybrys am ylys efnys afon.
Afon ae hechrys gᏮrys gᏮrth terra.
GᏮenᏮyn ychynbyt kylch byt eda.'

I saw sharp fighting in Nant Francon
At cockcrow 'twixt Gwytheint and Gwydion
On Thursday in sooth went they to Môn
Swiftly to contend with the wizards
Of Arianrhod beauty-famed beyond summer's dawn
The greatest disgrace the Death on the Brythons' side
Round his court the rainbow river hastens [1]
That river of dread strife hard by terra
Venom its essence around the world it goes.

The court here referred to is the court of Death, separated from this world by a mighty river called elsewhere the Eel River, in reference to some idea like that of the Norse World-snake [2]; and the Marth would seem to be here a personification of death. The word is doubtless of the same origin as the Latin *mors, mortis,* 'death.' So the compound Dor-marth must have meant the Marth at the door of Annwn or Hades, or still better, perhaps, the Marth which was the door of Annwn. This may be illustrated by a curious description of death, which is still current in the south of Cardiganshire, namely, *Bwlch Safan y Ci,* 'the Gap or Pass of the Dog's Mouth;' and it may be questioned whether such an English term as 'the jaws of death' or the German 'Rachen des Todes' originated in a mere

---

[1] This line seems to personify the Marth, while the preceding one only requires the word to mean mortality or slaughter on the Brythonic side, which would fit in with what we learn elsewhere as to Gwydion and Amaethon's contests with the dark powers : see *Hib. Lec.* pp. 244–50. We do not attempt to punctuate : the whole is obscure.

[2] Vigfusson and Powell's *Corpus Poeticum Boreale,* ii. 125, 200, 223, 232 : compare also the *Book of the Dun,* f. 85 ᵇ, where a passage in the Bruden Dá Derga speaks of *in leuidán timchella inn domon,* 'the Leviathan that surrounds the world.'

metaphor. At any rate, one is reminded of the mediæval pictures of hell with the entrance thereinto represented as consisting of the open jaws of a monster
mouth [1]. It is in some such a hideous fancy that one is
probably to seek the explanation of Dormarth, or door-
death, as the name of Gwyn's dog, though, in the
poem cited, the latter seems to have been rather represented hunting with his master. This agrees best
also with the modern Welsh superstition which sometimes makes the Dogs of Annwn, led by one dog far
bigger and louder than the rest, hunt at night overhead near the ground, and to stop giving tongue now
and then, as if to devour an overtaken victim, when
heart-rending screams fill the air [2].

To return to Pellinore, the uncanny nature of his
quest is emphasized by the account given of his
successor Palomydes, the Saracen and determined rival
of Tristram for the love of the fair Isoud. We have
now attempted to trace the damsel Eleyne back to a
father belonging to the same dark type as Pelles the
father of Elayne. But the relation of the lady of that
name to Lancelot varies widely, as already indicated
in the different treatments of her story; among other
things it may be mentioned that Lancelot lives many
years with Pelles' daughter in the Joyous Isle as does
Peredur with the Empress, while on the other hand the

---

[1] Take, for example, the picture at the bottom of folio 3 of the Cædmon
Manuscript, numbered Junius 11, in Bodley's Library, and supposed to date
early in the 11th century.

[2] See the Rev. Edmund Jones's *Relation of Apparitions of Spirits in the
County of Monmouth and the Principality of Wales* (Newport, 1813), pp.
39, 71, where the big hound is described as having 'a white tail and a white
snip down his nose,' and p. 82, where we have some more details, especially
about the big hound. The author was exceedingly spiritual, and his book,
as we are told on the title-page, was 'designed to confute and to prevent the
infidelity of denying the being and Apparition of Spirits, which tends to
Irreligion and Atheism.'

former never acknowledges himself in love with the
Fair Maid of Astolat, otherwise the Lady of Shalott,
nor was Pellinore's daughter wedded to the knight she
loved: he was to have wedded her, if only he had lived.
But, with the exception of the last-mentioned lady, whose
attitude is not mentioned, they agree in taking the
initiative in love-making, and that in the case, for instance, of the Fair Maid of Astolat in such an un-
feminine fashion, that we are loth to regard it as due to
the imagination of any romancer, so much as an integral
part of the ancient story when it reached the Ages of
Chivalry: such, in fact, as we find it in the epic story of
the Táin, where the Mórrígu makes proposals of love
to Cúchulainn.

The Elayne with whom Lancelot lived in the Joyous
Isle is usually treated in the romances as the mother of
Galahad, whose descent is a matter of considerable
mythological interest. A Welsh Triad, based on some
version of the Grail story, reads imperfectly to the
following effect:—The three knights of Arthur's court
who found the Grail, Galath, son of Lancelot du Lac,
and Peredur, son of Earl Evrawc, and Bort[1], son of
King Bort. The two knights first-named were virgin as
to their bodies, and the third was chaste, as he only
once committed carnal sin, and that owing to temptation,
when he begat . . .[2] on Brangor's daughter, who was
empress in Constantinople, and from whom came the
greatest family in the world. And they were descended
all three from the family of Joseph of Arimathea and
from the lineage of the Prophet David, as the historia of

---

[1] So runs Triad i. 61, but Triad iii. 122 calls him Bwrt son of Bwrt, king of
ILychlyn.

[2] The editors of the *Myv. Arch.* acknowledge that they were unable to fill
in the name, or more correctly speaking, perhaps, the names, to wit, both
of the son and his mother.

the Grail witnesseth.' The Empress of Constantinople referred to is, of course, the Empress represented in the story of Peredur as his wife: how she is to be identified with the Elen of Welsh mythology has already (p. 110) been suggested. But her father is here called Brangor, in whose name we clearly have an attempt to render into Welsh Malory's *Brandegore*[1], which he should have analysed into *Bran de Gore*, The writer of the Triad would seem to have done this, and construed *Bran Gor* rightly as Bran of *Gor*; he failed only to see that Gor, more correctly Goire[2], was the Welsh Gwyr, and that he should have written *Bran Gwyr*, that is to say 'Brân of Gower,' in allusion to the peninsula of that name in the Severn Sea.

In Brân we recognize one of the principal names of the Celtic Dis[3], and the propriety of connecting him with Gower will come under notice later. So we return to Malory's mention (xii. 9) of Brandegore, and the coming to his court of two brothers called Bors and Lionel, 'and there,' the story goes on to say, 'syr Bors was wel knowen / for he had geten a child vpon the kynges doughter fyten yere to forne / & his name was Helyn le blank / And whanne syre Bors sawe that child hit lyked hym passynge wel / And so the knyghtes had good chere of the kynge Brandegore / And on the morne syre Bors came afore kynge Brandegore and said

---

[1] See Malory, xii. 9, but in i. 14, 15 he has *Brandegorys*, which is shortened in xi. 4 to *Brangorys*, while in i. 12 the bearer of the name is more fully described as *Kynge Brandegoris of Stranggore*.

[2] M. Paris in discussing the name of Melwas's realm, *Rom.* xii. 467, mentions the reading *Goirre*, but considers that *Gorre* is the best reading of the MSS. of Chrétien's *Charrette*. From the point of view of the Welsh, *Goire* should be preferred to both, and the mistake probably arose from the similarity of *ir* in the old writing to *rr*, especially when the *rr* were closely joined together.

[3] *Hib. Lec.* pp. 94–8.

Here is my sone Helyn le blanck/that as it is sayd he
is my sone/And sythe hit is soo/I wille that ye wete
that I wil haue hym with me vnto the Courte of
kynge Arthur/Sir sayd the kyng/ye maye wel take
hym with you/but he is ouer tender of age/As for that
sayd syre Bors I wille haue hym with me/and brynge
hym to the hows of most worship of the world/Soo
whanne syre Bors shold departe/there was made grete
sorowe for the departynge of Helyn le blanck/and
grete wepynge was there made/But sire Bors and
syre Lyonel departed/And within a whyle they came
to Camelot/where was kynge Arthur/And whanne
kynge Arthur vnderstood that Helyn le blank was
kynge Bors sone/and neuewe vnto kynge Brandegore/
Thenne kynge Arthur lete hym make knyghte of the
round table/and soo he preued a good knyght/and
an aduenturous.'

Who, it may now be asked, was the Sir Bors of this
story? There can be no serious doubt that he was
the same person called Bort in the Welsh Triads, for
besides the similarity of the name, Bors like Bort was
one of those who found the Holy Grail[1]. Further,
Malory tells us, in his way, who Bors was[2]: he was
brother to Lancelot's father, king Ban of Benwyk.
He was king of Ganys, and the realms of both are
represented as being beyond the sea, and subject to the
ravages of a certain King Claudas. The brothers were
invited to this island by Arthur, that they might be of
help to him. The identity of Ban or Pan with Uthr
Ben or Uthr Pen-dragon is shown by his name, and

---

[1] Malory, xi. 5, xvii. 19 22, and Williams' *Seint Greal*, pp. 163-9, 542 5.

[2] It is hardly necessary to notice that he sometimes makes Bors into two
persons, Syr Bors de Ganys, as in iv. 19, and Kynge Bors of Gaule, as in
i. 10.

the story of his dying immediately after drinking from a certain well (p. 127)[1]. This has its counterpart in Geoffrey's account of Uthr Pendragon's death in consequence of his foes having poisoned the well he was wont to drink from[2]. Thus Bors readily falls into his place as Ambrosius[3] or Emrys, brother to Uthr Ben, especially as the two are described by Geoffrey as exiles in France, whence they are invited to come over to take possession of this country against Vortigern and his allies. But under the name Ambrosius or Emrys were confounded the historical Aurelius Ambrosius and the mythic Merlin Ambrosius, in whom we appear to have the Celtic Zeus in one of his many forms. This is also the mythic personage whom we have been led to consider as the one superseded by the Emperor Maxen in the Welsh story of Elen Lüyðog[4]. In fact, the legend as to Bors having a son by Elayne or Elen comes as a proof that our hypothesis fits the facts of the case. Thus we may say that Bors, Ambrosius, or Merlin Ambrose was the Emperor required to be correlated to the Empress in the Triads and the story of Peredur ; he was her husband by a right anterior to that which gives her Peredur as her consort. This was the last development of the Welsh story, those versions being probably more original which treated Elen or Elayne as in love with Lancelot without his requiting it. It affords some ground for the presumption, that the more ancient versions represented Bors or Ambrosius as the father of Elen's son or sons rather than Peredur or Lancelot, and Malory's chapter relating to the knighting of Helyn le Blank deserves attention here ; for it begins

---

[1] That story makes *Ban of Benwyk* into *Pant of Genewis*.
[2] Geoffrey, viii. 24, *R. B. Bruts*, p. 184.
[3] *Hib. Lec.* p 151.　　　　　[4] Ib. p. 166.

respecting Bors and his son Helyn, represented as the son of a mother whose name we have inferentially found to have been Elen.   In Malory's narrative she is made, as already related, greatly to lament the boy's departure with his father, namely, to Arthur's court to be knighted, as he was then just fifteen years of age.

The rest of the chapter, referring, so far as we can see, to contemporaneous incidents, describes certain knights of Arthur's court finding Lancelot settled with Elayne in the Joyous Isle, and inducing him to return with them to Arthur's court.   Now Elayne gives vent to her great sorrow on account of his departing just at the time when their son Galahad was to be knighted at the approaching pentecost, as he was by this time fifteen years of age.   Thus we gather that the stories describing the sons respectively of Bors and Lancelot as being fifteen seemingly at the same time, should be regarded as two accounts of one and the same Galahad. The explanation is to be sought in a confusion of two persons, such as might have happened in Irish legend if the Mórrígu had been confused with the lady who provided Cúchulainn with a bath and other comforts at the beginning of his labours on the Táin[1]. Thus it would seem that the lady whose love Lancelot failed to requite, ought not to have borne the same name as she who became the mother of his son: only one of the two should have had that name.   Which of them we have no sure means of deciding; but an indication of some value is afforded by the fact that the mother of Gwalchaved (Galahad) bears in Welsh the name Gwyar, which, as hinted later, induces us to compare her with the Mórrígu of Irish legend.

In that case, one has here to distinguish between two

---

[1] *Hib. Lec.* pp. 378, 468.

very different characters as bearing the name Elayne
in the romances. In other words, the amiable Elayne
of the Joyous Isle and the watery form of the Lady of
Shalott, which in some respects reminds one of the
Undine figure of the Fand of the Cúchulainn story,
should be regarded as outlines of one and the same
woman of the lake-lady type ; while she whose love
Lancelot repels should have borne a different name and
displayed a different temper. The same confusion,
however, of the two characters is to be traced in the
case of Peredur's wife the Empress, in that of Owein's
wife, and in that of Bors', where she is called Elayne.
The original form of the Peredur, we take it, made
distinct persons of the Empress and the damsel who gave
Peredur the concealing stone (p. 87), and perhaps made
Peredur persist to the end in repelling the advances of
the Empress, just as Cúchulainn did with the Mórrígu.

By identifying the two ladies the narrative of the Peredur gained doubtless in coherence, while it departed at
an important point from the mythological events of
which it was at first the exponent. The confusion in
some form or other dates probably very early, and may
have originated in the mythological shifting, which
sometimes resulted in placing the sun-hero in the place
of the ancient Zeus of the Celts. Practically, then,
the two versions of Galahad's pedigree come to this :
the one represents him as the son of the sun-hero by
his consort of the lake-lady type, that is Galahad as the
son of Lancelot and Elayne. The other makes him
son of the Celtic Zeus and his consort, and this we trace
partly in the story of Bors's son, and partly in the name
of Gwyar, mother of Galahad under the native form of
his name of Gwalchaved. Mythologically speaking, the
one descent is as little open to objection as the other.

If, moreover, Galahad as Gwalchaved be not treated as brother of Gwalchmei by the same mother, but abso-lutely identified with him, then we might have to admit a third pedigree, making Arthur his father and Gwyar his mother, as suggested in the first chapter. This would have to be explained as a result of another mythological provection, which in some instances thrust the Culture Hero into the place of the more ancient head of the Celtic pantheon.

CHAPTER VIII.

Galahad and Gwalchaved.

In the last chapter, Lancelot occupied our attention, and partly Galahad : let us now examine the story about the latter a little more closely, beginning with his name. This was at first Lancelot's likewise[1]; but we shall use it only as the younger hero's, and regard it merely as the romancers' way of reproducing the Welsh name of Gwalchavet or Gwalchaved (p. 13). *Galahad* or *Galaad* had also the form *Galahaut*, which was frequently made into *Galahalt*. Malory attempts to distinguish them as follows : Lancelot's son, the Grail knight, is oftenest called by him Galahad and Galahalt, and sometimes the epithet is added of *the haute prynce*[2]. But as a rule this is reserved by him for Breunor's son[3], whom he calls Galahaut or Galahalt and Galahad[4]: he is described as lord of the country of Surluse[5]. This second Gala-had of Surluse is the Galehaut mentioned in the prose version of the *Charrette* as King of the Far Away Isles,

---

[1] See Malory, xi. 3, also the *Romania*, x. 489, where M. Paris treats *Galaad* as a ' nom biblique,' but there must be some mistake here, as we can only find *Galaad* and *terra Galaad* (in the sense of ' Gilead ' and ' the Land of Gilead ') in the Vulgate.

[2] Malory, ii. 16, 19, xiii. 4, xvii. 1.

[3] Ib. viii. 26.

[4] Sommer also prints Galahaud and Galahault : see Malory, viii. 27 and vii. 28.

[5] Ib. x. 40.

and regarded by M. Paris as a comparatively late invention [1]. In other words, these two Galahads were at first but one, namely, the knight of Grail celebrity; and to him alone appertained, presumably, the epithet of *haute* or noble prince. Malory's pages, however, may almost be said to have a whole Galahad family figuring in them, as they speak of a Galihud and of a Galyhodyn [2], together with 'many moo of syre Launcelots blood.' Of the two principal forms of Galahad's name, the other, namely *Galahaut*, seems to come nearest to the Welsh *Gwalchaved* in its written form of *Gualchauet*, while to arrive at *Galahad* or *Galaad*, we seem to have something like a leap from Old French *avez* to *ad*, for Latin *habetis* and *habet* respectively.

The opinion here advanced as to the Welsh origin of the name Galahad is to some extent confirmed by the story of a hot spring called after him. Malory speaks of it thus [3]: 'And thenne Galahad putte hym in the erthe as a kynge oughte to be/and soo departede/& soo came in to a perillous foreste where he fond the welle/the whiche boylled with grete wawes as the tale telleth to fore/And as soone as Galahad sette his hand therto it seaced/so that it brente no more/and the hete departed/for that it brente hit was a sygne of lechery the whiche was that tyme moche vsed/but that hete myght not abyde his pure vyrgyntye/& this was taken in the countrey for a myrakle/ And soo euer after was it called Callahadys welle/Thenne by aduenture he cam in to the countrey of Gore.' Now Geoffrey speaks more than once of a well near which

---

[1] *Romania*, xii. 487. The name *Galehaut* is probably to be identified with the *Galehot* of the Huth *Merlin*, ii. 61.

[2] 'Galyhodyn was nyghe cosyn vnto Galahalt the haute prynce/And this Galyhodyn was kynge within the countrey of Surluse.'—Malory, x. 66.

[3] Malory, xvii. 18: see also Williams' *Seint Greal*, pp. 160, 540, and Nutt, p. 50.

Merlin was usually to be found. In his text it is called 'Fons Galabes,' and said to be 'in natione Gewisseorum[1].' Fons Galabes and Galahad's Well probably referred to the same spring, and in that case the name Galabes may be said to stand about half way between the Welsh Gwalchavet or Gwalchaved and Galahad or Galaad[2].

The Welsh form of the name is probably to be analysed into Gwalch-haved, from gwalch, 'a hawk or falcon,' and a vocable derived from hâv or hâf, 'summer.' The whole word may, accordingly, be interpreted as meaning the Hawk of Summer and forming a sort of synonym of *Gwalchmei*, which resolves itself into *Gwalch-mei*, 'the Hawk of the month of May[3].' It is further possible that some such a third name of Gwalchmei's as *Gwalch-gwyn*, 'White Hawk,' or *Gwalch-hevin*, 'Summer Hawk,' is implied by such romance forms of his name as Gauvain, Gawayne, and Walewein. The reason for this predilection for a hawk nomenclature in the case of the sun-god is not very apparent; but we may compare that of the Greek Helius, who was sometimes assigned the form of a hawk or falcon[4].

---

[1] See San-Marte's *Geoffrey*, viii. 10 ; but in vii. 4 we have ' Valles Galabes ' and 'Fons Galaes.'

[2] From Gwalchavet, with the usual difficulty of distinguishing in some manuscripts between *b* and *v*, was made Galabet, which, with the *s* of the old French nominative, became Galabets, written Galabez, whence Geoffrey's Galabes : compare such forms as Galaad and Gahariet, nominative Galaas and Gahariès in the Huth *Merlin*, ii. 59.

[3] See the note at p. 13, and compare ' the hawk whereof Castrar had such fear,' mentioned by Nutt, p. 9, in his abstract of the Pseudo-Chrétien's *Conte du Graal. Castrar* would seem to lend itself to identification with the *Casnar Wledic* mentioned at the end of the Mabinogi of Pwyʈʈ, *R. B. Mab.* p. 25.

[4] Preller, in his *Griechische Mythologie³*, ii. 191, quotes Porphyry, *De Abstinentia*, iv. 16 : καὶ θεοὺς δὲ οὕτω προσηγόρευσαν τὴν μὲν Ἄρτεμιν λύκαιναν, τὸν δὲ Ἥλιον σαῦρον, λέοντα, δράκοντα, ἱέρακα, τὴν δ' Ἑκάτην ἵππον, ταῦρον, λέαιναν, κύνα.

To return to Gwalchaved, it is unfortunate that he is, so far as we know, only mentioned once in our stories; namely, in that of Kulhwch, where he is thus mentioned with Gwalchmei in the list of warriors invoked by the hero of the tale[1]: 'Gwalchmei son of Gwyar, Gwalhauet son of Gwyar,' where Gwyar was one of the names of Gwalchmei's mother: Geoffrey of Monmouth calls her Anna, and makes her Arthur's sister and wife to King Loth[2]. *Gwyar*, however, is a word used by Welsh poets in the sense of shed blood; so that as a proper name it seems to refer to Gwalchmei's mother as a war-fury, a character very different from that ascribed to Galahad's mother under her name of Elayne in the romances. The interest of the name Gwyar, then, consists in its placing the bearer of it on the level of the Irish Mórrígu as a war-fury, and the consort of the Celtic Zeus regarded as a god of war, and in its exposing to our gaze a layer of Celtic mythology which has been mostly overlaid by later strata. To come back to the words in the story of Kulhwch, the habits of the story-teller are not such that we can regard him as proving, that Gwalchaved is not to be mythologically treated as merely another name of Gwalchmei's. The assumption of their original identity would, at any rate, meet the serious difficulty arising from the fact that Welsh literature has nothing hardly to say about Gwalchaved. On the other hand, the treatment of Gwalchmei and Gwalchaved as distinct persons would not be, so far as we can see, open to any serious objection of a mythological nature. That Gwalchaved is in either case to be regarded as originally a sun-hero, is highly probable; and among the stories pointing in this direction

---

[1] *R. B. Mab.* p. 112.
[2] See, however, *Brut Tysilio* in the *Myv. Arch.* ii. 311.

may be mentioned the one which represents the sword of Balyn miraculously preserved for Galahad : it could only be handled, it is said, by him and by Lancelot [1].

Something must now be said of the Holy Grail, in order to render intelligible the position of him, who brought the quest of it to a successful issue. The Grail was sometimes regarded as the eucharistic vessel, and sometimes as that in which Joseph of Arimathea was believed to have collected and preserved the blood of Christ. This vessel had all kinds of virtues ascribed it ; for example, it would by the ministration of angels come with all manner of sweetness and savour to the knights deemed worthy of that distinction at the hands of Heaven, and to them it was food and drink ; also an infallible cure from all ailments and diseases, whatever their nature might be ; but this was denied to all untrue knights and sinners. When the Saxon pagans began to invade the country, the holy vessel mysteriously disappeared, but it was to be discovered again in Arthur's time, for his knights were to undertake the search for it; and one of them was destined to find it, or to achieve the quest of it, as it was termed : he was no other than Galahad. All this was embodied in a romance called the *Queste du St. Graal,* whose author is not known ; but whoever he may have been, he cannot be said to have planned his plot badly, when he entrusted his quest to the knights of Arthur's court. For they were famous in Welsh story for undertaking things of the kind, and we have a sort of parallel to the quest of the Holy Grail in Arthur's expedition in search of the cauldron of Diwrnach the Goidel. The story of Kulhwch abundantly shows that Arthur's court was the nursery, so to say, of all kinds of pagan quests, if we may use the word in the

---

[1] Malory, ii. 19.

sense in which it was employed by the romancers. One
of these quests is especially in point here, but the nature
of it will be better understood in a later chapter.

Now the romances about the Holy Grail range themselves in two groups, relating respectively to the quest of
the Grail, and to its earlier history. Those purporting
to give its early history are the later ones in point of
date, and they would seem to owe their origin to an
after-thought. The romances describing the quest of
the Grail having made it famous, without narrating how
it found its way into Britain, there grew up a quantity of
literature pretending to give the history of the Grail
previous to the era of the quests, and this pretended
history took in the main two forms. One of the two made
Joseph of Arimathea the bringer of the Grail, for, with
the aid of his converts from the East, he brings about the
evangelization of Britain. This, in effect, is the well-
known Glastonbury legend, which was sometimes
fostered by the kings of England when they happened
to be at variance with the Pope and resisting the claims
of the Church of Rome. The other form of the early
history of the Grail knows nothing of the companions
of Joseph, and he is only indirectly concerned in the
Christianizing of this country, namely, through the instrumentality of kinsmen of his bearing decidedly Celtic
names[1], such as that of Bron, who receives the Grail
and becomes the leading personage. This proved the
less popular of the two stories with the romancers, but
one somewhat approaching it has met with a certain
amount of favour in Wales. As given in the Triads[2], it
represents Brân the Blessed, son of ILyr ILediaith, as
the first to bring the Christian faith to Britain, when he
had, as it is alleged, been some years in Rome as one

[1] Nutt's *Studies*, pp. 79, 80, 94.   [2] Triads, iii. 17, 18; see also iii. 61.

of the British hostages, when his son Caratacus was taken prisoner by Ostorius Scapula.

It is needless to say that this is all unhistorical, that Tacitus makes no mention of the father of Caratacus being present among the prisoners taken with him, and that Dion Cassius [1] states that his father was Cunobelinus, a comparatively well-known British king. But the curious way in which the story arose is not difficult to sketch : the old god Brân is called in the Mabinogi *Bendigeitvran*, or Brân the Blessed, a remarkable survival of the ancient paganism, which, however, does not stand alone in his case; for his head is called the *Urdawl Ben*, that is to say the Venerable or Dignified Head [2]. Nevertheless, any figure more unlike a historical man and especially anybody termed blessed in the hagiological sense of the word, it would be hard to imagine than this Brân, who was too big to enter a house or step on board a ship. This was softened down into a description of him merely as the biggest man ever seen, the most generous in giving, and the most hardy in war and distress [3]. What served to establish the fiction was the fact, that the Mabinogi gives Brân a son Caradawg or Caradog: he is more fully called Caradawg Vreichvras or C. of the Stout Arms, the Carados Brebras of the romances ; but the name Caradawg was also familiar as the later Welsh form of *Caratâcos*, written by Latin authors, *Caratacus*, usually reproduced in English books as *Caractacus*, a bit of gibberish out of fashion among scholars. So it was argued backwards that the father of the historical Caratacus was Brân the Blessed ; and the question seems next to have been asked, why the latter was

---

[1] *Hist. Romana*, Claudius, 20.
[2] *Hib. Lec.* p. 97.   [3] *Iolo MSS.* pp. 38, 414.

called blessed.   An answer to the purport above indicated was not hard to invent, and the legend was
complete, how Christianity was first brought to Britain.
The whole is so like Geoffrey of Monmouth's work, that
one feels disappointed not to find it in his writings.   As
it stands, then, we have no proof that the legend is old
enough to have influenced the romances dealing with
the early history of the Grail.

Now, of all the knights who entered on the quest of
the Grail, Galahad (Gwalchaved), Gwalchmei's brighter
brother or stronger self, is the one to whom the author
of the *Queste du St. Graal* has assigned the position
of pre-eminence, and this was in some degree facilitated
by thrusting him into the place occupied in other
stories by Peredur (Perceval).   Second to Gwalchaved
comes Gwalchmei; for, when the former had brought
the quest to a successful close and gone to Heaven, the
Grail was no more seen except once by Gwalchmei
alone [1].   The success of both is made the result of their
chastity, and the whole romance is a sustained exalta-
tion of that virtue.   But what can have been the
origin of this idea of glorifying the hero of chastity,
who would have found himself as uncongenially situated
among the knights and dames of Norman courts as he
would among the petted gallants of certain circles at
the present day?   The asceticism of certain of the
religious orders might perhaps have led up to the idea
of continence and chastity, but it could offer no explanation that would meet the question as it presents
itself in Welsh literature.   For it is found, with regard
to the principal knights whom we have ventured to
treat as late editions, so to say, of the sun-hero,
such as Gwalchmei, Peredur, and Owein, that they

[1] Williams' *Seint Greal,* pp. 169, 545.

have no serious indiscretions attributed to them as regards the other sex; nor can that be treated as a mere accident, since they are frequently placed in positions of great delicacy, not to say difficulty. Take Peredur, for instance, in the Welsh story of which we have given an abstract, or Gwalchmei both in Welsh literature and in the English romance called after the Green Knight, who put him to a severe test. According to the author of the *Queste du St. Graal*, Galahad (Gwalch-aved) excelled, but Welsh tradition, in its silence about him, gives Gwalchmei the palm, in that it ascribes to him neither wife nor mistress. This does not quite apply to the stories in their non-Welsh forms, for the romancers, French, Norman, and English, do not seem as a rule to have noticed the characteristic, here in question, of certain knights they undertook to follow in their narratives; and on the whole they treated them like the rest. How then came the Welsh story-tellers to represent Gwalchmei, Peredur, and other knights of the same class, as conducting themselves with such propriety as regards the fair women so often at their mercy? There is no reason to suppose that the morals of the Welsh in the Middle Ages were better than those of other nations; so students of our stories have on the whole been inclined to think that the latter do not in this respect faithfully represent the facts.

An instance will serve to make plain what we mean, and we take it from a work to which reference has already been made, namely, Mr. Nutt's *Studies on the Legend of the Holy Grail.* We select him all the more readily as he is one of the latest writers on the subject, and free from prejudice against the Celts: in speaking of Perceval at the town of Blanchefleur, he uses these words, p. 135:—'It may be noticed that in

this scene the Welsh story-teller is not only more chaste,
but shows much greater delicacy of feeling than the
French poet. Peredur's conduct is that of a gentleman according to nineteenth century standards. Chres-
tien, however, is probably nearer the historical reality,
and the conduct of his pair—

> " S'il l'a sor le covertoir mise
>   *   *   *   *
>   Ensi giurent tote la nuit,"

is so singularly like that of a Welsh *bundling* couple,
that it seems admissible to refer the colouring given to
this incident to Welsh sources.' The practice here
referred to was hardly confined to Wales: it has
certainly been Scotch and Scandinavian, and it has
probably been English too. In the next place, Welsh
story has its Medrod and its Melwas, its Goronwy and
its Gilvaethwy, and it may be readily granted that the
passage in the Peredur does not come so near, as
Chrétien's uglier words, to the historical reality, by
which we understand the average morality to be here
meant. We regard the treatment as exceptional, but
not due to any dishonesty of purpose on the part of
the Welsh story-teller or of a vain wish to whitewash
what would have probably appeared to him no more
hideous than it would to Chrétien; and the question
for us is, to what cause we are to trace the exceptional
nature of the treatment. As to our Welsh story-tellers,
we take it that their stories, on the whole, were
genuine echoes, however, inarticulate, of ancient myths:
in other words, the story-tellers were as a rule neither
prudes nor inventors, but merely editors, in their own
way, of materials which they found ready for use. So
we have next to enquire what in Celtic mythology could

have led them to deal in the way they did with certain
characters in their stories; and we have not far to go,
or long to search, for what we want [1].

A glance at the stories about the Welsh ILeu and the
Irish Cúchulainn will serve to show that one of the
characteristics of those sun-gods was their exceedingly
rapid growth: Cúchulainn, for example, was at seven
years of age a warrior of terrible skill and valour; and
it is, probably, in this childhood of the solar hero that
we are to look for the key to the peculiarity of the solar
knights in the Welsh romances. Those who fashioned
the myths into romances, whether that was the work of
literary men or of the popular mind, would naturally
normalize the age of the knights or say nothing about
it, a silence which would come to the same thing; but,
on the other hand, there was no equally forcible reason
to impel them to invent love intrigues for their heroes.
So the latter would thus, without any special intention
on anybody's part, and mostly perhaps without even
being perceived by the story-tellers themselves, appear
better behaved and more continent than the other
knights in their stories. As we have alluded to Cúchulainn, we must not object to this hypothesis being
tested by a reference to his character; but it must be
premised that the materials used in these lectures vary
widely in respect of the morals to which they testify.
Thus there is a very considerable gap between those of
society as it appears in the romances, and in the four

---

[1] In fact, Mr. Nutt narrowly escaped doing the work for us : witness the
following passage, in his note at p. 241, concerning Peredur (Percival) and
Blanchefleur : 'The older, mythic nature of Peredur's beloved, who might
woo without forfeiting womanly modesty, in virtue of her goddesshood, had
died away in the narrator's mind, the new ideal of courtly passion had not
won acceptance from him.' He refers to the scene as described in the
Welsh story of Peredur : see p. 80 above.

Mabinogion respectively. In the latter it is found to be morally on a far lower level, and it is with this stage that society as described in the Cúchulainn stories has to be compared: more accurately speaking, one may regard these last as the more primitive of the two by a good deal. At any rate one may say, with reference to the question before us, that no idea of such a virtue as chastity on the part of men is to be traced in the sagas of ancient Erinn, and indications of its being expected in the case of women are not very frequent or decided, except that occasionally an Irish king insists on wedding no woman favoured by any other man in his kingdom. All this relates to a country whose women in modern times are generally considered the most chaste in Christendom. Such, then, as we have suggested, being the social atmosphere in which we find Cúchulainn living and having his being, not much could be expected from him in the way of exemplary morals, especially as the stories treat him in most things like an adult when he is a child. Nevertheless, there are not wanting in‐ stances—and one of them has already been mentioned (p. 111)—of his declining overtures reaching him directly or indirectly from ladies who had fallen in love with him on account of his renown[1].

This is not all, for there was a peculiarity of Cúchu‐ lainn's which is here in point, and is curiously illustrated in connection with an Irish habit which we must now try, with the aid of the student of man, to explain. Mr. Herbert Spencer[2] finds in the behaviour of the small dog that throws itself on its back in the presence of an

[1] *Hib. Lec.* pp. 342, 464, 468-9, 479.
[2] See his *Ceremonial Institutions*, especially pages 113, 114, 116, 128, 129, 133, to which the author is indebted for the following illustrations out of many more with which the volume abounds.

N

alarmingly big dog, traces of the same motive as in
the corresponding attitudes assumed on occasion by
members of certain African tribes mentioned by Living-
stone. The attitude more particularly referred to is
interpreted to mean an appeal *ad misericordiam*, which
put into words would be: 'You need not subdue me,
I am subdued already.' Resistance, it is said, arouses
the destructive instincts, while prostration on the back
negatives resistance. One of the most remarkable
attitudes of this kind is that adopted by the common
people of Tonga Tabu, when they wish to show the
highest respect to their chief: they prostrate themselves
before him and put his foot on their necks. This
position represents completely that of the vanquished
beneath the victor; and other attitudes, more or less
helpless, serve to indicate the submission of the slave
to his master, of the ruled to the ruler, and even of any
one who wishes to show respect to another: take, for
instance, Benhadad's servants, in the Book of Kings,
girding sackcloth on their loins, and putting ropes on
their heads to appear before the king of Israel; not to
mention the prostrations still so widely prevalent, which
the modern European has reduced within the limits of
kneeling, curtseying, bowing, or merely nodding.

Reverting to the attitude of the victor over the vanquished, one may say that the former robs the latter of
his weapons, his arms, and any articles of clothing that
he thinks worth while taking: it was, for instance, the
habit of the ancient Assyrians to strip their captives:
witness Isaiah xx. 3, 4: 'And the Lord said, Like as
my servant Isaiah hath walked naked and barefoot
three years for a sign and a wonder upon Egypt and
upon Ethiopia; so shall the king of Assyria lead away
the captives of Egypt, and the exiles of Ethiopia, young

and old, naked and barefoot, and with buttocks uncovered, to the shame of Egypt.' The same prophet,
xxxii. 11, exhorts the Israelites to give ear unto his voice
in the words: 'Tremble, ye women that are at ease; be
troubled, ye careless ones: strip you, and make you
bare, and gird sackcloth upon your loins.'

Coming nearer to us, Mr. Spencer alludes among
other things to the vassal giving up belt, sword, gloves
and hat as marks of submission in the presence of his
lord, and cites the surrender to a victorious duke in
France, in 1467, of the head men of a town, who
'brought to his camp with them three hundred of the
best citizens in their shirts, bareheaded and barelegged,
who presented the keies of the citie to him, and yielded
themselves to his mercy.' This unclothing, as a ceremony indicating respect, has in European society been
reduced to unhatting in the case of men, while, in that
of women, the *décolleté* dress in which ladies have to be
presented at court is probably to be traced to the same
origin. Among nations in a low stage of civilization
this is much more marked: thus, in the case of the
Sultan of Melli, one is told by a traveller in the
Soudan, that women may only come unclothed to the
presence of his majesty, and that even his own
daughters have to conform to this custom; while at
another African court, that of Uganda, according to
another traveller, 'stark-naked, full-grown women are
the valets.'

Now unclothing, as an expression of submission or an
appeal *ad misericordiam*, was not unknown among the
ancient Irish: one finds their women resorting to this
method of appeasing Cúchulainn more than once. Thus
we read of the Ultonian captains riding in their chariots
on an unexpected visit to the court of Ailill and Medb

in Connaught, when, as soon as their coming and furious
driving were espied in the distance, Medb the queen
began to anticipate terrible bloodshed at her court, unless everybody got at once ready to attend on them: she
did her own part by going forth with her daughter and
thrice fifty other maidens to meet them. The Ultonian
chiefs are satisfied with their reception, and each selects
the lady that takes his fancy and leads her to the lodgings
assigned him. This remark applies especially to Cúchulainn, whose choice fell on the queen's daughter [1].

We mention this instance as it will serve to illustrate
the nature of the custom, though nothing is said on
this occasion about the dress of the ladies; but when
Cúchulainn is the hero chiefly concerned, there is no
such silence as to the dishevelled state they were wont
to meet him, when he was supposed to come home without having had fighting enough. Nor does the practice
appear to have been confined among the Celts to the
Goidelic branch; for we have the testimony of a Latin
author that it entered into a religious ceremony in this
country: we allude to Pliny, when he states in his *Historia Naturalis*, xxii. 1 (2), that the wives and daughters-
in-law of the Britons attended certain religious rites
without their clothing and with their bodies painted
black, as if in imitation of Ethiopians. The application
of the custom to religious uses does not alter its nature,
for the student of anthropology finds, that the attitude of
the conquered man, used by the slave before his master
and the subject before his ruler, becomes that of the
worshipper before his deity [2]. He also finds that, as
prayer is a request made to a deity as if he were a man,
so sacrifice is a gift made to a deity as if he were a

---

[1] See *Fled Bricrend* in Windisch's *Irische Texte*, pp. 275-281.

[2] Spencer, *Cerem. Institutions*, p. 116.

man[1]. Possibly the deity Pliny had in view was the
Celtic Dis, or some other dark divinity. In that case,
one may interpret the black pigment put on by the lady
worshippers as a piece of delicate flattery, meant to
influence the god they appealed to, as if he had been a
man, and in fact a black man.

To return to Cúchulainn: towards the close of the
day, when he was returning in the king's chariot from
his first raid into an enemy's country, he was descried
at a distance by the king's watchman at Emain: the
latter informed his lord that he saw a warrior approaching, and that he gathered from his manner of driving
that there would be bloodshed in the court at his hands,
unless attention were paid him and the women were
sent out dishevelled to meet him. The king gave orders
accordingly, and the ladies of the court, under the lead
of the queen, went forth to meet him ; and they bared
their breasts to him, while the queen addressed him,
saying: ' Here are warriors that will make head against
thee to-day.' Cúchulainn at the sight covered his face,
and the men of valour of Ulster put him in a bath of
cold water, so that his war fury departed from him
without harming anybody. This is represented taking
place when he was about seven years of age[2], and long
before the visit mentioned as paid by him and the other
Ultonians to the court of Ailill and Medb. But it is
treated as so well-known a peculiarity of Cúchulainn
that he would not look at a woman unclothed, that on
one occasion advantage was taken of it to make an
attack on his life: a man and a woman sought him out,
and while the former prepared to kill him the latter
began to undress herself. Cúchulainn covered his face,
and resolutely refused to listen to his charioteer, who

[1] Tylor, *Prim. Culture*, ii. 375.   [2] *Bk. of the Dun*, 63 ͣ.

warned him of his danger. This went on until the charioteer felled the woman with a stone, whereupon Cúchulainn began a duel fatal to the surviving foe [1].

We have here, it will be seen, to bridge over a gap in striking a comparison between an Irish myth or epic tale and a mediæval Welsh story, since the Irish contribution should be translated first into its equivalent Welsh myth or epic, and the latter then turned into a Welsh story of the usual kind, ready for the romancer to transform into a poem with a setting of his own. As one might therefore expect, our record, so to say, is imperfect; but it shows no serious inconsistency, and the conjecture, that Cúchulainn and Galahad mythologically belong to the same class of divinities, confirms the probable correctness of the suggestion here offered, that Cúchulainn's shyness, as already defined, is to be regarded as what Irish mythology has to set over against the chastity of Galahad in the romances. Nor would the force of our contention be annihilated by merely showing that we have erred as to the origin of the characteristics in question of Cúchulainn and Galahad respectively : it carries us, in any case, further back than the extreme development of the virtue of chastity in the hero of the *Queste du St. Graal.* The distance in point of morals and social setting, so to say, between an Irish epic tale and a Christian romance is, as already hinted, very great, but it does not prevent their running nearly parallel in virtue of the remote origin common to the mythic elements in both.

Of the other features of the romances, especially those relating to the Grail, one is a sort of Christian realism which is not only utterly non-Celtic, but disgusts the reader with sacramental fetishism of a low order and

[1] *Bk. of the Dun,* 20 [b].

wearies him with its infinite capacity for pious twaddle; but they have certain redeeming features, some of which they have inherited from the pagan tales of the Brythonic Celts. This is particularly the case with their choice of hero, the nature of his superiority and the position of pre-eminence it secures for Galahad, in whom we have Gwalchmei's brother or other self. The remark applies, with scarcely less force, to the highly favourable treatment dealt out to Gwalchmei himself. But as the romancers mostly adopted rather than invented, this can hardly be thought surprising; for neither has Celtic mythology nor Celtic legend, so far as we know, any more blameless character to show than that of Gwalchmei, the hero of tried continence and the constant peacemaker. It is needless to say that neither in his case nor in that of his brother Gwalchaved or Galahad can we for a moment permit the original to be considered Norman, French, or anything other than purely Brythonic. Chrétien's muse, warmed to her task by the smiles of Marie de France [1], gave its perilous finish to the *amour courtois*; but the author of the Quest of the Holy Grail, working on lines drawn for him by the genius of Celtic story, achieved a far higher ideal in the hero of perfect purity.

[1] See M. Paris's words in the *Rom.* xii 463, 508. 523.

CHAPTER IX.

CÚCHULAINN AND HERACLES.

In the *Hibbert Lectures*, Cúchulainn has been very briefly equated with the Greek hero Heracles, and that was found to carry with it the identification of the Mórrígu or Great Queen with Here, and Conchobar the Ultonian king with Zeus in the Olympic system, also of Fedelm of the Nine Forms with Zeus's daughter Athene. It is, however, not to be inferred from this that the Mórrígu was the wife of Conchobar. In fact, she is not correlated with any Great King in the Ultonian stories : she belongs to another sphere, and she does not mix with the Ultonians any more than the Empress does with the frequenters of Arthur's court. This discrepancy suggests an alternative treatment of Conchobar, namely, as a Culture Hero, like Arthur. But neither would this carry us through, for the way in which Conchobar acquires his throne marks him out unmistakably as playing the rôle of a sort of Celtic Zeus. If, then, this dilemma is to be insisted upon, Conchobar would have to be regarded as a Culture Hero thrust forward to occupy the place of the more ancient divinity; but it becomes important to bear in mind that he only occupies it in part.

So much for the relative positions of the leading

characters in the scheme, now proposed to be examined more minutely in the light shed upon it by a study of some of the details which it involves. It may be premised that Cúchulainn is, relatively speaking, on the same level as Heracles; and the comparisons instituted between them may be regarded as direct, while they are less direct with Owein, Peredur, and Gwalchmei in our Welsh stories, and Lancelot and Galahad in the romances. The more we come down towards modern civilization, the more considerably do the comparisons require to be rectified, by making what we may term the personal equation of the heroes as parts of a society, very differently constituted from that with which Cúchulainn and Heracles are associated. The story of Heracles aiding the gods by despatching the Giants for them, is of sufficient importance to be placed first: he was invited to this in his character of a mortal man.

On the Irish side we have the Ultonian braves *en couvade*, with Cúchulainn alone fighting for them against the invading hosts from the West. Only Cúchulainn and his father were able to be at their posts, for they differed in their nature from the rest of the Ultonians; but Irish story expresses the difference to the disadvantage of the latter, while we should have, in terms of Greek theology, to put it the other way, and say that they were immortals, and that Cúchulainn and his father were only mortals. The reason that a mortal was required to secure the victory for the gods is to be sought partly in the climatic nature of the contest, which made the presence of the sun-hero necessary to repel winter and its dark hosts, and partly in the descent of the sun-hero, who according to one account was reckoned the offspring of the Culture Hero, and therefore a man like his father and not immortal like the gods of older standing[1]. The parentage of the sun-hero is a subject of considerable difficulty, which will come under notice later.

In order to cover the ground, without missing any points of importance, it is thought advisable to take the so-called labours of Heracles one by one in the Greek order, and show what there is to compare with them on the Celtic side; first in the legends about Cúchulainn and secondly in the Arthurian stories and romances, which will be found not infrequently to supplement the Goidelic record with items of evidence of their own. We are well aware that the story of Heracles, or at any rate the most essential portions of it, are believed by some to be non-Aryan; for that reason we make the following comparisons, as comprehensive as we can, in the hope of learning from the advocates of the Asiatic theory what they can claim and what they cannot claim. The question is one which greatly stands in need of a careful sifting. The reader is therefore to bear in mind that these comparisons are entirely tentative, though it is not thought necessary to remind him of that fact in each instance as it comes forward for discussion [2].

1. The Nemean Lion.

One of the peculiarities of this lion was that his skin was invulnerable, so that the ordinary weapons of Heracles were of no avail. He had to pursue the beast into his den, whence he dragged him by main force and strangled him in his arms. But when he proceeded

---

[1] *Hib. Lec.* pp. 140, 363, 671, 678.

[2] For the sake of convenience the Greek side of the comparison is taken from Preller's *Griechische Mythologie*, which is usually sufficiently minute and accurate for our purpose.

to secure the beast's hide, he found that nothing was sharp enough to rip it up and sever it from the carcase, except the lion's own claws. When he had flayed it he clad himself in the skin, which served to make him invulnerable. So this labour takes its place naturally at the head of the list. According to another account, the hero once clothed himself in the hide of a different lion, namely, one which he killed on Mount Cithæron, when he was a youth among the herdsmen of Amphitryon watching his cattle[1]. The two stories are possibly to be regarded as versions of one and the same mythic incident. The Irish equivalent[2] is to be found in Cúchulainn's killing the terrible hound of Culann the Smith; this Culann appears to have been a form of the divinity of the other world, and his hound was the guardian of his house and property; and when he complained of the loss of his watch-dog, young Setanta undertook to guard his property for the Smith until he had another hound of the same breed to do the work: so Setanta's name was changed, at the Ultonian druid's suggestion, into that of Cúlann's Hound, in Irish *Cú Chulainn*, genitive *Con Culainn*. The story says nothing of the hero clothing himself with the hound's hide, but it invests him with the name and functions of the monster. In the story of Peredur we have no ferocious beast, but an insolent knight instead. The latter, as mentioned in a previous chapter (pp. 76–8), had been to Arthur's court and grossly insulted Gwenhwyvar, in order to provoke one of Arthur's knights to fight with him at a spot which he indicated to them. They were so taken aback that no one stirred, until Peredur in rustic attire happened to arrive, demanding loudly to be knighted by Arthur. Kei, in derision, told

---

[1] Preller, ii. 180.   [2] *Hib. Lec.* pp. 445–7.

him to go and fight the insolent knight. He did so,
and with one of the darts he had brought from home, he
killed him on the spot.   He had neither the armour nor
the weapons of a knight, so he tried to strip the fallen
knight of his coat of mail; but the more he tried, the
more he was convinced it must be a part of his person.
Owein, arriving in order to see what had happened to
the rustic youth, was surprised by his success, and
showed him how to strip the dead body. Then was Peredur first clad in a coat of mail and otherwise equipped
as a knight, at the expense of his fallen foe [1].

2. The Lernæan Water-snake.

This monster had nine heads, one of which was immortal, and as fast as Heracles cut them off more grew
in their stead; so Iolaus, the hero's charioteer, had to
assist by setting fire to the neighbouring forest and
bringing firebrands to sear the snake as fast as the
heads were cut off by his master. As to the head
which was immortal, Heracles buried it under a huge
block of rock. When he had thus accomplished his
task, he dipped his arrows in the gall of the hydra, and
thereby made the wounds inflicted by them incurable;
but owing to Iolaus having given his master important
help, Eurystheus would not allow this labour of Heracles
to count; although Here, on the other side, had sent to
the assistance of the hydra an enormous crab, which bit
him in the foot, when he was most sorely pressed by
the new heads of the hydra. The number of the latter
monster's heads is variously given, but nine is regarded
as the favourite one; and it would not be in that case
unnatural to interpret them as a reference to the nine
nights of the ancient week, while the immortal one cut

---

[1] *R. B. Mab.* pp. 197–9; Guest, i. 303-7.

off last might be compared with the Irish Mane, that comprised his eight brothers in the epic story of the Táin [1].

Now, the Irish equivalent of this labour is to be found in Cúchulainn's protracted conflict with Lóch Mór [2], whose armour was impenetrable, consisting as it did of a sort of horn-skin. Cúchulainn had fought with Lóch's brother, Long, and killed him at a ford ; so Lóch, bent on avenging his brother's fall, challenged Cúchulainn to a duel at a ford higher up the same river ; and when the hero began to be hard pressed by an antagonist on whom he could make no impression, the Mórrígu in the form of an eel gave three twists round his feet, so that he fell prostrate across the ford. Then Lóch plied him with his sword and reddened the stream with his blood, but recovering himself he seized the eel and crushed it in his hand ; the Mórrígu then came in other forms, and Cúchulainn, sustaining an unequal fight, bewails in doleful verses the solitary and unaided con-dition in which he is left, when Loeg, his charioteer, sent down to him with the stream the weapon called the *gái bolga*. He seized it, and at once directed it into Lóch's body from below, as the horn-skin made him otherwise invulnerable. So fell the great Lóch, one of the two most formidable antagonists Cúchulainn met on the Táin. The parallel between the Irish and the Greek story is so close that it requires no com-ment ; but it will be noticed that the Greek version has more regard for the dignity of the great goddess than the Irish one has for the Mórrígu : the former only sends a sea-crab to aid against the hero who was her pet aversion, while the latter becomes herself an eel to take a personal part in the conflict. No Welsh

---

[1] *Hib. Lec.* pp. 367-76.   [2] *Bk. of the Dun*, 74, 76, 77.

parallel can be pointed out with certainty, but it may be that we have one in Owein's killing the man-eating giant; or, perhaps, better in his slaying the two youths who would burn Lunet: in both conflicts a principal part was played by Owein's lion, who might here be regarded as rendering aid corresponding to the help given to Heracles and Cúchulainn by their respective charioteers.

3. The Boar of Erymanthus.

Heracles, on his way to hunt this destructive boar, comes among the Centaurs, and then follows his great slaughter of them, which they are made to bring on themselves. Afterwards he pursues the boar and brings him alive on his shoulders to Mycenæ. We have not succeeded in finding a key to any certain comparison with the story of Cúchulainn, although the Irish hero is more than once described bringing wild animals home alive. Nor are we much more successful with Peredur, where the boar might be expected in the form of some sort of a knight; and there we certainly find the Black Man of the Castle of Ysbidinongyl killed by Peredur at the bidding of the Black Maiden, after he had first resolved to leave him his life. The same incident appears in Chrétien's poem of the *Charrette*, and the man Ysbidinongyl is to be traced back through the romancers' Espinogre to the Welsh Yspyđaden Gawr or Hawthorn the Giant, more usually called Y. Pencawr or Chief of Giants, the story of whose death is told in the story of Kulhwch. How the name Yspyđaden or Hawthorn is to be interpreted here is not clear, but it might be that of a knight who, in his brute form, would be a bristly boar. It is needless to say that this is the merest guess, but it is not a little countenanced by the place it has in the list of Peredur's exploits, to wit immediately preceding the one next to be mentioned, where the comparison rests on a more solid foundation.

4. The Deer of Ceryneia.

This beast is curiously described by Greek authors as a hind with horns, namely of gold, and with feet of bronze; but ancient art sometimes represents it as a stag. It belonged to the goddess Artemis, and it was a special pet of hers; but Heracles, having pursued the animal a whole year to the land of the Hyperboreans and back to its favourite haunts in the Peloponnese, caught it at last, and began to make his way towards Mycenæ with it on his shoulders. Whether he had killed it or was carrying it alive is not quite certain, as the authorities differ; be that as it may, he was met on his way by Artemis in an angry mood and accompanied by her brother Apollo. She took her pet from Heracles, and freely expressed her displeasure at what he had done; but on his explaining that he had been compelled to do it, she was appeased and allowed him to take it to Eurystheus. Cúchulainn is more than once represented catching wild animals, and once in particular, when he first rode forth in a war-chariot: on that occasion he brought home a wild stag fastened to his chariot, but about that stag nothing is known that would enable one to compare it with the pet of Artemis, caught by Heracles.

Not so with the story of Peredur, who is asked by the Black Maiden to kill a formidable stag in a neighbouring forest: she gave him a dog to fetch the stag to meet him, for the animal was not given to running away. The Black Maiden described the stag as being as swift as the fastest bird on the wing, and as having a single horn in its forehead of the length of a spear and incomparably sharper : with that it cut down the branches of the trees and killed all the animals which came in its way, while those not thus killed died of fear and hunger. Her story[1] adds that this unicorn came every day and drank dry the fishpond, so that most of the fish died before enough water flowed in again to save them. When the fierce animal made a rush at Peredur, he avoided it and cut off its head as it passed ; but as he was gazing at the head, a lady came to him and proceeded to pick up the dog, the head of the stag, and the collar set with rubies that the stag had round its neck. She rebuked Peredur for killing the finest ornament of her domain: he excused himself, like Heracles, and asked if there was any way of his earning her forgiveness. She said it could be done by fighting with the Man from under the Stone (p. 107) : so he hurried away on that errand, leaving her to ride away in possession of the dog, the stag's head, and its collar. Some of the romances associate with the lady a knight, in whom we seem to have the counterpart of Apollo, as we certainly have that of Artemis in the lady who owns the dog and the stag. It is worth while noticing that she is merely called *arglôyðes*, 'domina,' while the lady Peredur is in quest of is *amherodres*, 'imperatrix,' the counterpart of the Mórrígu of Irish stories and of the Here of Greek mythology.

5. The Stymphalian Birds.

These were man-eating birds with wings of iron, and Heracles is said to have partly killed them with his arrows and partly frightened them away ; for numbers of them appear in the story of the Argonautic expedition

[1] *R. B. Mab.* p. 241 ; Guest, i. 367.

as the children of Mars, making their home in a Pontine island sacred to that fierce god. As the Greek story, however, stands, we can find no certain parallel in the legend of Cúchulainn, though he is represented catching a string of wild swans and bringing them home at the same time as the wild stag. If, however, one might suppose an older form of the story to have made Heracles bring the wild birds to Mycenæ and keep them in his own service afterwards, then one could show a Celtic parallel in Owein's army of ravens, which were more than a match for the rank and file of Arthur's forces, in the story called Rhonabwy's Dream[1]. At the end of that called after Owein, his power is represented as consisting of three hundred swords and the Host of Ravens: it is added, that wherever he came with those auxiliaries he prevailed[2]. How Owein acquired the Ravens or retained their allegiance we are not told; but we have them probably in the ravens that appeared in great numbers at the founding of Lugudunum, or the city dedicated to and called after the Gaulish sun-hero Lugus; also perhaps in Cúchulainn's two ravens of druidism or magic, which his foes attacked as soon as they heard them announce the coming of the hero[3].

6. The Augean Stables.

The story of the cleansing of these stables by Heracles, by directing a river to flow through them, has, so far as we have been able to discover, no certain equivalent in Irish or Welsh literature; but it would probably be too much to say that the story is not met with on Celtic ground, as the task of Heracles is

---

[1] *R. B. Mab.* pp. 155-8; Guest, ii. 409-14.

[2] *Hib. Lec.* p. 428.

[3] Windisch's *Irische Texte*, p. 220.

laid on the King's Son of Tethertown, in the Highland
tale called by Campbell[1] the Battle of the Birds. His
task-master, the giant, whose youngest daughter he had
asked to be given him to wife, one morning before
setting out from home showed his would-be son-in-law
a byre with the dung of a hundred cattle, which had
been accumulating for seven years : this byre he told him
he was to clean before he returned in the evening, and to
clean so thoroughly that a golden apple would run from
end to end of it. He did not try the expedient used by
Heracles, but the giant's youngest daughter came to
him in his despair, and made him sit down by her : he
fell asleep, and when he awoke he found that she had
the task done. The means adopted are not specified in
the story, but the daughter, who must be regarded as a
consummate magician, may be compared with Agamede,
daughter of Augeias, the owner of the stables cleaned
by Heracles. According to the *Iliad*, xi. 741, she was
acquainted with the magic properties of all kinds of
herbs :—

> Ἡ τόσα φάρμακα ᾔδη ὅσα τρέφει εὐρεῖα χθών.

Her father had promised Heracles a tenth of the cattle
for his work, but when it had been done, he refused to
give them, on the plea that Heracles had acted as the
servant of Eurystheus, who on the other hand declined
to count this as one of the ten labours, because it had
been performed for wages. Augeias in the sequel paid
for his treachery with his life, as did also the blood-
thirsty giant in the Highland tale.

7. The Cretan Bull.

The labour of bringing this animal to Mycenæ has, so
far as we can find, no certain Celtic equivalent ; or, to

---

[1] *Popular Tales of the West Highlands*, i. 29, 30, 34.

speak more exactly, we have not succeeded in finding
the key to a comparison with any of the Celtic stories
in which bulls figure; and the same remark applies to
the fetching by Heracles of

8. The Horses of Diomed the Thracian.

The capture by Cúchulainn of his two famous chargers
is, so far as one can guess, not in point, as will be
seen later. As if, however, to make up for our lack of
success under these last headings, the next one to be
mentioned lends itself not only to a comparison, but
to a sequence of comparisons of a striking nature.

9. The Queen of the Amazons' Girdle.

The Amazons and their queen, Hippolyte, had their
head-quarters at Themiskyra, near the mouth of the
river Thermodon in Asia Minor.   When Heracles
arrived and made known to the queen what the object
of his coming was, she is said to have been willing to
give the girdle to Heracles, though it was a present to
herself from Ares, the god of carnage.   But Here succeeded in creating alarm among the Amazons as to the
safety of their queen, and a battle followed in which
Heracles and his comrades overcame the Amazons and
left many of them, including Hippolyte, dead on the
field.   An ancient vase, however, tells the story differently, by representing an Amazon peaceably handing
the girdle to Heracles [1].   On his way back with the
girdle, Heracles came to Troy and found Laomedon,
the king of Troy, with his subjects, in great grief on
account of a sea-monster that used to come and swallow
both men and cattle.   At last an oracle announced that
this would cease if Laomedon would offer his daughter,

---

[1] *Denkmäler des Klassischen Altertums*, edited by A. Baumeister (Munich
and Leipsic, 1885), vol. i. p. 660; also *Arch. Zeitung*, 1856, plate 89.

Hesione, to the monster to devour.   He consented, and just as the princess had been exposed for this purpose on a rock near the sea, Heracles came to her rescue. The monster was so huge that he undertook to demolish it from within; so he sprang into its stomach, where, like Jonah, he spent three days, before he could cut his way out.   When that had been achieved, he was found to have lost all his hair from the intensity of the heat he had endured.   The monster having thus been slain and Hesione restored to her father, the latter was asked by Heracles for the promised reward; but he declined, and Heracles disappointed had to set out with the Amazon's girdle to Mycenæ.   On the way thither he took part in various adventures, but it was not long ere he and his friends returned to punish Laomedon for his bad faith.   This resulted in the storming of Troy and the death of the faithless king, together with most of his family except Hesione and her young brother, who figured afterwards as the Priam of the *Iliad.*   Heracles gave the princess to wife to one of his friends, called Telamon, on whom he had, at the taking of Troy, drawn his sword in a fit of anger, because he made his way into the doomed city before him.   Telamon took Hesione home to his island of Salamis, where she became the mother of Teucer, who figures on the Greek side in the *Iliad.*

The three points of importance in the story for our purpose are the girdle of the Amazon, the rescue of Hesione, and her being given finally by Heracles to his friend and rival Telamon.   These have their counterparts in the story of Cúchulainn; their sequence also is the same, though they are somewhat differently connected with one another.   Thus Hippolyte and her Amazons are represented on the Goidelic side by

Scáthach and her hosts. Scáthach was more famous
than any man as a teacher of the arts of war; so
Cúchulainn goes to her, not to procure her belt but
her instruction, which was to perfect him as a warrior;
but he only succeeds in getting her to teach him by
surprising her and threatening her with instant death:
she then, to save her life, granted his request. This
helps to an interpretation of Heracles forcing the Amazon to yield her girdle to him: it was the gift of Ares to
her as the one who excelled all her comrades in arms,
and in Apollodorus' words it was for her the σύμβολον
τοῦ πρωτεύειν ἀπασῶν [1]. So the transference of it to
Heracles marked him out as the champion thenceforth,
and this may perhaps be regarded as parallel to
Scáthach's imparting her skill to Cúchulainn. Possibly
the end of the story, which makes Heracles take the
girdle to Eurystheus for his daughter, was an addition
to bring this labour into a sort of conformity with the
other labours, and that we should rather regard it as
originally kept by Heracles for his own use as the
greatest of warriors, who was invited even to help
the gods in their dire need. The story of Peredur
keeps close to that of Cúchulainn, so far as the incident
in question is concerned: it brings the hero into
collision with the Witches of Gloucester, who are the
Welsh equivalents of the Amazons and of Scáthach
with her train. Peredur was about to slay one of the
witches, when she addressed him by name and told him
that it was destiny for them to suffer from him and for
him to learn from them to ride and wield his weapons.
He accordingly accompanies her to the Court of the
Witches, nor does he return till his martial education
is complete; but he has afterwards a more serious

---

[1] *Bibliotheca,* ii. 9.

encounter with the Witches than the one here alluded
to, as will be noticed later.

The other two points in the parallel were the rescuing
of Hesione by Heracles on his return from the Amazons, and his giving her afterwards to Telamon. Similarly Cúchulainn, on his return from the Isle of Scáthach,
queen of the Amazons in the Irish sense, visits the
court of the Red King of the Isles to find everybody
there plunged in grief; for the king had been obliged
to expose his daughter on the sea-shore as tribute to the
Fomori, three of whom were every moment expected
from islands far away to fetch her. In vain had the
king proclaimed that the princess would be given in
marriage to whomsoever should rescue her, until
Cúchulainn arrived and went to the princess to await
the coming of the three Fomori. The story of his
killing them is of the usual dragon-slaying type; but
when the king suggested to Cúchulainn that he should
take the princess away with him to Erinn, Cúchulainn
said he should prefer her coming after him in a year's
time. She did so, but owing to an accident which need
not be related here, Cúchulainn said that he could not
marry her; so he gave her to wife to his friend Lugaid,
who in later years proved his bitterest foe and made
himself active in the battle where Cúchulainn fell.
Here the parallel between the Greek and the Goidelic
is so close that no comment is needed to bring it
into relief.

The stories about sun-heroes were originally in all
probability much the same, so we venture here to inter-
polate, as it were, an incident from that of the Attic
sun-hero Theseus. Theseus is represented waging
war on the Amazons, or according to the later accounts
joining in the expedition of Heracles against them, and

carrying away one of them called Antiope, who is sometimes called their queen[1]. The story of Antiope's love for Theseus is much elaborated in ancient Greek literature, and she is said to have been the mother of his luckless son Hippolytus, who fell the victim of the hostility of his own misguided father. The Irish story in point is that Cúchulainn, when a pupil of Scáthach, that is to say, in Irish phraseology, when he was living at her court as her foster-son, assisted her against another queen who was at war with her, although the legend makes her out to be her own daughter[2]. Her name was Aife, and Cúchulainn succeeded in bringing her a captive to Scáthach's camp, where she was forced to make peace. Cúchulainn visited her country with her, and she became the mother of a son by him. Before departing, Cúchulainn gave her directions as to the disposal of the son that was to be born, which in some respects recall those given by Heracles to Echidna, when he left her about to be the mother of his Scythian offspring. When Cúchulainn's son, Conlaech, should reach the strength of manhood, he was to come to Erinn to his father, bringing with him a token which the latter left to Aife. He was to give way to nobody, to refuse nobody's challenge, and to tell nobody his name. He arrived in due time among the Ultonians, and was thought such an insolent stranger that Cúchulainn was sent to give account of him : the two fell to fighting. The father would have been beaten had he not asked Loeg, his charioteer, to give him the *gái bolga*, the fatal weapon he had received from Aife herself, and with it he slew his own son without discovering his identity[3]. On this comparison one has to notice, that Scáthach and

---

[1] Preller, ii. 233, 299.   [2] O'Curry, ii. 310-12.
[3] O'Conor's *Keating*, i. 196 8.

Aife correspond to Hippolyte and Antiope; but that in the Irish story the daughter is placed at variance with her mother rather than represent Cúchulainn making war on his foster-parent, which was a still more sacred tie according to ancient Goidelic ideas. Nevertheless, Cúchulainn's expedition to the Land of Scáth[1] looks suspiciously like one to Scáthach's country. It is further to be borne in mind, that the long and perilous journey into Scáthach's Isle is distinctly a journey to the other world. In Greek literature it sufficed however to place the home of the Amazons the other side of the sea in Asia Minor, while some legends brought them over on an expedition westwards, and pointed to their tombs here and there in Attica and other parts of Hellas. The later epic literature developed the Amazons into fine handsome women accessible to love; but the earlier authors, who represented them as rough and repellent[2], kept undoubtedly nearer to the original idea.

10. Geryon's Cattle.

Geryon was the name of the lord of an island called Erytheia; he was a giant with a triple body, that is to say he had three heads and a corresponding number of hands and feet, besides, according to some accounts, a powerful pair of wings: he possessed enormous strength and went in complete armour. He was the owner of numerous herds of fine fat cattle of a purple red colour, near which those of the Sun were also said to graze; and Geryon's name was associated by the Greek mind with sumptuous living and a dainty fare. Mythical geography was not very decided as to the position of Erytheia, but the prevalent notion was that it should be sought in the western ocean beyond the

----

[1] *Hib. Lec.* pp. 259–61.   [2] Preller, ii. 86.

Pillars of Hercules, and it was believed to enjoy a delicious and perfect climate. It was, however, the borderland of light and darkness, where the herds of Helius and those of Pluto grazed in the same pastures. Heracles, on arriving in the direction of the island, had to cross the sea to it in the golden bowl of the Sun; that is to say, the vessel in which the Sun was imagined to float back to the east during the hours of the night. On his landing, Heracles is attacked by Geryon's dog, Orthrus, which he kills, doing likewise with Eurytion, Geryon's herdsman, who hurries to the assistance of his hound.

Then Menœtius, who was there as the herdsman of Pluto, announces to Geryon what had happened, and how his cattle were being driven away. Geryon hastens after Heracles and attacks him, but he is slain by the hero, who then takes the cattle away to the strand, where he embarks with Geryon's daughter[1] and cattle in the golden bowl. Reaching the mainland, they commence a long journey through the territory of the Iberians, through Gaul and Italy into Sicily, whence they re-entered Italy and travelled round the Adriatic into Illyria and Epirus. Now, the goddess Here sent a gadfly among the cattle, so that they wandered into Thrace, and according to some accounts into Scythia, where Heracles, following them, fell in with Echidna, the maiden half woman, half snake, that became the mother of his Scythian offspring. On his way back towards the Peloponnese he dedicated Geryon's daughter, together with a part of the herd, to Aphrodite Phersephassa, at Hypata in Thessaly. These wanderings have been unsparingly elaborated, by introducing incidents which, probably, did not from the first belong

[1] Preller, ii. 211, 216.

to them ; but some of them must be regarded as of old
standing, such as the story of the semi-human Cacus,
son of Vulcan, stealing some of the cattle from Heracles.
What the original scene of this incident may have been
it would be impossible to tell, but Vergil fixed on the
Roman hill known as the Aventine, and describes with
eloquent detail, how the mighty robber had there a vast
cave in which he shut up eight of Heracles' cattle, how
he had cunningly dragged them in by their tails, that
their footprints might not betray their hiding-place, how
the hero finding them out lay the cave open to the light
of day, and how he slew Cacus in spite of the fire he
vomited and the darkness he spread around him [1]:—

> ' Panditur extemplo foribus domus atra revulsis,
> Abstractæque boves abjuratæque rapinæ
> Cælo ostenduntur, pedibusque informe cadaver
> Protrahitur. Nequeunt expleri corda tuendo
> Terribiles oculos, vultum, villosaque sætis
> Pectora semiferi, atque exstinctos faucibus ignes.'

The Cúchulainn legend gives several versions of the
Goidelic counterpart of this labour of Heracles : one of
them is related to Loegaire mac Néill, king of Erinn,
by the ghost of Cúchulainn, called up from the dead by
St. Patrick in his attempt to convert the monarch.   It
describes how the hero had among other things made
an expedition to Tír Scáith or the Land of Shadow,
and attacked the fortress there, how all kinds of
monsters were let loose at him and his comrades, how
there was a wonderful cauldron there which the king's
daughter gave to Cúchulainn, together with the three
cows that supplied the milk for the cooking done in the
cauldron, and how the cows had loads of pearls round
their necks.   The cauldron was taken and also the

---

[1] *Æneid*, viii. 193-267.

cows, who swam with Cúchulainn rowing behind them, until he was shipwrecked on the sea that was 'vast by the north.' So he had to swim to land, bringing with him as many of his comrades as could cling to his body[1].

Another version calls the king of the invaded realm Mider, one of the names of the chief of the fairies in Irish legend, as already shown (pp. 26-9). His daughter was Bláthnat, whose name is of the same class as that of the Welsh Blodeued in the Mabinogi of Mâth ab Mathonwy: compare also Fflûr and Blanchefleur, the name given by Chrétien to a lady loved by Perceval[2] (Peredur). Mider's country is called Inis Fer Falga, or the Isle of the Men of Falga. Cúchulainn and his friends took Mider's fortress, and carried away Mider's daughter, Mider's cauldron, and Mider's three cows. But on their way home, they were robbed of them all. Nor knew they where to look for them, since the robber was a cunning wizard, who, as Cúchulainn discovered later, was Cúrí or Cúroi mac Daire. His stronghold stood between Tralee and Dingle, in westernmost Kerry. Cúchulainn, with the aid of Bláthnat, slew Cúrí in his abode, and carried away the lady together with Mider's three cows and cauldron to his own Ulster. Cúrí was a great ancestral figure in the west, and the story has accordingly been carefully perverted in his favour, by representing Cúchulainn shamefully vanquished in the first instance, and convicted of owing his victory at the last to the blackest treachery. But traces are known of still another version, which is free from this feature: the cattle, according to this, were white, red-eared cows belonging to Echaid Echbél, who lived beyond the sea

---

[1] *Hib. Lec.* p. 261.   [2] Ib. pp. 153, 239; Nutt, p. 11, &c.

in Alban; but as they came sometimes to graze on one of the headlands of Antrim, Cúchulainn took possession of them and drove them away: then they were stolen by Cúrí mac Daire [1].

Here we have in Echaid Echbél, or E. with the Horse-mouth, a figure bodily peculiar about the head, and, so far as that is concerned, one to be compared with the monster Geryon; but we are not forced to lay any great stress on this comparison. We have elsewhere Geryon's more exact counterpart in the Cernunnos of Gaulish theology; and as Geryon was associated with abundance and plenty, especially of herds, so Cernunnos revelled in metallic wealth, as indicated by his statues, which are also embellished with ox heads, and sometimes with an ox and a stag feeding [2]. The statue of this ancient sitting god of the Gauls, which makes the nearest approach to the Greek representation of Geryon, is that found on an altar at Beaune in the Côte d'Or, which gives this divinity three complete heads [3]. It is more usual, however, to find him represented with merely three faces, and not three complete heads, but one head with or without horns. Sometimes also the head alone is elaborated, while the divinity is reduced to a Janus-like pillar, a form to be detected probably in the Venerable Head of Brân the Blessed. But as this latter has been discussed elsewhere [4], and is to come under notice later in this volume, it is needless to pursue it further at present.

Here may be mentioned another incident in the story of the return of Heracles from Erytheia, namely, that of his contest with his foes in the neighbourhood of

---

[1] *Hib. Lec.* pp. 473 7.   [2] Ib. p. 80.

[3] Bertrand's *Autel de Saintes* in the *Rev. Arch.* for 1880, p. 75.

[4] *Hib. Lec.* pp. 96-7.

Arles, where he sank on his knees from sheer weariness and despair; after having shot all his arrows and
looked round in vain for stones to cast at his enemies.
The story goes that Zeus out of pity sent down a
shower of stones, which has accounted for the stony
nature of that tract of country ever since, and enabled
Heracles at the time to rout the Ligyan foe[1]. After
crossing into Italy, he has a severe contest, among
the Ligurians, namely, with two sons of Poseidon, called
Alebion and Dercynus. But according to Pomponius
Mela, it is the two sons of Poseidon or Neptune, that
fight with Heracles near Arles: he calls them (in the
accusative) Albiona and Bergyon[2], in whom one cannot
help detecting some such names as Albion and Iberius
as eponyms of Britain and Ireland. This view is rendered possible by the ancient geographical notion,
which made Gaul and Spain into a long and narrow
peninsula, with Britain on the north-west, separated
from it by a comparatively narrow channel with its
southern outlet approximately opposite the Pyrenees.

This, however, need not detain us from returning to
the story of the shower of stones, which may be
recognized in the account of Cúchulainn on the Táin,
though it is there very differently put. Cúrí mac Daire
so sympathized with Ailill and Medb on the Táin, that
he gave them men to aid them in the war; and one day
he resolved to go and take part in it himself; but an
Ultonian hero of unknown attributes, except that he was
called Munremur, came to oppose him: they met in
mid-air and flung stones at each other   The stones met

---

[1] Æschylus, *Prometheus Unbound*, frag. 193; also Strabo, iv. 1. 7.

[2] As to the *g* of *Bergyon*, the author's remarks on *Avittoriges* as the Ogam
genitive of the name given in Latin as Avitoria, on the Eglwys Cymmun
Stone, may be consulted in the *Arch. Cambrensis* for 1889, pp. 225-32.

and fell on a spot midway between the three portions
of which the camp of the invaders was composed: it
was ever afterwards called Mag Clochar, from the
stones [1]. Munremur came to aid Cúchulainn and the
conflict greatly alarmed his foes. But neither this nor
the Greek version is of much importance in itself. It
looks, however, as though the story of the shower of
stones was a very ancient one, which was variously
placed, both as to locality and to its relation to other
incidents.

The original number of the labours of Heracles was
ten, and they were accomplished in a week of years, or
more exactly, eight years and one month [2]. But as
Eurystheus refused to count the killing of the hydra,
because Iolaus had given assistance, and the cleaning of
the Augean stables because Augeias had promised a
tenth of his herds to the hero for accomplishing the
task, two more labours are usually added: these bring
the number up to twelve. Which of the additional ones
should be reckoned the last, is not quite certain; but the
tendency was, on the whole, to give that place to the
one in which Cerberus figured. The other was concerned with the procuring of

11. The Apples of the Hesperides.

The first difficulty about these golden apples, supposed
to grow on a wonderful tree, guarded by a dragon attended by the maidens called the Hesperides, was the
fact that no one seemed to know where the Garden of
the Hesperides was situated. So Heracles comes to
the mythic river known as the Eridanus, and there he
finds certain nymphs, who advise him to go and surprise
Nereus, the old man of the sea, under one of his various

---

[1] *Bk. of the Dun,* 71 [b].   [2] Preller, ii. 164.

names, and compel him to put him on the way to find
the Garden of the Hesperides. He does so, and in
consequence of the information he got from Nereus, he
enters on a very long and varied series of travels. He
goes first to Libya, where he has to wrestle with a
terrible giant called Antæus. Having slain him, Heracles
appears next in Egypt, where he only escapes by main
force from being sacrificed by Busiris at the altar of
Zeus. Thence he proceeds up the country to Ethiopia,
and comes, after many adventures, to the sea-coast,
whence he sails in the golden bowl of the Sun to Asia.
There a ramble in India is attributed to him before
reaching the Caucasus and the scene of the torture
of Prometheus. He kills the bird that preyed on that
hero's liver, and obtains the release of the sufferer,
who informs Heracles how to find the Garden of the
Hesperides and what to do when he got there.

He was to go through Scythia to the Land of the
Hyperboreans, where he should find the Garden, and
he was not to pluck the apples himself, but to ask Atlas
to do it, who was there supporting on his shoulders the
burden of the heavens. Heracles did as he was directed,
but Atlas, having plucked the apples, felt that he should
like to take them to Eurystheus himself, and leave
Heracles under the weight of the world; but Heracles,
as he was not used to such a load, asked Atlas to take
it while he put on a cushion; the stupid Atlas having
taken back his burden, Heracles left him under it and
went his way with the three golden apples. But other
accounts made Heracles slay the dragon and pluck the
apples off the tree with his own hands, while as to the
situation of the Garden of the Hesperides, views also
varied widely : perhaps the most ancient of them was
that which fixed on the Libyan Atlas, or associated the

spot with the western ocean and a region not far distant from Erytheia and the abode of Geryon. Lastly,
when the apples had been shown to Eurystheus, Athene
took them back to the Hesperides, as nobody else
might have the keeping of the fruit, which may be
regarded as the symbol of everlasting youthfulness and
vigour.

When we come to compare the story of Cúchulainn,
we find no nearer counterpart to the three apples of
the Hesperides than the cauldron which Cúchulainn
brought from Mider's Fairy Isle, though much closer
parallels are to be found among the popular tales of
the Western Highlands, such as that of the King of
Erinn's Son, who fetches three bottles of the water
of the Green Isle. Besides the other treasures, he also
brings away a loaf that never diminishes and a cheese of
the same description, the narrative being made to close
with a feast that lasts seven days and seven years [1].
The Welsh story of Peredur offers more points of comparison than that of Cúchulainn, namely, when it speaks
of the charger with the head in it at the castle of
Peredur's second uncle; for in the head we have probably a blurred representation of Brân's Venerable Head,
which wherever it was borne meant continuous feasting
and delights, not to mention its relation to the romancers' ideas of the Holy Grail. The story, in other
respects, confirms this view in some measure: thus, as
in the case of Heracles and the Garden of the Hesperides, Peredur's first difficulty was that he did not
know where to look for the castle which should be his
destination; after a whole year's fruitless wandering
he is put on the way to find it by a knight wearing
the garb of religion, and represented in some of the

[1] Campbell, i. 164-74.

romances as brother to Peredur's mother. In this respect, the hermit acts as the counterpart of the Culture Hero Prometheus in the Heracles legend. Lastly, when Peredur at length reaches the Castle of Wonders he is not said to take away the charger with the head; at first sight this would seem to differ from the story of Heracles bringing the fruit to Eurystheus, but it is remarkable that Athene at once takes back that fruit where it was found, so that the bringing it away was possibly a point stretched in order to fall in with the general plan of the labours. Similarly with regard to the hell-hound,

12. Cerberus.

This was brought up from the other world to be exhibited at Mycenæ, and then to be at once led back into the darkness congenial to it. If the fetching of the monster from Hades was a part of the original story, one would have probably to regard it as a sort of duplicate of the conflict of Heracles with the Nemean lion; but even if it is to be regarded as an original part of the story, it cannot have been the principal moment in the labour, though it came near crowding out all else in it. Mythologically speaking, the interest of the incident centres in Heracles bringing back the other hero, Theseus, to this world. It recalls the story of Hermóðr descending to Hell to fetch back his murdered brother Balder, though he was not successful in his errand: it was in fact too soon, and all nature must weep for Balder before he obtained leave to return [1].

The Irish counterpart to Heracles releasing his friend from Hades is to be found in Cúchulainn going to the Isles of Hades and setting at liberty Dóel Dermait's

---

[1] *Hib. Lec.* p. 533.

Three Sons, in whom we seem to have a reference to the triple division by the Celts of the daylight portion of the twenty-four hours. On this occasion, Cúchulainn made his way to the Dolorous Glen, or what may be regarded as the uttermost part of the Irish Hades, and slew its king with the *gái bolga*, whereupon his captives hastened to bathe their wounds in the blood of the fallen despot : we are left to suppose that there were many of them besides the Three Sons of Dóel Dermait, mentioned always by themselves. The same event is referred to in Welsh in a blurred fashion in the account of Peredur slaying the Arrogant Black Fellow, and much more transparently in the story of Owein, where it makes Owein vanquish the Perverse Black Robber and release the twenty-four matrons imprisoned by him. In them we have, apparently, the twenty-four hours of the day, here treated as all alike captives of the king of darkness, and now allowed to come back again. In the romances this becomes the release of the captives of the realm of Goire on the arrival of Lancelot and his vanquishing Melwas. It is worth while noticing that the release of the captives ends the story of Owein, just as the bringing back of Theseus is associated with the last of the twelve labours of Heracles.

CHAPTER X.

Cúchulainn and Heracles (*continued*).

Beside the stock labours of Heracles, there were many other achievements ascribed to him in the numerous legends current about him in the different parts of the Greek world. One of these, relating what he had done in the war between the gods and the giants, has already been touched upon ; but its importance demands a somewhat more detailed notice from the comparative point of view. The early story-tellers of Greece could hardly have been expected to place it among the labours : the story went that it was Athene who invited Heracles to assist the Olympians, in consequence of an oracle that they could not dispose of their foes without the aid of a mortal. The Irish counterpart to this, as has already been suggested, was Cúchulainn fighting for the Ultonians when they were in their couvade, and against the invaders from the west under Ailill and Medb on the Táin : also his finally routing them, at the head of the Ultonians issuing from their couvade. But there comes the difficulty, that the Welsh story of Peredur presents the Welsh parallel as the last labour imposed upon Peredur, namely, that of annihilating the Witches of Gloucester. This he does with the help of the other hero, Gwalchmei, and Arthur's

men in force. Thus Peredur, who had been to complete his military education at the Court of the Witches,
is the one who leads a force to destroy them at the end
of the story; but this could hardly have taken place
in an Irish story which made Cúchulainn a foster-son
of the amazon Scáthach, so the corresponding war of
Cúchulainn's was with a mixed force of Fir Bolg and
others from the west, öf whom the real general was
another virago, namely Medb, wife of Ailill and queen
of Connaught. The Welsh story introduces the Witches
as 'Nine Witches of the Witches of Caer Loyw;' but we
are not told how many were present at the final encounter between them and Peredur. One is led, however, to gather from the narrative that they must have
mustered in great force. Further, we know from the
story of Kulhwch [1], that, when Arthur and his men
stormed Caer Loyw in order to rescue from a dungeon
there the sun-god Mabon, the Apollo Maponus of inscriptions of the Roman period, the place was defended
not by women but by men ; and here, possibly, we are
to regard Peredur's foes as consisting of the Amazons
called the Witches, helped by numerous allies of the
other sex, though the story-teller does not mention
them.

As a rule, the sun-hero fights unaided by numbers,
and this makes it the more important to take further
notice of such exceptions to that rule as have just been
mentioned. Among other things, it is not to be supposed that those exceptions are necessarily late; for in
the present case, for instance, the victory of Cúchulainn
at the head of the Ultonians and of Peredur at that of
Arthur's men, has its counterpart also amply expressed
in the *Iliad* of Homer. Of course, it is not pretended

[1] *R. B. Mab.* pp. 131-2 ; Guest, ii. 301.

that the story of that great epic is to be disposed of in a
few words here by the way; but it can be very briefly
shown how the story of the *Iliad* fits into the interpretation suggested in these pages. Helen has usually been
seized upon as the key to the situation, in her character
of a dawn goddess or the like; but the presence in such
contests of a female personage associating at one time
with dark beings, and at another with light or bright ones,
is so much the rule that it is of no adequate avail.

Let us approach the question from another direction, and first of all let us sweep aside all that part
of the poem which makes the gods of Olympus take
part in the war, and especially that which engages
Apollo on the wrong side, a feature probably to be
accounted for by the poet's ideas of the history and
ethnology of Asia Minor. This done, the Greeks themselves become our Olympians, and Agamemnon takes
the place of Zeus as the central figure, while the Asiatic
forces opposed to them make up an array in which the
Trojans and the Amazons are represented fighting side
by side. Let us now see how this fits as regards the
sun-hero: the chief person of that description in the
story is Achilles, son of Peleus and Thetis, the former a
mortal and the latter a goddess, who may perhaps be
here compared with the Lady of the Lake, who rears
Lancelot in the romances. Her first concern is for her
son's safety, and besides other precautions taken by her,
she endeavours to keep him from being forced into the
Trojan war: she went even so far as to have him
disguised in woman's clothing. Similarly, Dechtere
tried to prevent her child, Cúchulainn, from going to the
Ultonian champions at Emain Macha; but he could
not be turned from his choice, which was like that of
Achilles, a career brief and famous. The precautions,

taken in vain by Peredur's mother to keep him in utter
ignorance of all that appertained to knighthood and the
art of war, have already been mentioned. It may be
asked, where in the case of Achilles is the distinction of
race that should correspond to that between Heracles
and the gods, or between Cúchulainn and the other
Ultonians. It may be that no trace of it is left in
Greek literature, but it may also be that we have just
such a trace in his being made the leader of the people
called Myrmidons, one story of whose origin was that
they were descended from ants converted into men by
the fiat of Zeus. Whether that deserves to be taken
into account or not, Achilles was the saviour of the
Greeks when they were hard pressed ; and among
other scenes fondly elaborated by Greek poets and
artists was his slaying of Penthesilea, queen of the
Amazons, and his grief in observing her beauty and
youth. It is even suggested that he recognized in her
one whom he had met before on terms of amity and
more. This, if a part of the original Greek legend,
comes remarkably close to that of Peredur's two distinct
rencontres with the Witches of Gloucester, the first
resulting in friendship and the other in a fatal combat.

Though the slaying of Hector and the routing of the
Trojans together with their Amazon allies close the
Iliad, it was not the close of the Trojan war, for,
mythologically speaking, the story consists of several
threads wrought into a single one. Just as it is
conceivable that the fetching of Geryon's cattle by
Heracles and the procuring the apples of the Hesperides might have been combined into a compound
story, so the Trojan legend has several moments: the
triumph of Achilles over his Trojan antagonist was only
one of them, the recovery of Helen by her husband

Menelaus may have been another; but there was still
another, and that was the carrying away of the Palladium from the Citadel of Troy, which involved the
doom of the city. But the Palladium, as the Trojans
had been informed, could only be taken from them with
the help of the arrows of Heracles, which the Greeks
accordingly had to fetch; it was necessary also to have
the aid of Neoptolemus, the youthful son of Achilles.
He, under the direction of Odysseus, the wily Greek in
whom we have a form of the Culture Hero of the race,
was to wield the weapons of his father with fatal effect
against the doomed city. This solar hero, son of a solar
hero, brought the Trojan war accordingly to an end;
and in him, in spite of his savagery, one may recognize
a Greek counterpart to Galahad as the son of Lancelot
in the romances. For it was Galahad for whom the
sword of Balin was miraculously preserved, and Galahad it was that had been foretold as the coming knight
who was to achieve the quest of the Holy Grail,
and to put an end to the so-called Enchantments of
the Isle of Britain.

Greek literature emphasizes two crimes which it
attributes to Heracles, and divides his history accordingly into two parts. The one was his killing his
offspring by Megara when he was suffering from a fit
of madness, and according to some accounts it was to
expiate this crime that he had to submit to Eurystheus
as his taskmaster and to perform the labours he
assigned him. The other crime was his killing his
friend Iphitus, in a similar access of fury. For this he
was obliged, according to the direction of the Pythian
oracle, to submit to be sold into slavery. The story
goes that Hermes took him to the slave-market, and that
he was there bought by Omphale, queen of Lydia and

widow of king Tmolus, who had left her his throne. She loved Heracles and freed him; she was also loved of him, and gave himself up to the luxurious and idle life of a Lydian. Omphale amused herself by dressing herself in Heracles' lion's skin and equipping herself with his club, while he clothed himself in feminine attire and betook himself to spinning and other womanly occupations. This, and similar situations, formed the delight of Greek comedy; but Heracles also engaged in more serious undertakings while in Lydia, for he cleared the country of robbers and made successful expeditions against border raiders and others of the queen's enemies, including among them the Amazons. When the time of his exile in Lydia was over, the hero returned to his native land and his former sphere of action.

As to the Goidelic parallel, Cúchulainn, besides being subject to fits of dangerous frenzy, is described mad on two different occasions, which, however, do not succeed in the order indicated of the Greek incidents. He also slays his own son, owing rather to a mistake than to madness, as has already been mentioned. But the second madness of Heracles and his exile in Lydia have a parallel in the story of Cúchulainn of a very striking kind. His indisposition was caused by two fairies, Liban and Fand, of whom the former was the queen of Labraid of the Swift Hand on the Sword, who reigned over a sort of Elysian isle. Fand was sister to Liban and had been married to the great wizard of the sea, Manannán mac Lir; but he had forsaken her, and she had fallen in love with Cúchulainn on account of his fame and renown. Fand and Liban came in the form of swans, and lighted on a lake where Cúchulainn saw them; they made a sort of siren music, which caused the men of Erinn who heard them to fall asleep. Cúchulainn, much against the wish of his friends, cast a spear at them, and did so several times with a lack of success which was so unusual in his case, that it greatly surprised and chagrined him. He also then fell asleep. In that sleep he saw two women, one in red and the other in green, come to him and horsewhip him alternately for a long time; when he awoke, he was ill and asked to be carried to his bed, where he remained nearly a whole year without saying a word to any one. It was at last found out that the fairies had been the cause of his indisposition, so he was made to go and meet them at the spot where he had been horsewhipped by them in his sleep just twelve months before. They came to meet him, and would heal him on the condition of his coming to Labraid to aid him in a great battle on a given day, and of his abiding for a time with Fand in Labraid's Isle. After much reluctance, he allowed the invitation of Labraid to influence him; so he went and fought valiantly for him, and then he abode a month with Fand. When he took leave of her, he made arrangements to meet her again, and did so meet her. Now his wife Emer, having heard of it, also resorted there with her friends prepared to murder Fand; but when Fand was in this danger, her husband Manannán suddenly came and carried her away unseen of any one except Loeg, the charioteer of Cúchulainn. The scene ended with Cúchulainn becoming mad again and hurrying away from the abodes of men. He continued in this state till Conchobar's druid, with the aid of powerful ogams, got the best of him, and gave him and his wife a drink of forgetfulness to bring them back to their right minds [1].

[1] Windisch. p. 226; *Hib. Lec.* pp. 459–462.

On the Welsh side, this disappearance of Cúchulainn to live for a time with Fand is matched by Peredur reigning for a time with the Empress, and by Owein living with the Lady of the Fountain as his wife until Arthur and his men find him out and induce him to come away with them. Here, also, must be mentioned Lancelot afflicted with madness caused by a scene with Guinevere, resembling that between Cúchulainn and Emer when Fand was carried away by Manannán. He comes to Elayne, who heals him by means of the Grail; and he is then detained by her for years in the Joyous Isle, until in fact some of Arthur's men come to just with him and recognize him, with the result of inducing him to return with them. It is to be noticed that like Heracles in Lydia, both Owein and Peredur engaged in fighting during their absence from their own countries respectively, as Cúchulainn likewise fought during his stay in Labraid's Isle, and as Lancelot justed with all comers while he bore the name of the Chevalier Malfait. But it is not to be overlooked that the Welsh versions of the story imperceptibly merge the lady corresponding to Fand and Omphale, namely Elen, into another and a very different one, the Empress or Gwyar, who should rather correspond to the Mórrígu and Here (p. 169). The former, however, alone interests us at this point; and the Irish nature myth, in which Fand figures, teaches us that she was a personification of the tear, or possibly the dew-drop, and her name means probably water[1]; so that it may be compared with the description of Owein's wife as the Lady of the Fountain or Well, while in the pretty conceit of the fairy Lady of Shalott the glistening drop is made into a fairy mirror, which the reflection of the form of

[1] *Hib. Lec.* p. 463.

Lancelot irretrievably mars. Moreover, the parallel between Fand and Omphale extends further than has been indicated; thus Fand was the wife of the sea-god Manannán and the sister of the flood-goddess Liban, while Omphale was the daughter of the river-god Iardanus. Nay, her name may also probably compare with that of Fand, as it would seem to be of the same origin as the Greek ὄμβρος, 'rain,' Latin *imber*, 'a shower,' and Sanskrit *ambhas*, 'water.' So we have here, in various forms seemingly, a nature myth associating the sun with the world of waters. Lastly, though the mythological standing of Labraid is difficult to determine, his island is certainly to be regarded as belonging to the other world. One of the most common features of the geography of that world was that it lay on the other side of a water. So from Greece such lands as Lycia, Lydia, and the Troad, somewhere in the direction of the sun rising out of the sea in the morning, satisfied early Greek mythology as representatives of the other world just as well as an Erytheia first in the Adriatic, then removed, as geographical knowledge grew wider, to a spot in the far-away ocean of the west. It was in fact all the same, and the two directions met in the land of the Ethiopians of the *Odyssey*[1].

A word must now be said of the solar heroes as a group, and first of all with regard to their manner of fighting and travelling. Heracles appears to have been originally armed, like Apollo, with bow and arrows, while the club belongs to a later mode of equipping him[2]. Bellerophon uses the bow and the lance; sometimes also the sword[3]. Similarly Cúchulainn's weapons are missiles of various kinds, including stones; also the spear and the sword, and, in extreme cases, the

[1] *Hib. Lec.* p. 640.   [2] Preller, ii. 187 8.   [3] Ib. 83-4.

gái bolga [1], which he usually directs upwards into the
body of his antagonist, or exceptionally brings straight
down on his head.   This last mode of fighting reminds
one of Bellerophon on the back of the winged Pegasus
attacking the Chimæra from above.   On the Welsh side
Peredur, though unsurpassed in his day as a swordsman, derives his name from the spear which he wielded
with such deadly skill and force; when fully described
he is called Peredur Paladr-hir, or P. of the long Shaft.
The adjective originally involved a reference, perhaps,
to his unerring success in reaching his antagonist,
as did also probably that of Long-handed as applied
to the Irish sun-god Lug.   In fact, the connotation of
both epithets may have been originally much the same
as Apollo's epithet of ἑκατηβόλος, or far-shooting.   From
the position of the enemy assailed, it mattered little
whether the predicate *long* was applied to the distance
sped through by the assailant's missile, or else to the
weapon itself or the hand wielding it: in either case,
he might expect to be hit.

It was more usual in Greek mythology to represent
the sun-god driving in a chariot than riding on horseback ; but Perseus and Bellerophon are represented
each in his time riding on the winged horse Pegasus,
while Heracles, though often pictured fighting on foot,
has a chariot in readiness drawn by two chargers driven
by Iolaus, who sits beside his master.   When, however,

---

[1] See supra, p. 189 and the *Hib. Lec.* pp. 441, 481.   In spite of the exag-
gerated descriptions to be found of this weapon, it was not altogether an
imaginary one.   We are told in a passage translated by O'Curry in his
Manners and Customs of the Ancient Irish, ii. 309, that ' it made but the wound
of one dart in entering the body ; but it presented thirty inverted points against
coming back ; so that it could not be drawn from a person's body without
opening it.'   The author has been shown spears and harpoons in the Pitt-
Rivers Museum here, the working of which renders the principle of the *gái
bolga* fairly intelligible.

he came to a sea which he had to cross, he sometimes
borrowed the golden bowl of the Sun, and embarked in
that vessel as his boat. Lastly, Heracles is sometimes
represented, especially by oriental art, as seated· on the
back of a lion [1].

On Irish ground we have Cúchulainn usually fighting
from a chariot, drawn by two horses driven by Loeg,
who sat by the hero's side ; but on his long journey to
the isle of the amazon Scáthach, Cúchulainn all alone
travels in a variety of ways. Certain dangerous portions of the journey are safely made by him by following
the rolling of a wheel and of an apple respectively; but
over a much longer distance he travels on the back
of a savage beast resembling a lion. After he had
journeyed so for four whole days, the animal put him
down in an inhabited island, where those who saw the
savage beast thus serving a man were not a little surprised. With this animal should, perhaps, be compared
the two chargers which the hero tamed for his chariot
after his return to Erinn : they were both lake-horses ;
but the parallel is much closer between the wild beast
that carried Cúchulainn over land and sea and the animal ridden by the older sun-god Lug. This last was a
mare belonging to Lug's foster-father Manannán Son of
the Sea, and her name was *Énbarr* [2], which meant, possibly, that she had a bird's head. If so, she corresponded
to her name, as she was swift like the cold winds
of spring, and travelled with equal ease over land
and sea. The bird-like speed of this animal, the property of Manannán of the Sea, cannot help recalling
the wings of Pegasus, which is variously associated with

---

[1] Preller, ii. 190.

[2] See the *Atlantis*, iv. 163, where O'Curry prints *Aonbharr,* which he interprets ' One Mane ; ' but Cormac gives an *enbarr* meaning ' foam.'

springs of water in the Greek story, and made out to have been the offspring of the sea-god Poseidon.

As to the heroes of Welsh stories, they never drive in chariots, but ride on horseback. So Lug's Welsh counterpart Ileu had a celebrated horse, and it was called the Steed of the Yellow-white Footsteps : it has two things predicated of it, to which the Irish stories of Cúchulainn and Lug enable us to give a meaning: it is called a gift-horse[1], which the fact of Lug's horse being the property of Manannán[2], assists one to understand, and it has the adjective *lletuegin* applied to it, meaning tamed or domesticated, in the sense of bringing a wild animal up tame, a signification which the story of Cúchulainn riding on a wild beast like a lion towards Scáthach's Isle helps one to realize as applied to Ileu's horse. The Irish hero Conall Cernach had also a very peculiar steed, which drew his chariot without the help of another horse on the memorable occasion, for instance, of Conall's pursuing Lugaid, the slayer of Cúchulainn, and avenging on him the death of the latter earlier in the day. This horse of Conall's had a dog's head, and it used its teeth, like Darius' steed in Herodotus, to attack his master's antagonists. Thus Lugaid, having lost one hand just before, bound Conall to fight with him with one hand alone, the other being tied behind him: this was done, but in the course of the duel Conall's horse took a piece out of Lugaid's body with his teeth, and rendered him easily slain by his master. Riding to battle is probably more ancient among Aryan

---

[1] In the *Book of Taliessin*, poem xxv : see Skene, ii. 176, where the spelling of the MS. is incorrectly given as *letuegin*. The note at the foot of page 385 of the *Hibbert Lectures* was written before the author had guessed the point of the adjective.

[2] Triads, i. 94. ii. 50, and *R. B. Mab.* p. 306.

nations than driving in a chariot drawn by a pair of
horses; but a one-horse chariot used for the same purpose, as on the occasion of Conall's revenge, is quite
exceptional, and to be explained as a sort of compromise
between the two war chargers usual in the epic tales
of the Ultonian cycle, and Cúchulainn's savage beast
like a lion, or Owein's ally, who was a pure-white
lion.

In pursuing here as our leading thread the story of
Heracles, we have introduced several other heroes by
way of comparison, such as Perseus and Bellerophon.
Other personages also have been mentioned in consequence, at least partly, of the story bringing them in
contact with him: we allude especially to Theseus and
Apollo. The relations between Theseus and Heracles
have already been mentioned, and their mythological
interpretations suggested with the aid of Hermóđr and
Balder, while those between Heracles and Apollo, which
now claim our attention, present greater difficulties.
Allusion has already been made to Heracles in collision
with Artemis and Apollo, on account of the stag belonging to Artemis and caught by Heracles for Eurystheus;
but a more serious quarrel took place when Heracles,
in a disordered state of mind and body, consequent on
his committing the crime of murdering Iphitus, came
to the Pythian oracle at Delphi to enquire what he was
to do. The oracle turned away in horror refusing to
give a response, whereby Heracles was so angered that
he broke into the sanctuary, and snatching the holy
tripod, carried it away in order to set it up elsewhere for
his own service. Thereupon Apollo came to the rescue
of the sacred utensil, and a terrible duel would have
ensued had not Zeus intervened. But Heracles carried
his point of obtaining a response from the oracle, which

was to the effect, that he must serve again in order to
effect the expiation of his crime [1], and this it was that led
to his being sold to Omphale, queen of Lydia. Heracles
and Apollo are ever afterwards represented as the
greatest friends, and Heracles becomes a great propa-
gator of the cult of Apollo in various parts of the
Hellenic world.

With the quarrel between Heracles and Apollo is
probably not to be reckoned the standing hostility of
Apollo towards Achilles, which is to be traced rather to
the historical and ethnological prepossessions of the
poet of the *Iliad*; but it has its parallel in the Ultonian
cycle of Irish tales. For there we have no less than
three solar heroes intimately related with one another,
Cúchulainn, Conall, and Loegaire: the former two were
foster-brothers, which is a Goidelic way of representing
them as sworn allies. But they had their rivalries, and
one important story relates how the king and his most
influential men had repeatedly to intervene to prevent
the imminent fall of the three heroes by one another's
hands, and how they sent them to one uncanny being
after another to have the question of the champion's
morsel at the feasts of Emain decided for them. Cúchulainn issued victorious from all the terrible tests to
which he was submitted, but his rivals never admitted
the justice of the decisions in his favour; so Cúchulainn
said that he would no longer contend with them, and the
institution of the champion's morsel, with all that it
implied, fell into abeyance, and the heroes' friendship
was submitted to no further trials. Norse mythology
does not tell us of any rivalry between the solar
brothers, but it discloses their plurality; for besides
Balder and Hermóðr, his brother already mentioned,

[1] Preller, ii. 162-4.

there was a third brother Vali, who, born in the halls of the West and when but one night old, was to avenge Balder's death[1], which challenges comparison with Apollo's great feat of slaying the Pytho as soon as he was born.

Here, however, a difficulty presents itself, the mention of which must be no longer deferred: Balder and his brothers were, so to say, on the same level; and so were Owein, Peredur, and Gwalchmei, Lancelot and Galahad, while, according to Greek mythology, Heracles and Apollo were not. For Heracles was by birth a mortal, while Apollo was from the first one of the immortals. Both Celts and Greeks had a multiplicity of solar heroes; but as the ancient mythology does not appear to have required at once more than two, or at most three, the greater number of the solar heroes must be regarded as various editions, so to say, of one or two originals, however widely they may happen to differ in detail of treatment. One of the most ancient ideas respecting the solar hero was that which treated him as the offspring of the Culture Hero or the great medicine-man of the race; but such a primitive notion must have been liable at an early date to be obscured, especially among a progressive people such as the Greeks. Therefore, according to this view, one would, perhaps, be at liberty to suppose that Apollo's immortality was not original, but the result of an after-thought, though Greek literature gives no hint to that effect. But the admissibility of this view would seem to have in its favour various things in the story of Apollo. To begin with his birth, Here appears resorting to the same means of delaying that event as in the case of Heracles; and later, like Heracles subject to Eurystheus, Apollo serves Laomedon, king of Troy,

[1] Vigfusson and Powell's *Corpus Poeticum Boreale*, i. 183.

Q

whose cattle he pastures ; and later still he has to render
service at the house of Admetus of Pheræ in Thessaly.
Among other things he does for Admetus may be
mentioned the feat of yoking a lion and a wild boar to
the bridal chariot, without which Admetus was not to
obtain Alcestis, the daughter of Pelias [1], to wife. This
reminds one of the part played by Siegfried in wooing
Brynhild for Gunther. Lastly, the question of the immortality of the Greek heroes, here in question, may
be said to reduce itself almost to one of degree: thus
some of them, such as Perseus, Bellerophon, Theseus,
and Achilles, are not represented born immortal, or
acquiring immortality, while Heracles is born a mortal,
but acquires immortality : Apollo, on the other hand, is
immortal from the first. In any case, the distinction
between them in this respect is not so great as it might
at first sight seem to be.

Having mentioned some of the points which might be
urged in favour of the idea, that Apollo may have been
originally regarded as a mortal, like the heroes just
enumerated, it is right to add that another view is
possible and, on the whole, preferable, namely, that
Aryan theology of old admitted more than one account
of the origin of the Solar Hero. In fact, we have already
(p. 164) touched upon this in connection with the question of the parentage of Gwalchmei (Gauvain) and
Gwalchaved (Galahad). These accounts may be grouped
thus : (α) that which made the sun-hero a son or
avatar of another sun-hero, and (β) that which made
him son of the Culture Hero. To these may be added
an older one (γ) making him son of the Zeus of the Aryan
system, and like him a god from the first. The pedigree
making the sun-hero the offspring of the Zeus of the

---

[1] Preller, ii. 316.

system, is probably to be regarded as older than that which treats him as son of the Culture Hero, as the latter seems to postulate the former. In other words, when the Culture Hero of the Aryans or the medicine-man of the race, claimed to be the father of the Sun, he probably did so merely as a sequel to his placing himself on a level with the head of the Aryan pantheon, or of his being identified with that divinity as a manifestation or incarnation of him. This did not completely supersede the older theology, but it was the tendency; and as such it gathered at length force enough, for example, to make Indra head of the Hindu pantheon. It gave Woden the place of Tiu in Teutonic theology. It so advanced the Culture Hero in the estimation of the Celts that their Zeus is hard to identify in some of their tales, and wholly omitted in others, while his consort of the early period is left labouring, in some instances, under the title of Great Queen or Empress without a Great King or Emperor to call her his own. Greek literature takes for granted the solemn marriage of Zeus with his sister Here, but Celtic mythology fails to carry us back to a state of society where it could have been possible. Thus, in the case of Conchobar and his sister Dechtere, we only find a suspicion, but it was enough to cause the nobles of his realm great distress, until Dechtere was given in marriage to Sualdaim, the reputed father of Cúchulainn.

The suspicion mentioned is possibly to be regarded as the faint echo of a Zeus and Here marriage regularly sanctioned by the Celtic mythology of a previous period; but it is remarkable that, after the Culture Hero was elevated to the place of the ancient Zeus, the incest should reappear in several versions: to such an extent does the Culture Hero seem to take to the rôle of the god whom he supplants, that he even partially supersedes him as a husband; excepting, of course, that husband is not the word to use from the moment that incest, condemned as a crime, precluded the idea of a legitimate marriage. This is illustrated by the story of Cairbre Musc and Dubin in Irish, and by that of Arthur and Gwyar in Welsh[1]; but the latter case is not quite so simple: Gwyar may be taken to be one of the Welsh names of the Mórrígu and Here; and Arthur elevated to the rank and place of the Zeus of the system becomes her brother, so Medrod (Mordred) and, possibly, Gwalchmei, are of an unfortunate parentage. But the husband of Gwyar, king Loth, was still living: he had only ceased to be the Zeus of the Celtic system: he had been pushed to the background, and he now counted only as god of the sea or of the other world, which was the meaning of his being called king of Orkney and Ilychlyn. The case of Gwydion and Arianrhod, daughter of Dôn, is somewhat similar; the former attaining to the rank of a god becomes 'Son of Dôn,' and therefore brother to Arianrhod, the mother of his son Ileu, the sun-hero.

Lastly, the marriage of Here to Zeus is the keynote to her hostility to Apollo and Heracles, both her husband's offspring. Owing to her irritation on account of his diverse amours, her hostility to Apollo and Heracles dates before their birth; and she is accordingly represented resorting to means of delaying the birth of both the one and the other. But from what has already been said, Irish mythology, as we know it, could give no such reason for the Mórrígu or Great Queen's antagonism to Cúchulainn; so another was found, namely, that she had, in a weak moment, made love to him, and that he had given her a rebuff which she keenly

---

[1] *Hib. Lec.* p. 308, and p. 21 above.

resented. In the original story of Peredur, that knight probably acted analogously; but the story, as we have it, makes him, after insulting the Empress by despitefully treating her men, at last give way and become her husband. This is as if Heracles, when Zeus had disappeared forgotten, had to take Here to be his wife, and the key to this remarkable turn taken by the Welsh story has already (p. 164) been suggested, namely, the confusion of the Empress with a damsel of the lake-lady group.

A few words must now be said of those who commanded, and of those who encouraged and guided the sun-hero in his toils. In the Greek story of the labours of Heracles, the one who commands is Eurystheus, with Here in the background, and the one who encourages the hero is Athene. Let us begin with Athene, who accompanies Heracles in all his most arduous undertakings; and, when he is tired, she sees to his comfort, and even makes warm springs gush forth from the ground to give him a refreshing bath [1]. Among other acts of kindness to him, she is said to have saved him from being drowned in the Styx when he visited Hades. Athene had similarly aided Perseus in his labours, and helped Bellerophon to tame his winged steed [2]. It is, however, to be noticed that Greek literature gives no certain hint that Athene and her hero ever treated one another as lovers. The presence usually of Hermes, the Culture Hero, with Athene, as witnesses of Heracles' labours is also worthy of remark. Similarly, in the Cúchulainn legend Athene is once represented by Fedelm of the Nine Forms, daughter of Conchobar the king [3]: she has a bath secretly prepared for the hero during the night when he goes forth to defy the Fir Bolg forces from the West.

---

[1] *Hib. Lec.* p. 379; Preller, ii. 161.   [2] Preller, ii. 79.
[3] *Hib. Lec.* p. 378.

In Welsh we have Athene's counterpart in Lunet, who assists Owein in a variety of ways; and in the Peredur story she appears in the form of the princess who makes her bed near his cell when he is in prison. Both this anonymous princess and Lunet help their respective heroes on their errands, but the latter are not represented as their lovers. Nay even Chrétien, when he has to mention Lancelot in the embarassing situation of having to accept hospitality from a maiden hostess on the condition that he should share her bed, has not ventured to go so far, in this instance, as to remove his hero's self-restraint. The lady takes Lancelot on towards his destination on the following day, and wishes him success in his arduous undertaking (p. 102).

In the story of Cúchulainn, the presence of the Culture Hero is probably to be sought in his patron Conchobar, sometimes suspected of being his father. In Welsh the corresponding figure of the Culture Hero presents himself in the person of Arthur, who repeatedly fetches the Sun-hero back to the society of men from his sojourn in the other world as in the case of Owein, of Peredur, and of Lancelot whiling away his time with Elayne in the Joyous Isle. It is Arthur and his men that persuade the hero to return with them, just as it was one of the most important functions of Indra, as Culture Hero of the Hindus, to bring back the sun so as to be seen of men, and to hasten the course of the dawn that dallies all too long with the powers of night [1].

Eurystheus claims our attention next: he was king of Mycenæ, and descended from the same family of Perseus as Heracles himself. Owing to Here's wiliness and the short-sightedness of her husband Zeus, power was from

---

[1] *Hib. Lec.* pp. 299-300.

the first given to Eurystheus over Heracles, to the
weaker over the stronger, to the coward over the hero.
The story shows evident marks of much editing and
systematizing beyond what may be suspected in the
legends about most sun-heroes. But, allowing for this,
Eurystheus undoubtedly remains the principal task-
master of Heracles, and the question of his attributes
becomes one of importance for our comparisons. What
we learn about him is, that he was cruel and cowardly,
and that he was in such dread of Heracles that he had a
brass receptacle made for himself to slink into, when the
hero appeared at Mycenæ from time to time, as he
achieved his tasks. Then we read also that after the
death of Heracles his children were persecuted by
Eurystheus, who was, however, defeated by Theseus,
Iolaus and others, who exerted themselves on behalf of
the family of Heracles : the result was that Eurystheus
was slain by Heracles' son Hyllus, who carried his head
to Dejaneira his mother. On this one has to remark
that the story of the brass receptacle in which Greek
art represents Eurystheus hiding himself at the approach
of Heracles, suffices to show that we have mythologically
to regard him as one of the dark beings naturally hostile
to the Solar Hero.

This view is confirmed by the case of Polydectes,
for whom Perseus undertakes his labours. The story
of this latter hero's birth is almost exactly that of
Lug's birth, as related in a modern legend published by O'Donovan [1]. Acrisius, the grandfather of
Perseus, had been told that he would be killed by a
grandson of his, so he confined his only child, a daughter
named Danae, in a brass tower where no man should have

---

[1] *Hib. Lec.* p. 314.

access to her.   But this proved of no avail to keep Zeus
out; so Perseus was born, and Acrisius foiled exposed
him and his mother in a chest to the mercy of the sea,
in the expectation that they might both perish.   That,
however, did not come to pass, as they were cast ashore
on a rocky islet called Seriphus, where the despot of the
place, whose name was Polydectes, took a liking to Danae
and wished in time to get rid of her son, as he might
stand in the way of his advances[1].   He so arranged
matters that young Perseus was sent on a terrible adventure to fetch him the Gorgon head of Medusa.   In due time
he returned successful and delivered his mother from
the violence of Polydectes, whom he petrified with the
glance of Medusa's Head : in other words, he left him in
a condition somewhat analogous to that of a corpse god,
or that of the northern Sibyl, compelled to answer Woden,
when she described herself thus : ' I have been snowed
on with the snow, I have been beaten with the rain, I
have been drenched with the dew, long have I been
dead[2].'

Polydectes is represented as a hospitable king, and
his name describes him as one who receives many guests,
or in other words, one who keeps an open house; but
Polydectes and Polydegmon in this same sense of an
All-receiver were also names of Pluto, the god of the
other world, and we cannot be wrong in identifying them
with one another[3].   Of course, the barren island of Seriphus would scarcely suit as the seat of Pluto, when he
had been elaborately surrounded with all the adjuncts
of a great and imposing potentate, and when the practice

---

[1] Preller, ii. 60–2, 71.

[2] *Hib. Lec.* pp. 567-8; Vigfusson and Powell's *Corpus Poet. Bor.* i. 182.

[3] It is needless to say that Preller, i. 660, ii. 61, does not suggest identifying them.

of navigation had made the Greeks familiar with all the
Cyclades ; but that only goes to show that the idea of
Seriphus as a home of the departed must date from a
very early time.   At any rate, that rocky isle would have
been an ideal abode of Hades from a Celtic point of
view; and as to kingly hospitality and the means of
providing it in Seriphus, these questions offer no more
difficulty than in the case of Gwales.   Whence came
the supplies for the eighty years' banquet on the latter
inaccessible island[1] ?   This is the sort of contradiction
which usually characterises all ancient accounts of the
other world, which was nearly as much a subject of
imagination of old as it is to later generations.   We
venture, then, to regard Polydectes as a Plutonic personage, and the same may probably be said of Bellerophon's task-master, the Lycian king whom he succeeded; also of Laomedon, the king of Troy, whom
Apollo served, and probably of Admetus likewise.   So,
on the whole, when we can fix in Greek literature on the
solar hero's task-master, the latter proves to have been
probably a dark divinity.   This agrees with the character
and nature of Forgall the Trickster, who succeeds in
binding Cúchulainn by oath to expose himself to perils
which the dark wizard did not expect him to survive;
and the Welsh counterpart of Forgall has been discussed
already in its place in the story of Peredur (pp. 116-7).   If
it were necessary here to step on Teutonic ground, one
might point to the same relation between the dark
figure of Gunther and that of Siegfried, whose services
he secures.

The ways in which the dark divinity acquires his
power over the Solar Hero vary greatly, and in some

---

[1] *Hib. Lec.* p. 96 ; *R. B. Mab.* pp. 40-2 ; Guest, iii. 126-7.

stories the compulsion is slurred over or left wholly unmentioned. In the story of Heracles one finds not only Eurystheus, but also the stern figure of Here looming behind him : she is likewise potent in her hostility at the hour of Apollo's birth, as in the case of Heracles ; and to the latter she continues bitterly hostile throughout his earthly career. He resents it on his part, and on one occasion he even wounds her, as briefly told in the *Iliad*, v. 392-4 :

> Τλῆ δ' Ἥρη, ὅτε μιν κρατερὸς παῖς Ἀμφιτρύωνος
> Δεξιτερὸν κατὰ μαζὸν ὀϊστῷ τριγλώχινι
> Βεβλήκει· τότε καί μιν ἀνήκεστον λάβεν ἄλγος.

This is more than matched by the Irish legend, when it makes Cúchulainn roughly handle the Great Queen no less than thrice in the course of his duel with Lóch Mór[1]. The cause of her hostility to Cúchulainn at the time has already been noticed (p. 111), and so has the blurring of the record of that hostility in the Welsh story of Peredur (pp. 120-2).

Apart from the peculiar treatment of Here's counterparts in Celtic legends, her personality, studied even in the light of the most ancient Greek literature, offers great difficulties, especially when one begins to ask what she originally represented. But whatever she was in point of origin, she is described as fond of taking part in war and slaughter ; and in this respect she has her counterpart in the Empress, who will not have to husband anyone but the bravest and most stalwart of knights. We see her also in the Elen Leader of Hosts, whom her story elevates to the position of Empress, as the wife of an emperor of Rome[2] ; also in Gwalchmei and Gwalchaved's

---

[1] *Hib. Lec.* pp. 469-70.
[2] P. 110 above, also *Hib. Lec.* pp. 161-7.

mother Gwyar, whose name (p. 169) is redolent of the
delight, in bloodshed and battle, taken by the Mórrígu
or Great Queen in Irish, who early[1] in the story of the
Táin takes the form of a bird. Later, however, namely
in the incident of the duel between Cúchulainn and
Lóch Mór, she takes three other forms successively, that
of an eel, of a she-wolf, and of a hornless red heifer[2].
This last would seem to have had more importance than
appears from the Táin. For we find elsewhere the for-
tunes of a war depending on a hornless red cow. The
legend of the Déisi relates how Dil, the blind druid of
the Men of Erinn opposed to the Déisi, prepared by
spells and incantations a wisp against the Déisi, and how
this was to be burnt in sight of the Déisi's camp at the
same time that a hornless red cow was to be sent forth
towards the enemy: on the cow being wounded and
killed by the enemy, the latter would be done for. The
Déisi, however, were enabled to find all this out and to
steal the wisp; they then executed on their own behalf
the intentions of the blind druid of the Men of Erinn,
with the result that the latter quickly found that the war
was a hopeless one for them, and that they could not
help leaving the Déisi the territory which they had been
contesting[3].

No explanation is offered of the magic proceedings of
the druid; but a cow was essential, and it was also
essential that she should be a hornless red one, for the
Déisi not being able to find such a one at once, their
druid volunteered in consideration of certain privileges
to be granted to his family for ever, to take the form of

---

[1] *Bk. of the Dun,* 64ᵇ.

[2] Ib. 76ᵇ-77ᵃ. A different account occurs in the *Táin Bó Regamna* in the
Ir. Texte, ed. by Stokes and Windisch, ii. 246-7, 252-4.

[3] *Bk. of the Dun,* 54ᵇ.

a hornless red cow, and so to sacrifice his life in the enemy's camp, where one of the men, not knowing what was happening, wounded and slew the animal before Dil could get his order circulated, that it was not to be harmed on any account. So it is not improbable that the cow was one of the favourite forms of the Mórrígu, or at any rate that it was so closely associated, or even identified with her, that the slaying of the animal brought disaster on the slayers and the reverse to their foes. Why it should have been hornless and red does not appear, nor indeed why it should have been a cow at all; but one may compare the epithet βοῶπις, 'ox-eyed,' applied to Here, together with the story about the gods fleeing before Typho in brute forms, when the one assumed by Here was that of a cow. The other epithet, κυνῶπις, 'dog-eyed,' applied likewise to Here, comes nearer to the Mórrígu's form of a she-wolf in the epic tale of the Táin. To these coincidences must, lastly, be added the similarity of character between the Mórrígu and the Greek Here in her more unamiable moods.

The Mórrígu has no husband in Irish saga, but we are informed, archæologically so to speak, that she was the wife of Néit, a war-god of the old Irish [1]. This harmonizes with the fact that war was one of the chief departments of the activity of the Celtic Zeus, and that his wife continued a conspicuous figure after the place of her husband had been taken, partly by the Culture Hero, and partly by the Solar Hero. But the presence of the Mórrígu as a fairy or demon in the Cúchulainn legend awaits explanation, as does also that of her

---

[1] *Hib. Lec.* pp. 43, 215; Cormac's Glossary, p. 122 of the Stokes-O'Donovan edition.

Welsh counterpart, styled the Empress in the story of
Peredur.   They stand forth like the remains as it
were of an older formation, and, unable as we are to say
how they came where we find them, we can only
add the difficulty attaching to them to the mass of other
difficulties, which the question of mythological stratifica-
tion already presents.

CHAPTER XI.

Urien and his Congeners.

With regard to history as distinguished from mythology, the position of Owein is analogous to that of Peredur; and the former's father, Urien, has commonly been supposed to be the Urbgen whom Nennius represents[1] as one of the Brythonic leaders arrayed against the Angles of Deira, under their king named Hussa by Nennius. Undoubtedly, the Owein of Welsh story belongs to the domain of mythology, and the same thing may be said of Urien[2], who is described as son of Kynvarch Oer or ' K. the Cold,' son of Meirchion Gul or ' M. the Meagre.' Here the name Kynvarch may be treated as belonging to the same category as that of March ab Meirchion, from which it is in part derived. How March was the Midas of the Brythonic Celts, it is needless to repeat[3]. Further, Urien is commonly called king of Rheged, in Welsh, Urien Rheged; and Rheged was a region which the *Red Book* translation of Geoffrey of Monmouth's *Historia* places in the north of this island, and treats as synonymous with Mureif or Moray. According to Geoffrey, Mureif contained Ilyn Ilumonwy, or Loch Lomond, with its numerous islands,

---

[1] San-Marte's *Gildas et Nennius*, p. 72.   [2] *Hib. Lec.* p. 423.

[3] See supra, pp. 12, 70, and *Hib. Lec.* p. 593.

of which he gives a quaint account: the islands were sixty in number, with a rock in each with an eagle's nest on each rock; and the eagles congregated on the eve of the Calends of May to give the inhabitants auguries for the year then commencing [1].

Arthur and his men made war on the Picts and Scots, and, finding them taking refuge in the isles of Loch Lomond, they blockaded them until they forced them into subjection, in spite of the help brought to the northerners by an Irish king called Guillamurius. When this war was over, Arthur, we are told, restored their dominions to the three sons of Kynvarch, namely, Scotland to Auguselus (or Arawn) [2], Mureif (or Rheged) to Urianus [3] (or Urien), and Loudonesia to Lot (or ℓLeu).   Now Lot or Loth, though called ℓLeu or ℓLew [4] in Welsh, is probably to be identified with ℓLûd [5], and

---

[1] San-Marte's *Geoffrey*, ix. 6; *R. B. Bruts*, pp. 191-2. The Latin has also *sceptro Murefensium* in ix. 9, and in ix. 12, *Urianus rex Murefensium*, in both of which the Welsh is *Reget*: see *R. B. Bruts*, pp. 194, 200.

[2] Arawn is the name in the Welsh versions: see *R. B. Bruts*, pp. 194, 200, 208, 220, 224, 230. But one recognizes *Auguselus* (better, doubtless, *Anguselus*) in Malory's Anguyssaunce or Agwysaunce, king of Ireland, and in Anguysshe, king mostly of Ireland, but once of Scotland, namely in v. 2: it is needless to point out that *Scotland* and *Ireland* were once more or less synonymous, and how this fact kept a door open for confusion in later times. The longer forms in Malory seem to point to the genitive *Aengussa* of *Aengus*, while *Anguysshe* seems to derive from the later genitive *Aenguis*, with its *is* pronounced *ish*.

[3] From his *Urianus* Geoffrey distinguishes an *Urbgennius de Badone* in ix. 12 and x. 6, 9; and in iii. 19 he has *Urianus Andragii filius*, which becomes *Uryen* son of *Andryw* in *R. B. Bruts*, p. 81.

[4] The reason for this difference of names has not been discovered, but it is as old at any rate as the *Black Book of Carmarthen*, where *ℓLeu* and his two brothers are made into sons, not of Kynvarch, but of ℓLywarch Hên: see Evans' Aut. Fac. 54 a. It is worth noticing that ℓLywarch is another *March* compound, unless we are wrong in equating it with the *Loumarc* of the Harleian Genealogies in the *Cymmrodor*, ix. 171, and the Irish form *Lomarc* in the *Book of the Dun*, 67ᵃ, 73ᵃ, where mention is made of *Lugaid mc. Nóiss Ui Lomairc*.

[5] *Hib. Lec.* pp. 128-31.

considered the eponymus of Loudonesia or Lothian ; but he is also associated with Orkney and Llychlyn or Norway [1]. As to Arawn, he is represented in the Mabinogion as the king of Annwn or Hades [2] ; so here we have the North treated, by implication, in the usual way as the home of the departed. Further, Urien's realm may be presumed to have been of the same description, as may be inferred from the name Rheged, which appears to represent Mureif as the 'Accursed' country. The Welsh translator who identified Rheged with Mureif confounded it thereby with the province of Moray, and in effect he instituted a sort of rough division of the whole of the North between the Scots of Argyle and the Picts of Moray. But it is by no means improbable that underneath his Mureif there lay some such a mythic name as that of Murias [3], the marine country whence the Tuatha Dé Danann were said to have brought with them to Erinn the famous cauldron of the Dagda Mór.

It may possibly be regarded as somewhat less mythical that Urien should be styled Ruler of Catraeth [4], the name of which means the battle-strand. *Catraeth* has often been supposed to stand for the Cataracton-e or Cataracton-i of the Antonine Itinerary and the Κατουρακτόνιον of Ptolemy's Geography, surmised to be Catterick in Yorkshire ; but *Catraeth* cannot be derived from any form evidenced by those names [5]. The

---

[1] Supra, p. 11, and *Hib. Lec.* p. 355 ; see also Nutt's note in Mac Innes' *Argyllshire Folk and Hero Tales* (London, 1890), p. 420.

[2] *Hib. Lec.* pp. 338-41.

[3] Ib. pp. 257, 371.

[4] See Taliessin's poem, xxxvii. in Skene's *Four Anc. Bks. of Wales*, ii. 192.

[5] *Cataracton-* should make in Welsh *Cadraethon*, possibly *Cadraeth*, but not *Catraeth*, the *t* of which postulates a compound origin in the *d-d* of the *Caddraeth* marking an intermediate stage in the phonetic decay of an early

Gododin, or the poem devoted to the battle of Catraeth,
seems to point decidedly to the North, as does the rest
of the *Book of Aneurin*[1], in which the *Gododin* is contained, namely, to some spot in or near the Firth of
Forth. Witness the Aneurin allusion to the Iodeo[2], a
name to be equated, doubtless, with the Iudeu of the
Nennian account of the war between Penda and Oswiu,
which ended with the decisive battle of Winwæd in 655.
Iudeu, in its turn, is probably to be identified with the
'Urbs *Giudi*' of Bæda, who places it in the Firth of
Forth: he is usually supposed to have meant a stronghold on some such an island as Inchkeith. Catraeth
may have been a name of mythical origin, which had
become afterwards attached to a historical place, in the
same way that *Gwlâd yr Hâv,* 'the Land of Summer,'
became Somerset. This historical view is, however,
not favoured by the association of Catraeth with
Mordei[3], the name of which seems to mean sea-houses:

Catutract-. Compare *Cateyrn,* represented in the inscriptions by *Catotigirn-i,* a
personal name meaning war-lord or battle-king, from *catu-,* Mod. Welsh *cad,*
'battle,' and *tegirnio-s,* Mod. Welsh *tëyrn,* 'prince, lord or king,' formed
from *tegi-,* Mod. Welsh *ty,* 'house' (for an early *tegi- = tegez-`,* in the same
way that the Latin *dominus* derives from *domus.* Among others, the late
Mr. Thos. Stephens of Merthyr identifies Catraeth with Catterick in his
posthumous edition of the *Gododin,* a work seen through the press for the
Hon. Soc. of Cymmrodorion by Prof. Powel of Cardiff, who has spared no
pains to provide it with an exhaustive index and adequate notes.

[1] The manuscript is said to date from the latter part of the 13th century
or the beginning of the 14th; but the scribe has here and there left standing
proofs of his having copied parts at least of it from an original written in the
orthography of the glosses of the Old Welsh period, and dating therefore,
possibly, so far back as the 9th century. We allude to such forms as *erit
migam* for *yr edmygaf, mui hiam* for *mwyaf, nem* for *nef* (Skene, ii. 104),
erdyledam for what is written a few lines later *erdiledaf* (ib. p. 106), and
camb for the later *camm, cam* (ib. p. 70). The manuscript requires to be
thoroughly examined by a competent palæographer.

[2] The chief questions raised by this name will be found discussed in the
Archæologia Cambrensis for 1889, pp. 230-2.

[3] See Stephens' *Gododin,* pp. 144, 172, 176, 344. Mordei is also mentioned
in the *Book of Taliessin,* Skene, ii. 196 and 192, where one seems to detect

it sounds every whit as mythic as the Irish Murias. Mordei is described as *ewynvawr*, that is to say πολύαχνος, or 'of much foam,' and it partly recalls Taliessin's account of Caer Sidi and its wine feasts[1].

As to Nennius' Urbgen, it is by no means certain that the latter should be identified with Owein's father, even in the matter of names. For, while *Urbgen* may be traced to a Latin form *Urbigena*, 'City-born,' to be compared with *Aurelius Ambrosius*, the Latin name of another energetic opponent of English encroachment, there is nothing to prove that the name of the mythic Urien is related, rather than derived from an early Celtic form *Urogenos*, of the same origin as the *Urogenius* and *Urogenonertus* of Gallo-Roman inscriptions[2]. The latter of these names would seem to have a mythical basis, and it must have meant 'one endowed with the strength of an Urogen' or Urien. It has elsewhere[3] been suggested that Urogen implies a divinity analogous

---

Du Moroeð (p. 69 above) called *Du Merwyd*, and treated as Urien's charger. The words are exceedingly dark, but they would be a little more intelligible arranged in verses as follows :—

> Yscðydaðr yrac glyð gloyð glasgðen
> Gleð ryhaðt gleðhaf vn yð Vryen.
> Nym gorseif gðarthegyd. gordear
> Goryaðc gorlassaðc gorlassar
> Goriaga gordðyre. pop rei
> Sag [*read* sang] dileð du merwyd ymordei
> Vd tra blaðd yn yd el oth vod
> Vared melynaðr yn neuad [*read* neuod].

As to the houses of the Other World, they figure also in the story of Peredur, when that hero arrives unexpectedly in the Round Valley owned by a great big Grey Man, and beholds there 'large black houses of rough workmanship': see *R. B. Mab.* p. 215 ; Guest, i. 330 ; also p. 83 above.

[1] Skene, ii. 155, 181. The poet of the *Gododin*, according to his own repeated admission, freely enjoyed the wine and mead of Mordei (Stephens' *Gododin*, pp. 186, 188), which is to be regretted, as one would like to have understood better what he sang.

[2] See the *Rev. Celtique*, iii. 310, Glück's *Kelt. Namen*, p. 97, and Gruter, Nos. 490, 9, 570, 6.

[3] *Hib. Lec.* pp. 87-8.

to the stag-headed Cernunnos of the Gauls, only that in
this case the form affected was not that of the stag
so much as of the *urus* of our primeval forests.   Both
Urbigen- and Urogen- might be expected, in the course
of phonetic decay, to become Urien[1] in Welsh; and this
indicates one important way in which history and mythology may have been confused, as suggested already
in the case of Arthur's name.   In the one before us,
it may be the explanation of the fact that Urien is one
of the heroes termed in the Triads the Bull of Battle[2].

Urien is not alone lord of Rheged, for Owein is also
now and then so described[3].   This was presumably inferred from his being called son of Urien; and the same
explanation is probably to be given of the fact, that they
fight side by side against a foe called in Welsh poetry
Fflamdwyn, or the Flame-bearer.   For, mythologically
speaking, the sun-hero is not the natural ally of a dark
divinity, however close to one another they may appear
in the mythic pedigree; and the war with Fflamdwyn
would seem to have been Owein's war and not Urien's,
as the former is made to close with Fflamdwyn in fatal
combat[4].   As Fflamdwyn is represented defending[5]

---

[1] It is not certain that a form Verbigen- might not also result in *Urien*: the
former appears to have been Celtic, as may be inferred from the fact that
Cæsar, i. 27, gives *Verbigenus* as the name of one *pagus* of the Helvetii.

[2] Triads, i. 12, iii. 72.

[3] *Bk. of Taliessin*, poem xliv, Skene, ii. 199.

[4] The passage occurs in the Taliessin poem last referred to, but it is not
conclusive as to which of the two succumbed: see Powel's note in Stephens'
Gododin, p. 69.

[5] The passage, on which this is based, occurs in the Taliessin poem, No.
xxxv (Skene, ii. 189), and it runs thus:—

> 'dygryssöys flamdöyn yn petwar llu.
> godeu a reget y ymdullu.'

This has been rendered for Skene (i. 365) thus:—

> 'Flamdwyn hastened in four hosts
> Godeu and Reged to overwhelm.'

But it seems more correct to render *ymdullu* 'protecting,' as Skene has had

Godeu and Rheged against Owein and his father, this war is probably to be regarded as the same, in any case, as the war brought to a successful end by Arthur and his men, when Urien received from Arthur possession of his realm of Mureif or Rheged. This comparison would suggest that the Godeu and Rheged of the *Book of Taliessin* are to be treated as in a sense the equivalents respectively of the Mureif and Rheged of certain versions of Geoffrey.

The equation, which this suggests, of Godeu with Mureif or Moray will be found to serve as a key to the story of the Battle of Godeu. This was a thoroughly mythological event, and, as described in the eighth poem [1] in the *Book of Taliessin*, it shows a striking similarity to the conflict [2] in which Cúchulainn was the chief combatant, when he attacked the Stronghold of Scáth in Shadow-land. Just as Taliessin boasts himself present with Arthur, when they harried Hades and brought away the Cauldron of the Head of Hades, so he pretends to have also played no mean part in the Battle of Godeu: he speaks of his

---

ymdullya6 rendered in a passage in point in the Taliessin poem xxxvi (i. 351, ii. 191), which runs thus :—

'ysc6yt ynlla6 godeu a reget yn ymdullya6.
    neu vi aweleis 6r yn buartha6.'

The poet refers to Urien shepherding his people as if they were a herd or flock, and the lines may be rendered thus :—

'Shield in hand, protecting Godeu and Rheged,
    A man saw I penning (as it were his kine).'

Lastly, the battle to which the former passage refers is called, from the site, that of Argoed ILwyvein. This name means a place near to or bordering on the Wood of ILwyvein, and *ILwyvein*, also *ILwyvenyd* (Skene, ii. 190, 195) seems to be the Welsh for the district of the *Leven*, which discharges the waters of Loch Lomond into the Clyde : see Skene, ii. 413.

[1] Skene, ii. 137-144 : see also poem xiv, ib. p. 154 : likewise the *Hib. Lec.* p. 258, where a portion of poem viii is translated into English.

[2] Described in a poem which has been partly translated in the *Hib. Lec.* pp. 260-1.

fighting there in front of Prydein's Gwledig. The leaders on his side were Amaethon son of Dôn, and Gwydion his brother, the latter of whom was, when his party was hard pressed, told to resort to magic and convert the trees and shrubs of the country into warriors to aid him. That is done, and the poem gives a curious description of the conflict carried on by the taller trees, such as the oak, the alder and the birch; nor are the meaner trees and shrubs wholly forgotten. Elsewhere [1] the Battle of Godeu is identified with that of Achren, a slightly modified form, doubtless, of that of Ochren, one of the places mentioned in the Taliessin poem devoted to Arthur's harrying of Hades [2]. The Battle of Godeu or Achren was, we are further told [3], fought by Amaethon son of Dôn, and Gwydion his brother, against Arawn, king of Hades, aided by one called Brân; unless this is to be taken as merely another name of Arawn himself. We are also informed that the war was occasioned by Amaethon stealing certain animals which belonged to Hades. All this clearly shows that it was an engagement between the Culture Hero with his friends and the Head of Hades with his; and it is needless to repeat that the North of Britain was at one time regarded as a sort of Hades, or that the Welsh versions of Geoffrey locate Arawn's realm in Scotland.

Before leaving Godeu, it is worth while remarking that the hypothetical equation of that country with Mureif helps to solve a difficulty raised by an ancient enumeration [4] of the seven divisions of Scotland beyond the Forth : the seven are represented by seven

---

[1] See the *Myvyrian Arch.* i. 167 ; also the *Hib. Lec.* pp. 244-5, 257-8.
[2] *Hib. Lec.* p. 248 ; Skene, ii. 181-2.
[3] *Myv. Arch.* i. 167 : see also *Hib. Lec.* pp. 244-5.
[4] Skene's *Chronicles of the Picts and Scots*, pp. 4, 24-5, 396.

eponymous sons of the northern ancestor, Cruithne or Pict. Most of them are easily placed, as for example Fib in Fife, and Cait in Caithness ; but there is one whose proper place has always been uncertain. His name is given as Fidach, and it is remarkable that it phonologically admits of being identified with the Welsh Gođeu, both being derivable from a common form[1]. The view here suggested would require us to regard Gođeu as a word familiar to the Welsh, which it may well have been as that of a distant land identified with Rheged and the Other World. This leaves us, however, at liberty to suppose the name associated with a greater or less extent of the country covered later by Moray, Mar, and Buchan : at the present day it is possibly represented by the name of Glen-*Fiddich*, in Banffshire[2]. Be that as it may, the approach of the names Fidach and Gođeu to the Celtic words corresponding to the English word *wood*, namely Goidelic *fid*, and Welsh *gwyđ*, would seem to point to the origin of the quaint story of the trees and shrubs made to fight in aid of Gwydion and his men.

Let us add at this point that the explanation of the wars above mentioned, whether a harrying of Hades by Arthur and his men, or a great battle fought in the northern Gođeu by Amaethon ab Dôn against Arawn, king of Hades, is, that they are the mythic expression of the struggles of the Culture Hero to secure certain boons for his race from the dark divinities. But when the meaning of the myth was forgotten, Amaethon, for

[1] It would be some such a form as *Vidag* or *Vedag*, and the change in Welsh of *ag* into *ou*, later *eu*, would argue the word Gođeu a very old one in the language, which is countenanced by the fact, that Fidach has been forgotten so long ago in Scotland, that its location has become a matter of speculation.

[2] See the author's third Rhind Lecture in the *Scottish Review*, xvi, 249.

instance, whose name may be recognized distorted into Amangon (nominative Amangons), appeared in unfavourable light in the prologue to Chrétien's *Conte du Graal.* The passage, as summarized by Mr. Nutt[1], has a very ancient ring; and it may be the echo of a Welsh original with an undertone of mourning over the decadence of the cult of the chthonic divinities:—
'The story tells of the Graal, whose mysteries, if Master Blihis lie not, none may reveal; it . . . shows how the rich land of Logres was destroyed. In the wells and springs of that land harboured damsels who fed the wayfarer with meat and pasties and bread. But King Amangons did wrong to one and carried off her golden cup, so that never more came damsels out of the springs to comfort the wanderer. And the men of King Amangons followed his evil example. Therefore the springs dried up, and the grass withered, and the land became waste, and no more might be found the court of the Rich Fisher, which had filled the land with plenty and splendour.'

A word must now be added respecting Urien's children. Besides Owein he had a daughter Morvuḍ, twin sister to Owein, and among other sons he had two called Rhiwaḷḷon[2] and Elphin, whose name points to the North: it is probably to be identified with that of Alpin in Scotch history. The mother of Owein and Morvuḍ was Modron, but this was also the name of Mabon's mother, and it is not improbable that they were not two Modrons but one, though Mabon[3] belongs to a very different stratum of mythology from Owein. For,

---

[1] *Studies*, p. 8, where Mr. Nutt refers to Otto Küpp in the *Zeitschrift für deutsche Philologie*, vol. xvii. No. 1.

[2] *Hib. Lec.* p. 423; Triads, i. 10, ii. 21, iii. 70.

[3] *Hib. Lec.* pp. 27-9.

while the latter is given the standing of a Christian
knight, the former is left stranded on the old level of
an Apollo of ancient Celtic paganism[1].

Among the various descriptions given of Urien by
Welsh poets may be mentioned the following : In the
Red Book he is represented as the most distinguished
by far of the thirteen kings of the North[2]; and in the
Book of Taliessin he is called the gold-king of the
North[3], the head of Prydein[4], that is to say of Alban
or Pictland from Loch Lomond to the extreme of
Caithness.   More to the south he is possessor of Ꝉwyvenyđ[5], the district called in Gaelic Levenach and in
English Levenax[6], shortened into Lennox, and meaning
approximately what is now Dumbartonshire, with Loch
Lomond and its islands.   This may be regarded as in
part the outcome of the wish to give the mythic realm
of Rheged a geographical position in the North; but it
was also located sometimes in a very different part
of Britain, namely in South Wales, as we shall see
presently; and it remains to mention one remarkable
title which is given to Urien without any attempt to
connect it with geography, and that is Urien of the

---

[1] The Triads, i. 28, iii. 74, speak also of a Pasgen son of Urien, and the
same person seems to be alluded to in the *Red Book*, Skene, ii. 271 : see
also Stephens' *Gododin*, p. 239.   The only Pasgen known to Geoffrey was
Pascentius, son of Vortigern, vi. 12, viii. 13-16.

[2] Skene, ii. 293.

[3] Ib. p. 185, where Skene has *Eu teyrn gogled*: it should be *Eurteyrn
gogled.*

[4] Ib. p. 191; and Urien was probably meant by ' Prydein's Gwledig ' (in
Taliessin's poem viii) alluded to supra, p. 245.

[5] Ib. p. 192 : *teithiabc lḷoyfenyd* seems to mean this; and as to the district, it
is mentioned also at pp. 187, 190; and at p. 195 we read of *Lḷwyfenyd tired,*
or the Lands of Ꝉwyvenyđ.   On Argoed Ꝉwyvein, see note at p. 244
above, and Skene, ii. 191, 2.

[6] See Skene's note, ii. 412-3; also his *Chronicles of the Picts and Scots,*
pp. 291, 374, and his *Celtic Scotland,* iii. 69, 454.

Echwyd or Evening, also Urien Lord of the Evening [1], and Blessed Prince of the Evening [2].

Urien is, moreover, associated with a far distant city in the following verses in the *Book of Taliessin* [3] :

<table>
<tr><td>'Ac ef yn arbennic</td><td>*And he especially*</td></tr>
<tr><td>yn oruchel wledic.</td><td>*The supreme Guledig.*</td></tr>
<tr><td>yn dinas pellennic.</td><td>*In a distant city,*</td></tr>
<tr><td>yn keimyat kynteic.'</td><td>*A principal pilgrim.*</td></tr>
</table>

This translation into English has been published by Mr. Skene ; but we should be inclined to put it slightly differently, thus :

> *And he especially*
> *As supreme gwledig,*
> *In a distant city*
> *As pristine companion.*

In either case, the verses have a ring which recalls the *Rig-Veda* references to Yama as the first of the dead and their chief: the way to his abode was long and across rapid waters ; so he was the first to travel it and to show others how to arrive in his Elysium, where

---

[1] *Bk. of Taliessin*, Skene, ii. 184-5, 189. *Echwyd* meant the evening or the sunset, not *Abend-land,* or the west; and there is no reason for supposing, with Stephens, that it is the Welsh form of the Latin *equites,* and that Urien was accordingly a sort of Master of the Horse : see his *Gododin*, p. 118, and compare p. 67, where he renders *vd yr echbyd* ' lord of the plain ;' but that *echwyd* also meant a plain, remains to be proved. It is worth noticing, however, that Pughe gives the word as in some localities meaning 'the autumn ' or the *fall* of the year: it may have also meant a *fall* or depression in the ground. It is derived from the same *cwyd* as *cwydo* ' to fall.'

[2] See also the Taliessin poem No. xviii, where Skene, ii. 164, has besides other inaccuracies the form echbys instead of the echbyd of the manuscript. The couplet in question is remarkable for using *gwlat* in the personal sense of its Irish equivalent *flaith*, ' prince.' It runs thus :—

> ' Pan discynnbys Owein rac gbenwlat
> yr echbyd. Gorerefein bud oe tat.'

> *When Owein came down before the blessed prince*
> *Of the Evening, he achieved . . . benefit for his father.*

[3] Skene, ii. 184, i. 345.

he was represented welcoming the fathers of the human race to share in the endless delights of the country[1]. This has, however, a more distinct parallel in Welsh in the Blessed Brân wading through the two rivers Ili and Archan, separating Britain from Hades, called in his story Iwerđon, or Erinn. But such a parallel, to be admissible here, must be countenanced by equating Brân with Urien.

In order to do this, it will be necessary to re-produce a portion of Brân's story at length. How Brân crossed to Erinn, with the musicians of his court on his back, has been briefly told elsewhere[2], and we may begin the narrative with Brân's landing there. Thereupon followed the advance of his troops in quest of the Irish king Matholwch, and this created such an impression on the Irish, that they offered terms of peace. After futile attempts at an agreement, the Irish resolved to flatter Brân by building a house large enough for him; for till then he had never found one he could enter. He and his hosts were to go into it, and his brother-in-law, Matholwch, with his men, were to occupy another portion of it and publicly to do homage to Brân. This was all arranged by Branwen, Mathol-wch's wife and Brân's sister, in order to prevent ruin and bloodshed. So the house was built spacious and strong, but the Irish resorted to the following stratagem: On either side of each of the hundred columns support-ing the house they fixed a peg, and on each of the 200 pegs they hung a leathern bag containing an armed man. But Brân's half-brother, Evnyssien, taking into his head to visit the house before the arrival of the two armies, noticed the leathern bags and asked an

---

[1] *Hib. Lec.* pp. 654-5.   [2] *Hib. Lec.* pp. 95, 269.

Irishman present respecting one of them, what it contained: ' Meal, my friend,' said the Irishman.   Evnyssien,
however, felt the bag and found the man's head, which
he squeezed until he felt his fingers in the man's brain.
He came to the next bag, asked the same question, and
played the same trick with the inmate of the bag.   This
was repeated until he came to the 200th bag, where he
discovered that the man wore a helmet ; so he devoted
extra attention to him, and, when he had done for him,
he sang him an englyn as follows [1]:

> ' Yssit yn y boly hwnn amryw vlawt
> keimat kynnivyat disgynnat
> yn trin rac ketwyr kat barawt.'
>
> *In this bag there is another sort of meal—*
> *A comrade, a combatant, one alighting*
> *In the fray at the head of warriors war-prepared.*

Then came the hosts into the house, those of Britain
occupying the one part, and those of Erinn the other.
No sooner had they met than they were at one, and
the kingdom was delivered to Gwern, the infant son
of Matholwch and Branwen.   When this peace had
been made the boy passed, with the love and goodwill
of all following him, from Brân to Manawydan his
uncle.   Then Evnyssien called the boy to him, saying,
' Why does not my nephew, son of my sister, come to
me ?   Even though he were not king of Erinn, it were
pleasing to me to make friends with the boy.'   ' Let
him go to him, and gladly,' said Brân, whereupon the
boy willingly did so.   ' Heaven be my witness,' said
Evnyssien in his mind, ' a deed unexpected by the
family will I now perpetrate.'   Thereupon he rose, and

---

[1] See *R. B. Mab.* p. 38, where the original will be found to have the
plurals *keimeit kynniuyeit disgynneit,* also *kytwyr,* which we have altered into
ketwyr.

before any one present could seize hold of him, he
quickly took the boy by his feet and flung him, head
foremost, into the fire blazing there. When Branwen
saw the child burnt in the fire, she attempted to leap
into the fire from where she was sitting between her
two brothers; but Brân seized her with his one hand
and his shield with the other. Then everybody
struggled throughout the house, and it was the greatest
uproar ever heard in one house, as each man took
his arms; and it was then that Morđwyt Tyllion said:
'Gwern gwngwch uiwch uordwyt tyllion[1];' and while
everybody went for his arms, Brân held Branwen
between his shield and his shoulder. The Irish now
began to kindle fire under the Cauldron of Re-birth,
and the corpses of the slain were thrown into it until
it was full; for they would arise next day as fighting
men and as excellent as they ever were, except that
they would not be able to speak. So, when Evnyssien
saw the corpses of his own countrymen without a
birth for them anywhere he said in his mind, 'Oh
God! woe is me that I am the cause of this litter of the
men of the Isle of the Mighty[2], and disgrace upon me
if I seek not deliverance from this.' Thereupon he
thrust himself among the corpses of the Irish, when
two trouserless Irishmen came and cast him into the
cauldron, thinking that he was an Irishman. Therein he
stretched himself so that the cauldron burst into four
pieces, and his heart burst likewise. It was owing
to this that the men of the Isle of the Mighty obtained

---

[1] What this means nobody knows, but it looks as if it ought to be Welsh.

[2] This appellation of Britain only occurs in the Mabinogion of Branwen
and Manawyđan, while Kulhwch speaks of the Three Islands of the Mighty,
R. B. Mab. p. 113; but the former has also found its way into the *Seint
Greal*, Williams, pp. 192, 561.

what victory they did, and that only amounted to the
escape of seven of them, together with Brân, who
was wounded in his foot with a poisoned spear. The
seven men are mentioned by name, and Brân is
represented ordering them to cut his head off his
wounded body: 'Take the head,' said he, 'and bring
it to the White Hill in London, and bury it there
with the face looking towards France.' They obeyed,
and Branwen accompanied them to the Isle of the
Mighty, but as she took her last look at Erinn she
sighed and died, exclaiming, 'Woe is me that I was
ever born! the goods of two islands have been wasted
because of me.' For Ireland had been left without
inhabitants, save five widows in a cave, who escaped
to repeople the country. Their offspring divided the
island into five parts between them, and searching the
land where battles had been fought, they found gold
and silver, which made them rich[1]. As for Bran's
Head, it was a great many years ere it reached
London; but its history, and how it entertained
Manawyđan and his seven comrades, at a perennial
feast in a distant isle of the sea, need not be detailed
at this point.

Having given the story of Brân's death, we now
come to that of Urien, and we may first remark that
the person who is said to have been the cause of
Urien's death, is known in a poem in the *Red Book*
by the unusual name of Ƚouan Ƚawđivro[2], of whom

---

[1] Compare with this the passage in which the Norse poet of the Volospá
speaks of the Anses, after the restoration of things, finding ' in the grass
wonderful golden tables,' that is to say tables in the gambling sense and in
allusion to the pieces which had been used for playing in previous days: see
Vigfusson and Powell, i. 201 ; also *Hib. Lec.* p. 534.

[2] See the poem in Skene's *Four Anc. Bks. of Wales*, ii. 272, where *difro*
rhymes with *bro* and *agro*, also the *Red Book* Triads, which give the word

nothing else is known. The epithet is of obscure meaning and origin, but it reminds one of that of Ỻeu Ỻawgyffes[1]. Further, *Ỻouan* may be supposed to be, etymologically speaking, nearly related to the name Ỻeu, which in the Welsh of the 9th or 10th century would have been Ỻou, so that the derivative from it would be Ỻouan. This we take Ỻouan to be, namely, a reproduction of such a name just as it occurred in manuscripts of those centuries; for had it continued in common use, and subject to the ordinary phonetic changes, it would have come down to later times as Ỻeuan and not Ỻouan. Accordingly, the death of Urien at the hands of Ỻouan may be regarded as in a sense another version of the slaying of Goronwy Pevr by Ỻeu Ỻawgyffes; and it is somewhat remarkable that the scene of his death is called Aber Ỻeu[2], or the mouth of a river called possibly after Ỻeu: compare the name of the Snowdonian glen called Nantỻe, formerly Nant-ỻeu, after Ỻeu Ỻawgyffes, as explained in his story in the Mabinogi of Mâth[3].

To come to the manner of Urien's death, and the parallel with the story of Brân, the *Red Book* poem to which we have referred, consists of fifty-eight stanzas,

---

the same form (*R. B. Mab.* p. 303). The Triads in the *Myvyrian*, i. 38, ii. 29, iii. 47, call the man in question Ỻofan Ỻawdino, and Ỻouan Ỻawdiffro, while Stephens in his *Gododin*, p. 76, has been able to find Ỻovan Ỻaw Difrod; but it is not clear where. We may connect *difro* with the Irish *dibairgim*, 'I cast or shoot,' and the later Irish *dibrachad*, 'the act of shooting.' According to this surmise, the name Ỻouan Ỻaw Difro might be explained to mean the Ỻouan whose hands were famed for their skill in shooting an arrow or hurling a dart. Ỻabddifro, written Ỻautiuro, misread or miscopied *Lancinro, Lancinlo,* simplified *Lancilo,* and completed into *Lancilos* (by adding the *s* of the O. French nominative) is the nearest approach the author can suggest to the origin of the name *Lancelot,* nominative *Lanceloz.* It is needless to say that Ỻawdifrod would have fitted still better.

[1] *Hib. Lec.* pp. 237-40.
[2] See the same *Red Book* poem, Skene, ii. 270.
[3] *R. B. Mab.* pp. 78-9; Guest, iii. 246 8.

mostly triplets, in which the former's death at Aber
ILeu is bewailed. The deed has usually been ascribed
to ILywarch Hên, and the fact, that the person who
is made to speak calls Urien his cousin, agrees with
the respective places assigned to Urien and ILywarch
in the stock pedigrees[1]. The poem represents ILywarch lamenting his being the slayer of Urien, whom
he calls not only his cousin but his lord, his supporter,
the pillar of Prydein, the son of Kynvarch and the
father of Owein. More than once he uses such
a refrain as

> 'Gwae vy ffaw ffad vy arglwyd !'
> *Woe to my hand that it has slain my lord!*

But Dr. Pughe discovered a way of mistranslating it
thus —'Woe to my hand that my lord is slain.' This
rendering has met with pretty general acceptance,
though it defies the evident meaning of the words,
and hardly harmonizes with the poet's repeated mention
of his carrying his lord's head about with him, that is to
say, if he regarded himself with regret as the murderer
of his lord. Add to this that the effective cause of
Urien's death is alluded to as being ILouan ILawdivro,
of whom warriors, as the poet states, are in quest in
every land[2]. The whole difficulty, however, disappears
if we only suppose the circumstances, under which
Urien was beheaded, to have been somewhat the same
as in the case of Brân. We then have Urien, wounded
in battle, ordering his own head to be cut off: one of his

---

[1] Stephens' *Gododin*, 174; Skene, i. 168.
[2] See the original in Skene's *Four Anc. Bks. of Wales*, ii. 272, from the
Red Book, col. 1040 :—

> 'Angerd Uryen ys agro.
> gennyf. kyrchynat ympob bro!
> yn wysc ffouan lȧ difro.'

friends obeys reluctantly, and feels uneasy in his mind on account of the deed, though he had not committed it of his own free will. There seems to be no objection to the bearer of Urien's head being identified with Llywarch Hên, who thereby becomes in this story the counterpart of Manawyđan, the chief of the seven in charge of Brân's head in the Mabinogi of Branwen. The poem gives Urien, as one of his attributes, a black crow or raven on his breast: the Welsh for it is *brân*, and the possibility suggests itself, that the *brân* which was originally but an attribute of the dark god gave him his name of Brân. In that case, the latter was a secondary and newer name of his; and this derives confirmation from the fact that Bran or Bron[1], brother to Manannán, the counterpart of the Welsh Manawyđan, is all but unknown to Irish literature. The view here suggested, whatever may be thought of it, would make for the original identity of Urien and Brân.

It is further inevitable that we should identify with Brân, or Brân's Head, a divinity called the Wonderful Head, in Welsh, Uthr Ben and Uthr Ben-dragon, to whom allusion has been made elsewhere[2], but here we wish to draw attention only to one point of similarity between Urien and Uthr Ben, namely, as to complexion: the Taliessin poem about Uthr Ben makes him sing his own elegy, and in it he describes himself as *arđu*, 'black, dark, or dusky.' He also represents himself called *gorlassar*, which seems to have denoted a dark blue or livid colour, and it is twice used in connection with Urien, once of his person, and once of the spear wielded by him to despatch a foe[3].

---

[1] See the *Hib. Lec.* p. 666.   [2] *Hib. Lec.* pp. 97, 269.
[3] See Skene, ii. 189, 192, 203.

But the fancy which reduced the sable divinity into a mere head, or a Janus-like stump, need not detain us here, as it has been touched upon elsewhere, in connection with the monumental representations of it, with which Gaulish archæology have made us familiar [1]. But before leaving the *Red Book* triplets it may be worth while to direct attention to the following words, out of which little sense has hitherto been extracted [2]:

> 'Ar yr echwyð ethyw gwaꝉ
> O vraw marchawc ysguaꝉ:
> A vyð vyth uryen araꝉ?'

> *On the Echwyð evil has fallen*
> *From the dread of a savage knight:*
> *Will there ever be another Urien?*

The allusion to the furious knight, and the widespread results of his deed, is best understood in the light of

---

[1] *Hib. Lec.* pp. 93-4.

[2] Skene, ii. 271, from col. 1041 of the *Red Book*: the reading given in the text is the result of the minimum emendation requisite to make the passage intelligible: see Pughe's Dictionary under the word *ysguaꝉ*, which, meaning furious, fierce, savage, is evidently a good equivalent for *saueage* in the name of Balyn le Saueage; also in that of Lorayne le Saueage, whom Malory describes, iii. 15. treacherously killing the lover of a lady called Eleyne (p. 153 above). In fact, the name Lorayne probably represents the Welsh Iꝇenan, but the story, as given by Malory, would seem to have undergone no little perversion. We are not bound to read *ysguaꝉ*, as one might also construe *ys cuaꝉ*, 'who is savage,' *cuaꝉ* being a word the genuineness and meaning of which are beyond doubt. Iꝇouan's name is also to be detected in certain versions of the *Queste du S. Graal*, as that of Labran who slays *Urban*, or of Laban, who (by some error of the scribe's) is slain by *Uꝏlain* instead of *vice versa* (Nutt, p. 47). Nor is this the whole complication, as will be seen from Nutt, pp. 83-4. *Urban* and *Urlain*, in which the *l* is the result of misreading *ba* written conjointly, stand for some form of Urien's name (see p. 242), if not rather for *Uthr Ben*. This latter is countenanced, perhaps, by *Urban* being once given as the Maimed King's name (Nutt, pp. 48, 84). For the reason why Uthr Ben, or U. Bendragon, might be described a maimed king, see the *Hib. Lec.* p. 567, and compare Geoffrey's 'rex semimortuus,' viii. 23.

the story of Balyn le Saveage wounding Pellam, with
the instantaneous effect already described (p. 119), that
the latter's entire castle collapsed and his realm fell
into decay, for as Balyn rode away through 'the fayr
countreyes and cytees,' as the narrator tells[1] us, he
'fond the peple dede slayne on euery syde/and alle
that were on lyue cryed O balyn thow hast caused
grete dommage in these contrayes for the dolorous
stroke thow gauest vnto kynge Pellam thre countreyes
are destroyed.' The corresponding deed of Ỻouan
Ỻawđivro, which brought ruin and confusion on Urien's
realm, holds the rank of Balyn's Dolorous Stroke in
the Welsh Triads[2], where it is termed one of the
Three atrocious Slaughters of Britain. Another account
of the Dolorous Stroke is given in the *Petit S. Graal*,
in which Urien appears as Urban of the Black Thorn,
a name which may, perhaps, be the direct representative rather of *Uthr Ben*, but that matters not;
neither does it matter that the assailant is not called
there Ỻouan, but Perceval or Peredur, as will be seen
from the following[3]: 'Perceval comes to a ford and
is challenged by its guardian, whom he overcomes.
His name is Urban of the Black Thorn; his lady
had set him to guard the ford. Her castle vanishes
with a great noise, and she comes to her lover's aid
with her maidens in shape of birds. Perceval slays
one who becomes a woman, and is carried off by
the others to Avallon.' Here, it may be observed, that
the Black Thorn in Urban's full designation reminds
one of Yspyđaden and Espinogre (p. 190), whereas
the birds should probably be the fairy birds of
Rhiannon. This places Urban over against Rhiannon's

---

[1] Malory, ii. 16.   [2] Triads, i. 38, ii. 29, iii. 47.

[3] Nutt, p. 30.

husband, Pwyll, whose name is to be brought under the reader's notice later. Further, the whole scene, as compared with the story of Balyn's Dolorous Stroke, to which Pellam succumbed at the same time that his castle collapsed, makes for the equation of Urban with Pellam. We mention this as an instance of the impossibility of drawing a hard and fast line of distinction between certain mythological characters of the same group, such as Urien, Uthr Ben, Bràn the Blessed, Pwyll, and Pellam on the one hand, and such on the other as Balyn, Ilouan, Peredur, and the like knights. In other words, the difficulty arises from the same divinity having a variety of names serving to express overlapping aggregates of attributes.

The whole incident may be regarded as the expression of a nature myth to be compared with that of Ilacheu slaying the giant of darkness and sleeping on his body, the western sea (p. 61). This, however, is more elaborate: in Urien's realm Urien is a great monarch. His castles are of imposing proportions, and his country seems an Elysium; but the onslaught of the sun-hero reduces the sable chief's dimensions, levels his castles with the ground, and exposes his realm as the abode of desolation. For the name of that realm is *yr Echwyd*, the evening and the dusk, the twilight which is essential to the illusion and glamour on which this whole cosmos of unreality is founded.

Urien is remarkable above all others who figure in the *Book of Taliessin*, as being the subject of no less than eight of the poems in that collection. In other words, his are the praises sung in one-seventh of the whole number of poems in the manuscript. This is out of all proportion as compared with the other heroes, who happen to be the most popular in the Taliessin poems. There must have been a reason for it: what may it be? It has already been mentioned that Brân the Blessed is said in the Mabinogi of Branwen to have carried the musicians of his court on his back across to Erinn. But they were musicians: for the poets and the bards we turn to the Taliessin poem already mentioned as put into the mouth of Brân's other self, namely, Uthr Ben. The latter describes himself as both bard and harper, piper and crowder, and, in short, no less than seven score artistes in his own person. Now, even allowing for the possibility of our being misled in this instance, by the obscurity of the language, the association between Uthr Ben and the professional class, including bards and musicians of various descriptions, remains undeniable. The unavoidable conclusion to be drawn therefrom is, that the bards thought themselves, as a class, to be under the special protection of the dark divinity under his various forms and names, such as Urien, Brân, Uthr Ben, and others. The dark divinity is the god both of beginning and ending, of life and death: as the former he is the god of plenty, and as the latter he is the god of the departed, who adds to the number of his subjects by frequenting, among other places, the field of battle. He acquires therefore the character of a god of carnage, as, for instance, under the name of Gwyn ab Nûd, otherwise known as the king of the fairies and the demons of the Other World. Carnage and slaughter form the boasted sphere of Uthr Ben's delight, and Urien is praised mainly for two things, his activity in war and his lavishness to the bards. All this is in harmony with what may be learned in Irish literature, which relates how Cúchulainn was sent to the fierce Domnall to be taught the warlike feats in which he ex-

celled. Domnall fills the same sort of place with regard
to Cúchulainn in the Irish story as the uncle of Peredur
does with regard to Peredur, when the latter is put by
him through the sword exercise. What is here still
more to the point, is, that Domnall is probably to be
identified with the dread figure specially associated with
bardism, and described as 'Domnall in his chariot[1].'
Domnall is in Welsh Dyvnwal, surnamed *Moelmud*, or
Bald-and-dumb, an epithet akin to others given to the
dark god in some of his many forms. Geoffrey describes Dyvnwal as a prince, who first signalized his
warlike capacities by reducing all the monarchs of
Britain under his single sceptre, and then distinguished
himself as a great legislator[2], with whom one of the
Triads, iii. 58, connects the organization of the bardic
system in Britain.

Thus it may be surmised, that the reason why so
many of the Taliessin poems were sung in honour of
Urien, is, that he was the special god of the bards under
one or more of his names in the pagan period. Hymns
had doubtless been wont to be sung in his praise, and
it is to a continuation of this habit in Christian times we
seem to owe the poems in question. The pagan and
semi-pagan traditions of bardism among the Welsh
have lingered long, and the *Book of Taliessin* is the
most complete *répertoire* that we have of them : it is only
unfortunate that its language is so obscure. One has,
as will have been seen already, other interesting traces
of the paganism here in point: take, for example, the
name given in the Mabinogi of Branwen to Brân's head,
namely *Urđawl Ben*, the Dignified or Venerable Head.
Still more remarkable is Brân's constant designation

---

[1] *Hib. Lec.* pp. 323, 449.

[2] San-Marte's *Geoffrey*, ii. 17, iii. 5 ; *R. B. Bruts*, pp. 70 1, 73.

of *Bendigeitvran* in the same, signifying Blessed-Bran, or Brân the Blessed. For it is needless to repeat that Brân was not 'blessed' in the hagiological sense of that word, and that it would be hardly possible to imagine any personage more unlike a saint of the Christian Church than he. One is, in fact, left to draw the inevitable conclusion, that the name Bendigeitvran has come down to us from a time when the bearer of it was still an object of worship, at any rate to one powerful class of the community, the bards.

It is not to be supposed that Urien, Brân, and Uthr Ben exhaust the list of pagan names in the *Book of Taliessin*. Among others of the same class may be mentioned as figuring therein, Goronwy Pevr, the foe and rival of Ꝉleu Ꝉlawgyffes. The former is made lord of Penꝉlyn, or the district in which Bala Lake lies ; the same district is also in other stories represented as that of Tegid[1] the Bald, whose epithet suggests his belonging likewise to the category of dark divinities. Tegid's abode is represented by tradition as having been where Bala Lake now bears his name, called as it is in Welsh Ꝉlyn Tegid. His wife, Kerridwen, was the goddess of Welsh bardism, and the owner of the so-called Cauldron of Sciences. Among other children she had a son called Avagꝺu, whose name in Welsh has become synonymous with darkness and hell. He is mentioned in the Taliessin poem entitled 'Kerridwen's Chair;' but he is likewise alluded to in another Taliessin poem, to which reference has already been made as the Elegy of Uthr Ben, where he is associated with the dark god under that name[2]. Considering, therefore, the nature

---

[1] This name must literally mean beauty, from *teg*, 'fair, beautiful :' it cannot be derived from the Latin *Tacitus*.

[2] Skene, ii. 158, 203 ; *Hib. Lec.* pp. 97, 151, 269, 567.

of the materials of these poems, and the mythology to
which they belong, one would be almost warranted in
treating Tegid and Uthr as distinct merely in name.
The tradition that Tegid's abode has sunk, where
the lake bears his name, is the euhemerism that has
grown up to cover the old notion, common enough with
regard to Welsh fairies, that he lived in or beneath the
lake.

This recalls another weird figure of the same class,
and one who is mentioned also in the *Book of Taliessin*,
namely, Gwyđno Garanhir, whose territory one version
of his story represents overrun by the sea near the
mouth of the Dovey; and hard by the story of Taliessin
describes that bard discovered as an infant. He was
taken to Gwyđno by his son Elphin, to be brought up
by him, and on the Cardiganshire side of the river is
Tre' Taliessin, or Taliessin's Town, while not far off
stands on the coast the village of Borth, called now in
Welsh *y Borth*, 'the Port,' the full name of which
appears to have been Porth Wyđno yng Ngheredigion,
or Gwyđno's Port in Cardiganshire. So much of this
locality of Gwyđno: the next to be mentioned was on
the coast of North Wales; for a little to the east of
Bangor is a small river known as Gwenwyn Meirch
Gwyđno, or the Poison of Gwyđno's Steeds, so-called
in reference to the bursting of Kerridwen's Cauldron,
the contents of which are described in the story of
Taliessin as virulent to such a degree, that they poisoned
the Steeds of Gwyđno. This term is probably to be
understood to mean the billows of the sea, and the
legend implies that the scene of the accident to Kerridwen's Cauldron was so placed, that the poison from it
flowed into the stream, still named with reference to
that fabulous event. Add to this, for what it is worth,

that Gwyđno is said to have given land to Taliessin[1] in Arđechweđ, which comprises, roughly speaking, the land looking towards the sea between ℒandudno and Bangor. Moreover, according to the story of Taliessin in the so-called History[2] of him, Elphin and Taliessin appear to have lived within a fairly easy reach of Maelgwn of Gwyneđ, who held his court at some one of his towns on the north coast of what is now the county of Carnarvon. Lastly, Gwyđno was reckoned among the kings of the North[3], where also a version of the Triads locate a Porth Wyđno, or Gwyđno's Port[4]. This association of Gwyđno with the north of the island comes out also in another way: Gwyđno, like Urien, had a son called Elphin, whose name, as already hinted, is probably the Welsh form of Alpin, so prominent in the early history of Scotland. For our purpose the two Elphins may be treated as one, seeing that Urien may be said to have his other self in Gwyđno.

With regard to the Dolorous Blow and its equivalents in the various versions, it will have been seen that the narrator's sympathy is all spent on the dark divinity and not on his antagonist. It is so in the case of Balyn: he is accursed, on account of his deed, to the day of his death at his own brother's hands. So with regard to ℒouan ℒawđivro, whose wounding of Urien ranks in the Triads as one of the Three atrocious Slaughters of Britain. The case of the wounding of Brân is not essentially different, though the fact of the scene being in Ireland seems to have left the story-teller so little interest in Brân's antagonist, that he does not even mention his name; and the Triads[5] shift the critical

---

[1] *Iolo MSS* pp. 78, 467, where *Gwyđno* is called *Gwyđnyw*.
[2] Printed in Guest's *Mab.* iii. 321-55. [3] Skene, i. 166-9.
[4] Triads, i. 5. [5] i. 51, ii. 13, iii. 49.

point to the slap which Matholwch gave Branwen. This
they call one of the Three criminal Blows of Britain ;
for it was treated as the immediate cause of bringing
her brother Brân over to Erinn. These instances
raise the question why the action of the foe of the
dark divinity was regarded with horror and not the
reverse. To this Malory's answer is ready: Balyn's
victim ' kynge Pellam was nyghe of Ioseph kynne/and
that was the moost worshipful man that lyued in tho
dayes [1].' Then as to the story of Urien, as given in
the *Book of Taliessin*, we have the answer in the
emphasis laid there on Urien's hostility to the Saxon
and the Angle, to the Pict and the Scot, and on his
liberality to the bardic fraternity. But neither of these
answers can be regarded as going to the root of the
matter, while the third case, that of Brân, suggests no
obvious answer except that he was Brân the Blessed,
and that his antagonist in Ireland is represented as
being in the wrong. At any rate, Brân was out of his
own country, and therefore among a people naturally
hostile to him. This would also apply to another probable scene of the Meal-bag slaughter, namely, where
the name *Blatobulgium* [2], or the 'Meal-bag' Station,
fixes it at Middleby Kirk, near the river Annan, in a
district which was considerably west of the Brythonic
boundary.

The Teutonic counterpart of the mutual slaughter of
the Welsh and the Irish in the Meal-bag Pavilion in
Erinn is to be found, possibly, in the carnage at Etzel's
Court in the Land of the Huns, as described in the
Nibelungen Lied. The comparison does not admit
of being instituted in detail, but passing over some

---

[1] *Malory*, ii. 16. [2] *Hib. Lec.* p. 597.

differences, one may signalize the following as the principal points of correspondence :—

The Burgundians, with Gunther their king at their head, go to the court of Etzel, king of the Huns, and in the course of their journey they have to cross a great river : Brân and his men proceed to Erinn, on the way to which they have to cross two intervening rivers (p. 250).

Both Gunther and Brân set out from home at the instance of their sisters, respectively Kriemhild and Branwen, the former of whom had given her hand to the king of the Huns, just as the latter had given hers to the Irish king, Matholwch.

Peace and amity are thought to be cemented by the presence in the former case of Ortlieb, the infant son of Etzel and Kriemhild, at the meeting of the hosts, when the child is mocked at, and presently slain by Gunther's kinsman Hagan. In like manner peace is made between Brân and Matholwch on condition, that the latter resign his kingdom in favour of Gwern, his infant son by Branwen, an arrangement which is suddenly brought to nought by Brân's half-brother Evnyssien, who causes the instant death of the boy.

The death of the child is, in both cases, the signal for general carnage, which, in the case of the Huns, leaves as survivors only Etzel and his warrior Dietrich, in whom, judging from his name [1], we have possibly the sun-hero of the German story, and the counterpart of the Celtic Balyn of the romances—whom we may here introduce, to supplement the Brân story, which leaves the Irish no male survivors.

The gold treasure of the Burgundians, which fills so great a place in the Nibelung story, has its counterpart

---

[1] *Hib. Lec.* p. 30.

on the Celtic side in the perpetual feast provided for
Brân's friends.

Lastly, the treasure remains with the Burgundians to
the end, deposited in the river Rhine ; and, on the other
side, the feast presided over by Brân's Head continued
long in Britain, or in an adjacent isle, where it might be
still going on but for the usual curiosity through which
a paradise is lost.

If one might venture to go back behind the distinction between Burgundians and Huns, with which the
German story has made one familiar, and treat the disposition of the parties in the struggle as an open question, one might be tempted to ask why Gunther and
his friends, the murderers of Siegfried, should not have
been the Huns, and Etzel and Dietrich the Burgundians.   This exactly matches the question which the
Welsh story also raises, Why have Brân and his men
not been treated as the Irish, and their foes as the
Welsh?   Such an arrangement would have allowed one
to identify the sun-hero with the party which the narrator might have been expected to favour.   All this is,
however, inseparable from the fact of Gunther and
Brân being out of their own country in another land ;
and the question practically returns in another form,
What was the original meaning of this remoteness of
the scene of the conflict?   As an answer, we can only
give the conjecture, that the dark divinity and his subjects are to be regarded as identified with that portion
of the human race which has passed away and departed
for another world.   In that case, Gunther's long journey
and his crossing the river on his way to the Huns, and
Brân's wading through the waters in order to reach the
west, might be compared, as has already been partially done, with what the *Rig-Veda* has darkly to relate

of Yama. He was the first of the departed, both in point of time and of power, to cross the rapid waters and show others how to come, following in his footsteps, to the happy land, where he sits in festive guise ready to receive the fathers of the race at a perpetual banquet, whose dainties arrest old age and decay, whose delights permit no reckoning of time [1]. Suppose the rays of the sun—for we are brought again face to face with the nature myth—to be let in on such a scene, the whole is clean gone as in a fairy tale; and a fairy tale, in fact, it is. The visit of the solar hero has annihilated a whole landscape of enchantment in the twinkling of an eye. Balyn, with one thrust of his long lance, has undone a whole world: why should not the curse of its fall pursue him evermore?

Brân the Blessed, when ordering his friends to take away his head, told them that they would find the Head as sociable and interesting a companion as it had ever been whilst it was yet on his body; that they would sit with it seven years over dinner at Harlech, listening to the Three Birds of Rhiannon; that they would thence go to Gwales in Penvro, and feast in the society of the Head eighty years, until, in fact, they opened a certain door that looked towards Aber Henvelen, in the direction of Cornwall; but as soon as that was done the Head would begin to decay, and they would have to hasten to bury it in London. The story goes on to relate how all this came to pass. They sat at dinner, as it had been foretold, seven years at Harlech, enjoying the warbling of the Birds of Rhiannon, which they could see far away from them out at sea; but they were as clearly visible to them as if they had

---

[1] *Hib. Lec.* pp. 654-9.

been with them on the spot. These were the birds said
to sing the dead into life, and to sing the living into the
sleep of death [1]. From Harlech, after their seven-year
feast, they went to Gwales, where they had a fair
kingly place above the sea. They entered a spacious
hall there, and found two of its doors open; but the
third was shut, and they recognized it as the one looking
towards Cornwall, which was not to be opened. There
they remained for four-score years, feasting and passing
the happiest time they ever spent. For they had no
thought or memory of anything unpleasant that had
ever happened to them, and the society of the Head was
no less agreeable to them, than when Brân was alive
and whole. But one day, one of the seven comrades,
Heilyn, son of Gwyn Hên, said: 'Disgrace on my
beard if I do not open the door, to see whether what is
said of it be true.' He did so, and looked towards
Cornwall and Aber Henvelen. No sooner was that
done than they were as well aware of their misfortunes, of the disasters that had befallen them, and
especially of the loss of their lord, as if it had all
happened only the day before. They could no longer
tarry, so they hurried away to London to bury the
Head.

One or two remarks, by way of explanation, will
suffice on this story. Gwales, in Penvro or the cantred
of Pembroke, appears to have meant Gresholm, the
Pembrokeshire isle which lies furthest out at sea. The
position of Aber Henvelen, 'the mouth or confluence
of Henvelen,' is uncertain, and so is the exact significance of the allusion to it in the story of Brân. All we
can say is, that Taliessin, in a poem to which reference

---

[1] The *White Book of Rhyderch* in the Hengwrt Collection, folio 291ᵃ.

has already been made, speaks of himself singing
before the Sons of Ⅼyr, at Ebyr Henvelen¹, or the
Confluences of Henvelen. First and foremost among
the sons of Ⅼyr were Brân and Manawyđan; but
whether looking from Gwales in the direction of Aber
Henvelen was to remind the Venerable Head's seven
associates of past prosperity or of past disaster we are
not told.

With Gwales as the scene of perennial feasting, may
be compared the open house kept by Polydectes on the
small isle of Seriphus (p. 232). Various echoes of this
fairy tale, of an ancient type, have come down to modern
times in Demetia ; thus sailors on the coast of Pembrokeshire and Carmarthenshire have been heard to talk of
the Green Meadows of Enchantment, lying out at sea
west of Pembrokeshire, and of men who had landed on
them or seen them suddenly vanishing. Some of the
people of Milford could, as they used to believe, see
the Green Islands of the fairies distinctly; and the latter
were supposed to go to and fro between their islands
and the shore, through a subterranean gallery under
the sea. One of their objects in doing so was to make
purchases in the markets at Milford or Laugharne ;
this they did sometimes without being seen, and always
without speaking, for they seemed to know the prices
of the things they wished to buy, so that they invariably
laid down the exact sums of money payable. The ancient
story in the Mabinogi of Branwen speaks of incessant
feasting, but nothing of any catering or attendance ; for

¹ The Mabinogi of Branwen (*R. B. Mab.* pp. 40, 42) leaves it doubtful
whether we should read *Henvelen* or *Henveleu*, but the rhyme in the *Book of
Taliessin*, Skene, ii. 153, proves *Henvelen* to be the correct form. It will
have been noticed that the prose passages have *aber*, and the verse the
plural *ebyr*.

the old notion of fairy feasts was that the food came to
the table without the intervention of any attendants.
But the modern version is now and then so far euhemerized as to regard the island fairies as living in
densely crowded towns, for which supplies have to be
imported [1].

Beliefs of this kind used to be current on the
coast on both sides of the Teivi; and there the fairies
were known by the name of Plant Rhys Đwvn, or
the Children of Rhys the Deep (in the sense of shrewd
or cunning), and their market town used to be Cardigan.
So, when the price of corn was high and the supply
happened to be cleared away early in the day, the poor
would say to one another on their way home, 'Oh!
they were there to-day;' meaning the Children of Rhys
Đwvn, to whom they preferred not to refer by name.
Rhys Đwvn's realm was not extensive; but it produced, among other things, a rare herb, which rendered
the country invisible to strangers. This was not
known to grow elsewhere, except at a spot of about
a square yard in area in the Hundred of Kemmes, in
the north of Pembrokeshire. If a man chanced to stand
all alone on this spot of ground he could see at a glance
the whole territory of Rhys Đwvn's Children; but
once he moved away, it would be in vain to try to find
it again. These fairies might, perhaps, steal children,
but they were reckoned very honest traders; so much
so, in fact, that they were supposed at the last to have
been so disgusted with the greed of the farmers around
Cardigan that they came there no more, but went to
Fishguard in preference; at any rate, old people observed that strange customers were seen to visit the

[1] The *Cymmrodor*, v. 116-7 : see also Wirt Sikes' *British Goblins*, pp
8-10.

Fishguard market [1]. The fairies of North Wales appear to have been, in some instances, less honest in their trade; but the author has been told that Bala was one of their favourite markets, until the colleges set up there drove them away. This brief sketch of the later story, should it answer no other purpose, will serve to show how hard the ancient mythology dies.

---

[1] The *Cymmrodor*, v. 109, 114 8.

CHAPTER XII.

Pwyll and Pelles.

Allusion has more than once been made to Peredur's uncles, the Lame or Maimed King and his
brother; but their story deserves a somewhat more
thorough examination. In the Peredur, the uncle first
visited by the hero was engaged, when he found him, in
watching certain of his men fishing on the water near
the castle (p. 78). Later in the story, Peredur finds
another of his uncles, and it was in the latter's castle
that he saw the head brought in on a charger and the
Bleeding Lance (p. 79). Both uncles are described as
lame, which is possibly due merely to the narrator's
carelessness; but he only calls the second uncle the
Lame King, and the distinction drawn by him between
the Lame King and the Fisher was probably inten-
tional[1]; for it is found to coincide with the treatment of
the two brothers in the *Queste du S. Graal.* Thus, one
French version speaks of the Maimed King, where the
Seint Greal, a Welsh translation of a lost French
original, gives the name Peleur[2]; and where the former
speaks of the Fisher King, or of Pelles, the Welsh calls

---

[1] *R. B Mab.* pp. 200-3, 232, 242.
[2] He is once given the name Mesior in the *Seint Greal* : see pp. 256, 603.

T

him Peles[1], and treats him as brother to Peleur. He
is represented becoming a hermit, while Peleur continues an invalid king. They had a sister called the
Widow of Camalot, Peredur's mother; also a wicked
brother, called the King of the Dead Castle, who was
a pagan. He was always trying to rob King Peleur of
the Holy Grail and of the Bleeding Lance[2], both which he
ultimately succeeded in taking, but in vain, as his place
was stormed by Peredur, who brought Peleur's people
back to the Christian faith[3]. In the *Grand St. Graal*
we read not of Peleur, but Pellean, said to have been
called the Maimed King on account of his having been
'wounded in the two thighs in a battle of Rome[4].' The
other king in the same context is called Pelles; but he
is there made a descendant of Pellean, and not brother
to him. In the Huth manuscript of the *Merlin*, recently published, Pellean reads Pellehan, king of Listi-
nois[5], which after Balyn's dolorous stroke was known
as the Terre Gastee and the Terre Foraine. This
romance calls Pellehan's demon brother Garlan or
Gallan, who appears as Garlon in Malory's narrative,
where the good brother, who trying to avenge Garlon's
death is wounded by Balyn, is called Pellam. The other
good brother, Pelles, has, as will appear from the comparisons to be made later, to be sought here under the
names Pelles and Pelleas, though the latter can only be
a modification of the French nominative Pelleans, of the
name Pellean of the Maimed King, of which Malory
makes Pellam; nor is this the whole of the confusion
in Malory's pages, for he treats Pellam and Pelleas as

[1] Nutt, pp. 39, 50.
[2] *Seint Greal*, pp. 205, 570; 223, 581.
[3] Ib. pp. 309-11, 638-9; 335-8, 655-7; also p. 118 above.
[4] Nutt, pp. 64, 90.
[5] Vol. ii. pp. 24, 30; also p. 7, where a variant *Pellohin* is given of *Pellehan*.

in no way related to one another, while he confuses Pelles and Pellam[1]. But all this, and a good deal more, may be regarded as the result of his having compiled from different sources[2].

Everything about Pelles and Pellean, Peles and Peleur, seem to suggest the probability of a Welsh origin; but who, in Welsh literature, can they be? At first sight, the resemblance of the name Pelles to the Welsh pell, 'far, distant,' would seem to refer us back to Pellehan as King of the Foreign Country, or to the Distant City associated with Urien's name (p. 249). Such a name as *y Brenin Pell*, or the Far Away King, sounds a very possible Welsh appellation of a western Yama; but as we have never found any trace of its occurrence, we are forced back to such names as actually meet us in Welsh literature. The two which seem to answer to Pelles and Pellean are, undoubtedly, those of Pwyll and Pryderi. The simplest way, probably, to examine the correspondence between them respectively will be to bring together, as briefly as possible, what is said about the former in the romances and about the latter in Welsh prose and verse. We have already mentioned the leading members of the family of Peles and Peleur, as they are called in the *Seint Greal*, and we now come to a description of Peleur's court, as given in a passage relating how Gwalchmei (Gauvain) succeeded in reaching it. We are told of two places belonging to King Peleur: the

---

[1] Thus, after making Pellam the victim of Balyn's dolorous stroke in the early part of his narrative, he calls him Pelles later, xiii. 5. He also makes Pelles the Maimed King, xvii. 5, and King of the Foreign Country, xi. 2, both of which descriptions would seem to have belonged rather to Pellam.

[2] For some remarks on Malory's sources, see M. Paris' introduction to the Huth *Merlin*, i. pp. lxx-lxxij.

first to which Gwalchmei comes is called the Sincere Castle, or the Castle of Questions[1], and it has its entrance guarded by a lion with two villeins made of latten on either side, and so constructed as to attack any one who should approach to enter. In order to get admission, Gwalchmei had to procure a special talisman, the sword with which John the Baptist had been beheaded; so, when he arrived in possession of that weapon, he found the lion had vanished and the villeins had left off shooting, while the gate was wide open, with the priests of the place coming forth to welcome him as the bearer of the sword.

From this first or frontier castle of Peleur's, Gwalchmei had to cross, on his way to the king's own abode, the fairest meadows he had ever seen; and after more than a day's journey he came to a fair valley, abounding in all good things and within sight of Peleur's residence, from which he was, however, separated by three rivers. These were spanned by as many bridges, of which the first was an arrow-shot in length, but only a foot wide, as mentioned in a previous chapter (p. 56). While he was gazing at it in dismay, a grave-looking man, coming to the other end of the bridge called the Eel Bridge, bade him cross at once, as it was already late in the day. He assured Gwalchmei there was no other way of traversing; and the latter, having crossed himself and breathed a prayer, urged his horse on to the narrow bridge; but no sooner had the beast set his feet on it than it became wide enough for two cartwains to travel side by side. On crossing this, he found the other two bridges equally formidable, for he observed a boiling current striking under the bridges, while they

---

[1] *Seint Greal*, pp. 224, 582, 237, 591.

seemed weak at their foundations and to consist of ice.
He crossed, however, unscathed, and approached the
gate of the castle, where he found a huge lion standing;
but no sooner had the lion seen Gwalchmei than he
laid him down with his head between his forefeet, resolved to offer the stranger no harm. The latter was in
due course presented to King Peleur, whom he found
lying on a bed. Everything in the Court was magni-
ficent; and in the course of the evening Gwalchmei
saw the Holy Grail, the Bleeding Spear, and other
wonders[1]. On his way from Peleur's castle, Gwalchmei came to a castle, not very far off, called the Castle
of Joy[2].

We ought to have mentioned that, at an early
stage in his wanderings, Gwalchmei had been entertained by a hermit, who described himself as having
years before been a knight in the service of Uthr Bendragon. He had since, as he said, become a priest to
King Peleur by the command of Christ; and he continued as follows[3]: 'So perfect is that place wherein
is that king [Peleur], that no one who had been there
a year would suppose it to have been six months; for
there in the chapel is the Holy Grail, and it is therefore
am I so young as thou beholdest me.' Gwalchmei at
once seized the opportunity of learning the way to
Peleur's abode, and told the hermit that was the place
he had set out to seek; but the answer he received runs
thus: 'By my faith, I know not how to direct thee; and
I can only say that thou wilt never arrive there unless
God bring thee there.' In the language of Irish story,
Peleur's castle would be treated as a fairy or enchanted
palace, made inaccessible by the magic of its druid

---

[1] *Seint Greal*, pp. 245, 596.   [2] Ib. pp. 248, 598.
[3] Ib. pp. 201, 567.

owner, like that, say, of Bodb the Red [1], or that of Ailill, which was visible from afar, but not to be found when one approached. Compare the Rich Fisher's character for magic, as already cited at p. 117.

Let us now come back to Malory, and take first his Pelleas, on whose name we have already remarked. In the eighteenth chapter of the fourth book we read of three knights—Marhaus [2], Vwayne (Owein), and Gawayne (Gwalchmei)—arriving together in the outskirts of 'a grete foreste that was named the countreye and foreste of Arroy and the countrey of straunge auentures.' Entering it, they come across three ladies, who undertake severally to lead the knights in their quest of adventure. The offer is accepted; and the first sight to challenge Gawayne's attention and his lady companion's was that of a single knight discomfitting ten others, and then allowing himself to be insulted and taken captive by them. It was explained to Gwalchmei by his companion that the ten were the men of a lady called Ettard, with whom the knight led captive was in unrequited love, and that the reason, why he submitted to be taken in that guise to her castle, was in order to have a sight of her. This knight was no other than

---

[1] *Hib. Lec.* pp. 171-2.

[2] This name is Morhout, nominative Morhous, in the Huth *Merlin*, ii. 234-46. Marhaus or Morhous reflects the name Merchiaun (one of the old spellings of Meirchion), in the full name March Meirchion, usually expanded into March ab Meirchion. He is probably to be regarded the same person as March and the King Mark of Cornwall, but, curiously enough, he is brought into collision with Mark; for Marhaus was sent by the king of Ireland to Cornwall to demand the tribute of that country, which had fallen seven years in arrears. The question of the tribute was settled by single combat between Marhaus and Tristram in an island on the coast, and Tristram proved victorious (Malory, viii. 4-8). The place assigned the truage or tribute in this story of Marhaus reminds one unavoidably of the tribute exacted in Ireland by his Irish namesake, Morc or Margg, and his ally Conaing, the chiefs of the Fomori: see the *Hib. Lec.* pp. 262, 584.

Pelleas. Gawayne undertook to assist him, which resulted in Pelleas finding out that the lady had at
once preferred Gawayne to him. 'Ryght soo syr Pelleas vnarmed hym selfe and wente vnto his bedde
makynge merueyllous dole and sorowe.' A lake lady,
named Nyneue or Nymue, comes to Pelleas' rescue, filling him with love for her and loathing for Ettard [1]. The
latter then changed her mind, and died of love for Pelleas,
while Nyneue became his consort and brought him away
to Arthur's court, where he was found so strong that
few knights could withstand him. His account of himself and his country is given in these words: 'my
name is Syre Pelleas borne in the Iles/and of many
Iles I am lord [2].' We are also told that Pelleas was
a worshipful knight, 'one of the four that encheued the
sancgreal [3],' a statement to be explained only by identifying Pelleas with Pelles, at whose castle the Holy
Grail was kept.

According to Malory, Pelles was the father of Elayne,
mother of Galahad, and he lived in a city of strange
adventures, to some of which Lancelot put an end; it
was called Corbyn [4] or Carbonek [5], where also the
Maimed King lay, that is to say, Pellam ; and as the
Holy Grail and the Bleeding Lance were there also [6],
one may treat them as being in the charge of both Pelles
and Pellam. In a passage which treats the former as
the Maimed King, we read as follows [7]: 'Syr sayd she
there was a kynge that hyghte Pelles the maymed
kynge/And whyle he myghte ryde/he supported moche

---

[1] Malory, iv. 21-4.   [2] Ib. iv. 22.   [3] Ib. iv. 29.
[4] Ib. xi. 1.   [5] Ib. xvii. 16-21.
[6] With xiv. 2 compare xvii. 19, 20, where Pelles and the Maimed King
are certainly both in the castle when the Grail and the Lance are seen; but
Malory's text here offers considerable difficulties as to journeys and distances.
[7] Malory, xvii. 5.

crystendome and holy chirche/Soo vpon a daye he
hunted in a woode of his whiche lasted vnto the see/
and at the last he loste his houndes/and his knyghtes/
sauf only one/and there he and his knyghte wente tyl
that they cam toward Irland.'

This forms a sort of complement to the account of
Pelleas being found in the Land of Strange Adventures,
which must now be described a little more in detail.
The account of Gawayne, Uwayne, and Marhaus entering it reads thus[1]: 'In this countrey sayd syr Marhaus
cam neuer knyghte syn it was crystened/but he fonde
straunge auentures/and soo they rode/and cam in
to a depe valey ful of stones/and ther by they sawe a
fayr streme of water/aboue ther by was the hede of
the streme a fayr fontayne/& thre damoysels syttynge
therby/And thenne they rode to them/and eyther
salewed other/and the eldest had a garland of gold
aboute her hede/and she was thre score wynter of age/
or more and her here was whyte vnder the garland/
The second damoysel was of thyrtty wynter of age with
a serkelet of gold aboute her hede/The thyrd damoysel
was but xv yere of age/and a garland of floures aboute
her hede/when these knyghtes had soo beholde them/
they asked them the cause why they sat at that fon-
tayne/we be here sayd the damoysels for thys cause/
yf we may see ony erraunt knyghtes to teche[2] hem vnto
straunge auentures/and ye be thre knyghtes that seken
auentures and we be thre damoysels/and therfore eche
one of yow must chese one of vs/And whan ye haue
done soo/we wylle lede yow vnto thre hyhe wayes/and
there eche of yow shall chese a wey and his damoysel

---

[1] Malory, iv. 18, 19.
[2] Compare with these the Well Maidens mentioned by the Pseudo-
Chrétien in Nutt's *Studies*, p. 8: see the passage quoted at p. 247 above.

with hym/And this day twelue monethe ye must mete
here ageyn/and god sende yow your lyues/and there to
ye must pliȝte your trouthe.' They did so, and returned
to the fountain at the end of a year to the day, Gawayne
having in the meantime made the acquaintance of
Pelleas and earned his hatred in the way already
mentioned.

Let us now compare the story of Pwyll, prince of
Dyved and head of Annwn or Hades, as narrated in
the Mabinogi called after him[1]. But, before doing so,
it may be as well to say, that, for the purposes of the
comparison, one has to apportion Malory's incidents
thus: the things said of both Pelles and Pelleas are to be
put down to Pelles. It is he that the lady Nyneue takes
in hand, and it is he that hunts; whereas Pellam, as the
victim of Balyn's attack, is the Lame or Maimed King
and the King of the Foreign or Waste Country. To
come back to the Mabinogi of Pwyll, it relates how
the latter went to hunt and lost his companions; how
he met Arawn, king of Hades, and agreed with him to
exchange kingships for a year, Arawn undertaking that
no one should discover the exchange; how he bound
Pwyll to meet his (Arawn's) enemy, Havgan or Summer-
white, and kill him at the ford where they annually
fought; how Arawn and Pwyll agreed to meet again in
the same spot in the forest on that day twelvemonth.
The story goes on to narrate how all this happened as
they had arranged, and how the title of Head of Hades
clung ever after to Pwyll, as he had not only ruled
there for a year but added to the realm of Hades the
dominions of Havgan.

The exchange of personal features, which is effected

---

[1] *R. B. Mab.* pp. 1-8; Guest, iii. 37-46; *Hib. Lec.* pp. 338-41.

for a time, between Arawn and Pwyll, through the magic skill of the former, is made the occasion of one of the best stories in the Mabinogion; but, mythologically speaking, it was probably a mere expedient to get over the difficulty that the dark divinity was called Arawn and Pwyll, and that as Pwyll he was also termed king of Dyved, it being no longer understood how Dyved could belong to the geography of the other world. Going, then, back as it were behind this, one may treat Pwyll as another name of Arawn, and Dyved as another name of Hades. Add to this that some of the Welsh versions of Geoffrey of Monmouth make Arawn king of Scotland, a name which may have meant either North Britain or Ireland, the original home of the Scotti, which helps to explain why Malory makes Pelles hunt until he comes towards Ireland. The view here advocated as to Pwyll is confirmed by the fact, that, wherever we meet with Pwyll or Pryderi his son, we are forced by the context, mythologically speaking, to treat them as belonging to the class of dark divinities. Further, the identity of the mythic region in which Gawayne (Gwalchmei) finds Pelleas (Pelles) with that in which Pwyll hunts, is placed beyond doubt by the fact, that, though the thickly wooded glen into which he enters is Glyn Cúch, on the confines of the counties of Pembroke and Carmarthen, the point from which he sets out on the hunt is called *Pen Llwyn Diarwya,* or the End of the Wood of Diarwya, in which name one cannot be mistaken in seeing that of the country and forest of Arroy of Malory's version, and the 'forest grant et parfonde que on apieloit Aroie' of the Huth *Merlin*[1].

---

[1] See vol. ii. 244. In Guest's *Mab.* iii. 3, 37, *Diarwya* is wrongly printed *Diarwyd*; and the French *Aroie* was evidently obtained by discarding the

Another glance at the Mabinogi of Pwyll, and one notices the name of a certain Teyrnon Twryf-vliant or Twryf-bliant, an epithet not easy to explain [1]. It emerges however in the romances used by Malory, to wit, in the name of the 'Castel of Blyaunt [2].' For in the transition the Welsh appears to have been treated as if it had been *Twr Bliant*, that is to say, the Tower of Bliant, whence the designation which Malory has rendered the Castle of Blyaunt. Further, as that sort of description might be taken to suggest that the castle was called after its owner, Blyaunt came to be treated as the latter's name, so that an equivalent for the Welsh Teyrnon was no further necessary, though the castle might require an additional name: Malory sometimes calls it *Castel Blank* [3]. Now the Castle of Blyaunt it was that Pelles gave Lancelot to inhabit, with his daughter Elayne, in the Joyous Isle [4]. Blyaunt must therefore be regarded as under the rule of Pelles, and the relation

---

initial syllable of *Diarwya* or *Dearwya*, as if it had been the preposition *de*, 'of.' The name is obscure, but it may be for *Diarvwya*, with the second part identical with that of *Clegyr-Voia*, a fortified rock at St. David's so-called after an Irish Pict named Boya or Baia. See Giraldus' *Vita S. Davidis*, lec. iv; *Liber Landavensis*, pp. 94-5; *Lives of the Cambro-British Saints*, pp. 106-7, 124-6; Jones & Freeman's *St. David's*, pp. 4, 32-3, and Rhys's *Celtic Britain*, pp. 229, 255. As to *Diar* or *Dear*, it is not an unusual name for a stream.

[1] See *R. B. Mab.* pp. 20-24; also p. 109. *Tóryf Bliant* would seem to mean only 'the noise of linen,' which is not promising as an epithet. *Tóryf Vliant* yields no better sense, and in addition involves a difficulty of gender: so we are disposed to think that the original was *Tóru liant*, or *lliant*, which would admit of the whole name being rendered Teyrnon of the Thunder-flood, or of the Thunder of the Waters, whatever that may have originally meant. In this connection it is, perhaps, worthy of note that poem xv. in the *Book of Taliessin* (Skene, ii. 156) is entitled 'The Chair of Teyrnon,' and contains the following couplet :—

> 'Póy enó y teir kaer.
> róg lliant a llaer.'
>
> *What is the name of the three cities*
> *Between the flood and the ——— ?*

[2] Malory, xii. 5, 6.   [3] Ib. xii. 1, 2.   [4] Ib. xii. 5, 6.

between Pwyłł and Teyrnon was the same; for Teyrnon
was one of Pwyłł's lieges, and the fact, so far as it goes,
goes to countenance the identity here conjectured of
Pelles with Pwyłł.

Further, the Lady of the Lake associated with Pelleas
may be compared with Rhiannon, wife of Pwyłł. Even
the names of the former, distorted as they are to *Nyneue*
in Malory and *Niviene* in the Huth *Merlin*, admit of
being traced back by easy steps of misreading and
miscopying to that of Rhiannon, which in the 12th
century and later would be written Riannon[1]. As to
the rôle of Rhiannon, she offers her hand to Pwyłł,
even as the Lake Damsel does to Pelleas; and that
Rhiannon was a kind of lake lady may be gathered
from the fact that her action in the story of Pwyłł
equates in one curious particular with that of Liban[2],
namely, when the former undertakes to carry on her
shoulders into her husband's presence all the visitors
who presented themselves at the gate[3] of his castle.

[1] Thus Nyneue and Niviene point back to the prototypes niñen and ninien
respectively, as anyone will see who knows anything about our old manuscripts. But besides the common confusion of *n* and *u*, of *in*, *ni* and *ui*,
there was also that of the open *a* with *u*, which makes niñen the possible
result of misreading niunen for niane or nianen. Further, the consonant
ŋ, in the writing usual in Wales till the advent of the Normans, was easily
mistaken for an *n* in case the first limb was carelessly left insufficiently
prolonged below the line. This is one of the misreadings evidenced elsewhere in the romancers' reproduction of Welsh names, and assuming it here,
we step from nianen to ŋianen. Lastly, the scribe's predilection for
certain forms must always count for something, and other instances, such as
Natiien, or Nascien, for Welsh Nwython, illustrate the substitution of *ien* (for
on), making nianon into nianien : so we pass from ŋianien to rianon,
which comes sufficiently near Riannon, the old Welsh spelling of Rhiannon.
See also the preface to the Huth *Merlin*, p. xlv, where preference is given
to *Ninienne* over *Nivienne*, and where forms such as *Niniane*, *Niniene*,
Nimenne, *Nimainne*, *Jumenne*, are mentioned; also *Viviane* and *Vivienne*,
the worst and most popular in print.

[2] *Hib. Lec.* p. 641.

[3] Ib. pp. 498, 500.

In the next place, the three Birds of Rhiannon, whose warbling sings the dead to life and the living to sleep, make music for Brân's friends at their long feast at Harlech; but the birds were not with them on the land: the banqueters had a far reaching sense of eye and ear, and they could see that the birds singing to them were far out above the sea. It may be inferred that they were supposed to be in the atmosphere of Rhiannon's realm, somewhere in the bosom of Cardigan Bay.

We come next to Pwyll's son, Pryderi, who should correspond to Malory's Pellam, the Maimed King. Now, in the story of Pryderi's war with Gwydion son of Dôn, in the Mabinogi of Mâth, Pryderi has with him a prince called Gwrgi Gwastra who seems to be made to succeed Pryderi as his next of kin[1]. In this Gwrgi we have, probably, the same person as Gwrgi Garwlwyd, with whom has already been equated Garlon the black faced knight and demon brother of Pellam, of whose disabling he was the indirect cause (p. 118). This coincidence goes but a short way to confirm our equation of Pellam with Pryderi, and it would be clearly more convincing if it could be shown that the Dolorous Stroke dealt by Balyn to Pellam has its equivalent in the case of Pryderi. This can be done, but it must be premised that the wounding of Pellam is to be reckoned as only a part of the incident. With the wounding of the king his whole palace collapsed into a heap of ruins, his entire domain fell into decay, and his subjects died, while he himself remained infirm for many years. The counterpart to this will virtually be found elaborated at considerable

[1] *R. B. Mab.* pp. 64, 5; Guest, iii. 225, 6, where *dylyedaöc*, 'prince,' is translated 'hostages'!

length in the Mabinogi of Manawydan[1]. For Pryderi
had at his court of Arberth not only his wife Kigva,
but his mother Rhiannon, and also Manawydan, to
whom he had given his mother to wife, after the death
of his father, Pwyll.

One evening after dinner, so the story runs, Pwyll
and his friends ascended the mound of Arberth,
which was a place well known for the strange events
of which it was the scene. As they sat there, they
heard a clap of thunder, and it was so tremendous
that it was followed by mist, which made it impossible for one to see the other, but presently it
became light again. When they looked around them,
where previously they had beheld flocks and herds
and habitations, they saw nothing, no house or house-
beast, no smoke or fire, no human being, or the work
of human hands, except the buildings of the court
empty, desolate, untenanted of man or beast. Their
own household had disappeared, and they four alone
remained, to wit, Pryderi and Manawydan with their
wives. They searched the country in vain for houses
and habitations : wild beasts alone they found. So they
took to hunting, fishing, and gathering wild honey;
and when that failed them they went to England, where
they spent some time. Eventually they revisited
Dyved, and lived the lives of hunters and fishermen,
as they had tried before, and that continued until
Pryderi and Rhiannon his mother had been lost, taken
prisoners by him who had begun their ruin. Who he
was, will appear in the last scene, to which we are
now coming.

Manawydan and Kigva, wife of Pryderi, having
lost their respective consorts and their dogs, betook

---

[1] *R. B. Mab.* pp. 46-58 ; Guest, iii. 164 84.

themselves to England again, where Manawyđan earned his-living for some time, as he was the most skilful of all workmen. When a year had passed, the two returned to Dyved, and Manawyđan brought with him a bag of wheat; then he began to dig[1] three plots of ground, in which he sowed it. The wheat throve as no wheat had ever thriven, and when the time of harvest came round, Manawyđan went to look at his plots and found one of them ripe. He left the corn, resolved to return to reap it on the morrow. With the break of day he came back in order to begin the work, but what was his surprise to find nothing there but straw, every stalk having been cut short close to the ear and every ear carried away! He wondered greatly, and went to look at another of the plots: that was ripe, and he resolved to return the next day to reap the corn, but when he came he found only earless straw as in the previous case. 'Alas!' he exclaimed, 'who is completing my ruin? I know who it is: he who began my ruin is completing it, and he has ruined the country with me.' Thereupon he went to look at the remaining plot: nobody had ever seen finer wheat, he thought, and it was ripe. 'Disgrace upon me!' said he, 'if I do not watch to-night: he who stole the other will come to steal this, and I shall know what it is.'

He returned later in the evening to watch the corn, and just as it was midnight he heard the loudest thunder in the world. He turned to look, and beheld coming a host of mice that nobody could number; he had hardly time to bethink himself, ere each mouse made for a stalk of the wheat, and climbed it so that

---

[1] The Welsh word, *R. B. Mab.* p. 52, is an unusual one, *ryuorya6*, but it is clearly of the same origin as the Irish *rómhair*, 'to dig,' Scotch Gaelic, *ruamhar*, 'to delve,' Manx, *reuyrey*, the same.

it bent to the ground; then each mouse cut off the
ear and ran away with it. They all did so, leaving
the straw bare, and it seemed to him that there was
not a single straw for which there was not a mouse.
Angrily he struck among them, but he could no more
fix his sight on any of them than on flies or birds in
the air, excepting one of them, which seemed so heavy
as not to be able to travel. That one he pursued and
caught; he then put it in his glove, and secured it by
tying the opening of the glove with a string. Having
taken it home he aroused Kigva's curiosity, and explained to her what had happened, and how he would
on the morrow hang the thief he had captured. She
tried to persuade him not to meddle with the vermin
but to let it go, as it scarcely became a man of his
dignity. But he insisted that he would hang it, as
he would also have done with the other mice if he
had caught them.

So the next morning he took the mouse to the
top of the Mound of Arberth, on the highest part
of which he planted two wooden forks in the ground
and set up the gallows on which he was going to
hang the mouse. In the meantime he beheld a
clerk coming to him in old threadbare clothes—
it was seven years since he had seen a human
being there, except his friends who had been lost,
and Kigva who still remained. The clerk bade him
'good day,' and on being asked whence he had come,
he said that he was going home to his country from
England, where he had been singing. 'My lord,' said
the clerk, 'what art thou doing?' 'Hanging a thief,'
said Manawyđan, 'that I found stealing from me.'
'What sort of a thief?' said he, 'it is a vermin like
a mouse that I see in thy hand, and it ill befits a man

of thy estate to touch that kind of vermin: let it go.'
' By my faith, I will not,' replied the other: 'stealing
from me I found it, and to the penalty of a thief I
shall subject it, namely, hanging.' 'Here is a pound
I have got by begging, I will give it thee if thou wilt
let go that vermin.' 'By my faith, I will neither let
it go nor sell it,' said Manawyđan. 'Do as it listeth
thee,' said the clerk; 'were it not to prevent a man
of thy estate handling that vermin I should not care.'
Having so spoken he walked away, and as Manawyđan
was placing the cross stick on the forks, behold a priest
came to him well-mounted on horseback. A similar
conversation takes place with him, and he offers more
money, namely, three pounds, but takes his leave
rebuffed.

Now Manawyđan makes a noose round the mouse's
neck, and as he is doing that he beholds a bishop's
rutter[1], his pack-horses, and his retinue, with the
bishop himself coming to him. The conversation
begins much as in the previous cases: the bishop
offers Manawyđan successively seven and twenty-four
pounds, and all his horses and property he had with
him there; but Manawyđan was inflexible. So the

---

[1] The Welsh word is *rótter*, which we have not met with elsewhere : it is
clearly the English *rutter*, and what that means may be approximately
learned from lines 120-5 of Marlowe's *Doctor Faustus*, for the reference to
which the author has to thank Mr. Mayhew :—

> 'As Indian Moors obey their Spanish lords,
> So shall the spirits of every element
> Be always serviceable to us three;
> Like lions shall they guard us when we please;
> Like Almain rutters with their horsemen's staves,
> Or Lapland giants, trotting by our sides.'

The editors of Marlowe explain *Almain rutters* to mean German troopers;
see also Haliwell's Dic. But Lady Charlotte Guest or her authority slurs, as
usual, over the difficulty in the Mabinogi and renders *rótter* by 'retinue,' as
if the word were quite a familiar one in Welsh: see Guest's *Mab.* iii. 180.

U

bishop at last told him to name any price he chose.
'That I will,' said Manawyđan: 'the price is the
liberation of Rhiannon and Pryderi.' 'Thou shalt
have it,' said the bishop. 'Not that alone, by my faith,'
said Manawyđan. 'What then wilt thou?' 'The
removal of the Enchantment and glamour off the seven
cantrevs of Dyved.' 'Thou shalt have it, if thou wilt
only let go the mouse.' 'I will not,' said Manawyđan;
'for I must know who the mouse is.' 'She is my wife,
for otherwise I would not ransom her.' 'How came
she to me?' 'To steal from thee,' said the bishop. 'I am
Ꞔwyd son of Kil-coed, and it is I that put the Enchantment on the seven cantrevs of Dyved: it was to avenge
Gwawl son of Clûd, by reason of my friendship with
him, that I put on the Enchantment; and on Pryderi
have I avenged the baiting of Gwawl as "a brock in
a bag," which was done to him by PwyꟄ Head of
Hades, through evil counsel, at the Court of Heveyđ
Hên[1]. When it was known that thou wert inhabiting
the country, my household came to me requesting me
to transform them into mice to consume thy corn. The
first night my household came alone, and so they did
the second night, destroying the first and the second
plot of corn. The third night came my wife together
with the ladies of the court, asking me to transform
them, which I did. She was with child, otherwise thou
wouldst not have overtaken her. I will yield thee
Pryderi and Rhiannon, and also remove the Enchantment and glamour from off Dyved. I have told thee
moreover who it is, so let her now go.' 'No, by
my faith,' said Manawyđan. 'What wilt thou then?'
said Ꞔwyd. 'I will,' said Manawyđan, 'that there
be never more enchantment on the seven cantrevs of

[1] See *R. B. Mab.* pp. 12–16; Guest, iii. 52–8.

Dyved, and that it be never put on it.' 'Thou shalt
have that granted, only let her go.' 'No, by my faith.'
'What more then, wilt thou?' said the bishop. 'This
is what I will have, that there be no vengeance taken
on Pryderi and Rhiannon, or on me for ever.' 'All
that shalt thou have,' said ILwyd, 'and well, by my
faith, hast thou bethought thee, for the whole trouble
would have come upon thee.' 'Verily,' said Manawydan, 'that is why I have been exact in my words.'
'Release me my wife now,' said ILwyd. 'No, by my
faith, I will not till I see Pryderi and Rhiannon free
before my eyes.' 'Here they are coming,' said ILwyd,
and when Manawydan had warmly welcomed them
he let go the mouse, which ILwyd, striking with his
magic wand, turned into her proper shape, namely,
that of the fairest young woman any one had ever seen.
'Look around thee at the country,' said ILwyd, 'and
thou wilt find the dwellings and habitations as they
were at their best;' and this proved to be true.

Such was the Welsh story of the Enchantments of
Britain, as the romancers are wont to call them, a story
so well known to the Welsh bards of the 14th century in its connection with Dyved, that D. ab Gwilym
repeatedly calls the south-west of Wales the Land of
Illusion and the Realm of Glamour[1]. It has been
deemed necessary to give the latter part of the contest
between Manawydan and ILwyd at so great a length,
for the sake of showing the importance attached to the
exact terms used by the former in order to obtain the
permanent removal of the Enchantments, under which
the tale represents the country as labouring. Now,
some versions of the Grail legend make the undoing[2] of

---

[1] See poems CCXXVIII and CCXXXII; also poem XLVII.
[2] It is otherwise termed 'ending the wonders of Great Britain' (Nutt,

the Enchantments of Britain, and the healing of the
invalid king, depend on certain questions being asked
by a knight from Arthur's court.   It is not to be denied
that the idea of uttering a given word, with magical
effect, is fairly widespread ; but in that case one would
perhaps rather expect a single word, or a brief command like 'Open Sesame!' in the story of *Ali Baba
and the Forty Thieves*.   In the case before us it is not
so, the effective words being certain questions as to the
use of the Holy Grail, the Bleeding Lance, and the
other wondrous things carried past the visitor at the
Maimed King's court.   On the whole, we cannot help
thinking that a version of the contest between Manawyđan and ILwyd served, in the first instance, to give
the cue to the Grail romancers.   This explanation
has in its favour the fact that in the Welsh story the
words are not, in any sense, a formula to remove the
Enchantment, used as they are in the ordinary way as
the terms of a bargain, which binds the author of the
Enchantment to remove it himself.

Let us return to ILwyd and follow him a little further,
and first as to his name, which means grey, probably in
reference to his hair and the venerable appearance of
his person, as indicated in the story by its clothing him
in the garb of a bishop.   But besides *ILwyt*, son of
Kil coet, his name takes the form of *ILwydeu* son of
Kel coet, and under that name the story of Kulhwch
and Olwen places his house at Porth Kerdin, the Dyved
harbour in which Arthur lands on his return with
Diwrnach's Cauldron from Ireland [1].   Now there was

p. 39), 'achieving the great adventures of the Kingdom of Logres,' or
'casting out the evil adventures of the Island of Britain' (ib. p. 50), and
'freeing us from the evil destinies and adventures that were in this island'
(*Seint Greal*, pp. 7, 441).

[1] *R. B. Mab.* pp. 110, 136.

in the Land of the Cornish Brythons a Dinn map
Liathâin according to Cormac's Glossary[1], which explains the name to mean the Fortress of the Son of
Liathân; and Nennius[2] gives the name of Sons of
Liethan to the Irish conquerors of Dyved. This
Liathân or Liethan would imply a Welsh *Llwydan*,
which in that case might be regarded as a third form
to be added to those of Llwyd and Llwydeu. The Sons
of Liathan probably belonged to the powerful tribe that
called itself Hy-Liathâin, or the Descendants of Liathân,
and owned a part of the present county of Cork, namely,
a district which included the Great Island and *Caslean
Ui-Liathâin*, 'O'Liathain's Little Castle,' a village whose
name has been Anglicized into Castle-Lyons[3]. But
whether any Liathân can be identified with Llwyd son of
Kil-coed, the latter's name undoubtedly appears in Irish
literature in the form of Liath mac Celtchair of Cualand.
There was a district of Cualand within what is now the
county of Wicklow, and Liath is represented as one of
the comeliest princes of his race. He is said to have
been in love with Bri, daughter of Mider, the fairy king
already mentioned more than once, and the story about
the lovers relates how Mider prevented their meeting,
and how Bri died broken-hearted on that account[4]. On
the whole it seems probable, that the name Llwyd son
of Kil-coed, for the personage opposed to Manawyđan,
comes from the Irish conquerors of Dyved, and that, in
the forms known to us, it is the result of an attempt to

---

[1] See the Stokes-O'Donovan edition, p. 111.

[2] San-Marte's *Nennius et Gildas*, § 14 (p. 36).

[3] See O'Donovan's ed. of the *Four Masters*, A.M. 2859 (note *e*, p. 11),
and A.D. 1579 (note *c*, pp. 1722-3), where the editor states that the tribe
took its name from a certain Echaid Liathanach, son of Daire Cearba.

[4] See the Autotype Facsimile of the *Bk. of Ballymote*, 408[b], 409[a]; O'Curry,
iii. 355-6.

render into Welsh the Irish name *Liath mac Celtchair.*
But how much of the Welsh story is to be traced to the
same Goidelic source, it is, perhaps, impossible to say.

But who was ℓLwyd in the mythological sense? To
answer this we have first to ask who Gwawl son of
Clûd was, on whose behalf he exerted himself. Now,
the latter's name would mark him out as a counterpart
of Balyn; for Gwawl means light, like that of ℓLeu
ℓLawgyffes; and *Clut* or Clûd is the Welsh form of the
name written by the ancients Clota, for the river now
known as the Clyde: so it probably meant a goddess with
whom that river was associated. Thus in the description Gwawl son of Clûd, we have a sort of parallel to
that of Mabon son of Modron. This last is the Welsh
form of a name which in its ancient form was probably
matrona, and the designation of the river called by that
name in its abbreviated French form is *Marne,* while
Mabon is found inscriptionally described as Apollo
Maponus. One thing in the story of Gwawl's contest
with Pwyℓℓ for the hand of Rhiannon is worth noticing:
the former is overcome by being deluded into puting
his feet in a beggar's bag, into which he instantaneously
disappears. This incident, while betraying the nature-
myth account of the sun setting, reminds one in some
degree of Helius, according to one Greek account,
descending into his cup. From the story of Balyn, one
would have expected Gwawl to be his own avenger.
What we, however, have is a more powerful friend acting
for him, but probably one of kindred attributes with himself, as it were a Zeus aiding Heracles. The hypothesis
of ℓLwyd being a sort of reflection of the Zeus of the
ancient Celts, would harmonize well enough with the
rôle assigned to the former in the story, where he is
a great magician, a wielder of thunder, the friend of

the Solar Hero, and the enemy of the dark beings, among whom Manawyđan may be classed, in so far as he is befriended by Pryderi as a sort of Cronus or Saturn hospitably received by Janus. There is this important difference, however, namely, that the Mabinogi closes with the victory of the dark divinity ; and that is a part of the larger question of the entire sequence of the Welsh story. Thus Gwawl first defeats Pwyłł in the competition for Rhiannon's hand, while Pwyłł wins in the next scene, and the third begins with Łwyd vic-toriously avenging Gwawl on Pryderi, while the closing scene shows Łwyd baffled by Manawyđan, who is enabled to release his friend Pryderi, and otherwise undo what Łwyd had done. This sequence carries with it the reversal of the true meaning of the action of the respective parties in the struggle. For the appear-ance of Pryderi's realm as a wilderness and a desolation is its truer aspect, with its hideousness exposed in the light of Łwyd's triumphing countenance. The re-moval of the Enchantment, so as to make the landscape seem to teem again with life and abundance, is more truly to put the Enchantment on it. It is, in a word, to bring on the glamour and illusion which are essential to the magnificence in which the king of the Other World reigns.

A word now as to the names Pelles and Pellean, which, as we think, represent, however inaccurately, the Welsh names Pwyłł and Pryderi respectively. Now the former, Pelles, looks at first sight as though its con-nection with Pwyłł required no explanation, but as a matter of fact it is not easy, palæographically speak-ing, to show how it can have been derived from the Welsh name, as one would have expected not Pelles but Pools, Poils, or Poels. Perhaps the most natural view to take is, that it has been assimilated in form to the nominative Pelleans of the other name associated with it. This latter admits of being derived by easy steps of misreading and miscopying from the Welsh Pryderi, which would have also been spelled Prederi in the 12th century, but Pryteri and Preteri were likewise admissible. A trace of the last-mentioned form is to be detected possibly in the greeting sent by Galahad to his grandfather and to his uncle or grand-uncle. According to Malory[1], it ran thus: 'Recommaunde me vnto my graunt sir kynge Pelles and vnto my lord Petchere.' In one version of the *Queste du St. Graal* he calls them his grandfather King Pelles, and his uncle the Rich Fisher[2]; just as if some such a name as Petchere had been taken to be the French *peschéour* or fisher. However there is no evident reason why Malory should have failed to recognize the French for fisher any more in this context than elsewhere. In the same *Queste*, the sister of Peredur (Perceval) is made to tell him, that they are the offspring of King Pellehem[3]; but as Pellehem can hardly be anything but one of the forms of the name of Perceval's uncle, better known as Pellean and Pellehan[4],

---

[1] Malory, xiii. 4.

[2] Nutt, pp. 39, 83. [3] Ib. p. 47.

[4] Of the different spellings of the Welsh names let us take first Preteri: written ꝥteri, it would be liable to be read *peteri* or *petere*, the accented vowel of which might be made by the romancers into *ee* and even *ehe*, yielding *petehere*, whence Malory's Petchere by misreading an *e* into *c*. If we next take Prederi, this would be written either ꝥderi or ꝥderi, where the *ri* would be liable (see note 1, p. 284) to be read *ni*, *in* or *m*, as in Pellohin and Pellehem; but the change of *d* into *l* remains unexplained unless we suppose Pederi misread Pecleri, and the *c* then elided. The difficulty of deciding between an upright *d* and *cl* is well known: witness *amdet ar wŷdun* in Skene's *Four Anc. Books*, ii. 19, for *am clet ar wŷ clun* (see Evans' Autotype of the *Black Book*, 25a). There is another, and perhaps a more satisfactory hypothesis, namely, that ꝥderi was read ꝥcleri, which was subsequently made into *peleri* by confusing *c* and *e*, which is very

the name Pellehem in this connection is probably an error for Pellinore. For that is the name more usually given to Perceval's father, who was the king engaged in the pursuit of the Questing Beast, followed after his death by his next of kin, Palomydes the Saracen (p. 154). But the name Pellinore or Pellinor can scarcely be identified with Pellean or Pellehem: rather does it point to the Welsh name of the father of Peredur and Gwrgi, namely, Eliver Gosgorðvawr, or E. of the great Retinue (p. 71), after whom were called the Sons of Eliver, as a recognized description of a group of warriors, the most frequently mentioned of whom were Peredur and Gwrgi. They were, however, seven in all, as we learn from the first poem in the *Black Book of Carmarthen*[1], where their praises are

difficult to avoid in some manuscripts, for instance, the *Red Book*. But whatever the exact steps may have been which gave the first part of the name its form of *pel* or *pell*, no great difficulty attaches to the latter part : thus ɲi making for example *in*, would help us to a form Pelein, which comes near Pelloin, and this last with an inserted *h* gives us Pellohin, one of the forms attested. Lastly, certain vowels in proper names in the romances are doubled, probably to indicate length or stress. Thus Malory's Balyn is found not only as Balain, but also as Balaain, representing an ancient Celtic Belīnos; and Brân, Balyn's brother, is called Balan and Balaan, to the influence of which possibly the *ae* of Balaain is partly due. Take also Ἰωνᾶς, which became not only Jonas and Jonans, but also Jonaans. The same thing seems to have been done with the accented vowel of Prederi, though it has never been long in Welsh, thus Peleri became Peleeri, whence Peleem, to which may be traced Pelleam; and this last approaches both Pellean and Malory's Pellam. With *h* inserted, Pelleem becomes Pellehem, with which must be connected Pellehan. Where the Peleur of the *S. Greal* branches off is not clear; but its single *l* is worthy of note as accounting by association for the single *l* of Peles in the same manuscript, where the name should otherwise have had *ll*. With regard to the insertion of *h* in Pellohin, Pellehem, Pellehan, and Petehere, a good instance occurs in Malory's *Kehydius*, a knight, whose name is simply the old Welsh *Keidiau*: as to the fashion of inserting *h* between vowels in old Welsh (and in Breton), see Rhŷs' *Lec. on Welsh Philology*, p. 232.

[1] Evans' Autotype, p. 3 a, where Eliver is written Eliffer, but in that MS. *ff* is not necessarily different in value from *f* = *v*. The same is the spelling in the Triad ii. 11, in the *Red Book* (see *R. B. Mab.* p. 301); but *Effra6c* for *Evra6c* in the *Red Book* (ib. p. 193) is not quite parallel.

comprehensively sung. To return to Eliver, his name
when written Eliuer was easily misread into Eliner,
which comes near Elinor or Ellinore. Nothing, in fact,
is wanting, but an initial *p*, in order to spell Pellinore,
and that consonant one would probably be right in
regarding as supplied by the association of Pellinore's
name with that of Palomydes, his next of kin. Malory
gives the latter name usually as Palamydes and
Palomydes, which is, palæographically speaking, clearly
derived from the Welsh name Pabo Prydein, or Pabo
of Pictland, for the fuller designation Pabo Post
Prydein or Pabo Pillar of Pictland. Pabo is represented to have been brother to Eliver[1], and the
name occurs in Wales in connection with Ilanbabo
or Pabo's Church, a chapel in Anglesey. The tradition is that Pabo was a king who became a saint, and
this answers to Malory's story, that Palomydes was
a Saracen who was converted to Christianity. One day
after fighting with a knight called Galleron of Galway,
Palomydes encountered his rival Tristram, and fought
also with him; but being worsted in the conflict,
Palomydes made friends with Tristram, and went without delay with him and Galleron to Carlisle, where
he was christened[2]. Most probably the Welsh tradition
mixes myth and history together; but one's opinion of

---

[1] This is according to the Genealogies of the Men of the North in a
Hengwrt MS., which Skene believed to have been transcribed about 1300
(*Four Anc. Books*, i. 166-9); but the Genealogies in the Harleian MS. 3859,
are somewhat different (see Phillimore's edition of them in the *Cymmrodor*,
ix. 169-182). According to the latter, *Pabo Post Prydein* is there written
Pappo ꝥ priten; but on the whole the spelling which seems to have served
as the basis of *Palomides* was pabo priden. For *bo*, written conjointly,
as for instance in *Llyvyr yr Agkyr* would be very readily mistaken for *lo*;
and p2 blurred or smudged would appear to give the elements of an *m*. Add
the *s* of the French nominative and we have Palomidēs which comes
sufficiently near *Palomydes*, one of the forms which prevail in Malory's pages.

[2] Malory, xii. 12-14.

the amount of history involved is not raised by the fact, that in the reign of Charles II a stone bearing the inscription, HIC JACET PABO POST PRUD CORPORS . . . . , was dug up at Ilanbabo. It is believed to date from Edward the Third's reign, though the saint commemorated is said to have lived in the 6th century [1].

It is almost needless to remark, that the treatment of Welsh proper names by the Anglo-Norman romancers was a very loose one, subject to nothing of the nature of an etymological law so much as to the accidents of the handwriting in which such names appeared, or through which they eventually passed.

[1] See Rees' *Welsh Saints*, p. 168; Westwood's *Lapidarium Walliæ*, p. 193, and the *Arch. Cambrensis* for 1861, p. 300, and for 1874, p. 110.

CHAPTER XIII.

The Origin of the Holy Grail.

Now that we have practically discovered the form taken by the Dolorous Blow in the story of Pryderi, we have to produce from the same the counterpart of the Holy Grail. The romances are not very clear in whose keeping the Grail was, for some of them place it in that of Peles (Pelles), and some in that of Peleur (Pellean); so we should probably not greatly err in supposing it associated with both, a view which is easy to admit on Welsh ground, where Pwyll and Pryderi are always treated as standing in the relation of father and son to one another. But had Pwyll and Pryderi anything that might be set over against the Grail? Most assuredly they had, as witness the Taliessin poem which describes Arthur harrying Hades. The principal treasure, which he and his men carried away thence, was the Cauldron of the Head of Hades, that is to say, of Pwyll. In that poem, xxx, Pwyll and Pryderi are associated together, and the cauldron is found at a place called Caer Pedryvan, the Four-horned or Four-cornered Castle, in Ynys Pybyrdor or the Isle of the Active Door, the dwellers of which are represented quaffing sparkling wine in a clime that blends the grey twilight of the evening with the jet-black darkness of night; so lamps burn in the front of the gates of Uffern or Hell. Besides the names Caer Pedryvan and Uffern, it has these others : Caer Veðwit, meaning probably the Castle of Revelry, in reference to the wine-drinking there; Caer Golud, or the Castle of Riches; Caer Ochren (p. 245), Caer Rigor, and Caer Vanðwy [1], all three of unknown interpretation; and, lastly, Caer Sidi, which is interesting as occurring in another Taliessin poem of similarly mythological import. The bard in this latter poem, xiv, represents himself singing before princes over their mead-cups, and the verses in point run thus :—

> 'Ys kyweir vyg kadeir ygkaer sidi.
> Nys plawd heint a heneint a uo yndi.
> Ys gwyr manawyt[an] a phryderi.
> Teir oryan y am tan agan recdi.
> Ac am y banneu ffrydyeu gweilgi.
> Ar ffynnhawn ffrwythlawn yssyd oduchti.
> Ys whegach nor gwin gwyn yllyn yndi.'

> *Perfect is my chair* [2] *in Caer Sidi :*
> *Plague and age hurt him not who's in it—*
> *They know, Manawyðan and Pryderi.*
> *Three organs round a fire sing before it,*
> *And about its points are ocean's streams*
> *And the abundant well above it—*
> *Sweeter than white wine the drink in it.*

We do not pretend to understand this description, though the words used present no serious difficulty; but it is to be noticed that the name Sidi refers to the castle as a revolving one : compare the Welsh word *sidytt*, 'a spinning wheel.' This leads one to compare the words in the Taliessin poem with the account in

---

[1] Also mentioned in poem xxxiii of the *Black Book* : see Evans' Autotype, p. 50 a.

[2] There is, so far as we know, no warrant for treating cadeir, 'a chair,' as a seat in the sense of an abode or mansion.

the Welsh *Seint Greal*[1] of a revolving castle, which
Peredur entered. The passage runs thus : ' And they
rode through the wild forests, and from one forest to
another until they arrived on clear ground outside the
forest.   And then they beheld a castle coming within
their view on level ground in the middle of a meadow ;
and around the castle flowed a large river, and inside
the castle they beheld large spacious halls with windows
large and fair. They drew nearer towards the castle,
and they perceived the castle turning with greater
speed than the fastest wind they had ever known.
And above on the castle they saw archers shooting so
vigorously, that no armour would protect against one
of the discharges they made. Besides this, there were
men there blowing in horns so vigorously, that one
might think one felt the ground tremble. At the gates
were lions, in iron chains, roaring and howling so
violently that one might fancy the forest and the
castle uprooted by them.' We are not told that
either the warriors or the trumpeters were figures in
metal, but we have here the music, which, in the poem,
is produced by the three organs. We find nothing,
however, to throw any light on the sweet fountain of
Caer Sidi.

One would probably not greatly err in regarding the Turning Castle as a form of the abode of the
king of the dead, and the swiftness of its revolution
would explain such a name as that of the Isle of the
Active or strenuous Door. The large river flowing
round it reminds one of the castle of Peleur, entered
by Gwalchmei ; and the sequel of the story of the
Turning Castle, showing, among other things, how the
lions and the warriors offered no obstruction to Peredur

---

[1] See Williams, pp. 325, 6 ; and for his translation see p. 649.

when he galloped up to the gate, also recalls the behaviour of the lion and the metal men in the case
of Gwalchmei's entry to the other castle (p. 276). It
remains to mention a remarkable circumstance in connection with Peredur's entrance into the Turning
Castle, namely, that he was led by a lady, who took
from him his spear and his shield to carry them
before him. In other words, the warrior is protected
by a woman, as when, in a well-known Irish story, Liban,
leading Loeg, Cúchulainn's charioteer, to the other world,
and arriving at a perilous point in the journey, took
him by the shoulder. Loeg objected, reminding her
that this was not what he had been most used to do,
namely, to accept protection from a woman ; thereupon
she assured him, that, if he was to return alive, it must be
so [1]. It has already been pointed out, that we have
a blurred version of the same sort of thing in Rhiannon
carrying the visitors to Pwyll's court on her back from
the horseblock to the hall ; and a line hitherto unexplained, in the beginning of the same Taliessin poem
xxx, seems to refer to this goddess with free access to
both worlds. The bard, before describing Arthur's
expedition to Caer Sidi or Caer Pedryvan, observes
that before him nobody had been there, that is, nobody
who returned, excepting one whom he calls Gweir.
He would seem to have entered with the aid of Rhiannon, strangely called in this story the 'apostle' or
messenger of Pwyll and Pryderi; and he only returned
after a terrible imprisonment there, an initiation which
made him for ever a bard. In the other poem mentioned we have, instead of Pwyll and Pryderi as here,
Manawyđan and Pryderi as in the Mabinogi bearing
the former's name.

[1] *Hib. Lec.* p. 641; see also Windisch's *Irische Texte*, pp. 210, 219.

The same poem, in the lines already cited, speaks likewise of the sea surrounding the points or corners of Caer Sidi. The word used is *banneu* the plural of *ban*, the Welsh equivalent of the Goidelic *benn*, ' a horn, peak, or gable,' so wellknown as the word used in naming mountains in Scotland; *ban*, and especially *banneu*, is so used also in Wales, as in the case of *Banneu Brycheiniog*, 'the Beacons of Brecknock,' where the word refers to the tops of those mountains; but it may mean more indefinitely the ends of anything, as in the phrase *pedwar ban y byd*, ' the four ends or corners of the world.' We have it also in the name *Caer Pedryvan*, or the castle of the fourfold *ban*. What this may have ex- actly meant is not clear, as it might mean simply square, in reference to its having four corners or angles. Most probably it meant more, and it is worth while mentioning that the Irish story of Maildun's Boat speaks of an ' Isle of the Four Precious Walls.' These latter met in its centre and consisted respectively of gold, silver, copper, and crystal, the four parts into which they divided the island being allotted severally to kings and queens, youths and maidens [1]. The adjective from *ban* was *bannawc* [2], in modern Welsh *bannog*, ' having points, peaks, or horns;' and the Kulhwch story refers to a mountain in the north called Bannawc. Bannawc was also probably the name which became the Benwyk of Malory's *Morte Darthur*, the Benoic of the Huth *Merlin*, as the name of the country of King Ban. The same adjective qualifying *caer* would in old Welsh yield Caer Bannauc, written later Caer Vannawc

---

[1] Joyce's *Old Celtic Romances*, p. 139.

[2] This, mutated, becomes *vannawc* (written also *fannawc*) as does *mannawc*, with which it is not to be confounded. The latter is derived from *man*, as in *man geni*, ' a birth-mark,' Latin *menda*, ' a fault or blemish.'

or Vannawg, and it is the former we probably have in the name given by the romancers as Carbonek. Malory calls the place both Carbonek and Corbyn, while in Manessier's continuation of Chrétien's *Conte du Graal* it even becomes Corbiere[1]; but the *Queste du Saint Graal*, edited by Dr. Furnivall for the Roxburghe Club, retains a form Corbenic, which is less estropié; and this is also the name given in the *Grand St. Graal*[2], where it is stated that Corbenic was situated in the Terre Foraine[3]. Now Carbonek was the name of the castle where Pelles lived and kept the Holy Grail, and Carbonek seems practically the same as Taliessin's Caer Pedryvan or the *Banneu* of Caer Sidi, with which we have found Pwyll Head of Hades associated, as well as his famous Cauldron.

With regard to that vessel, Taliessin, in poem xxx, mentions the following things respecting it. The Cauldron of the Head of Hades had a rim set with pearls adorning it; the fire beneath it was kindled by the breath of nine maidens; utterances might be heard issuing from it; and it would not boil food for a coward. The other poem does not mention the cauldron as being at Caer Sidi, but says that he who has his seat there has nought to fear from plague or old age. Compare with this what is said of the Grail in the romances, where Pelles and his brother figure. The Grail, when it comes, feeds those at the table with whatever kind of food each one desires[4]. But those who are not worthy are not allowed by it to remain or to approach too near with impunity[5]. Similarly those who worship at the Grail Chapel at King Peleur's remain young nor mark the lapse of time[6]. Add to this that the Grail heals

---

[1] Nutt, p. 22.   [2] Ib. pp. 43, 50.   [3] Ib. p. 63.   [4] Ib. pp. 20, 39.
[5] Ib. pp. 49, 50, 57.   [6] Williams' *Seint Greal*, pp. 201, 567.

X

the sick and wounded [1]. By means of accounts other
than those in which the Grail belongs to Pelles or
Peleur, the correspondence between it and the Cauldron of Pwyłł Head of Hades, might, perhaps, be more
strikingly shown ; but the foregoing is sufficiently near
for our purpose. Now, as the original identity of Pelles
and Peleur with Pwyłł and Pryderi has been shown to
be probable, as has also the identity of Carbonek, where
the Holy Grail was kept, with Caer Pedryvan, where
Pwyłł's Cauldron was found by Arthur and his men, the
conclusion is all but inevitable, that the famous Cauldron served as a prototype of the far more famous
Grail.

In the romances to which we have had to refer in
connection with Pelles and Peleur or Pellean, the owner
of the Grail is called the Lame or Maimed King ; but
there are others which style him the Fisher King or
the Rich Fisher. These latter appellations appear to
be derived from a different Welsh original, and they
subdivide themselves into two groups—those in which
the counterparts of Pelles and Pellean are called Gonemans or Goon and the Fisher respectively ; and those
in which they are represented as being a father and son,
called Bron and Alain. Let us begin with the latter,
and first with Bron, in whose name we have one of
the romancers' versions of the Welsh name Brân.

The banquet of seven years' duration around Brân's
Head at Harlech, and the festivities of eighty years on
the lonely isle of Gwales, are left undefined as to the
means or manner of providing for them : the presence
of the Venerable Head appears to have sufficed without
even a reference to a magic cauldron or any other
vessel of mysterious virtues. A remarkable cauldron,

---

[1] Malory, xii. 4; Nutt, p. 42.

however, does figure earlier in the story of Brân more than once, but it answers quite another purpose there, namely, to bring Brân's fallen foes back to life, which will be found matched, in Gerbert's Perceval, by the potion already mentioned as used by a hag working by the order of the King of the Waste City[1]. This incident of the quickening of the dead occurs elsewhere, especially in Irish literature, as for example in the story of a war between the Cruithni or Picts and the mythic Men of Fidga: under the direction and spells of a druid called Drostan, the resuscitation is brought about by means of a bath of new milk at a place called Ard Lemnachta, or Sweetmilk Hill, in Leinster[2]. It occurs also in the story of the battle of Moytura between the Fomori and the Tuatha Dé Danann, under the leadership of their king Nuadu and Lug the Long-handed[3]: in this instance the quickening of the dead warriors is brought about by dipping them at night in a well of marvellous virtues; and it is resorted to until those on the other side find out what is going on, whereupon they pile a cairn of stones over the well.

This, however, does not help us very much in the matter: so let us try the vessels which are made by Welsh story the objects of quests in the romancers' sense of the word. One of them has just been discussed, the Cauldron of the Head of Hades, and allusion has been made in the previous chapter to another which is treated so in the story of Kulhwch and Olwen, namely the Cauldron of Diwrnach the Goidel. For this Arthur and his men had to undertake

---

[1] See Nutt, p. 23, and p. 121 above.

[2] *Bk. of Leinster*, 196ᵃ: see also O'Curry's *MS. Materials*, p. 450.

[3] *Hib. Lec.* p. 587. The whole story is about to be published by Stokes in the *Rev. Celtique.*

a dangerous expedition to Erinn, as already mentioned. The Kulhwch story[1], however, mentions the perilous quests of other vessels of various virtues, though it closes without showing how they were all achieved. Among others may be cited the *cib* or bushel of Ilwyr son of Ilwyryon, which alone would be found capable of holding the mead to be brewed for Kulhwch and Olwen's wedding; the horn of Gwlgawt Gogodin, to supply the guests with drink at the feast; the *botheu* or bottles of Rhinnon Rhin Barnawt[2], in which no drink was ever known to turn sour; and the bottles of Gwidolwyn the Dwarf, which would keep the drink put in them in the east without losing its warmth till it arrived in the west. This mysterious reference calls to mind the story of Joseph of Arimathea collecting the blood of Christ in the Holy Grail and bringing it himself to the west, or else giving it to another to bring.

The latter was none other than Bron, in whom, as already hinted, we have the Brân of Welsh literature; and, according to some of the romances, Bron, with all his people, is ordered to go to the West; and punning references are not wanting to Glastonbury under the name of *Avalon*, as the land of sunset, *ou li soleil avaloit*[3]. Their passage over the sea to these parts was rather peculiar: a certain number of the company is said to have floated across on a shirt stripped from the back of Joseph son of Joseph of Arimathea, and the bearers of the Grail, with Bron at their head, were conducted on their way by the mystic

---

[1] *R. B. Mab.* pp. 121-3 ; Guest, ii. 282-6.

[2] Can this be an estropié form of *Rhiannon Rhian Varnawt*, or Rh. the sentenced Lady? See *R. B. Mab.* p. 19, Guest, iii. 62 ; but note that the Kulhwch story (*R. B. Mab.* p. 123) makes Rhinnon a male.

[3] Nutt, p. 78.

virtues of that holy vessel[1]. This voyage at once recalls that of Brân the Blessed to Erinn, when his troops went over in ships, whilst the king himself waded across, carrying the musicians of his court on his shoulders. Further, Brân, as the centre of a perpetual banquet, has already been placed in juxtaposition with the Grail as means of feeding the faithful; and here we have the rarer attribute of conducting a following in the sea superadded to the other characteristics of both alike, and serving to establish the soundness of the comparison. We have in reality to go further: it is not a case of similarity so much as of identity. The voyage of Bron is but a Christian version of the voyage of Brân, and one cannot be surprised to find one of the romances of the Quest of the Holy Grail stating that the vessel was in the keeping of Bron, represented as dwelling 'in these isles of Ireland[2].' This description, which may be regarded without any violence as including not only Erinn, but also Gwales and the other isles from Lundy and the Scillies to Bardsey and Man; not to mention the mythic meadows to which allusion has been made as moored in the same seas.

The story of Brân, however, as we have it, shows no vessel to set over against the Grail of Bron and his son Alain: what sort of vessel it should have been may be

---

[1] Nutt, pp. 53, 60, 79.

[2] See Nutt, p. 28, where he gives an abstract of the *Petit Saint Graal*, also termed by him the Didot-Perceval. The *Saint Greal* has made of Bron and Brân the curious conglomerate *Brwns Brandalis*, who has a brother, *Brendalis* of Wales (pp. 173, 548), both uncles to Peredur on his father's side. Now Brwns is nothing but the French nominative *Brons*, from *Bron*, and *Brandalis* of *Wales* suggests that the more correct form was Bran Galis, or Brân of Wales, if indeed one should not rather say Bran of Gwales in reference to the Isle of the Banquet. Brandalis appears in Malory's narrative as Brandyles, but he gives him no very distinctive attributes.

gathered from the properties of Bron's Grail[1]. Take
the following instances: on one occasion ten or a dozen
loaves, placed on the table on which stood the Grail,
were found to suffice for more than five hundred
hungry people. Another time, when the multitude
clamoured that they and their children were dying of
hunger, Bron was to go into the water and catch a fish,
and the first he caught was to be set on the table; then
the Grail also was to be set on the table and covered
with a towel while the fish was placed opposite to it.
This was duly done, and the people were bidden to seat
themselves; and those of them who were not defiled
with sin were filled with sweetness and the desire of
their heart[2]. Here putting the fish near the Grail
would seem to indicate, that what was originally conceived as done was putting the fish simply in the vessel
to cook; but such a commonplace treatment would not
do, once the vessel had come to be reckoned holy.
That the Grail would not feed those 'polluted with
sin' looks like a spiritualized version of such a property
as that of which the Cauldron of the Head of Hades
gave proofs in declining to cook for the craven or
coward. In the version extant of the Brân story no
such a vessel is mentioned, and we are left to suppose
that the food and drink came before the banqueters
around the Venerable Head without the intervention
of any visible service, after the manner of feasts in
Welsh fairy tales and, for that matter, in Irish ones too,
where the usual order is continuous feasting without
attendance[3].

---

[1] See the *Queste du St. Graal*, summarized by Nutt, p. 43; also the *Grand
St. Graal*, p. 60.

[2] See Robert de Borron's poem, summarized by Nutt, p. 64[b]; and compare his summary of the *Grand St. Graal*, p. 62.

[3] The Irish phrase for 'without attendance' was *cen rithgnom*: see

The case is not represented as otherwise with the Grail, for when that vessel goes round feeding those deemed worthy, 'none may see who carries it[1].' Just as we hear nothing about attendance in the Brân story, so neither do we hear of vessels. Another version may very possibly have alluded to one or more; for how were Brân's friends supposed to carry his head about with them? Certainly not on a pole, as that of a foe. Most likely it was on a dish; nay, it is not improbable that Brân's head on a dish, and the poisoned spear with which he had been wounded, formed the originals which suggested the Head brought in on a dish and the Bleeding Spear at the court of Peredur's second uncle, as mentioned in a previous chapter. The former, in fact, holds in that story the place occupied by the Grail in most of the versions of Perceval's visit to that court. Enough in any case has been said to show that the origin of Bron's Grail is to be sought in a Welsh story about Brân the Blessed, though no such is extant in the precise form which that of the Grail would seem to postulate.

There remains to be mentioned more particularly another quest in the Kulhwch story, and this brings us at length to Gonemans and Goon: Yspyďaden, chief of giants, lays it down as one of the conditions on which Kulhwch is to wed his daughter Olwen, that his would-be son-in-law should procure for him the *Mwys* of Gwyďno Garan-hir, for the truculent father-in-law would not consent to eat out of any other vessel on the night of his daughter's wedding. So Kulhwch under-

---

Tochmarc Bec-fola, ed. by O'Looney in the *Irish MSS. Series* of the Royal Irish Academy, i. 180; also the story of Condla Ruad in Windisch's *Irische Grammatik*, p. 119, where he prints *can rithgnom*. Compare Rhŷs' Welsh Fairy Tales in the *Cymmrodor*, v. 82, vi. 195.

[1] Nutt, p. 39.

takes to procure it in due course, though the story makes
no allusion later to the achievement of this quest. It
does, however, what is more important for our purpose;
it describes the *mwys* thus [1]: it was such a vessel that
though all the world should approach it, thrice nine
men at a time, they would find in it the food each liked
best. A later account of the *mwys* is to the effect, that
one man's food put into it would be found to be no less
than enough for a hundred, when the *mwys* came to be
opened. It was thought to have finally disappeared
with Merlin when he entered the Glass House in
Bardsey [2], as were also the other treasures of Britain:
the entire number was usually held to be thirteen [3].

This account of Gwyđno's *Mwys* is the most exact
which Welsh literature probably contains of the pagan
prototype of the Grail of Christian romance. In the
first place, its supposed disappearance into the isle of
Bardsey, off the westernmost point of North Wales,
recalls 'those isles of Erinn' where Bron was supposed to reside in charge of the Grail. In the next
place, it will be noticed that the *mwys* was not a vessel
for cooking food but for holding it, just as the Grail
was. The later Welsh account speaks of it as a vessel
to be opened, so that it might be regarded as some
kind of a basket, box, or cask; and this harmonizes with
the modern use of the word, which is explained by
Dr. Pughe to mean 'a kind of covered basket, pannier,
or hamper, also the quantity contained in such vessel:
mwys o ysgadain [sic], a mease or five-score of herrings.'
Similarly Dr. Davies explains it as a 'vas quoddam,

---

[1] *R. B. Mab.* p. 122.   [2] *Hib. Lec.* p. 155.

[3] They will be found enumerated in the *Brython* for 1860, pp. 372-3, and
in the *Greal* (London, 1805), p. 188; also in Lady Charlotte Guest's *Mabinogion*, ii. 354.

quoddam mensuræ genus,' adding that *mwys o ysgadan*
is five hundred herrings, in which he was more correct
than Dr. Pughe: he also gives *mwys bara* as meaning
panarium, that is to say a bread *mwys* or bread-basket.
In old Cornish the word was *muis* or *moys*, and
meant a table. In Old Irish it was *mias*, and it had
the meanings of table and of dish. So in modern
Irish the charger on which the Baptist's head is placed,
in Matt. xiv. 8, is called a *mias*, as also in the Scotch
Gaelic version, but not in Manx Gaelic, where, however, the word occurs as *meays*, meaning a mease or
five hundred fishes.

This meeting of the meanings of table, dish, basket,
and hamper, would seem to receive its explanation in the etymology of the words *mwys* and *mias*,
both of which are probably the Latin *mensa*, 'table,'
borrowed[1]. As the ancient Brythons, like the Irish
and presumably the Norsemen, had no tables in the
Roman sense of the word, the borrowed word not only
served to denote the borrowed idea of table, but it was
also partly applied to that of the native substitute for
a table, namely a dish or platter; and this would undoubtedly appear to have been the meaning of the
word *mwys* in Yspyđaden's demand that Kulhwch
should obtain the Mwys of Gwyđno, for him to eat out
of it at the wedding feast. In other words, *Mwys
Gwyđno* in the Kulhwch story meant neither more
nor less than Gwyđno's vessel. The only property

[1] If this prove incorrect, then one has to regard the Irish *mias*, 'table,'
and *mias*, 'dish,' as distinct words, and to treat them somewhat as indicated
by Ducange, who gives a *mēsa*, 'table,' from Spain chiefly, and another
mēsa or *meisa halecum*, which he explains to have meant a *doliolum*, or cask:
this latter was in Old French *meise* (*maise*) and *moise*. Note that the 'thrice
nine men' at the *Mwys* may be taken as if meant to be a multiple of the
Roman triclinium, the 'thrice' being introduced to render the exaggeration
required.

recorded of it was its power of multiplying a hundred-
fold, or even more, any food placed in it; and this
is in entire agreement with what is said of the
Fisher King's Grail in the *Conte du S. Graal*: Chrétien
speaks of it feeding the Fisher King's father and sustaining his life[1], while two of the other authors of that
poem represent the Grail serving the guests abundantly
with bread[2], and even with wine and all sorts of food[3].
One of the two, Gautier, goes further, and characterizes
the Grail in a way which recalls the spiritual properties
of Bron's Grail, for he states that the devil might not
lead any man astray on the same day he had seen the
Grail. The passage has, however, been suspected of not
being homogeneous with Gautier's other verses[4]; but
in any case it can throw no serious difficulty in the way
of our identifying, in point of origin, the anonymous
Fisher King's Grail with Gwyðno Garanhir's *Mwys*.

The question of the mutual influence of the various
versions of the Grail legend is a difficult and compli-
cate one; but we have an instance probably of the
influence of the French romances on the Welsh story
of Peredur, where it represents the first of his two
uncles as lame and also associates him with fishing[5],
for the two things seem to have belonged to different
versions of the story. It is owing also possibly to
a similar mixture of different versions, that both
Gonemans or Gwyn and Bron bear the same title of
fisher. At any rate, Welsh literature enables one to
see a reason for it only in the case of the former;
but let us first see how it has hitherto been treated.

---

[1] Nutt, p. 74, citing lines 7796-7800.
[2] Ib. p. 74, citing lines 20,114-6 (Gautier).
[3] Ib. p. 74, citing lines 171-4 (Pseudo-Gautier).
[4] Ib. pp. 17, 74-6: Gautier's lines in question are quoted as 28,778-81.
[5] *R. B. Mab.* p. 200; Guest, i. 309.

Some have supposed that the fishing incident in which
Bron plays the part already described (p. 310), is to
be taken as a sufficient explanation of the name. The
title of Rich Fisher is given in one of the romances both
to Bron and to his successors. We allude to the *Grand
St. Graal* representing Bron's youngest son, who had
been made keeper of the Grail, ordered to take the
net which was on the Grail table and to fish with
it. Alain, for that was his name, did so, and caught
one big fish ; but the people murmured that it would
not be enough. When, however, Alain had divided
the fish into three parts and prayed that it might suffice,
all the people were fed, including the sinners that
time [1]. So not only Bron, but also Alain acquired the
title of Rich Fisher, and it was inherited by the
Grail-keepers after him ; but it is added, that they
were more blessed than Alain, as they were all
crowned kings, whereas he never wore a crown [2].

Such are the explanations hitherto attempted, and it
is significant, that in the opinion of one of the most
recent students of the Grail legend, they are not
satisfactory ; for Mr. Nutt thinks it simpler to believe
that in the original Celtic tradition the surname of
Rich Fisher had a significance now lost [3]. This appeal
to Celtic tradition we gladly accept, believing as we
do, that its significance is even now not altogether
lost. Let us premise, that while the Fisher King's
name is not given, that of a person treated sometimes
as his brother is mentioned : Chrétien, in his *Conte
du Graal*, calls him Gonemans of Gelbort [4] ; Gerbert,

---

[1] Nutt, p. 62.   [2] Ib. p. 62, also p. 208.
[3] See Nutt, p. 123, who quotes with approval this view (ib. p. 126) from
E. Martin's work *Zur Gralsage, Untersuchungen* (Strasburg, 1880).
[4] Nutt, p. 11.

in his portion of the same poem, calls him Gornumant[1],
and Manessier, in his portion of it, calls him Goon
Desert[2], that is in other words, Goon of the Terre
Gastee or the Waste Land. These names stand unmistakably for the Welsh Gwynwas and Gwyn (p. 121),
which, as explained in another chapter, meant one
and the same personage; namely, that most usually
known to Welsh literature as Gwyn son of Nûd,
king of the fairies and the demons of the Other World.

Gwyn and Gwydno are not represented in Welsh
as brothers, as are Goon and the Fisher King by
Manessier; but one of the most remarkable poems
in the *Black Book of Carmarthen* consists of a dialogue
between them, in the course of which they become
great friends[3]. So far, then, we have not made
much progress towards the identification of Gwydno
with the anonymous Fisher; but let us come to the
fishing. In the first place it may be worth mentioning,
that Gwydno has the standing epithet or surname
of Garan-hir, which seems to have meant Long-crane[4]
or Tall-heron. This, to say the least of it, is the
reverse of incompatible with the idea of fishing. In
the next place Gwydno was famous as the owner,
not only of the *Mwys*, but also of a weir in which fish
to the value of a hundred pounds used to be caught
on the Eve of the First of May every year; and
connected with this is the well known story of finding
the baby-bard Taliessin there[5]. For in those days,

---

[1] Nutt, p. 23.　　　　　　　　[2] Ib. p. 20.

[3] See Evans' Autotype, pp. 49 a–50 b, also pp. 155, 6 above.

[4] *À propos* of this crane, one is inclined to ask what may be the origin of
the Crane in the *Seint Greal*, pp. 231, 587, that used to give the alarm to
a whole country. See also *Hib. Lec.* p. 334, where the three baleful *birdcz*
of Thornton's *Morte Arthure* should be corrected into *bridez* or damsels.

[5] *Hib. Lec.* p. 545.

we are told, Gwyđno had an only son Elphin, who was the wildest and neediest of the young men of his time. So his father, anxious about him and fearing that he had been born in an evil hour, permitted him to draw the weir one First of May, in order to see whether no luck would fall to his share. Elphin with his men went at the proper time to examine the weir, and the latter were about to leave in sad disappointment, persuaded that Elphin had interrupted the luck of his father's weir, when Elphin observed a leathern bag on one of the poles of the weir. It is needless to relate, how he found the bag to contain the baby Taliessin, who at once began to address Elphin in elaborate verse, and to inform him that he would be of greater value to him than the fish caught in the weir had ever been to Gwyđno.

Here then in this story, some of the essentials of which occur in a Taliessin poem[1], we have an adequate explanation of the fact, that the Grail owner was called the Fisher King or the Rich Fisher. It will, however, have been noticed that the two fishers in the Welsh story are Gwyđno and his son Elphin, while the Grail legend only associates with the anonymous Fisher his brother Goon, but no son. So here again one has probably to fall back on the mutual influence of the Grail romances, for in the version previously discussed, we had not two brothers, but a father and son, named Bron and Alain, to wit that Alain who was less blessed than the other heads of his family, inasmuch as he never wore a crown, as they are represented doing. In this Alain or Alein, surnamed *le Gros*, Malory's Hellyas le Grose[2],

---

[1] See poem vii, Skene, ii. 136–7; i. 532–3.

[2] Nutt, pp. 31, 45, 60-4, 64c, Malory, xv. 4, and Williams' *Seint Greal*, where Alain le Gros is called Julien ly Gros, pp. 277, 617.

we seem to have the representative of Gwyðno's son Elphin, who is described as less fortunate than the rest of his family, and as a sort of a luckless youth. Alain, however, is sometimes treated as the father of Perceval[1] (Peredur), and the name is probably a distorted form, not of *Elphin* but of *Eliver* (p. 298): perhaps one would not be far wrong in regarding Eliver and Elphin as confounded here with one another[2]. But we are not aware that Welsh literature mentions a son of Brân, called either Eliver or Elphin, any more than it gives Brân the surname of Fisher: so we are on the whole inclined to ascribe both to the influence of the romance in the form in which it reached Chrétien, Gerbert and Manessier, on that other form in which it was known to Robert de Borron and the author of the *Grand St. Graal.* This agrees with the fact of the probable priority of that of Chrétien and his continuators[3], while on the other side one has to admit that the latter make no allusion to Alain; but this is no decisive proof that he did not figure in some of the versions which they worked into the poem of the *Conte du Graal.*

In this chapter the various versions of the Holy Grail have been treated as falling readily into three groups, namely, those in which the Grail belongs respectively to Pelles, to Bron, and to the anonymous Fisher. The Welsh origin of the Grail of the first and the third groups has been pointed out, while in the second group the Grail has been traced to the quarter in which alone its origin is to be sought. So this

---

[1] Nutt, pp. 28, 30.

[2] The *Grand St. Graal* tries to distinguish two Alains: see Nutt, p. 62. The principal stages through which *Eliver* passed into *Alain* or *Alein* were probably Eliuer, Eliuen, Elaien, Elain or Elein.

[3] See Martin's views on this point, quoted with approval by Nutt, p. 122.

chapter might end at this point, were it not that we may here conveniently append a few more identifications of Grail names, which could not have been advantageously introduced at an earlier stage. They may have a bearing on the difficult question of the influence on one another of the Grail stories of the three groups just mentioned. In any case the reader may rest assured, that it only requires more patience, and more acquaintance with the French versions than the author possesses, to identify most of the Grail proper names in them.

Let us begin where we left off with Goon of the Desert or Gonemans of Gelbort, in whom we seem to have Gwyn ab Nûd. The following short and savage episode in the story of Kulhwch and Olwen[1] makes Gwyn king of the North, and subject to Arthur as his suzerain: 'A little previously Creiđylad daughter of Lûd the Silver-handed had gone with Gwythur son of Greidiawl, but before he had slept with her, Gwyn son of Nûd came and carried her away by force. Gwythur collected an army and fought with Gwyn; but Gwyn prevailed, and captured Greid, son of Eri, Glinneu eil Taran, Gwrgwst Ledlwm, and Dyvnarth his son. He captured also . . . . . son of Nethawc, Nwython, and Kyledr the Wild his son. He killed Nwython, took out his heart, and forced Kyledr to eat his father's heart, and it is therefore Kyledr became wild. Arthur heard of this, and came to the North and summoned Gwyn son of Nûd before him: he released his men from his prison and made peace between Gwyn son of Nûd and Gwythur son of Greidiawl. This was the peace that was made, that the damsel be left at her father's house, untouched by either side; that the two

[1] *R. B. Mab.* pp. 113, 134; Guest, ii. 269, 305.

suitors fight every First of May for ever thenceforth till
the Day of Doom; and he who then proves victorious—let him take the damsel.'

Leaving this mythological joke for a while, we turn
to a passage relative to Lancelot and his lineage in the
Queste du Saint Graal, which will serve among other
things as a specimen of the taste of some of the
romancers who undertook to christianize pagan
stories: Lancelot, after having a vision in which
he saw a man surrounded with stars, and accompanied by seven kings and two knights, 'comes to a
hermitage, confesses, tells his vision, and learns that it
has a great meaning in respect of his lineage, which
must be expounded at much length: forty-two years
after the Passion of Christ, Joseph of Arimathea left
Jerusalem, came to Sarras, helped Evelac, who received
baptism at the hands of Josephes, together with his
brother-in-law, Seraphe (who took the name Nasciens),
and who became a pillar of the holy faith, so that the
great secrets of the Holy Grail were opened to him,
which none but Joseph had beheld before, and no knight
after save in dream.   Now Evelac dreamed that out
of his nephew, son of Nasciens, came forth a great lake,
whence issued nine streams, eight of the same size, and
the last greater than all the rest put together; our Lord
came and washed in the lake which King Mordrains
[this is another name for Evelac] thus saw flowing
from Celidoine's belly. This Celidoine was the man
surrounded by stars in Lancelot's vision, and this because he knew the course of the stars and the manner
of the planets, and he was first King of Scotland,
and the nine streams were his nine descendants, of
whom seven [were] Kings and two knights:—first, Warpus; second, Chrestiens [another version gives the

preferable reading *Nasciens*]; third, Alain li Gros; fourth, Helyas; fifth, Jonaans, who went to Wales and there took to wife King Moroneus' daughter; sixth, Lancelot, who had the King of Ireland's daughter to wife; seventh, Bans. These were the seven Kings who appeared to Lancelot. The eighth stream was Lancelot himself, the elder of the knights of the vision. The ninth stream was Galahad, begot by Lancelot upon the Fisher King's daughter, lion-like in power, deepest of all the streams [1].'

In the *Grand St. Graal* the names of Nascien's descendants, as given by Mr. Nutt [2], are Celidoine, Marpus, Nasciens, Alains li Gros, Ysaies, Jonans, Lancelot, Bans, Lancelot and Galahad. Now Warpus or Marpus, as the name is here given, can hardly be regarded as anything else than a faulty reproduction of the name given as Gwrgwst in the Welsh story: it was the name also of the father of a powerful king of Fortrenn in the 8th century, Ungust, son of Wrgust or Uurgust, or as he is usually called Aengus son of Fergus, according to the Anglo-Gaelic forms of the names. In the next place *Nascien* appears, as given by Manessier, in the form *Natiien*, which is evidently the same name as Bæda's Naiton [3]; for so he calls the Pictish king driven from his throne by Aengus son of Fergus in the year 729. The same name is probably to be found in the Nwython of the Welsh story of Gwyn and Gwythur; further, the Celidoine of the *Grand St. Graal*, wrongly explained to mean Heaven-given, is to be set over against Kyledr, as a faulty reproduction of a Welsh name. Thus Natiien and his

---

[1] Nutt, p. 45, where he gives an abstract of the *Queste*, from Furnivall's text, pp. 38-52.   [2] Ib. p. 60.

[3] *Hist. Ecclesiastica*, v. 21, where Moberly prints also the form Naitan.

son Celidoine are Nwython and his son Kyledr, and
this is favoured by a sort of correspondence between
their story and that of their Welsh counterparts. For the
Grand St. Graal mentions Nascien and his son Celidoine thrown into prison by a hater of Christians, who
was called Kalafier. Nascien, however, is not killed like
Nwython by his foe, for he is miraculously rescued by
a hand which appears out of a cloud and strikes off his
fetters, while Celidoine is also released and borne
through the air by nine hands to the land of a King
Label, whose daughter he marries later in this confused
narrative [1], whereas Kalafier dies killed by fire from
heaven.

It is probable, with regard to Celidoine as the first
king of Scotland, that we have to regard the original
as Kelyđon who appears at the opening of the
story of Kulhwch as Kelyđon Wledig or Prince Kelyđon. This latter is doubtless to be treated as the
eponymus hero of Caledonia ; and the conclusion one is
forced to draw is, that the Grail name Celidoine covers
the two Welsh ones of Kelyđon and Kyledr [2]; if indeed
they be two, and the latter, which is obscure, be not
rather an error to be corrected into Kelyđon. Thus
it will be seen that all of them about which anything
can be predicated point to the North. But the *Grand
St. Graal* connects Bron in a sort of way with them,

---

[1] Here we apparently have Gwyn appearing under the name of Kalafier,
which is obscure, while King Label and his daughter may perhaps be ILûđ
and his daughter Creiđylad; for ILûđ's surname in its Welsh form of
ILaƂereint may be regarded as in part reflected by that of Label: the form
to be expected was Laberēz, or Laberenz, the earlier portion of which is
fairly represented by Label. The daughter's name does not appear, as the
French romancer probably found it untractable, though in other hands it
has yielded the well-known name of Cordelia.

[2] Kyledyr looks like a sort of compromise between *Kelydon* and *Kynedyr*
or *Kyuedyr*: see *R. B. Mab.* pp. 112, 124.

while the Welsh Brân is not usually associated with the North. This would seem to indicate that here Bron has been substituted for the anonymous Fisher, whom we have identified with Gwyđno. The name, however, of Gwyđno has already passed before us, but heavily disguised: the romancers give it at least two forms differing considerably from one another. The first to be mentioned, as the easier to recognize, is that of Nentre (nominative *Nentres*) king of Garlot. The kingdom of Gwyđno is in Welsh called the Hundred of the Bottom, for which the modern Welsh is Gwaelod, in older Welsh spelling Gwaelawt, which is the key to Malory's Garlot, Garlott, and Garloth. The oldest recorded spelling of Gwyđno's name occurs in the *Black Book of Carmarthen*, 49ᵇ, as *Guitnev*, which according to the usual spellings and misreadings might result in Nentres and Neutres [1].

The other disguise of Gwyđno's name is to be detected in the form of Mordrain, mentioned in a passage just quoted from the *Queste*, for it was a name of great importance in the Grail stories purporting to give the early history of the vessel. It is also Mordrain in the *Grand St. Graal*, but Manessier makes it Noodran [2], which comes considerably

---

[1] For Nentres see Malory, i. 2, 8, 12, 18, and xix. 11: it is Neutres in the Huth *Merlin*, i. 120. The Welsh pronunciation of Gwyđneu would, in the orthography of the Venedotian version of the Welsh Laws be represented by Guetneu, which, misread Gnetnen, might result in a nominative Netnēs or Nētnes, Nentnes; and by the phonetic change of *tn* into *tr* we should have Nentres. Compare Castrar for Casnar or Castnar: see p. 168 above, and Nutt, p. 9. Gwyđneu should, according to analogy, drop its final *u*, but it is not certain that this would occur early enough; but in case it did, the change to Nentres would be somewhat simpler. The same system of Welsh spelling would make Gwaelawt into Guaylaut, which a romancer might reduce to Gailot or Goilot, whence by the easy misreading of *i* into *ı* one would get Garlot.

[2] See Nutt, p. 20. The Welsh spelling here implied would probably be that

nearer the Welsh prototype. Now Mordrain or Noodran is represented as the designation adopted by Evalach or Evalac when he was baptized. But this is the Welsh Avallach or Avallon, which would imply the identification of Gwydno with Avallach. Nor is this all, for the Huth *Merlin* makes Neutre king of Sorhaut[1] the only time it mentions him, and it represents Garlot as the kingdom ruled over by Urien and his wife Morgue or Morgain la Fee. Add to this that the Huth *Merlin* had in the first instance made of Morgue or Morgain and Morgan two sisters, and given the one to Neutre to wife, and the other to Urien. This attribution of the same kingdom of Garlot, and virtually of the same wife, Morgen, to Neutre and Urien, suggests the identity of Neutre with Urien, and recalls the allusion (p. 264) to Elphin as the name of a son of Urien, as well as one of Gwydno's.

Pwyll is found as Pelles in the Venedotian district of Gwydno, but whether this is to be ascribed to the mutual influence of the Grail stories, it is difficult to decide, and all that we can say is that it is not the district with which Welsh literature is wont to associate Pwyll: that, as we have seen, was Dyved in South

of Gwydneu or Guydneu; and Noodran is probably for Noodrain = Noodren, *by* being misread into *oo*, as is easily done, in the *Red Book* for example, and as was actually done in making *Gbyn* into *Goon*. As to *ai* and *a* for *e* compare Morgain and Morgan in the Huth *Merlin* (i. 120, ii. 225, &c.), for Welsh Morgen. With Mordrain compare Marpus (and Warpus), for Gwrgwst or Guorgust, but the former perhaps started from the mutated forms *Wydneu* and *Wrgust*. Lastly, with the *rdr* for *dr* compare the *rdr* of Mordred for Modred (Welsh Medrod), also the *ntr* of Nentres

[1] Urien and his wife are made king and queen of *Gore* (Gower) by Malory, whereas here we have not a peninsula, but islands; for *Sorhaut* doubtless stands for some such a form—as *Sorlianc*—of the name of the Scillies, called *Sorlingues* in modern French. The accusative singular, according to the best reading of the MSS. of Sulpicius Severus, was *Sylinancim*: see his *Chronica* (ii. 51), ed. by Halm.

Wales, far enough from Arllechwed and Gwydno's land, where one finds Peleur's Castle, together with a group of localities associated with it [1]. In the *Seint Greal* the chief of these latter are called the Turning Castle, the Dead Castle, the Maidens' Castle, and Glannog's Isle. Now the king of the Dead Castle used to make war on his brother Peleur, after whose death he took possession of his castle, and held it until it was stormed by Peredur; the same wicked tyrant used to war also on the Queen of the Maidens of the Castle of Maidens; and among other places visited weekly by him was Glannog's Isle, overlooking which from the mainland was situated the Queen's Castle, which should accordingly have been situated near Penmon and the eastern point of Anglesey. For Glannog's Isle, in Welsh Ynys Lannog [2], is known to have been a name of the island otherwise called Ynys Seirioel, or St. Seiriol's Isle, in English Priestholm, more commonly known as Puffin Island, which is separated from Anglesey by a channel less than a mile wide. In the Welsh chronicle, published under the name of *Annales Cambriæ*, we are told that Cadwallon was blockaded in Glannog's Isle in the year 629 by the fleet of Edwin of Northumbria, but unsuccessfully, as the Welsh king made his escape to Ireland: *Obsessio Catguollaun regis in insula Glannauc.* Of this Glannauc or Glannog nothing is known except that he is called the father of Helig of

---

[1] Williams' *Seint Greal*, pp. 616, 621, 648-9, 670, 672, 714, 720.

[2] See the *Seint Greal*, p. 276, where the words are *ynys yrhonn aelwir lanoc*, and so in the version in Lord Mostyn's Library (MS. 284); but had the scribe recognized the name he ought to have given it in his sentence the unmutated form of *Glannoc*, which seems to have been equally unknown to the editor of the *Seint Greal*: witness p. 616, where he translates the above words, 'an island that is called Lanoc.' Neither seems to have bethought him that *Ynys* and *Glannoc* must, when joined together, become *Ynys Lannoc*, according to the rules of *sandhi* usual in Welsh.

Tyno Helig, or Helig's Hollow, the name of a country supposed in Welsh legend to have been overrun by the sea on the coast of North Wales[1]. Helig is styled in full Helig Voel or H. the Bald, which reminds one of the name of Tegid the Bald, whose land was likewise regarded as submerged, namely, beneath the lake bearing his name near Bala, as mentioned in a previous chapter (p. 262). On the other hand, we seem to have the other selves of Gwyđno and his son Elphin in Glannog and his son Helig. Lastly, the association of the Turning Castle with the flourishing country of which Glannog's Isle is the most conspicuous remnant, is worthy of note; for it has been essayed (p. 302) to identify the Turning Castle with Caer Sidi, where Taliessin, according to one of his boasts, had a firm seat: this is probably the key to the tradition (p. 264), that the bard had land given him in Arłlechweđ by Gwyđno.

The reader may perhaps, on perusing this chapter, think it strange that Celtic literature, at one time, busied itself so much about vessels, and especially cauldrons. But it can be shown that such vessels may have had a spiritual or intellectual significance, as for instance in connection with the notion of poetry. Thus allusion is made in the *Book of Taliessin* to three muses rising out of the cauldron of Ogyrven the Giant, whose name is associated with bardism and the origin of writing. Outside the Celtic domain one may point to the Dwarf's Cup as one of the old Norse terms symbolic of thought, wisdom, and especially the inspiration of poetry; and one might bring into the comparison the soma of Hindu religion. All these cases connecting the sacred vessel or its contents with poetry and inspiration, point

---

[1] See the *Iolo MSS.* pp. 42, 419-20, and Rees' *Essay on the Welsh Saints*, p. 298.

possibly back to some primitive drink brewed by the
early Aryan, and taken by the medicine-man in order
to produce a state of ecstasy or intoxication [1]. Lastly,
the religion of ancient Greece may be said to offer, in
its holy tripods, a curious parallel to the cauldrons of
Taliessin. It is true that nothing quite so intractable as
a cauldron is associated with the oracle, for example, of
Apollo at Delphi; but what was a tripod but a contri-
vance for holding a vessel over a fire? In the case of
Delphi the tripod was placed over a chasm in the
ground, the exhalations from which may be regarded
as a substitute for the blaze of fire fed, according to
Taliessin, by the breath of nine maidens. In Hellas
the tripod, instead of bearing the weight of a cauldron
from which utterances issued or three muses ascended [2],
had seated on it the medium in person, and she was
supposed to give her responses according as the invisible influence of the divinity prompted her. The
Celtic treatment being more primitive, the cauldron
remained, and one may presume that it required the
services of a druid as its interpreter.

[1] *Hib. Lec.* pp. 286-7, 296-9, 356-9.

[2] This may have suggested the scenes of mystery commonly described
in connection with the Holy Grail, as for instance by Malory, xvii. 20,
where one reads, 'thenne loked they and sawe a man come oute of the
holy vessel that had alle the sygnes of the passion of Ihesu Cryste bledynge
alle openly.'

CHAPTER XIV.

GLASTONBURY AND GOWER.

AMONG the peculiarities of Arthurian geography nothing is, perhaps, more remarkable than the various hints given as to the nature and position of the realm of Melwas ; and Malory, when he made Westminster the head-quarters of Arthur, placed the castle of Melwas (Mellygraunce) seven miles away on the other side of the Thames. That river thus became, after a fashion, the river of hell to be crossed by Lancelot on his horse when he hurried to rescue the queen. In that direction also was Guildford, whose name one detects disguised in the *Grand St. Graal* as Castle Galafort, and in the Gelbort whence Chrétien's Gonemans hails[1] ; and Malory makes Astolat also to have been Guildford. Modern Welsh writers, however, represent Melwas as coming from Scotland, and this view would seem to admit of being explained in somewhat the same way as that in which Medrod, from Geoffrey's time down, was more or less closely associated with Picts and Scots : he is sometimes called a Pictish prince. We have a trace probably of the same idea in Cormac's *Glossary* when he calls Glastonbury the Glastonbury of

---

[1] Nutt, pp. 11, 60, 1 ; Malory, xviii. 8, 9.

the Goidels or the Gaels, that is to say in Latin the
Scotti : this we take to be the Irish echo of a Brythonic
belief that Melwas, under whatever name, was a Goidel
or *Scottus*. It would be hard to decide how far this
may be taken to point to an occupation of Gower or
Somerset by invaders from Ireland. But, even leaving
this out of consideration, the form assumed by the myth
is no more surprising than the substitution of Ireland
for Hades in the story of Bran's expedition on behalf
of his sister Branwen. But once Hades became Ireland, its head would naturally be regarded as a Goidel.

However, neither the author of the *Vita Gildæ*
nor that of the *Conte de la Charrette* knew anything of
Ireland as the realm of Melwas : they located it nearer
to Arthur's court. According to the former, Melwas
was king of the *Æstiva Regio*, whereby he seems to have
meant Somerset with Glastonbury as its most impregnable stronghold, while the latter, Chrétien, sang of
him as king of Goire, whence nobody returns[1], and as
living with his father in his capital of Bade[2]. It is
admitted on all hands that Bade means the ancient city
of Bath, and it can hardly be doubted that Goire points
to the peninsula of Gwyr, sometimes called Goer, in
English Gower. At first sight, this looks hopelessly
inconsistent ; but in reality it is merely a jumble of two
stories. For the Celts had undoubtedly two ideas
about the realm of the dead, and according to one of
them they regarded Hades as an island beneath the sea
or simply beyond the sea. Such was the Brittia to
which the souls of the departed were wont, according
to Procopius' well-known story, to be shipped from the

---

[1] See lines 639–41, cited by M. Paris, from the *Charrette*, in the *Romania*,
xii. 467.

[2] Ib. xii. 474, 481, 512.

shores of the Continent, and such would be Gower as
viewed hazily from the land on the other side of the
Severn Sea: so Gower would be the realm of Melwas.
The other notion, equally old or perhaps even older,
was that of a fairy settlement entered through a hill or
a mound, such as Mider inhabited in some Irish legends,
and such as the fairies are most commonly believed to
inhabit in Wales, though in certain districts, such as the
neighbourhood of Snowdon, the belief used to be that
they lived beneath the lakes.

Glastonbury might be said to admit of both descriptions.
For the waters and swamps around Glastonbury made
it into an island, while the hill now known as Glastonbury Tor would form a fairy hill: either feature would
justify its being described in Welsh as an *ynys*, which,
in Welsh topography, means not only an island but
also any rising ground with low-lying land around it,
though not necessarily covered with water. William of
Malmesbury tells us that the ancient name of Glastonbury was Ynesuuitrin[1], which he explains as *Insula
Vitrea*. It is also Chrétien's Isle de Voirre or Glass
Island, which he describes in his *Erec* as a happy land
subject to no tempest or thunder, where no noxious
beast remains, where the heat is not excessive and
winter is unknown: Maheloas (Melwas) was lord of that
land of perpetual summer and fine weather:—

> 'Avec ces que m'oez nommer
> Vint Maheloas, uns hauz ber,
> Li sire de l'isle de voirre[2].

---

[1] This we understand to be the prevalent reading of the Cambridge MS.

[2] See Chrétien's *Erec*, lines 1933-9 cited in the *Rom.* x. 491, but Giraldus,
in his *Speculum Ecclesiæ*, Rolls Ed. ii. 9 (p. 49), explains away the mythical
colouring of the Welsh name when he says of the words *Ynys Wydrin*, or, as
he writes it, *Inis Gutrin*, 'hoc est *insula vitrea*, propter amnem scilicet, quasi
vitrei coloris in marisco circumfluentem.' A similar conjecture is given in

> En cele isle n'ot l'en tonoirre,
> Ne n'i chiet foudre ne tempeste,
> Ne boz ne serpenz n'i areste ;
> N'i fait trop chaut, ne n'i iverne.'

The monks pretended that their founder was Joseph of Arimathea, whom they represented, as already mentioned, as the first to convert the people of this country to Christianity. According to their fabulous assertions, the claims of the Church of Rome to supremacy in matters relating to the faith in this realm had no foundation in history ; and this fell in well with the views of Henry II, whose differences with the Papacy culminated in the murder of the Archbishop of Canterbury. The King is said to have had the pretensions of Glastonbury examined and approved ; for they struck not only at Rome but also at St. David's and the traditions of the Welsh, who were a source of annoyance to Henry. So in the year 1189 the said monks requited the King's favour by discovering at Glastonbury the tombs of Arthur and his wife, together with that of his favourite Gwalchmei. This discovery was calculated to discourage the troublesome Welshmen, who were credited with looking forward to the return of Arthur to lead them to victory over all their enemies [1].

There is no reason to suppose that the ingenious monks of Glastonbury were the first to identify Insula Avallonia or Ynys Avallach with that place: they were

Dr. Pughe's Dictionary under the word *gwydrawl*, 'vitreous, or glassy' : it comes from a Welsh version of the Account of Arthur's end, and is to the following effect :—' It was usual formerly to call that place the Glassy Island (*Ynys Wydrin*), on account of being surrounded by rivers, the water of which was of a blue vitreous colour.'

[1] Giraldus, ib. ii. 9 (p. 50), relates that the inscription—what has become of it !—on Arthur's coffin read: Hɪᴄ ᴊᴀᴄᴇᴛ sᴇᴘᴜʟᴛᴜs ɪɴᴄʟʏᴛᴜs ʀᴇx Aʀᴛʜᴜʀɪᴜs, ɪɴ ɪɴsᴜʟᴀ Aᴠᴀʟʟᴏɴɪᴀ, ᴄᴜᴍ Wᴇɴɴᴇᴠᴇʀᴇɪᴀ ᴜxᴏʀᴇ sᴜᴀ sᴇᴄᴜɴᴅᴀ: see also the *Romania*, i. 463.

in this merely following what had possibly for ages
previously been the popular idea. William of Malmesbury gives as one of the explanations of the name, that
it was called *Insula Pomorum* from the native word
which he writes *avala* 'apples,' the Welsh word for
apple being *aval* or *afal*. But as Avallonia appears to
be more correctly written so than with a single *l*, the
Welsh word required would be rather *avaĺĺ* or *afaĺĺ*.
'an apple tree,' and this would agree even better with
the strange story of the name as related by the same
writer [1], who gives his readers to understand that his
statements were based on the authority of Brythonic

---

[1] It runs as follows in his work, *De Antiquitate Glastoniensis Ecclesiæ*, in
Gale's *Historia Britanniæ*, &c. (Oxford, 1691), p. 295 (see also *Romania*, xii.
510):—'Legitur in antiquis Britonum gestis, quod a Boreali Britanniæ parte
venerunt in occidentem duodecim fratres, et tenuerunt plurimas regiones.
Venedociam, Demetiam, Buthir [*read* Guhir], Kedweli, quas proavus eorum
Cuneda tenuerunt : nomina eorum fratrum inferius annotantur, Ludnertb
[*read* Iudnerth], Morgen, Catgur, Cathmor, Merguid, Morvined, Morehel,
Morcant, Boten, Morgen, Mortineil [*read* Mormeil], Glasteing [*read*
Glastenig]. Hic est ille Glasteing [*read* Glastenig], qui per mediterraneos
Anglos, secus villam quæ dicitur *Escebtiorne*, scrofam suam usque ad Wellis,
et a Wellis per inviam et aquosam viam, quæ *Sugewege*, id est, Scrofæ via,
dicitur, sequens porcellos suos, juxta ecclesiam de qua nobis sermo est, lac-
tentem sub malo invenit, unde usque ad nos emanavit, quod mala mali illius
Ealdcyrcenes epple, id est Veteris Ecclesiæ poma vocantur : sus quoque *ealdcyre*
[sic] *suge* idcirco nominabatur, quæ cum cæteræ sues quatuor pedes habeant,
mirum dictu, ista habuit octo. Hic igitur Glasteing, postquam insulam illam
ingressus, eam multimodis bonis vidit affluentem, cum omni familia sua in
ea venit habitare, cursumque vitæ suæ ibidem peregit. Ex ejus progenie
et familia ei succedente locus ille primitus dicitur populatus, hæc de antiquis
Britonum libris sunt.' The writer then proceeds to speak, 'De diversis
nominibus ejusdem Insulæ ' in the following words :—' Hæc itaque insula
primo Ynesuuitrin a Britonibus dicta, demum ab Anglis terram sibi sub-
jugantibus, interpretato priore vocabulo, dicta est sua lingua Glastynbiry, vel
de Glasteing [*read* Glastenig], de quo præmisimus etiam, insula Avallonia
celebriter nominatur, cujus vocabuli hæc fuit origo. Supradictum est quod
Glasteing [Glastenig] scrofam suam sub arbore pomifera juxta vetustam
ecclesiam invenit, ubi quia primum adveniens poma in partibus illis rarissima
reperit, insulam Avalloniæ [sic] sua lingua, id est, insulam pomorum nomi-
navit ; *Avalla* [*read* avaleu] enim Britonice poma interpretatur Latine, vel
cognominatur de quodam Avalloc, qui ibidem cum suis filiabus propter loci
secretum, fertur inhabitasse.'

manuscripts. These last have not been identified, but we have one, nearly like them, namely a manuscript in the British Museum [1]. It contains pedigrees and enables one to see that the Englishman has made the mistake of regarding a genealogy traced back to Glast as a list of the sons of Cuneda, who are very differently named on the next page of the same manuscript, and are thus spoken of in words partly copied by Malmesbury: ' Et tenuerunt plurimas regiones in occidentali plaga Brittannie.' A very obscure note [2] on Glast connects with his name a longer one, Glastenic, which enables one with tolerable certainty to correct Malmesbury's *Glasteing* into *Glastenig* for an older *Glastenic*. The whole has to do with an attempt, apparently, to explain the etymology of the name of Glastonbury. But, though such names as *Glast*, *Glastenic*, and *Glastonia* would, especially with the aid of English, suggest ' glass,' we are not forced to suppose that the idea of a glass island was not a part of the myth previous to any English explanation of its names: compare the Glass Tower in

---

[1] Harl. 3859, fol. 194[b].

[2] The words in question, from *Glast* onwards, are :—unu' st.' glastenic. qui uener'/q: uocat' loyt/coyt. Mr. Phillimore in the *Cymmrodor*, ix. 180, expands them thus :—unum sunt glastenic. qui uenerunt que uocatur. loyt coyt. By expanding them somewhat differently and supposing, as he has suggested, *unu'* to be an error for *unde*, we should arrive at the following as the probable original of what the scribe tried to copy : ' unde sunt glastenic, qui uenerabiliterque uoca[n]tur loyt coyt.' This would mean—' whence, i.e. from Glast, are derived Glastenic, which are reverently called the Grey Trees ': compare Malmesbury's *celebriter nominatur* in the last note but one. Loyt coyt and Glastenic would thus be two names of one and the same place, which was held sacred, probably Glastonbury itself : the former requires no explanation, and as to the latter it is clearly derived from the *glasten*, which in Breton meant ' oak ' : cf. Cornish *glastanen*, ' an oak.' The Glastenig of William of Malmesbury is, doubtless, the place-name Glastenic made into the name of an eponymus for Glastonbury. It may well be that the Glast of the pedigree had nothing to do with any of the names here in point. It occurs as a man's name in Brittany : see M. de Courson's *Cart. de l'Abbaye de Redon*, p. 309, where he assigns a benefaction of a certain Glast's to the years 990-992.

the middle of the sea, spoken of in the *Historia Brittonum* of Nennius [1]. Much the same kind of remark applies to the name Avallonia; for it is not improbable that Glastonbury may have been noted for its apples or apple trees, as Malmesbury and others would lead one to believe. It is also possible, that, in some versions of the myth, an apple tree figured, or at any rate some kind of tree of a remarkable or sacred nature [2]; but we are persuaded, nevertheless, that the tree had nothing directly to do with the etymology of *Avallonia.* Whether the term *Insula Pomorum* was founded on the false etymology, or derived from a reference to a tree in the original myth, it would be hard to decide.

It dates, however, as far back as the time of Geoffrey, in whose *Vita Merlini* the island to which Arthur is carried to be cured of his wounds by the fairy leech Morgen, is termed *Insula Pomorum.* There, after a mention of the sea-girt spot where a dragon guards the apples of the Hesperides, and a short allusion to Taprobana or Ceylon, our fairy realm is introduced in the following verses [3]:—

> 'Insula Pomorum quæ Fortunata vocatur,
> Ex re nomen habet, quia per se singula profert:
> Non opus est illi sulcantibus arva colonis;
> Omnis abest cultus nisi quem natura ministrat:
> Ultro fœcundas segetes producit et uvas,
> Nataque poma suis prætonso germine silvis;
> Omnia gignit humus vice graminis ultro redundans.
> Annis centenis aut ultra vivitur illuc,
> Illic jura novem geniali lege sorores
> Dant his qui veniunt nostris ea partibus ad se.'

---

[1] See San-Marte's *Nennius et Gildas,* p. 35 (§ 13); also *Hib. Lec.* p. 263.

[2] See the remark on the etymology of Glastenic in the last note but one, and, on the subject of the sacred trees of the Celts, see the *Hib. Lec.* p. 219-21; also Mr. Arthur J. Evans' paper on Stonehenge in Nutt's *Archæological Review* for 1889, pp. 327-30.

[3] *Vita Merlini* (ed. by Grenville for the Roxburghe Club, London, 1830), ll. 908-17 (p. 41): see also the *Romania,* i. 464.

A similar account of this fortunate isle is given by
an anonymous poet who also describes the medical
maiden Morgen, whose charms are represented as the
cause of Arthur's delaying his return. His verses run
as follows [1]:—

> 'Cingitur oceano memorabilis insula nullis
> Desolata bonis; non fur, nec prædo, nec hostis
> Insidiatur ibi; nec vis, nec bruma, nec æstas
> Immoderata furit; pax et concordia, pubes,
> Ver manet æternum, nec flos nec lilia desunt . . . .
> Semper ibi juvenes cum virgine, nulla senectus
> Nullaque vis morbi, nullus dolor, omnia plena
> Lætitiæ; nihil hic proprium, communia quæque.
> Regia virgo locis et rebus præsidet istis,
> Virginibus stipata suis pulcherrima pulchris . . . .
> Immodice læsus Arthurus tendit ad aulam
> Regis Avallonis: ubi virgo regia, vulnus
> Illius tractans, sanati membra reservat
> Ipsa sibi: vivuntque simul, si credere fas est.'

From the lines last cited, it does not appear whether
the poet called the king *rex Avallonis* or *rex Avallo*:
probably the latter is to be preferred. At any rate, it
coincides with Giraldus' alternative explanation of the
name of Avallonia, according to which it meant Avallo's
Isle [2], and this in its turn is favoured by Malmesbury's
like alternative, 'vel cognominatur de quodam Avalloc,
qui ibidem cum suis filiabus, propter loci secretum,
fertur inhabitasse [3].' Thus it appears that *Insula Avallonia* and *Ynys Avallach* signified the island belonging
to the king called in Latin Avallo and in Welsh Avallon
and Avallach or Avalloc; but had the original name

---

[1] Cited in the *Romania*, i. 464, from San-Marte's Geoffrey, pp. 425, 6,
where it is cited from Usher's *Prim.* (c. 14, p. 273) and ascribed to the
Pseudo-Gildas.

[2] Giraldus, *Spec. Ecclesiæ*, ii. 9 (p. 49), where the editor prints 'a *Vallone*
quodom.'

[3] Gale, ib. p. 295.

meant the Isle of Apples or of Apple-trees, it is hardly probable that the Brythons would have given it up for that of Avallach's Isle, where *Avallach* had ceased probably at a comparatively early date to convey any meaning of its own. Be that as it may, we should, doubtless, be right in regarding the *aula regis Avallonis* to which the wounded Arthur was borne as being no other than that of the Avalloc or Avallach said to inhabit Avallonia with his daughters; and these last may be identified without much hesitation with the beautiful maidens around the more beautiful Morgen, as mentioned in the verses already cited :—

'Regia virgo locis et rebus præsidet istis
Virginibus stipata suis pulcherrima pulchris.'

It would follow that Avallach, Avalloc, or Avallo is to be regarded as a name of a Celtic dark divinity, a notion which is countenanced by the fact that the same manuscript which mentions Glast places near the remote end of a pedigree the name Avallach in the two forms *Aballac* and *Amalech*. The pedigree ends thus: 'son of Eugein [i. e. *Owein*], son of Aballac, son of Amalech, who was the son of Beli the Great, and his mother was Anna, who is said to have been cousin to the Virgin Mary, mother of our Lord Jesus Christ[1].' Beli the Great need not delay us at this point[2], and the Anna here treated as his wife, had of course nothing to do with the other Anna, except that the name of the former accidentally resembled hers. The Celtic Anna, said to have been sister to Arthur, has already been mentioned more than once as mother of Gwalchmei

---

[1] Harl. 3859, fol. 193[b]; but at 194[a], Aballac is made son of Beli and Anna, without any allusion to the duplicate form Amalech : see the *Cymmrodor*, ix. 170, 174.

[2] *Hib. Lec.* pp. 90, 285. 644.

and Medrod, and as wife of Loth (p. 19), that is to say
of Ỻûđ or Nûđ, originally the Zeus of the Celts. So
Anna's association with him at one time, and at another
with Beli, the dark god, is just as might be expected;
and it is Avaỻach the son of Beli and Anna that gave
his name to the Isle of Avallon. But his parentage
would leave it uncertain whether Avaỻach should rank
on the side of darkness and death or of light and life.
His association with Glastonbury, however, inclines
one to the former view; and that is not all, for one dis-
covers Avaỻach in the bedridden tercentenarian, whom
Grail story introduces under the slightly modified
form of his name as Euelake[1] (Evalach). It gives him
a bed in a chapel where Peredur (Perceval) saw him
with his body covered with wounds and scars[2]. Evalach
had been converted by Joseph of Arimathea, and he
had repaid the saint for the kindly interest he took in
his salvation by delivering him from the prison into
which he was cast by a pagan; but it would take up
too much of our space to enter into the details of the
treatment whereby such unpromising materials of the
old theology of Celtic heathendom was worked into the
fabric of a Christian romance. Suffice it to say that in
the description of Evalach the Unknown, for so he was
called, because it was not known where he was born
or whence he came[3], one cannot help recognizing the
same idea of a god of death or of the dead, as in the
living corpse of Uthr Bendragon[4].

---

[1] *Anelac,* doubtless for *Auelac,* also seems to occur: see Nutt, p. 268.

[2] Malory, xiii. 10, xiv. 3; Williams' *Seint Greal,* pp. 53-6, 470-3.

[3] Lonelich's *Holy Grail* (E. Eng. Text Soc.: Extra Series, xx), pp. 47, 8.

[4] *Hib. Lec.* p. 567. We have another version, so to say, of *Uthr* in Malory's *Urre,* who is cured of his festering wounds by Lancelot: see Malory, xix. 10–13. It is to be noticed that he comes from the Huns' Country.

The foregoing remarks tend to show that the realm to
which Melwas carried Arthur's queen was considered
the land of darkness and death: the same idea is
brought into relief in a story which occurs in a Welsh
life of St. Collen[1], who has left his name to the church
and pleasant Vale of Llangollen in North Wales. It
relates how the saint went to the mountain of Glastonbury, which is doubtless to be identified with Glastonbury Tor, and made his cell beneath a rock away from
the road. As he was one day in his cell he heard two
men conversing about Gwyn ab Nûd, and saying that
he was the king of Annwn and the fairies. Collen put
his head out and bade them hold their peace, as those
were only demons. They told him to hold his peace,
and assured him that he would have to meet Gwyn face
to face. By and by Collen heard a knocking at his
door, followed by the enquiry whether he was in. He
answered in the affirmative, and wished to know who
it was that asked the question. The reply was: 'I am
here, the messenger of Gwyn ab Nûd, king of Hades,
to bid thee come by the middle of the day to speak
with him on the top of the hill.' The saint did not go;
and the same message was delivered to him by the
same messenger on the day after, but in vain as before.
The third day the messenger added to Gwyn's command to Collen the threat that if he did not obey, it
would be the worse for him. The menace disconcerted
the saint, who now proceeded to consecrate some water,
and when he was ready he took it with him up the hill.

On reaching the top, Collen beheld there the fairest
castle he had ever seen, with the best appointed
troops, a great number of musicians with all kinds of
stringed instruments, steeds with young men riding

[1] *Y Greal* (London, 1805), pp. 337-41.

them of the handsomest description, maidens also of
the most gentle and sprightly aspect, light of foot and
lightly clad, all in the bloom of youth, and in addition
everything else that became the state appertaining to
the court of a sumptuous king. Aloft on the castle wall
he descried a gentleman who bad him enter, as the king
was waiting for his coming to dine. Collen entered,
and found the king seated in a gold chair: he welcomed the saint with due honour and told him to go to
the table, adding that beside what he saw there served
for him, he should have the rarest of all dainties he
could desire, and plenty of every kind of drink and
sweet beverage his heart could wish, and that further
there were in readiness for him all kinds of service and
entertainment in order to do due honour to a guest of
his wisdom, 'I will not,' said Collen, 'eat the tree-
leaves.' 'Hast thou ever,' asked the king, 'seen men
better dressed than these here in red and blue?' 'Their
dress is good enough,' said Collen, 'for its kind.'
'What kind of dress is that?' rejoined the king. Collen
then answered and said, that the red on the one side
betokened burning, and the blue on the other betokened cold. Then he sprinkled holy water over them
and they all vanished, leaving behind them no castle or
troops, no men or maidens, no music and melody, no
steeds and riders, nothing in the world but clumps of
grass.

Such is the story of Collen's meeting with the
King of the Fairies; and probably few spots could be
conceived better adapted to be the scene than Glastonbury Tor, on which a site was in due time found for
a chapel dedicated to the Archangel Michael, who
appears in more places than one in Celtic lands as the
supplanter of the dark powers. Another instance, worthy

of mention here, occurs in the story of Arthur slaying the cannibal giant that had taken Howel's sister Helena or Elen to his island stronghold on the coast of Normandy: Christianity, associating the spot with the archangel, has given it the name of Mont S.-Michel[1]. This in its turn suggests the islet known as St. Michael's Mount on the coast of Cornwall, though we are not aware of the survival of any story associated with the name. One may add a third instance, namely, from the south-western coast of Ireland, where a rocky islet lies, called the Great Skellig: it was known in Irish as Sgelic Mhichil, or the Skellig of Michael; and tradition made it the burial-place of Ir, son of Mil[2]. To return to Mont S.-Michel, Wace[3] gives the giant slain there the name of Dinabuc, which one can scarcely err in recognizing in the name of the Welsh towns of Denbigh and Tenby, both called in Welsh Dinbych. In the case of Denbigh, a legend survives[4] to the effect that the place was at one time the scene of the ravages of a monster after which it was called Dinbych. The virtual identity of this name with that of Dinabuc[5] argues the probable similarity of its bearers

---

[1] *Hib. Lec.* p. 161 ; Geoffrey, x. 3 ; Malory, v. 5. According to Malory, this giant fed mostly on babies, and the same sort of cannibal appears in some Welsh stories as a giantess : two such have been mentioned by the author in the *Cymmrodor*, ii. 33–7, in a paper which is otherwise best forgotten. It may be said that such giants and giantesses simply point back to a habit of cannibalism in this country in the time of St. Coten ; but we prefer to regard them as death divinities euhemerized.

[2] *The Four Masters*, A. D. 950, 1044 ; O'Connor's (1723) *Keating*, p. 102.

[3] *Le Roman de Brut* (Rouen, 1836), vol. ii. p. 146, l. 11,598.

[4] It is known to us only in the sadly modern form in which it is given at the opening of John Williams' *Ancient and Modern Denbigh*, published there in 1856.

[5] The author is reminded by a friend of a name in Dumbartonshire, which would seem to challenge inclusion here, namely, that of Dumbuck between Dunglass and Dumbarton : see Joseph Irving's *Dumbartonshire* (Dumbarton, 1860), p. 9.

with one another; and it is possibly but an accident that neither Denbigh nor Tenby shows a dedication to the archangel.

It is not hard to understand why Michael should appear as the supplanter of Gwyn ab Nûd; for the archangel was the general of the heavenly host: he was the vanquisher of Satan, and he was supposed to keep the activity of him and his demons within bounds. Similarly, Gwyn was supposed to delight in the battle-field; and the restraining of the demons of Annwn or Hades is represented in the story of Kulhwch as one of his functions. Yspydaden addresses his would-be son-in-law thus: 'Twrch Trwyth will never be hunted until you have found Gwyn son of Nûd, in whom God has put the instinct of the demons of Annwn, lest the present world should be destroyed: he will not be spared thence [1].' Above all, the Archangel Michael played the part of a kind of psychopompus for Christendom. For as Gwyn ab Nûd with his hell-hounds hunted disembodied souls, so Michael with his angels undertook to save them. He is made to be present to separate the good from the bad when the souls are being weighed in the scales, and he is pictured especially engaged in keeping in check the wiles of the elves busy on all such occasions [2]. It is not surprising, therefore, that the archangel was popular in Wales, and that the number of the Welsh churches and chapels called Ilan Fihangel, 'Michael the Angel's Church,' or dedicated to him, is considered

---

[1] *R. B. Mab.* p. 124, and Guest, ii. 289, where the translation given is 'Gwyn, the son of Nudd, whom God has placed over the brood of the devils in Annwn:' it is glaringly wrong.

[2] As an instance, we may refer to the Last Judgment on the well-known west window of Fairford Church in Gloucestershire.

remarkable[1]. It is probably to be explained by the
view here advanced, that he was regarded as *par
excellence* the defender of Christians against the sprites
and demons with which Celtic imagination peopled the
shades of night, the gloom of the forest, and even the
straggling mist on the tops of the hills. Perhaps it
would not be rash to suppose that most of the old
foundations associated with his name occupy sites of
sinister reputation, inherited from the time when
paganism prevailed in the land, sites which were considered to be dangerous and to form the favourite
haunts of evil spirits.

We have tried to show the nature of the connection of
Glastonbury with Avallach, and with Gwyn ab Nûd;
but we may be told that there is nothing to identify
either of them with Melwas. This touches one of
the difficulties attaching to the Celtic Dis, namely, the
multiplicity of his forms and names. Avallach, whom
the romancers call not only Evalach, but also Mordrain
and Noodran (p. 323), differs both in form and name from
Gwyn; but we are by no means certain that the difference between Gwyn and Melwas was anything more
than one of name alone. *Melwas* was the Cornish pronunciation of what was in Welsh Maelwas, but in the
pages of Geoffrey one detects Gwyn under the longer
name Gwynwas, which might be interpreted the white
or fair youth, while Maelwas would seem to have meant
a princely youth, as already hinted (p. 51). According
to the view here suggested as possible, the Brythonic
divinity in question had the two names, Maelwas and
Gwynwas, of which the former survived in Cornish as
Melwas, while in Welsh the preference was very
decidedly given to Gwyn, which had the advantage

[1] See Rees' *Welsh Saints*, pp. 36-43.

of being short. It is not essential that Melwas and
Gwynwas, the Gonemans already mentioned (p. 121),
should be proved originally one; nor, on the other hand,
can it be regarded as a serious objection to that conjecture that Geoffrey treats them as two. His references
to them are very instructive as to how history has been
mixed with mythology. Melwas is called by him in a
passage or two Melga, which is derived from the form
Melgwas or *Maelgwas*, and Gwynwas is treated as
Guanius: the former is king of the Picts, and the latter
of the Huns.

They find Ursula and her virgin companions shipwrecked on their way to their friends on the Continent,
and they murder them all. The two kings then land
in Albania, and invade the rest of Britain; but, being
repulsed by the legions of Rome, they take refuge in
Ireland[1], whence they return with Scots and Scandin-
avians and devastate Britain from sea to sea. They are
again repulsed, and a wall is made between Albania and
Deira: Melwas and Gwynwas settle in the former
country[2] and infest the Wall, while Constantine, the
grandfather of Arthur, clears the rest of the island of
invaders[3]. Later, the two kings are to be detected as
Arthur's vassals, called by Geoffrey this time Malvasius,
king of Iceland, and Gunvasius, king of Orkney[4]. The
following points are worth mentioning in connection
with Geoffrey's narrative: Ursula is treated as the
daughter of Dionotus, in the Welsh version Dunawt,

---

[1] Geoffrey, v. 16. The Welsh versions usually have *Melwas* and *Gwynwas*:
it is the latter name also, probably, that meets us in Malory's Gwinas, i. 15,
and Gwenbaus, brother to Ban and Bors, i. 11.

[2] Ib. vi. 1.

[3] Ib. vi. 5.

[4] Ib. ix. 12. The Welsh version has here *Melwas* and *Gôynw[as]* : see
the *R. B. Bruts*, p. 201.

king of Cornwall, and, according to an account of her
death written [1] on the Continent a little earlier than
Geoffrey's narrative, she and her companions were
murdered by the Huns under Attila at Cologne, while
Ursula herself is made to be the daughter of Nothus, in
whose name we have a decapitated form to be restored
into Dinothus, identical, virtually, with the Welsh
Dunawt [2]. One may compare and contrast the story of
Gwyn carrying away Creiḋylad, daughter of ILûḋ, whose
name was originally Nûḋ or rather Nodens, but it is
probably not to be sought in *Nothus*. As to Melwas
and Gwynwas, in the position of vassals to Arthur, the
latter thus appears in that story (p. 319), while the former
is mentioned among Arthur's men in the story of
Kulhwch, where he is called Maelwys, son of Baedan [3].
More correctly speaking, *Maelwys* is to be reckoned an
error for some such a form as *Maelyf* or *Maeluf*, standing for the Irish name *Maeluma*, borne by a historical
person, the son of Baedan or Baettan, a well-known
Ulidian king, who waged war in this country on behalf
of the Dalriad Scots, as did also his son. It is to this
confusion of Maeluma with Melwas, that we are to
trace the name of the latter's father, Bademagu or
Bagdemagu, in the mouths of the romancers: it is

---

[1] By Sigebert of Gemblours (Pertz's *Monumenta Germaniæ Historica,
Scriptorum tom.* vi. p. 310), for the reference to whom the author is
indebted to the kindness of Mr. H. L. D. Ward, of the British Museum; as
he is also for the hint as to the origin of the name Bademagu of Melwas'
father in the romances, and for other valuable suggestions bearing on this
part of Geoffrey's narrative.

[2] Geoffrey's *Dionotus* should have been *Dinotus*; the modern Welsh
spelling is Dunawd or Dunod, and it is the same name as that borne by the
Abbot of Bangor, said to have met Augustine. Bæda's spelling of the
former's name is Dinoot, and the original of the Welsh form was the Latin
Dōnātus.

[3] *R. B. Mab.* p. 106.

probably but their way of reproducing the full designation, Baedan mac Cairill [1].

According to Geoffrey, Ursula and the survivors of
her train were shipwrecked on islands belonging to
barbarians, where Melwas and Gwynwas found them ;
but otherwise, his narrative connects them with the
north of Britain, with Orkney, and even with Iceland,
all of which admirably fit into the Celtic geography of
the other world. Add to this that the Picts and the
Scots play the same rôle from a Welsh point of view as
the Huns do in the myths and romances of the Continent. But we are here more particularly interested in
Glastonbury, the identification of which with Avallach's
Isle, and all that term was supposed to connote, would
naturally lead to the further conclusion that it was also
the *Æstiva Regio*. This is in Welsh *Gwlad yr Hâv*, or
the Land of Summer, which in the form Somerset has
become fixed as the name of the county to which
Glastonbury belongs. Originally *Gwlad yr Hâv* was,
doubtless, as mythical a name as Llychlyn before that
term came to mean Scandinavia. The most curious
account of this fabulous Land of Summer occurs in the
Triads, iii. 4, where we are told that Hu the Mighty
brought the Kymry to Britain from 'Gwlad yr Hâv,
which is called Deffrobani, where Constantinople stands.'
The latter part of the statement was probably a gloss
made by somebody who did not know that Deffrobani
meant Taprobane, or the Island of Ceylon ; but the

---

[1] To explain the manufacture of the name, one must set out from the
appearance of Baedan's name in the old Irish spelling, where *ll* admits of
being misread *u*, and where *air* is represented by a *q* with a stroke through
its limb and a small *i* placed over the upper part of the letter. Thus
written, *Baedan mac Cairill* would look approximately Baedāmaccᶣiu, which
might be simplified into something like Bademagu, unless one should rather
regard Bagdemagu as a more original form, implying the misreading of *tt*
into *ct*, to be reduced afterwards into *gd*.

introduction of the reference to the latter reminds one of
Geoffrey's poem in the *Vita Merlini*, where Taprobane
and the Insula Pomorum are mentioned in succession,
and in a way, be it noticed, which does not exclude all
possible doubt that the poet did not mean by both names
one and the same happy land. Even now the term
Gwlad yr Hâv has not completely lost its mythical force
and hazy signification of a fabulous country [1] somewhere far away, to which a troublesome person may be
asked to betake himself. Melwas, as lord of the winter-
less Glass Island, identified with Glastonbury, would, in
other words, be regarded as king of the *Æstiva Regio*,
which thereby would come to mean the country around
Glastonbury; nor could he well remain long king of the
Æstiva Regio, in that sense, without having the celebrated
city of Bath reckoned as his capital. But, on the other
hand, a different tradition made him king of Goire, or
the peninsula of Gower, which loomed in the distance
across the Severn Sea. Thus by mixing the two versions of the myth, the writers of the romances came to
speak of the kingdom of Melwas as Goire, and of his
capital as Bade or Bath.

Everything goes to show that the story of Melwas, as
we have it, is mostly Cornish, like his name, rather than
Welsh; and one might naturally surmise that it was
from the Cornish side that Gower, accessible by land on
the Welsh side, derived its mythical importance as a part
of the other world. It was the Cornish Brythons also
possibly that associated the dark divinity of Brân with

---

[1] Such it seems to be in the following rhyme, which is well known in
North Cardiganshire :—

'Cèr i Wlad yr Hâ	*Go to reap ferns,*
I fedi rhedin,	*To the Land of Summer,*
Lle ma cwn dion	*Where black dogs*
Yn c——u menin.'	*Do s—— butter.*

Gower, whence Malory's *Brandegore*, for *Bran de Gore*
or *Goire* (p. 160). Cornish, likewise, we presume the
story of Morgan le Fay to have been, when it describes
her withdrawing under the fear of her brother Arthur
to the same land of Goire : 'there was she rychely
receyved,' we are told, and there she 'maade her castels
and townes passynge stronge:' in fact, she is called
the queen of Goire [1], in which Welsh legend agrees
when it makes Urien, her husband, king of Gower.

Lastly, one of the places which figures among the
graves mentioned in the *Black Book of Carmarthen* is
called Gwanas Gwyr, or the 'Point of Gower' : it is also
called Gwanas without any qualification, and it is introduced here as the probable antecedent of the place-name
which Malory reproduces as Ganys, as, for example,
when he speaks of Bors of Ganys or of the two brothers
Bleoberys and Blamore of Ganys.   The lines [2] alluded
to in the *Black Book* place at Gwanas the resting-place
of Gwrgi and others, including the Household of Oeth
and Anoeth.   With this strange group one is naturally
led to associate the Prison of Oeth and Anoeth, by which
Welsh legend understands a huge structure built of
human bones.   In that ghastly prison one cannot help
recognizing a picture of the abode of the dead [3] : it is
probably but another aspect of the vast castle that
collapses simultaneously with the wounding of its lord
by Balyn.

---

[1] Malory, iv. 15; see also vi. 3.   [2] Evans' Autotype, p. 33 b.
[3] *Hib. Lec.* pp. 667-8.

CHAPTER XV.

The Isles of the Dead.

Reference was made in the last chapter to Morgan le Fay: her name would be more correctly written Morgen, as it is the same name in fact as that of the lady in the Isle of Avallon, who had the charge of healing Arthur of his wounds; and considering how predicates, frankly inconsistent and contradictory, are applied to everything connected with the other world, there is no occasion to regard these two Morgens as forming distinct persons rather than one and the same fairy differently described. In a word, she is viewed at one time as kind and benevolent and at another as hostile and truculent. The same sort of remark applies to the same sort of person under the name of the Lady of the Lake, of whose figure Malory gives, so to say, widely different views. Accordingly, one Lady of the Lake sends Arthur the sword Excalibur and asks for Balyn's head in return for it[1]; another Lady of the Lake confines Merlin in his stone prison[2]; a third, Nyneue, busies herself about Arthur's safety[3], and a fourth about that of Lancelot[4]. They may all be taken as different aspects of the one mythic figure, the lake lady Morgen. The name Morgen means the offspring

---

[1] Malory, ii. 3.
[2] Ib. iv. 5.
[3] Ib. ix. 16.
[4] Ib. xix. 11.

of the sea, as in the case of Morgen as the native name of Pelagius, in later Welsh *Morien*, the only difference being one of gender. Still more to the point here is the fact that the name Morgen, in its Irish form of Muirgen, was that of a lake lady otherwise called Liban, of whom mention will have to be made later. Her story[1] is, that, having the charge of a magic well and neglecting it, she was overwhelmed by the waters that formed the lake now known as Lough Neagh: she roamed about for some three hundred years in the world of waters in order in due time to be caught in the net of a saint who baptized her, half woman and half salmon as she was then found to be. Thus she was enabled to die in the odour of sanctity and leave her name to a church. This probably means that a common name has led to a saintly woman being confounded with a lake lady or mermaid. This Liban, called Muirgen, is not identified in Irish literature with the Liban who lived in an island with her husband Labraid of the Swift Hand on the Sword and her sister Fand (p. 217), though the two Libans were perhaps originally one.

Let us now come back to Muirgen's Welsh counterpart: Morgen as a truculent person is treated by Malory as queen of Goire (Gower), and her husband Vryence or Vryens he calls king of Goire, from which district he generally brings him when he appears at Arthur's tournaments. Uryence is no other than the Urien of Welsh literature, which connects him as we have already shown with a country called Rheged in the North ; and a passage in the Huth *Merlin*, ii. 143, reads as though Rheged was called also Goire, for it

---

[1] *Bk. of the Dun,* 39ᵃ–41ᵇ; Joyce's *Old Celtic Romances,* pp. 97–105; *Martyrology of Donegal,* Jan. 27 (p. 28).

states that Goire was situated the other side of North-umberland from Logres or England. But besides a Rheged in the North there was also a Rheged in Wales, and the surmise at once suggests itself that it was our Goire or Gower, on the Severn Sea. We have, however, not succeeded in finding any evidence [1] to that effect, whereas on the other hand the name Rheged can be shown to have been once associated with another spot in Wales. We allude to a pas-sage in a poem by a prince who lived and reigned in the 12th century, Howel, son of Owen Gwyned, prince of North Wales; for his son Howel speaks of his reaching the Land of Rheged in one ride from Maelienyd, a part of the present county of Rad-nor; and a 16th century bard gives us a clue to a Rheged which was an island and nearer to Maelienyd than any part of Gower peninsula could be : it was the site of the present town of Aberystwyth, which the bard describes as *Caer Reged uwch cwrr eigiawn* [2], or ' the Castle of Rheged over the brink of the ocean.'

As to the site of Aberystwyth, it is to be noticed that the time cannot be very far past since it was an island, at least at high tide, while, no longer ago than the

---

[1] The only approach to it would be certain tracts in the volume of the *Iolo MSS.* pp. 69-71, 73, 78, which assign to Urien the district between the Towy and the Tawĕ, together with Gower. This was given him by Arthur, we are told, as a reward for having cleared it of Irish invaders But the story is clearly an adaptation of that of Geoffrey, ix. 6, 10, also *R. B. Bruts*, pp. 191-4, where Arthur is described conquering the Picts and Scots in the isles of Loch Lomond, and giving the northern Rheged to Urien, who had been driven from his throne there. Even Geoffrey's Irish king, Guil-lamurius, appears in one of the Iolo tracts under the name Gilmwr : see the *Iolo MSS.* p. 70. All that the tracts in question can, therefore, be said to indicate, is, that the writer or writers of them had heard of a southern Rheged.

[2] Cited s. v. 'Caer Reged' in Lewis Morris' *Celtic Remains*, p. 68, where he gives the poet's name as Morus ILwyd William.

summer of 1886, it became for a time an island, to the terror and peril of a considerable portion of the population. The present name signifies the Mouth of the Ystwyth, which occurs in Ptolemy's Geography as Στουκκία for a more correct form Στοῦκτα or Στουκτία; but, as at present situated, the town would be more correctly called Aber Rheidol[1], as it is rather on the Rheidol than the Ystwyth. The explanation probably is that the two rivers formerly joined their waters before reaching the sea, which appears to have greatly encroached on this part of the coast: even within the memory of the author the grounds between the remains of the castle and the sea have been greatly reduced in extent. A part of the town lies on the south side of the Rheidol: it is called y Dre' Vychan[2] or 'the Little Town,' and connected with the rest by a bridge, where there appears to have been a bridge in the beginning of the 12th century. For we read of it as the only approach made use of in an attack on the castle of Aberystwyth and the Normans in possession at the time, by Gruffud ab Rhys ab Tewdwr in the year 1113[3]: it is thus not improbable that the town was then

---

[1] A *Castell Aber Reidawl* is mentioned under the year 1163, in *Brut y Tywysogion*, but it is not to be assumed that it was identical with Castell Aberystwyth. A site for a small castle might probably have been found in the neighbourhood of the town, as for example at Plas y Crûg, or on the knoll where the Ilanbadarn vicarage now stands.

[2] This is an old name, for the modern Welsh of Keredigion would make it into *y Dre' Vach*.

[3] See the *R. B. Bruts*, p. 311: the chronicler would seem to have known the neighbourhood of Aberystwyth, since, among other places there, he mentions Ystrat Peithyll, Glasgruc, and Ystrat Antarron, which are now known as Peithyll, Glasgrug, and Antaron respectively (ib. p 299). Wales is dotted with many a *caer* and many a *dinas*, the ancient name of which is now unknown, and nothing disappoints the enquirer more than the answer that it is only called *y Gaer*, 'the Castle,' or *y Dinas*, 'the Fortress:' so the author takes this opportunity of stating that he thinks he has discovered that the hill overlooking Aberystwyth from the south of

inaccessible from the mainland on the other side. That this island, the highest part of which is now occupied by the ruins of the castle and a church dedicated to the Archangel Michael, was the spot meant by Howel, is rendered all the more probable by the fact of its being on record, that in the year 1142 he took violent possession of some of the land of his uncle Cadwaladr in that part of Wales and burnt his castle at Aberystwyth[1]. Rheged was even in Howel's time a name of the past, but it was one which a poet might, as we have seen, employ some four centuries later; but Howel gives us a little more than the mere name, for he speaks, if we do not misinterpret his words, of the place he had in view as 'the land of Rheged between night and day[1].' This remarkable description takes us back, perhaps,

the Rheidol, and now called *Pen y Dinas*, on account of the prehistoric earthworks crowning its top, was anciently called *Dinas Maelawr*. This he infers from a 15th century poem, which will be found printed in the *Cylchgrawn* (for 1834) i. 23. The name Dinas Maelawr will help one to understand that of Rhiw Vaelawr in Keredigion, in the Triads, i. 93; ii. 11 : see *R. B. Mab.* p. 301.

[1] The words in the Welsh, as printed in Stephens' *Literature of the Kymry*, p. 53 (see also the *Myv. Arch.* i. 277), read as follows, with his rendering of them into English :—

> ' Esgynneis ar velyn o vaelyenyt
>   Hyd ynhir Reged rwng nos a dyt.'

> *I mounted the yellow steed, and from Maelienyð*
> *Reached the land of Reged between night and day.*

More literally still they would read in English thus :—

> *I mounted on a yellow (steed) from Maelienyð*
> *Even to the land of Rheged between night and day.*

The words *o Vaelyenyt* do not necessarily mean that Howel began his ride from Maelienyð, but only that his horse was one from that district, though the former interpretation is, perhaps on the whole, the more probable. It is hard, granting this, to understand how *rwng nos a dyt* yield the 'night's ride' which Mr. Stephens assumes in his note. But all that difficulty disappears if they are taken in immediate connection with *Reged*, as their position in the line would seem to indicate. The author, however, feels by no means certain that this gives the meaning the poet meant to convey, though he thinks his view, on the whole, preferable to that advocated by Mr. Stephens.

ages beyond the time of Prince Howel into the thick
of Celtic heathendom; and his words might have proved
a hopeless riddle were it not that we are helped to
understand them by another name of the country over
which the dark divinity of Urien is supreme, namely,
that of *yr Echwyd*, or the realm of Sunset.

Up to this point we have mostly devoted this
chapter to two or three islands, or to tracts of land
which may, with a little aid from a hazy imagination,
have been regarded as islands, Glastonbury, Gower,
and the western Rheged. They have forced themselves on our attention as supposed abodes of the
departed; but they by no means exhaust this category
of islands, as will have been seen by the references
already made to others which assume the same character; not to mention the fairy isles playing hide-
and-seek with the bewildered mariner off the coast
of South Wales. Among the former may be mentioned the following, and the list might easily be
extended:—

(1) The Isle of Gwales, or Gresholm (p. 269), which,
with its perennial banqueting, may be compared to the
never failing hospitality of Polydectes on the barren
Isle of Seriphus (p. 232) in Greek legend. It was otherwise by no means unusual to treat the sun-hero's home
as an isle of the sea.

(2) The country of Surluse, in Malory's narrative, is
probably to be identified with the Scilly Isles, or the
Sorlingues as they are called in French, the Syllingar
of the Norsemen, and the Sylinancis Insula of the
Romans, who used them as a place of banishment.
According to Malory, Galahalt, the haute prince, was
lord of Surluse, which is explained by his also calling
him otherwise King of the Long Islands, in the sense

of islands which were a long way off, in French *les Isles Lointaines.* Galahalt, the haute prince, is a slightly disguised alias of Galahad the Grail knight, and in Surluse we have an imperfect reproduction of the same name as Sorlingues [1], which we have also found made into Sorhaut [2].

(3) Bardsey, where Merlin and his nine bards were fabled to have entered the Glass House, taking with them the thirteen treasures of Britain [3]; but the island is called in Welsh Ynys Enlli or Venlli [4], which is probably the more original form of the name, meaning the Isle of Benlli. But Benlli is otherwise known as the Giant, after whom one of the heights of the Moel Vammau range in Flintshire is called. One of the stories of Nennius [5] relates how Benlli, having resisted St. Germanus, was, together with his whole court, burnt to ashes by fire from heaven, as is elsewhere told of Vortigern. The two may probably be regarded as belonging to the same category of dark figures in the Celtic pantheon.

(4) Ynys Lannog, or Glannog's Isle, has already been mentioned (p. 325) as that now known in English as Puffin Island, a few miles to the north-east of Beaumaris. Thither, according to one Grail story, came every week the King of the Dead Castle, in order to

----

[1] The Huth *Merlin*, ii. 159, has Sorelois, and Malory mostly Surluse, but once also Surleuse, which points back to a Surlenge, the *g* of which was either misread *s*, or being written *ʒ* was misread *s*, which was afterwards made into *s*. Compare the name Menzies—for Mengies—and the like.

[2] As to Sorhaut, see p. 324 above.

[3] *Hib. Lec.* p. 155.

[4] See Lewis Morris' *Celtic Remains*, s. v. *Benlli*, p. 33. The elision of the *v* occurs in other instances, such as *Bodorgan* for *Bod Vorgan*, *Rhuabon* for *Rhiw Vabon.* Morris refers to a life of St. Cynhafal, which the author has not been able to consult.

[5] San-Marte's ed. §§ 32, 3 (pp. 48, 9).

harass his neighbours, especially the Queen of the Castle of Maidens, whose knights he slew one after another. But Peredur, having arrived in the course of his wanderings at the Queen's Castle, heard what his uncle the King of the Dead Castle used to do; so he rowed out and landed on the island to fight with him. Peredur prevailed, but the wicked uncle was able to reach his galley before his nephew could slay him. Thus the island may be regarded as having been one of the head-quarters of the truculent King of the Dead [1].

(5) The Isle of Man had the like character, but mostly from the Irish point of view, according to which it was the home of the great fairy druid or magician Manannán mac Lir. It was from Man also, that the Great Ultonian smith Culann was supposed to hail, from whom Cú-Chulainn took his name. According to some accounts, the Isle of Man as a mythic country was that called the Isle of the Men of Falga or Failge, over whom reigned Mider, king of the fairies, when Cúchulainn carried away his daughter Bláthnat, together with his Cauldron and his Three Cows that filled it with their milk [2]. This name of Failge was otherwise explained to mean the Western Isles of Scotland. It may also have been identified with the mythic City of Falias, from which the Tuatha Dé Danann were said to have brought to Ireland one of their treasures, the *Lia Fáil* [3].

(6) To the north-west of Ireland, off the coast of Donegal, stands Tory Island, where the baleful monster Balor lived, and where his grandson the sun-hero, Lug the Long-handed, was, according to one account,

---

[1] Williams' *Seint Greal*, pp. 276-7, 616-7.   [2] *Hib. Lec.* p. 476.
[3] Keating (Dublin, 1880), pp. 112-19.

fabled to have been born.   That isle, according to another set of stories, was the head-quarters of the Fomorian leaders Conaing and Morc, after the former of whom was called Tor Conaing, or Conaing's Tower, which the children of Nemed went to destroy.   The assailants were all overwhelmed by the waves of the sea[1].

(7) Conaing also gave its Irish designation to Anglesey, namely, that of Moin Conaing, or Conaing's Mona. The association of Conaing's name with Anglesey is not known to Welsh literature ; but we have the next thing to this in the fact that the name of Morc, in its Welsh form of March ab Meirchion, is connected with the island as that of its sometime lord, by the 14th century poet D. ab Gwilym.   For he makes the owl, as Blodeued[2], give her pedigree in the following couplet[3] :—

> ' Merch i arglwyd ail Meirchion,
>   Wyf i, myn Dewi ! o Fôn.'
>
> *Daughter of the lord, son of Meirchion,*
> *Am I, by St. David ! from Mona.*

We have, possibly, a faint echo of an ancient superstition about the island as the realm of March ab Meirchion in a poem by the 15th century bard L. Glyn Cothi, which apostrophizes Anglesey as 'the Dark Island[4].'   However, it is to be borne in mind that March would, on this side of the Irish Sea, seem to have been fonder of peninsulas than islands, for he is associated both with the western portion of Carnarvonshire, called Lleyn, and with Cornwall.   In the former,

---

[1] *Hib. Lec.* p. 264 ; also p. 333 above.

[2] *Hib. Lec.* pp. 239, 241.

[3] *Bardoniaeth D. ab Gwilym* (London, 1789), poem clxxxiij. p. 365).

[4] See the *Cylchgrawn* for 1834, i. 92 : the words will also be found quoted in Lewis Morris' *Celtic Remains*, s. v. *Ynys Dowell*, p. 436.

a fine old-fashioned farm-house which looks as if it
had once enjoyed far greater importance than it can
boast at present, stands on the southern side of the
peninsula, and bears the name of Castellmarch, or
March's Castle. With regard to the said March, whose
name means horse, it is fabled that he had horse's
ears. The story goes on to relate, how he used to have
every barber who shaved him killed, lest he should
betray the secret as to his ears. Now on the spot
where the bodies of the murdered barbers were buried,
there grew reeds, from among which a certain of
March's bards chose one to make a pipe. Now the
reed, when it was ready for use as a musical instrument,
would discourse of nought but March ab Meirchion's
equine ears. This so enraged March that he would
have killed the musician had he not been persuaded
to try the pipe himself, when he was at once convinced
that it was the fault of the instrument and not of the
man who blew in it[1]. As to Cornwall, Malory has
much to say about Mark, as the cowardly, treacherous,
and cruel king of that country. That the Cornish
Mark is essentially the same person with the March
of Ileyn, admits of almost absolute proof, which is
worth mentioning here, as it explains a passage in
Malory's narrative, which in this instance has lost its
point and much of its meaning. When King Mark,
who was also called King Fox, on account of his wiles,
had greatly angered Arthur and Lancelot, a knight
called Dynadan who was a famous jester took him
in hand, saying[2]: 'I will make a lay for hym & whan
hit is made I shalle make an harper to synge hit afore
hym Soo anone he wente and made hit and taughte

---

[1] See the *Cymmrodor*, vi. 183, also the *Brython* (for 1860), p. 431.
[2] Malory, x. 27 : see also p. 70 above.

hit an harper that hyght Elyot/And whanne he coude
hit/he taught hit to many harpers. And so by the
wylle of sire Launcelot and of Arthur the harpers went
streyghte in to walys/and in to Cornewaile to syng the
laye that sire Dynadan made kynge Marke/the whiche
was the werste lay that euer harper sange with harp
or with ony other Instrumentys.' Naturally Malory
who made believe he was busying himself with Christian
knights, could not condescend to know that one of
them was a monster with horse's ears, and much less
to tell us the import of what was sung about him;
so he becomes vague and uncommunicative on the
subject of the so-called lay. We know, however, from
the story current in Wales and Ireland[1] that the
burden of it was nothing more or less than this: King
Mark has horse's ears.

The Celtic notion of locating the spirits of the departed on islands is inseparable from the widespread
superstition, that water formed an effective barrier
against their movements; to be conveyed to such
islands they must be ferried across, and once they had
gone, one felt no apprehension of their ever returning
to disturb the living. Procopius, writing in the 6th
century, proves the prevalence of this notion among
some of the Celts of the Continent; and Pliny, writing
in the 1st century, and quoting a Greek writer called
Philemon, is supposed to take us back to the 2nd
century B.C. in one of his references to the northern
ocean. We allude to the following passage[2]: ' Philemon Morimarusam a Cimbris vocari, hoc est, mortuum
mare, usque ad promontorium Rubeas: ultra deinde
Cronium.' It is not clear whether the explanation
' mortuum mare ' emanates from Pliny or was merely

---

[1] *Hib. Lec.* p. 593.   [2] *Historia Naturalis,* iv. 27.

taken by him from the author he was perusing; but whichever of the two it came from, it is scarcely possible to admit that it is quite accurate. The name Mori Marusam, here attributed to the Cimbri, is purely Celtic [1], meaning, probably, not Mortuum Mare but Mortuorum Mare, or the Sea of the Dead; that is, as one may suppose, the sea which the dead had to cross on their way to the home of the Yama of the race.

Leaving the isles and the peninsulas, which have hitherto occupied us, let us now turn our attention to the other notion of the home of the departed and the fairies, namely, in lands supposed to have been overwhelmed by water. This subdivides itself, according as the water is regarded as forming a lake or only an extension of the domain of the sea. Under the first heading come such lakes as Ilyn Tegid, hard by Bala in Merioneth, of which a sufficient mention perhaps has already been made (p. 262). But probably all the other lakes of Wales were supposed to have had inhabitants wealthy in herds of cattle [2], and in our time each mere is

---

[1] Mori is in Welsh mor, ' sea,' Irish muir; while the *marus* of Marusam is represented in the same languages by *marw* and *marbh*, ' dead,' the disappearance of Aryan *s* or *z* between vowels being the rule in the Neoceltic tongues. Marusam as a genitive plural was probably pronounced Marusăm, and the only other early Celtic form to be compared would seem to be the ogmic Irish *Tria maqva Mailagni*, meaning ' Trium Filiorum Mælagni.' The *us* of Marusam seems to represent the weak form of the suffix *ues* of the perfect participle of *mer*, ' to die,' as in the corresponding Sanskrit *mamrushăm*, ' moribundorum : ' the Celtic word should literally mean ' of those who have died.' For a comprehensive study of forms of this kind, see Brugmann's *Grundriss der vergl. Grammatik*, ii. 410–18.

[2] Plenty of instances in point will be found in the author's Welsh Fairy Tales in vols. iv, v, and vi of the *Cymmrodor*. The last example which has come under his notice is that of Ilyn Eidwen, in which the river Aeron rises : it is a mere fragment of the ancient belief, to the effect that at one time ' wild cattle ' used to come out of the lake and rush back into it when disturbed.

supposed to have been formed by the subsidence of a city, whose bells may even now be at times heard merrily pealing. Under the second head fall such instances as the overflowing of Gwyđno's land by the waves of the Irish Sea. That country is known in Welsh as Cantre'r Gwaelod, or the Bottom Hundred, and according to the more common legend, it extended indefinitely from Aberdovey, where the bells ringing *ûn, dau, tri, pedwar, pump*, probably belonged to Gwyđno's realm. The euhemeristic account of the submersion of Gwyđno's Plain is that it occurred in consequence of the negligence of a certain Seithennyn, whose business it was to take care of the embankments and their floodgates; he, one day heavy with drink, forgot all about his charge, and the catastrophe took place. The oldest account, however, is contained in a short poem [1] in the *Black Book of Carmarthen*; and it is by no means such a commonplace story: for the author of the poem knows nothing of Seithennyn's drunkenness, as he merely characterizes him as a person of weak intellect, while he lays the entire blame on a damsel whom he terms the Well Minister or Fountain Servant. What her duties exactly were, we are not told; but she had probably the charge of a magic well, as in the corresponding Irish story [2] of Lough Neagh (p. 129), in which the neglect to keep the lid on the magic spring resulted in an inundation, a catastrophe foretold by the idiot of the family, who occupies there the place of Seithennyn in the Welsh version. Now, the name of the woman who had charge of the well in the Irish story was Liban, which is in Welsh ILïon [3], and occurs in the

---

[1] Evans' *Autotype Facsimile*, pp. 53 b-54 a.

[2] *Bk. of the Dun*, 39ᵃ-41ᵇ; Joyce's *Old Celtic Romances*, pp. 97-105.

[3] Liban is perhaps more correctly written Líban; and the Welsh corresponding (on the supposition of an Irish *b* for an earlier *v*, as in *Eber* and

Welsh account of the deluge resulting from the bursting of ILyn ILïon, or ILïon's Lake[1]. Further, it is this lady's name probably in some one of its forms, or a derivative from it, that meets us in Malory's *Liones*. She has a sister whom he calls Linet, the messenger and confidante of Dame Liones; but Linet is only a slightly altered form of that of the Lunet or Luned[2] who figures in the Welsh story of Owein, namely, as the messenger and confidante of her mistress, the Lady of the Fountain. So in this round-about way we arrive at a partial equation of Dame Liones with the Lady of the Fountain and wife of the Black Knight, whom Owein slays in the Welsh story, and with Liban the attendant on the magic well of Lough Neagh in the Irish one; or better in point of character perhaps with Liban, the queen of Labraid of the Swift Hand on the Sword, and sister of the water lady Fand[3]. Now Malory

Duibne, Hib. Lec. p. 526) to Liban would be ILiwan, which occurs : witness the lake-name ILyn ILiĜan in the story of Kulhwch (*R. B. Mab.* p. 140). The Latin text of Geoffrey, as edited by San-Marte, calls the same water Linligwan (ix. 7), while the Welsh versions partly agree and partly differ; for one reads (*Myv. Arch.* ii. 310) ILyn ILivan, while the other has ILyn ILiaĜn (*R. B. Bruts*, p. 193); and this ILyn ILiaĜn would in its modern form yield exactly the ILyn ILïon of the latest version of the Triads (iii. 13, 97). On the whole, however, ILiĜan or ILiwan seems to be the correct form, supported as it is by the Stagnum *Liuan* of the Nennian *Mirabilia* (*Nennius & Gildas*, § 69, p. 76), where the junction of the waters in question with the Severn is named *Operlinnliuan*, 'the *aber* of the pool of *Liuan*.' Add to this that the commot of ILivon (or ILifon) in Anglesey is called *Lywan* in the *Record of Carnarvon*, pp. 45, 51; for the passage of ILiwan into ILivan is easy, intervocalic *w* being usually made into *v* (written *f*) in North Wales. L. Morris, in his *Celtic Remains*, p. 273, gives the commot's name as ILifon or ILiwon; but, what his authority for the latter may have been, we are not told. He regards the commot as taking its name from a stream called ILivon, which is also the name of a river on the opposite coast of Carnarvonshire. The two ILivons and the ILyn ILiwan above mentioned, probably took their name from one and the same mythic lady, who was in Irish called not only Liban but also Muirgen, meaning Sea-born or Offspring of the Sea.

[1] Triads iii. 13, 97.

[2] See p. 103 above; also the *Hib. Lec.* p. 351.   [3] *Hib. Lec.* p. 463.

makes Dame Liones the owner of a Castle Perilous, hard by the Isle of Avallon, and he also speaks of a country of Liones and a Castle of Liones. This last is spoken of as not far from Tintagel in Cornwall, and the three names of the lady, the castle, and the country are probably not to be severed, though Malory suggests, be it marked, no connection between the lady and the castle or the country. The reason for this is probably to be sought in the fact that he, or the authority he followed, had fixed the Isle of Avallon at Glastonbury; but from what has already been said, it will be seen that we are warranted in unmooring it and attaching it to the west coast of Cornwall; there Dame Liones comes readily by her own in a castle and a country of the same name with herself and lying somewhere under the sea between Lundy and the Isles of Scilly. From that mythic land comes Tristram, just as Galahalt, the haute prince, hails from the Far Away Isles, and Lancelot from the verdant abode of the Lake Lady who was his foster-mother. Without dwelling on the probably extreme antiquity of the myths underlying these romances, one may venture to point out that we seem to have evidence, dating from the early portion of the Roman occupation of this country, to the equation of some such a hero as Tristram or Lancelot with the Heracles of classical mythology; witness the fact that Ptolemy calls Hartland Point Ἡρακλέους Ἄκρον, or the Promontory of Heracles.

It has been suggested that Gower, regarded as belonging to the other world, may have owed that character to the imagination of those who lived on the southern side of the Severn Sea; but this fails to explain how Dyved, or the whole south-west corner of Wales, should have also been regarded in the same light. It

is not hard to understand how a wild inhospitable
country in the north of the Island, separated as it was
from the Brythons by impenetrable forests and lofty
mountain ranges, should have come by the character
given by Procopius to all the region west of the wall
drawn across his Brittia from north to south[1]. But if
the well-marked natural features of the North fail us in
the case of Dyved, we derive a hint from the ancient
station of Blatobulgium. This name seems, as already
hinted (p. 265), to mark the place out as one of the
scenes of the Nibelung-like slaughter of the Meal-bag
Hall. Blatobulgium is supposed to have been at Middleby Kirk, not far from the river Annan, that is to say,
in a district which was probably never inhabited by a
Bythonic population. So we take it that ancient Dyved,
or the land of the Demetæ, was inhabited by a people
hostile to those who gave the latter's country the
character of being the home of the departed. What
formed the boundary between the Demetæ, and the
Silures is unknown : it may have been a dark forest,
or it may have been chiefly a river. The modern map
would suggest the Towy ; but that river is very probably too far west, at any rate its lower course ; and the
Tawy or Tawë, as it is now called, suggests perhaps a
more probable boundary, which would obviate the neces-
sity of postulating two homes of the departed, or two
lands of enchantment, Gower and Dyved, instead of one,
namely, the ancient Demetia embracing both. This
conjecture is not entirely disposed of, even when we
suppose no people north of the Severn Sea to have
looked at Gower in the sinister light in which we
have surmised (p. 329) the Cornish Bythons to have
regarded it.

[1] Procopius, ed. Dindorf (Bonn, 1833), ii. 559 (620), 565 (623 C).

A passage in the *Black Book* poem, mentioned in a previous chapter (p. 60), favours the preference here given to the Tawë. In the dialogue between Gwyn ab Nûd and Gwyđno Garan-hir, Gwyn addresses Gwyđno as follows [1] :—

> 'Hasten to my ridge, the Tavwy abode;
> Not the nearest Tavwe name I to thee,
> But that Tavwe which is the farthest.'

The mention of Gwyn's dwelling on a ridge reminds one of his fairy castle on Glastonbury Tor; and the association with the river Tavwy of the abode of one who was king of the fairies and frequenter of the field of slaughter, recalls the association of the river Dee with a *deva* or divinity, namely, Aerven, who interested herself in war and let her ' wizard stream ' annually indicate the fortune of the struggles between the Welsh and the English, according to the side on which the floods encroached [2]. The name Tavwy is pretty certainly the antecedent of the modern Tawy or Tawë [3] on which Swansea stands, called in Welsh Aber Tawë. But whether the river meant in the dialogue was the Tawë or the Devon river Taw, or some other river of similar name, each of them was probably so called by reason of

---

[1] Evans' *Autotype*, p. 49 b, where the river-name is first written tawuẏ and then tawue twice.

[2] See Rhys' *Celtic Britain*, p. 68, and Giraldus' *Itin. Kambriæ*, ii. 11 (p. 139).

[3] The *Black Book* Tavwẏ, or Tavwe, cannot be the Towy which was the Τόβιος of Ptolemy's Geography. The Welsh forms of its name are Tywi and Towy, the latter being the more colloquial, and bearing the same relation to the other as *Howel, Owein,* and *bowyd* do to *Hywel, Ywein,* and *bywyd* : see *Hib. Lec.* pp. 63, 162. The elision of the *v* of Tavwy and Tavwe, to make Tawy and Tawe, has plenty of analogy: witness such words as *awyn,* 'a rein,' for *avwyn* (afwyn), from the Latin *habēna* ; and *awch,* ' edge, sharpness,' for *avwch* (afwch). We have possibly a more serious rival of the Tawë in the Devonshire Taw, the Welsh form of whose name is unfortunately unknown to the author.

the association with it of the abode of Gwyn, king of the fairies. So far then as this goes it favours the fitness, mythologically speaking, of the Tawë, to have formed part of an ancient boundary.

To these remarks may fittingly be added a word on the Severn in the same capacity of a boundary water. Here our attention is at once challenged by the location on its banks of the home of the Witches and the prison of Mabon son of Modron (p. 294). Both were at Gloucester, called in Welsh Caer Loyw or Loew [1], of which the English name is a kind of translation; for it means the Castle of Gloyw [2]. In the Brythonic tongue of the close of the Roman occupation, it would have sounded *Castra Glēvi*, which agrees with Glevum [3] as the attested form of the Latin name of the place. By the father of the Witches we are probably to understand no other person than Gloyw: he presumably belonged to the same class of divinities as Gwyn ab Nûḍ, and his name, meaning 'bright or shining,' seems to invite comparison with Gwyn's, which meant 'white,' both being contradictory of what one would, perhaps, have expected. The Mabinogi of Pwyłł makes Pryderi marry Kigva, grand-daughter of Gloyw Wałłt-lydan [4], while Geoffrey of Monmouth has identified a Gloyw with Claudius Cæsar, and

---

[1] See pp. 81, 122, 212 above; also *R. B. Mab.* p. 210; Guest, i. 323.

[2] The Cair Gloui of Nennius is probably editorial gibberish for Caer Gloiu, where Gloiu would be exactly the old spelling of the Welsh *Gloew* or *Gloyw*. The diphthong represented by *oi, oe,* or *oy* is one of the regular developments of *ē* in Welsh, somewhat as in French words like *loi, roi,* and others of the same kind.

[3] See Hübner's *Inscrip. Lat. Brit.* (vol. vii. of the Berlin *Corpus*), pp. 29, 30, and Inscr. 54.

[4] So in the *R. B. Mab.* p. 25, but elsewhere he is more usually called Gloyw Gwlad-lydan, as for instance in *R. B. Bruts*, p. 96: the former means Gloyw Broad-hair, while the latter would be Gloyw Broad-realm, or possibly Gloyw Widely-ruling.

the Welsh translations call him Gloyw throughout[1]; but the association of the emperor with Gloucester seems to rest on no historical basis, except the finding of many coins of his reign on the spot. Geoffrey further cements a peace, made between Gloyw (Claudius) and the native king Gweiryđ[2], by giving the latter the former's daughter, called Genuissa[3], to wife; but the name Gweiryđ is probably but another form of Gwri, one of Pryderi's names[4]. So Geoffrey's is only another version of the story of Pryderi marrying a grand-daughter of Gloyw Waƚt-lydan. The mythic element still further betrays itself in his narrative, when it describes Gweiryđ helping to bring Orkney and the other islands into subjection to Gloyw (Claudius), and also when on

[1] See Geoffrey, iv. 12–16, *R. B. Bruts*, pp. 94–8, and the *Myv. Arch.* ii. 187–194.

[2] It is right to say that the name Gweiryđ does not occur in the Latin text, which has that of Arviragus instead: for this last it cites from the fourth satire of Juvenal the passage, ll. 126–7:—

> 'Regem aliquem capies, aut de temone Britanno
> Excidet Arviragus.'

[3] So in San-Marte's Latin text, but the *Red Book* (*R. B. Bruts*, p. 96) has G6enwissa, and the *Myv. Arch.* ii. 191, Gennylles.

[4] *R. B. Mab.* pp. 21, 24; Guest, iii. 65, 69. Gwri was called in full Gwri Waƚt-euryn, or G. of the Golden Hair, while the Welsh versions of Geoffrey give Gweiryđ an obscure epithet: the *Red Book* Geoffrey seems to make it *Adarweinda6c*, or *Adarweinda6t* (*R. B. Bruts*, pp. 94, 97), while the *Myv. Arch.* gives the variants *gweryd adar weudawt* and *adarweinida6c* (ii. 188–9). What must be the same name occurs in the Kulhwch as *g6eir dathar wennida6c* and *gweir dathar wenida6c* (*R. B. Mab.* pp. 110, 112), but it is equally obscure. On the whole, the name may, perhaps, be supposed to have been Gweiryđ (or Gweir) Adarweinidawc, meaning 'Gweiryđ who is the servant of birds,' or possibly 'Gweiryđ who has birds as servants.' In either case, the person in question would seem to equate not only with Pryderi but with Urban of the Black Thorn, as to whose birds see p. 258. Pryderi, by being named Gwri Waƚt-euryn, looks as if he bore the name of one of his mother's birds, the famous Birds of Rhiannon. It is these birds, probably, that sometimes appear in modern Wales as embodiments of angels attending on good men, and answering to the call of 'Wryd, Wryd!' For an instance in point, see a story contributed by the author to the *Cymmrodor*, vi. 170.

one occasion it makes Gweirŷd send his soldiers to pass the winter in Ireland. For, after what has already been said, the Hadesian interpretation of the allusion to the islands need not be discussed any further. Let the remark suffice, that even as the importance of Glevum to the Romans belonged to the time before they had obtained possession of Isca Silurum, so Caer Loyw probably marks a boundary of much earlier importance to the Celts than any spot near the Tawë. In a word, the Severn and the Tawë may be taken as marking successive stages in the westward march of the Celtic settlers.

Before closing this chapter we return for a moment to the superstitious beliefs attaching to the islands lying near Britain, and the fact of their association with the dark divinities and the dead; so we append, to the remarks already made on that subject, the words of a writer who lived in the first century of our era. We allude to Plutarch, whose words are to the following effect [1]:—

'Demetrius further said, that of the islands around Britain many lie scattered about uninhabited, of which

---

[1] The author has to thank Mr. Farnell of Exeter College for kindly calling his attention to the passage. The text, as printed in the Didot Edition of Plutarch, vol. iii. p. 511 (*De Defectu Oraculorum, xviij.*), runs as follows :—

Ὁ δὲ Δημήτριος ἔφη, τῶν περὶ τὴν Βρεττανίαν νήσων εἶναι πολλὰς ἐρήμους σποράδας, ὧν ἐνίας δαιμόνων καὶ ἡρώων ὀνομάζεσθαι· πλεῦσαι δὲ αὐτὸς ἱστορίας καὶ θέας ἕνεκα, πομπῇ τοῦ βασιλέως, εἰς τὴν ἐγγιστα κειμένην τῶν ἐρήμων, ἔχουσαν οὐ πολλοὺς ἐποικοῦντας, ἱεροὺς δὲ καὶ ἀσύλους πάντας ὑπὸ τῶν Βρεττανῶν ὄντας· ἀφικομένου δ' αὐτοῦ νεωστὶ, σύγχυσιν μεγάλην περὶ τὸν ἀέρα καὶ διοσημείας πολλὰς γενέσθαι, καὶ πνεύματα καταρραγῆναι καὶ πεσεῖν πρηστῆρας. Ἐπεὶ δ' ἐλώφησε, λέγειν τοὺς νησιώτας, ὅτι τῶν κρεισσόνων τινὸς ἔκλειψις γέγονεν. Ὡς γὰρ λύχνος ἀναπτόμενος, φάναι, δεινὸν οὐδὲν ἔχει, σβεννύμενος δὲ πολλοῖς λυπηρός ἐστιν, οὕτως αἱ μεγάλαι ψυχαὶ τὰς μὲν ἀναλάμψεις εὐμενεῖς καὶ ἀλύπους ἔχουσιν, αἱ δὲ σβέσεις αὐτῶν καὶ φθοραὶ πολλάκις μὲν, ὡς νυνὶ, πνεύματα καὶ ζάλας τρέπουσι, πολλάκις δὲ λοιμικοῖς πάθεσι τὸν ἀέρα φαρμάττουσιν. Ἐκεῖ μέντοι μίαν εἶναι νῆσον, ἐν ᾗ τὸν Κρόνον καθεῖρχθαι φρουρούμενον ὑπὸ τοῦ Βριάρεω καθεύδοντα· δεσμὸν γὰρ αὐτῷ τὸν ὕπνον μεμηχανῆσθαι, πολλοὺς δὲ περὶ αὐτὸν εἶναι δαίμονας ὀπαδοὺς καὶ θεράποντας.

some are named after deities and heroes. He told us also, that, being sent by the emperor with the object of reconnoitring and inspecting, he went to the island which lay nearest to those uninhabited, and found it occupied by few inhabitants, who were, however, sacrosanct and inviolable in the eyes of the Britons. Soon after his arrival a great disturbance of the atmosphere took place, accompanied by many portents, by the winds bursting forth into hurricanes, and by fiery bolts falling. When it was over, the islanders said that some one of the mighty had passed away. For as a lamp on being lit, they said, brings with it no danger, while on being extinguished it is grievous to many, just so with regard to great souls, their beginning to shine forth is pleasant and the reverse of grievous, whereas the extinction and destruction of them frequently disturb the winds and the surge as at present ; oftentimes also do they infect the atmosphere with pestilential diseases. Moreover there is there, they said, an island in which Cronus is imprisoned with Briareus keeping guard over him as he sleeps ; for, as they put it, sleep is the bond forged for Cronus. They add that around him are many deities, his henchmen and attendants.'

The last words of this passage remind us of many a Welsh shepherd's vision of Arthur and his Men dozing away in a cave until the peal of destiny ring them forth to the field of battle. The more important parallel, however, is the one which may be drawn between the slumbering Cronus as here described, and the owner of the Holy Grail, who under the name of Bron dwells in one of those 'isles of Erinn,' or Merlin with his bardic satellites entering the Glass House in Bardsey, never more to appear among men. This brief story of Demetrius might serve as the text for a dissertation on the ancient mythology of the British Isles, but we shall be content to advert only to the sacredness of the persons of the dwellers in the small isles of the sea near our shores. This is paralleled by what Pomponius Mela[1] has left on record as to the inhabitants of the islands on the coast of Brittany, and it discloses a motive which may possibly have been present to the early recluses, who were fond of withdrawing to the islands; for it is not wholly improbable, that some of them expected to derive advantage from the wall of inviolability which the pagans of former ages had built round the person of the islander. At any rate, it would be hazardous to treat that consideration as a *quantité négligeable* before the sanguinary advent of the Norsemen; and it lends some countenance to our conjecture, expressed elsewhere[2] to the following effect :—'Irish druidism absorbed a certain amount of Christianity; and it would be a problem of considerable difficulty to fix on the point where it ceased to be druidism, and from which onwards it could be said to be Christianity in any restricted sense of that term.' This has been characterized[3] as an extreme view, but, after toning it down a little, we should be disposed to extend it so as to take in the Celts not only of Ireland, but of Britain too.

---

[1] Frick's edition, chap. iii. 48; see also Vigfusson and Powell's *Corpus Poet. Boreale*, i. 121, and the *Hib. Lec.* pp. 195-9.

[2] *Hib. Lec.* p. 224.

[3] By Mr. Newell in his *Saint Patrick* (in the S. P. C. K. series entitled 'The Fathers for English Readers'), p. 221.

CHAPTER XVI.

GREAT BRITAIN AND LITTLE BRITAIN.

THE question how the stories about Arthur and his men reached the Normans is one of considerable difficulty; and perhaps we could not do better than give here a summary of the principal views concerning it. Let us take first that of M. Gaston Paris, as expressed in the thirtieth volume of the History of French Literature[1]. According to M. Paris, the appearance of these stories in a French dress belongs to a period comprising a little more than a century: it began about the middle of the 12th century, and ended before the close of the ensuing one. This species of French literature has been known in France as 'la matière de Bretagne,' a term which he construes with exclusive reference to Great Britain and not to Little Britain or Brittany, as we now more briefly call the country of our Armorican kindred. It was, he thinks, as one of the results of the conquests of the Normans in Wales, that lays and stories devoted to Arthurian themes reached the Continent; and it was only after these had stimulated the literary appetite of France, and, through it, that of cultured Europe generally, that Brittany began to be invited to contribute her share of the entertainment. But there is no reason to believe that the lays and stories in question found their way all of

[1] *Histoire littéraire de la France*, xxx. (Paris, 1888), more especially pp. 1-22.

a sudden into French literature: they must have been, so to say, in the air some time before the middle of the 12th century. The following consideration with regard to Geoffrey of Monmouth favours this view: Geoffrey published his *Historia Regum Britanniæ* about 1136; and, written as it was in Latin, it was soon translated into French; nevertheless, it exercised very little influence on the materials which went into the fabric of the romances. Thus it may be inferred that they were even then so popular and so widely known, that Geoffrey's more ambitious efforts were powerless to affect them to any extent worth mentioning. At any rate, in 1155 Wace published a rhymed translation of Geoffrey's *Historia* under the name of *le Roman de Brut*, or the Story of Brutus, and from divers passages in it we perceive, that there was even then a great *embarras de richesse* in the matter of fables about Arthur. Wace in fact tells his readers, that the *fableor* or story-tellers had so elaborated their stories about Arthur that they had succeeded in making even what might be true seem to be of their own fabling. This raises the question who the story-tellers were: M. Gaston Paris believes that they were Welshmen, and he goes so far as to mention reasons for his belief, that Welshmen of this class had been in the habit of crossing the boundary into England even before the Norman Conquest; and after that event it was not long, he thinks, before they found their way to the Continent, to pursue their profession there at the courts, great and small, of the north of France.

One class of these wandering professionals sang their *lais bretons*, which, M. Paris says, consisted of pieces of music accompanied with words. So a Welshman might compare them in that respect to the

Penillion Singing which still lingers at the Eistedvod in
Wales, and has the characteristic that the accompani-
ment is not the music but the verse. Though the
music of the lays discussed by M. Paris formed their
chief characteristic, the words were not without their
importance, and those who did not understand them
required to be told what they meant. Thus it was the
first French versions destined to be the materials of
the lays in their French form came into existence, to
wit, through the instrumentality of the minstrels themselves. How these last acquitted themselves in their
efforts to write French we have no means of judging,
as we have nothing to go by except the *lais bretons* in
their French form, of which French literature boasts
a considerable wealth. They usually refer to some
story of love or misfortune, but they retain no trace
of the music. They consist nearly all of rhyming
couplets of eight syllables a line. This, however, does
not mark the end of the French development, for the
lays and the stories in prose served as the materials,
which, according to M. Paris, the romancers used in the
composition of their poems. Far the most important
of the romancers was Chrétien de Troyes, whose
earliest productions date somewhat before the middle of
the 12th century. He has not only left us the largest
number of rhymed romances, but his style of work
soon became the model and standard for all the subsequent romancers. Speaking of the romances generally, and especially with regard to their groundwork,
M. Paris divides them into two classes, namely, biographic and episodic. The biographic romance is a
poem pieced together by means of the various lays
and tales relating to a single hero, whose life is thus
more or less continuously described from his birth or,

at least, from his appearance at Arthur's court to the
day of his death: such are the romances of Durmart,
Guinglain and Mériadeuc. The romances of the other
class restrict themselves to episodes in the life of certain knights, of whom the favourite in this respect was
Gauvain (Gwalchmei); and it is needless to say that on
the whole these romances are shorter than the biographic
ones. Like the lays, the romances, without distinction
of class, consist as a rule of rhyming couplets of octosyl-
labic lines, and they were intended to be read, not sung.

To return to the *lais bretons*, they were, as already
hinted, not the only channels through which M. Paris
makes the stories of Wales reach the Normans, whether
in England or on the Continent; for Wace and others
give ample proofs in their poems, that Brythonic story-
tellers were busy at work at all the courts where a
cultured society was found willing to listen to them.
The name of the most famous has been identified by M. Paris in two authors; for Giraldus Cambrensis[1] describes him as 'famosus ille fabulator
Bledhericus, qui tempora nostra paulo prævenit.' His
name was therefore Bledri, or more correctly speaking
Bleðri, which one readily recognizes in the French
forms of Bléri or Bréri in the following passage in the
fragmentary romance of Tristan by a certain Thomas,
who, according to M. Paris, wrote in England about
the year 1170:—

> 'Entre cels qui solent cunter
> E del cunte Tristran parler,
> Il en cuntent diversement,
> Oï en ai de plusur gent;
> Asez sai que chescun en dit,
> Et ço qu'il unt mis en escrit.
> Mès sulum ço que j'ai oï

[1] *Descriptio Kambriæ*, i. 17.

Nel dient pas sulum Breri,
Ky solt les gestes e les cuntes
De toz les reis, de toz les cuntes
Ki orent esté en Bretaingne.'

Such are the views held by M. Gaston Paris as to
the origin of the Arthurian romances; but very different
ones have lately been put forward by Prof. Foerster in
the introduction to his recently published edition of
Chrétien's *Erec* and at greater length by Prof. Zimmer[1].
Without going into details, let it suffice to say, that, on
the negative side, the latter challenges the production
of any evidence to show, that Welsh bards or minstrels
used to sing to the Saxons in England before the
Norman Conquest, or even after that event to either
Normans or Saxons at a time early enough for the
purpose of M. Paris' argument[2]. He contends that the
term 'lais bretons' and 'la matière de Bretagne' had
nothing to do with Wales, but everything with the
Bretons and Brittany. Then as to the lays and the romances, and the suggestion that the latter are derived
from the former, he denies it, partly because neither he
nor Foerster knows of any lays which can be said to have
been originally Arthurian; partly also—and this brings
us to the positive side of Zimmer's contention—because
he is convinced that the romances were based on stories
in prose rather than verse. He even goes so far as
to call attention to what he considers an ancient and
far-reaching distinction between Celts and Teutons,

---

[1] His researches are to be found in this year's *Göttingische gelehrte Anzeigen*,
pp. 488-528, being a review of Mr. Nutt's *Studies on the Legend of the Holy
Grail*, and pp. 785-832, being a review of M. Paris' contribution to the 30th
vol. of the *Hist. lit. de la France*; but the latter article is finished in *another*
publication, called the *Zeitschrift für französische Sprache und Litteratur* (edited
by Körting and Koschwitz at Oppeln and Leipsic), pp. 231-56.

[2] The nearest approach to such evidence in Welsh is, perhaps, the case
of the minstrel mentioned in the Mabinogi of Math, and brought before the
reader at p. 288 above.

namely, that while the Teutonic way of dealing with the heroic was to express it in the form of an epic poem, the Celtic ideal was that of an epic story in prose. To suit the Norman the Celtic originals had not only to be translated into his language, but also transformed into the epic form of his predilection. The versification was his own business, or that of his French neighbours; but the translation was quite a different matter belonging to an antecedent stage, and this is believed by Zimmer to have been gradually done, in the first instance, by the Bretons of the eastern portion of Brittany when they gave up their own Brythonic speech to adopt Norman French in its stead, and when their nobles became dependent on Normandy.

Accordingly Dr. Zimmer lays great emphasis on the difference between the Arthur of the romances, whom he tries to trace to Breton sources, and the Welsh Arthur whom Nennius, for instance, mentions hunting the *Porcus Troit*[1]. This, however, does not go quite far enough, as the rôle he assigns to the Normanized Bretons of east Brittany does not exclude the Welsh from playing a similar rôle with regard to the Normans later, namely, after the advent of the latter into Wales: witness the case of the Welshman Bledri. The twofold Brythonic origin of the romances makes itself perceptible in a way which the readers of these chapters may have already noticed, especially in the matter of proper names. Looked at from our point of view, the latter divide themselves into two groups:—

---

[1] When Zimmer says in the *Gött. g. Anz.* p. 522, that Nennius' *Troit* is regular, as to consonants and vowels, for the *Trwyth* of later Welsh, that is so far from being correct that the later form should be not *Trwyth*, but *Trwyd*, which in fact occurs. So one may, perhaps, compare the name *Twrch Trwyd* with Cormac's *Orc Tréith*.

1. Well-known names like Gauvain and Modred[1], the forms of which do not admit of being explained as the result of misreading or miscopying of Welsh originals: they may be the French forms which the Normanizing Bretons gave them—without the direct intervention of scribes or literary men of any kind—when they adopted French as their language. 2. Names like Gonemans, Bron, and Palomydes, together with place-names like Aroie, which readily admit of being explained from Welsh originals: these mostly belong to the romances more or less closely connected with the story of the Holy Grail, which itself we have endeavoured to trace to Welsh sources. This opens up a new and difficult question, which may be confidently left to future research.

When the prose story is regarded as the epic form preferred by the ancient Celts, it is by no means meant that verse was excluded: the contrary is frequently found to have been the case, as they were very fond of relieving the heavy march of the prose narrative with the livelier canter of lyric poetry. The epic story, loosely strung together as it was, admitted of this readily enough, but when the verses are found to make up in point of quantity a considerable portion of the narrative, it may prove difficult to decide whether the story was originally all in verse or not. This would

---

[1] But when Dr. Zimmer builds repeatedly, as, for instance, in the *Gött. g. Ans.*, p. 527, on the supposition that *Ouein* or *Owein* takes the place in Welsh of *Eugein* or *Ywein* after the year 982, as though the latter in the form *Ywain* were not still a Welsh name to be set over against the Breton *Yvain*, one can only say that he has not observed the facts; and when, after dealing with an oversight of ours as to its etymology, he suggests, ib. p. 818, that it is but the Greek-Latin *Eugenius*, we may say that idea is by no means new to us. We must, however, confess that we have never felt so certain as Zimmer does, as to the phonological possibility of deriving *Ywain* from *Eugenius*.

apply, perhaps, to some Irish tales and in Welsh to the *History of Taliessin*; but not to the oldest Welsh stories known as the *Four Branches of the Mabinogi*[1]. One or two of them contain a few verses, and the story of Kulhwch and Olwen is not without an instance, which, as we wish to say something concerning this kind of Welsh poetry, may be here cited. It refers to Kei returning from a successful quest and presenting Arthur with a trophy consisting of the beard of a giant called Dillus[2]: Kei represented the giant to have been shaved with wooden razors whilst he was still alive, so Arthur drove Kei into great rage by singing the following *englyn* on the occasion:—

> ' Kynnllyuan aoruc kei.
> O uaryf dillus uab eurei.
> Pei iach dy angheu uydei.'
>
> *The leash made by thee, O Kei,*
> *Of Dillus, son of Evrei's beard,*
> *Were he alive, thy death would be.*

A late Triad attributes to Arthur another englyn about his knights, as follows[3]:—

> ' Sef yw : vyn tri chatuarchawc
> Mened. a llud llurugawc.
> A cholovyn kymry karadawc.'
>
> *These my war-knights, three in number,*
> *Mened and Llud Mail-wearer,*
> *And Caradog Cambria's pillar.*

As a longer specimen of the same metre, may be mentioned the *englynion* forming the dialogue between

---

[1] The author's theory as to the meaning and proper use of the words *Mabinogi* and *Mabinogion*, as set forth in his preface to the Oxford text of the *Red Book Mabinogion*, is adopted by Zimmer in the *Gött. g. Anz.*, pp. 512-5, where he accuses M. Loth of using in his French version, entitled *Les Mabinogion*, that term in all the misleading senses which inaccurate writers have succeeded in associating with it.

[2] *R. B. Mab.* p. 133; Guest, ii. 304.

[3] *R. B. Mab.* p. 308; *Myv. Arch.* ii. 21 (Triad ii. 57).

Arthur and Gwenhwyvar, cited in an early chapter (pp. 57, 8). A similar string of englynion is that of a dialogue between Arthur and the Eagle into which Arthur's nephew Eliwlod had been transformed when he died. The Eagle, however, does not relate a story but girds himself to the saintlier task of giving Arthur various pieces of moral advice. A better instance, in point of matter and action, is a dialogue between Gwalchmei and Drystan (Tristram) in a scene like the meeting of Gwalchmei with Peredur, when the latter had half-killed Kei (p. 82), only that in the verses Tristram takes the place occupied by Peredur in the story called after that knight. We are not concerned here with the question of the origin of the story, but in passing we wish to refer to the statement frequently made, that Tristram never had anything to do with Arthur originally. That, no doubt, is the impression left on one's mind by the way in which Malory tries to bring Tristram in contact with Arthur ; but those who absolutely sever Arthur and Tristram, ought to tell us what to make of the Triad which mentions Tristram watching the swine of March ab Meirchion, with Arthur trying by fair means and foul to obtain possession of some of their number[1]. The scribe or scribes who gave the Triad its present form were capable of a good deal of muddling, but we are sceptical as to their power of absolutely inventing. To return to the dialogue, the following are some of the triplets[2] :—

'GWALCHMEI.

Trystan gyfaill rhianedd,
Cyn mynd yngwaith gorfedd,
Goreu dim yw tangnefedd.'

---

[1] *R. B. Mab.* p. 307 ; *Myv. Arch.* ii. 6, 20, 73 (Triads i. 30, ii. 56, iii. 101).
[2] From the *Myv. Arch.* i. 178, 9.

> Drystan, the friend of the fair,
> Before thou go to the grave
> The best of all things is peace.

'DRYSTAN.

O caf fy nghleð ar fy nghlun,
Am ꞁaw ðeau i 'm ðiffyn,
Ai gwaeth finneu nag undyn?'

> If my sword be at my side,
> And my right hand me defend,
> Must I yield to other men?

'GWALCHMEI.

Trystan gynneðfau eglur,
Cyn cynnaws ꞁiaws ꞁafur,
Na wrthod yn gar Arthur.'

> Drystan of noble qualities,
> Ere thou hast many a hardship,
> Refuse not Arthur's friendship.

'DRYSTAN.

Gwalchmai o honot y pwyꞁaf,
Ag om pen y ꞁafuriaf:
Fal i'm carer y caraf.'

> Gwalchmei, 'tis of thee I think,
> My brain's labour is of thee:
> I will love as one loves me.

'GWALCHMEI.

Trystan gynneðfau blaengar,
Gorwlychyd cafod cann dâr:
Tyred i ymweled ath gâr.'

> Drystan of prime qualities,
> The rain wets a hundred oaks:
> Come with me to see thy friend.

'DRYSTAN.

Gwalchmai attebion ——,
Gorwlychyd cafod cann rhych:
Minneu af ir lle mynnych.'

> Gwalchmei of —— replies,
> Rain wets a hundred furrows:
> Whither thou wilt, will I go.

Gwalchmei then leads Drystan to Arthur, and the conversation proceeds as follows :—

'GWALCHMEI.

Arthur attebion cymmen,
Gorwlychyd cafod cann penn :
ILyma Drystan byð lawen.'

Arthur of the neat replies,
The rain wets a hundred heads :
Here is Drystan, now rejoice.

'ARTHUR.

Gwalchmai attebion difai,
Gorwlychyd cafod cann tai :
Croesaw wrth Drystan fy Nai.'

Gwalchmei of blameless replies,
The rain wets a hundred roofs :
Welcome is Drystan my Nephew.

We have quoted this dialogue at so great a length in order to call attention to a very common feature of Welsh verse of the kind, and one which to our mind proves that it was to be sung to music, probably that of the harp : it is the fact, that the sense intended to be sustained is left to be conveyed by the last line of every triplet. The other two may help, but it is not necessary they should ; so the action of the little drama is almost confined to the lines :—

G. The best of all things is peace.
D. Must I yield to other men ?
G. Refuse not Arthur's friendship.
D. I will love as one loves me.
G. Come with me to see thy friend.
D. Whither thou wilt, will I go.
G. Here is Drystan, now rejoice.
A. Welcome is Drystan my nephew.

In the first two verses of the triplet, the voice of the singer and the music of the harp may have played at a game of baffling each other over otiose epithets or com-

monplaces about rain or snow, or anything else to which
the whim of the poet chose to resort; but unless the
singer succeeded in making his words clearly intelligible
in the last line, he probably forfeited the attention of his
audience, just as a Penillion Singer would nowadays
not fail to do at an Eisteddvod.

It is right to say that except the rare triplets in the
Welsh stories to which reference has been made, none
of those mentioned or cited by us are known to occur
in ancient manuscripts. On the other hand, it is to
be noticed that others of the same kind do so occur.
For instance, the *Red Book* contains a large number of
them, several series of which form dialogues. They are
well represented also in the *Black Book of Carmarthen,*
from which some have been cited, especially from the
dialogue between Gwyn ab Nûd and Gwydno Garan-hir
(pp. 155, 364), and that is not the only dialogue of the
kind in that manuscript.   The same is also the metre of
most of the Englynion of the Graves in the *Black Book.*
Many triplets, both in the *Black Book* and the *Red,* could
be produced to illustrate the comparative importance of
the third line, as indicated in connection with the Drystan
dialogue.   It is remarkable, however, that hardly any
instances of this metre occur in the *Book of Aneurin*
or that of *Taliessin,* both manuscripts belonging to
the 13th century.   The official bards were inclined
to cultivate more difficult metres, stricter rhymes, and
greater obscurity of speech, while the triplet in its
commonest form was simple, smooth, and intelligible.
It was, therefore, probably popular, and, in the case of
the dialogue form which it affected, it must have been
attended with the dramatic effect of a rudimentary
opera.

In its simplest form, the triplet consists of lines of

seven syllables each, but eight occasionally occur. In
the instances quoted the three lines rhyme, and this
appears to have been the more common form; but it
was by no means obligatory, for we find that the first
or second line does not always rhyme. Lastly, it is not
uncommon here and there among triplets to find stanzas
of four or more lines, as in the following from the
Englynion of the Graves [1] :—

> 'E beteu ẏnhir vẏnẏt.
> ẏn llvẏr ẏ guẏr lluossit.
> bet gvrẏen gvrhẏd engu*avt*.
> a llvẏt*auc* uab lliwelit.'

> *The graves on the Long Mountain* [2],
> *Well do multitudes know them—*
> *The grave of Gwrien famed in war,*
> *And Llwydawg son of Lywelyd.*

Here the fourth line contains an assonance with the
last syllable of the third line, and two similar stanzas
occur in the body of the Mabinogi of Mâth ab
Mathonwy, together with another stanza of the same
kind, except that the four lines end in a common rhyme [3].
There are other variations, which require, however, no
special mention; and all the englynion of three or four
lines to which we have thus far called attention may,
roughly speaking, be characterized as parisyllabic.

We now come to a species which is regularly impari-
syllabic; for in this case the stanza consists of a line of
nine or ten syllables followed by one of six and that by one
line (or two) of seven or eight. The one coincides with
the four-lined *englyn* which is popular in modern Welsh,
but the other represents the more ancient form, falling,
as it does, under the wider description of a triplet. It has

---

[1] Evans' *Aut. Facsimile,* p. 33 b.
[2] Can this be the Longmynd?
[3] See the *Hib. Lec.* p. 399.

the peculiarity, that of the nine or ten syllables of the first line, one, two, or even three are considered hypermetric: most commonly in old Welsh the excess, or *gair cyrch* as it is called, is one word of two syllables, which may or may not be supported by an assonance in the short line. In writing modern Welsh, the *gair cyrch* is separated from the rest of the line by a —, which has no reference to the sense. Now, leaving the *gair cyrch* out of consideration, this kind of triplet follows, in the matter of rhyme, much the same rules as the parisyllabic one, as will be seen from the following specimen from the Gwyn-Gwyðno dialogue, where Gwyn describes himself thus[1] :—

> 'Mi awum lle llas milvir—prid*ein*.
> or duÿr*ein* ir gogl*et*.
> Mi. wi. wiw. vintev. y. b*et*.'

> *I have been where fell the soldiers of Britain,*
> *From the east to the north:*
> *I am the escort of the grave.*

Here the first line of the triplet does not rhyme with the other two, as the words in question are *milvir, goglet, bet*; but the hypermetric word *pridein* has an assonance in *duyrein* in the short line. In the next instance to be cited the three lines rhyme, but the *gair cyrch* has no echo in the short line[1] :—

> ' Niguorcosam nemheunaur—henoid
> Mitelu nit gurmaur
> Mi amfranc dam ancalaur.'

> *No maenawr do I possess* (?) *to-night*
> *My household is not too large—*
> *My Frank and I round our cauldron.*

This is the first of three englynion of this kind in the 9th century manuscript of the Juvencus Paraphrase

---

[1] Evans' *Aut. Facsimile*, p. 50 b. The — is ours, and the Italics are meant to call attention to the rhymes and assonances.

in the University Library at Cambridge[1]. It contains also nine others of a religious nature, among which the following occurs :—

> 'Gur dicones remedau[t]—elbid
> Anguorit anguoraut
> Niguru gnim molim trinta[ut].'

> *He who made the wonder of the world—*
> *He who saved us—will save us:*
> *No hard work to praise the Trinity.*

This is not the place to point out the various ways in which alliteration and assonance have been elaborated in Welsh verse since the 9th century ; but we may remark that the long line and the short one taken together are known in Welsh as the *paladr*, 'shaft or spear,' of the englyn. The latter word, *englyn*, was loosely used formerly in Welsh to signify any short stanza marked off by the rhyme, the music or the sense as complete in itself: it seems to mean what is 'connected or joined' together. Both the englyn of four lines and that of three are metrically speaking composite metres, the latter being made up of a *paladr*, and a line added to make it a triplet. This may, perhaps, be regarded as the outcome of the same tendency which made Triads once the fashion in Welsh : in the Triad we have the number three applied to the subject-matter, and in the triplet to the metrical form. At any rate, the couplet with the *gair cyrch* seems to date far earlier than the 9th century triplet ; for we detect it in an epitaph which Hübner[2] places in the earliest group of our post-Roman inscriptions, supposed by him

---

[1] This and the following englyn are printed here from Skene's *Four Anc. Books of Wales,* ii. 1, 2. They are very obscure, and the translation is only tentative.

[2] See his *Inscriptiones Britanniæ Christianæ,* No. 131 (p. 46); also his chronological classification, pp. xx, xxi.

to belong to the 5th or the 6th century. It occurs on a stone at a place called Ilech Idris, between Trawsfynyd and Dolgelley in Merioneth, and reads as follows:—

> 'PORIVS
> HIC IN TVMVLO IACIT
> HOMO XP*IST*IANVS FVIT'

The position of the name *Porius* on the stone becomes at once intelligible when the epitaph is written after the fashion of the *paladr* of an englyn, with ivs and ian reckoned as one syllable each, thus:—

> 'Hic in tumulo iac*it*—Pori*us*
> Homo Christian*us* fu*it*.'

One may compare with it the first two lines of one of the 9th century triplets already cited:—

> 'Gur dicones remed*aut*—elbid
> Anguorit anguor*aut*.'

Or take those of the one previously cited from the same manuscript:—

> 'Niguorcosam nemheun*aur*—henoid
> Mitelu nit gurm*aur*.'

The metre is much the same in the three instances, but neither *elbid* nor *henoid* has an assonance in the next line, which is the case, however, with Pori*us* and Christian*us*. This may be a mere accident, but it is to be noticed that it sometimes occurs in Welsh triplets, as for example in the one last quoted from the *Black Book*:—

> 'Mi awum lle llas milvir—pride*in*.
> or duÿre*in* ir goglet.'

Or take the following from the *Red Book*, as an instance where there is also rhyme:—

> 'Iluest gatwallawn ar ffynn*awn*—uet*wyr*.
> rac mil*wyr* magei d*awn*.'

It has been rendered thus [1] :—

> *Cadwallawn encamped by the well*
> *Of Bedwyr; before soldiers he cherished virtue.*

We abstain from any remarks on the nature of such a metre as that of the Porius epitaph or the possibility of its being derived from a Latin origin. We are only concerned with it as a proof, that verse-making was practised in Wales at an early date, and as one of the metres used in the triplet. With regard to the triplet generally, the sum and substance of what need here be said is, that it was employed for lyric poetry and that as such it might be introduced at will into epic story.

The kind of lyric verse which was popular among the Welsh and woven into their oldest stories has now been sufficiently illustrated, and we only wish to call attention to one species of verse which cannot be shown to have ever been a special favourite with them, to wit, that which consists of rhyming couplets of eight syllables, like the *lais bretons* of old French literature. The reverse would seem to have been the case among the Bretons, since the greater portion of the popular poetry of Brittany, in such collections as that published by M. Luzel in 1868, turns out to be in that very metre. It may be readily granted, that some allowance has to be made for a possible tendency in Brittany to imitate the poetry of the Normans or the French, but even then a residuum of proof seems to remain, making for the theory championed by Foerster and Zimmer. In favour likewise of the latter's conjecture, that the Celtic exponent of the heroic was rather

---

[1] *Red Book*, column 1043 : it is to be found in Skene's vol. ii, p. 278, and the above translation is in his vol. i, p. 434.

the epic story than the epic poem, may be mentioned the rôle assigned more than once to Gwydion in the Mabinogi of Mâth. Thus he undertakes to go as a bard at the head of a dozen bardic subordinates on a difficult mission to the court of Pryderi, king of Dyved. The first evening after their arrival, Gwydion is placed to sit by the king, and when they had done eating the following conversation takes place between them [1] :—

'Well,' said Pryderi, 'we should be glad to have a *kyvarwyðyt* from some of those young men.'

'It is our custom, Lord,' said Gwydion, 'the first night one comes to a great man's house, for the chief professional to tell—I will tell a *kyvarwyðyt* with pleasure.'

The story then proceeds thus :—'Now Gwydion was the best *kyvarwyð* in the world, and that night he entertained the court with amusing conversations and *kyvarwyðyt*, in such a way that he was admired of all at the court, and that Pryderi found it entertaining to converse with him.' On another occasion [2] he and Ꟙeu, in the guise of bards from Glamorgan, visit Arianrhod daughter of Dôn, at her court in Arvon, and then we are told that she conversed with Gwydion concerning news and *kyvarwyðyt*. In both instances *kyvarwyðyt* means history or story—it would be useless to insist on the distinction—and a *kyvarwyð* was a person skilled in relating such *kyvarwyðyt*. But it is to be noticed chiefly that not one of the words used, noun or verb, allows us to suppose that Gwydion sang in any sense of the term: his eloquence took the form of

---

[1] *R. B. Mab.* p. 61 ; Guest, iii. 220.

[2] *R. B. Mab.* p. 72 ; Guest, iii. 237, where *chwedleu*, 'news,' is rendered 'tales,' but it refers doubtless to the news which Arianrhod expected from Gwydion concerning the country he was supposed to come from : compare the term *chwedleu porth*, 'news from the gate,' for which it was usual to ask the porter of a castle whenever he made his appearance in the hall.

prose. The Mabinogion are contained in manuscripts only of the 13th and the 14th century, but they show indications of being copied from originals belonging to the 12th: we have no evidence to enable us to go further back, though it may be surmised that the state of society they represent must have existed considerably earlier. Be that as it may, the Mabinogion, such as they are, place before us a stage of Welsh culture where the chief bardic professional, one who associated with princes on terms of equality, would not think it beneath him to play the part of a story-teller. This harmonizes, to say the least of it, with the importance which we suppose to have belonged to epic story among the Celts from early times.

Putting aside the questions of the form of ancient Celtic story and of the channels through which it reached the Normans and the French, we may perhaps be excused a word or two as to the important rôle it played in the world of letters, both on the Continent and in Great Britain. The 12th century author of the *Chanson des Saxons*[1] has, at the opening of that poem, left on record his deliberate opinion, that for the men of genius of his time there were but three themes from which to choose, France, Brittany, and imperial Rome :—

> ' Ne sont que .iij. matieres a nul home entendant,
> De France et de Bretaigne et de Rome la grant.'

To this position, given in the French world of letters to the Celtic theme, must be added the hearty reception so readily accorded to the *Matière de Bretagne* in Germany and elsewhere outside France ; and when

---

[1] Published by Francisque Michel (Paris, 1839), and ascribed by him to Jean Bodel as its author; but this has since then been contested, as for instance by M. Raynaud in the *Romania*, ix. 218.

we turn to our own country, the case is even more
striking. The literature of the English before the
Norman Conquest is fairly well known. They had, for
instance, the great epic of Beowulf, and, as indicated by
the fragments extant, an epic on the battle of Finnes-
burh, and another on the death of Bryhtnoth, together
with epics of an ecclesiastic and biblical nature; also,
shorter poems about the battles of Brunanburh and
Maldon; while under the head of lyric poetry, of which
they had various kinds, one may mention the Traveller's
Song.

But what was the influence of these and the other
literary treasures of earlier English on the literature
after the Conquest? It was nil, or the next thing
to nil. For the English literature of the Middle Ages
the Beowulf Epic was practically as dead as the Hep-
tarchy for the purposes of modern politics. In fact, it
remained for a comparatively recent generation to discover the Beowulf and brush away from the forgotten
features of that poem the accumulated dust of ages.
To our thinking, this diverting of the stream of English
letters by the Conquest so that it never flowed again in
the old channels, is a clear proof of the thoroughness
with which English culture was extinguished by the
Normans.

The latter, however, do not appear as men who
themselves introduced anything that could be fixed
upon as very distinctly Norse or Teutonic in the
literary sense: rather may they be regarded as Gallic
Celts, excepting of course the Breton auxiliaries who
helped to fight their battles: these were Celts of
Celtic blood derived from Brythonic ancestry.

English literature, subsequent to the Conquest, resolves itself, roughly speaking, into four principal cycles

or groups, consisting of Dares Phrygius' tale of Troy, the sagas concerning Alexander the Great, and those that gathered round Charlemagne and his Peers: these three groups were importations from the Continent. The fourth group was Celtic, that is in this instance Breton and British, as it comprised the Arthurian romances and Geoffrey of Monmouth's writings. The influence of this last group was far more powerful and widespread in England than that of any one of the others: nay, we should probably not err in saying that it outweighed in importance the other three put together.

There was also, it is needless to say, a variety of biblical and religious literature, but even here the Celt came in, bringing with him the Enchantments of Britain and the inebriating odours of the Holy Grail. Nor is this all, for the Celtic strain in English literature has since the Middle Ages been greatly reinforced from time to time by the genius of such men as Shakspear and Spenser, Tennyson and Swinburne. Whatever, then, may be said of the pedigree of the English people, the pedigree of English literature is well established: Teutonic it cannot be to any great extent, whereas we have seen how largely it must be Celtic. Any attempt, therefore, to throw light on the genesis and history of the Arthurian legend may be expected to appeal not only to those who have an interest in Celtic, but also to some whose interest clings chiefly to the English language and the grand literature which is the reflection of her fairest features.

ADDITIONS AND CORRECTIONS.

—◆—

P. 11. The eponymus of Lothian was more probably ILeuđun, whence the territorial name was in Welsh ILeuđuniawn, which was sooner or later reduced to *Lothian* : see Mr. Phillimore's note in the *Cymmrodor*, xi. 51.

P. 22. In the story of Gereint and Enid (*R. B. Mab.* pp. 261, 286, 7 ; Guest, ii. 92, 129) Arthur's head physician is called Morgant Tut, and Prof. Zimmer, in a communication published by Foerster in the introduction to his edition of Erec (pp. xxvii-xxxi), makes the suggestion that the person originally meant was no other than Morgan la Fée, with a change of sex occasioned by the ignorance of the Welsh story-teller, a view which we are inclined to accept. Now *Morgan* is a man's name in Welsh, and it has passed through the stages *Morcant* and *Morgant* ; but Lady Charlotte Guest, in her English translation, has naturally chosen the modern forms *Morgan Tud*. Dr. Zimmer takes this and states that in French it would mean *Morgan le pays*, which we do not quite understand. Had he looked, however, at the original, he would have there twice found *Morgant Tut*, which we should now regard rather as representing an older and more correct spelling *Morgant Hut*, of exactly the same pronunciation. *Hut*, now *hûd*, means illusion or enchantment ; but there must have been a *hud* also meaning one who practised illusion or enchantment, an elf or fairy. For Gwyn ab Nûđ, in the dialogue so often quoted already, is made to say of himself (Evans' *Aut. Fac. of the Black Book*, p. 49 b):—

> 'Hud im gelwire. guin mab nud.'
> *Fairy am I called, Gwyn son of Nûđ.*

Thus *Morgant Tut*, as an incorrect spelling of *Morgant Hut*, meant 'Morgan, the elf or the fairy,' not 'Morgan le pays.'

P. 38. Whatever the origin of the name *Medrawt* or *Medrod* may be, the Breton and Cornish forms involve a difficulty which should have been noticed. The Cornish one appears early as *Modred* (*Revue Celtique*, i. 335), apparently under the influence of such English names as Ælfred and Æthelred. Otherwise it must have followed suit with the old Breton form, which was *Modrot*. The Welsh forms *Medrawt* and *Medrod* point to an earlier stage, Mĕdrōt or Mĕdrāt; but Mĕdrōt will explain the Breton form too, if only we suppose its second vowel to have attracted its first to its own sound. Be that as it may, Dr. Zimmer's explanation in the *Zeit. f. fr. Sprache und Lit.* xii. 254 is of no avail: he invokes the analogy of old Breton *Funton* (from the Latin *fontana*) without noticing whither it leads. For *fontana* is in Welsh *ffynnhon* or *ffynnon* 'a well,' whereas the other word does not become *Mydrod*, but obstinately remains *Medrod*.

P. 111. In his paper 'On the Linguistic Value of the Irish Annals,' read before the (London) Philological Society, June 6th, 1890, Dr. Whitley Stokes (p. 8) derives *Fomoir* from the same origin as the *mare* of the English night*mare*; but when he suggests a similar etymology for Mórrígan or Mórrígu, we hesitate to follow without further light on the phonological changes implied.

Pp. 113, 121. The evidence for the blackness of the face of Forgall is removed by Dr. K. Meyer in the *Revue Celtique*, xi. 435.

Pp. 116, 302, 325. References to revolving castles are by no means very scarce, but we would call attention to one, which has, so far as we know, been overlooked. We allude to a passage in *Fled Bricrend* in the Irish manuscript of the *Book of the Dun*, fol. 111ᵃ, which Windisch (*Irische Texte*, p. 295, also Glossary, s. v. *cáinim* and *demithir*) has not made out. It reads in the facsimile—*Cipé aird do airdib indomain tra imbeth cu rui docháineth for achatraig cachnaidchi combo demithir brôin mulind connafogbaithe addorus dogrés iar fuiniud ngrene.* The chief emendation required is to make *demithir* into *déinithir*, and the passage then will read : 'Whatever airt of the airts of the world Cúroi might be in, he was wont to sing a charm on his city every night, with the result that it would be swifter than a millstone, so that its door might never be found after sunset.' This is corroborated by the other manuscript used by Windisch, so far as we can understand it.

P. 132. The substance of Mr. Phillimore's communication may now be read in the *Cymmrodor*, xi. 46. Dr. Zimmer, in the *Gött.*

g. Anz. p. 527, wants to make *Karadigan* into *Kaeragned*, and to treat that as standing for *Oppidum Montis Agned*; but that seems to us rather a desperate suggestion for which there is no very urgent need.

P. 134.   Owing to an oversight, the Romance of *Durmart* has been wrongly ascribed to Chrétien.   On the question of its authorship and composition see Stengel's edition, pp. 500-18.

Pp. 150, 328.   The original of the name which variously appears as *Shalott, Escalot, Astolat,* and other forms, was probably *Alclut,* the old Welsh name of the Rock of Dumbarton in the Clyde.   It is alluded to in the *Vita Merlini* of Geoffrey, edited for the Roxburghe Club from the Cottonian MS. Vesp. E. iv. See lines 612, 3, which run as follows :—

> 'Corruet urbs Acelud, nec eam reparabit in ævum
> Rex aliquis, donec subdatur Scottus apello.'

One of the other readings of *Acelud,* as we learn from the editor's note, is *ascelud.*

P. 157.   *Efnys* is probably the same word which has been made into *enfys* 'rainbow,' and in that case *efnys afon* might be translated 'the hateful or hostile river.'   The word would seem to be related to *naws* 'disposition or temperament,' in the same way as gwrth*n*ysig 'refractory, of a perverse disposition,' and from it is derived *Nyssien*; also *Evnyssien* (p. 250) borne by the evil genius of Brân's household in the Mabinogi of Branwen.   It would thus appear that *enfys* for rainbow stands for some longer name such as *efnys afon,* and that it referred to some superstition which treated the rainbow as an object of dread.

P. 168.   There is no occasion to postulate *Gwalch-gwyn* or *Gwalch-hevin,* as Dr. Zimmer has hit on a better explanation when he supposes the second syllable of *Gauvain* indebted for its form to the association of the name with that of *Yvain.*

Ib.   As to the name Gahariet, we may remark that the Huth *Merlin* gives Gauvain two brothers, called respectively *Gahariès* and *Guerrehès,* and they appear in Malory as *Gareth* and *Gaherys.*   In point of fact, however, they seem to be variants of a single name best represented by *Gaharies* in the nominative and *Gahariet* in the other cases.   Now *Gahariet* admits of being traced back through easy stages of misreading or miscopying to Galiauet, (which must be a form of *Gwalchavet* or *Gwalchaved*), namely, by reading *li* into *h,* a mistake very easily committed in the manuscripts (compare *Houel* and *Lionel*), and *u* into *n* and then into *r* or *ri.*   The identification here suggested leads up to questions which space does not permit us to pursue at this stage. As to the elision of the Brythonic guttural spirant, a similar treatment has been detected by Zimmer (*Gött. g. Anz.* p. 797) in the case of *Guigemar* for *Guihomarc[h]us*, to which may be added *Rigomer* as the equivalent of the Welsh name *Rhygyvarch*.

P. 172. Since writing the words relating to the spelling of the name *Caratacus*, we have had the good fortune to read the genitive *Carataci* on an ancient inscribed stone among the hills of Exmoor in west Somerset. A notice of it is to appear in the *Archæologia Cambrensis*.

P. 184. Our attention has been called by Mr. Phillimore to the fact that Conchobar mac Nessa is mentioned in the story of Kulhwch and Olwen under the name Cnychὸr mab Nes, in company with other Irish heroes: see *R. B. Mab.* p. 106, and Guest, ii. 259, where he is made into 'Crychwr, the son of Nes,' but not wholly without excuse.

P. 256. Uthr Ben singing his own elegy has a deliberate air about it, which seems to suggest that it was preparatory to some scene like that of the beheading of Brân at his own request.

P. 261. Is it possible that *Dyvnwal Moelmud* is merely the Welsh form given to some such an Irish name as Domnall *mael Muaid?* Compare *Maelmuaid* in the very common Irish name *Ua Maelmhuaidh*, Anglicized *O'Molloy*.

P. 269. In support of the identification of Gwales with Gresholm, Mr. Phillimore has kindly called our attention to an excellent authority dating from 1602, namely George Owen's *History of Pembrokeshire*, as published in the *Cambrian Register* for 1796. See more especially ii. 129, where one reads:—'Far off in the sea standeth the iland Gresholme, soe called of Mr. Saxton, but of the neighbours, Walleyes, eight miles from the maine, and for the remotenes thereof, and smalle profit it yeeldeth, seldom frequented.'

P. 273. Can the name *Mesior* of Peleur have anything to do with the *mwys* (p. 313) in one of the late Latin or Romance forms of that word? There was, according to Ducange, a *mensarius*, 'qui *mensam* escariam curabat.'

P. 283. The form *Twryf-vliant* was in fact simplified on Welsh ground; for we find that Tὸr Bliant is the form actually occurring in the story of Kulhwch and Olwen, as given in the *White Book* (Hengwrt MS. 4), col. 324.

Ib. *Dear* and *Dearwya*, it should have been specified, are based only on the analogy of similar words: witness the compound *gor-dear* in the Taliessin verses cited on p. 242 above.

P. 298. It is to be observed that the *ι* mentioned in note 1 is in the manuscripts much more like the third limb of an *m* than we have been able to represent it in type. The same remark applies to it as compared with an *i*, as in the case of *Garlot* in the note on p. 323.

P. 330. The *Erec* has since been published by Wendelin Foerster under the title of *Erec und Enide von Christian von Troyes*, and forms vol. iii. of the series of *Christian von Troyes Sämtliche Werke* (Niemeyer, Halle, 1890): the lines cited occur at p. 72.

P. 335. Thanks to the kindness of a friend at the Bodleian Library, we have been enabled to trace the verses cited by Usher to a poem called *Gesta Regum Britanniæ*, printed for the Cambrian Archæological Association as the extra volume of the *Archæologia Cambrensis* for 1862, and edited by Francisque Michel, who considers the author to be unknown. The lines quoted begin on p. 153.

P. 337. As to the dark divinity of Beli, one may consult a note by Mr. Phillimore in the *Cymmrodor*, xi. 53, where he mentions a *Kair belli* on which John of Cornwall touches in connection with another description of it, namely, as *Fatale Castrum*: the passage will be found published by Stokes in the *Revue Celtique*, iii. 86, with other curious notes relating to Cornwall.

P. 347. We are by no means certain that the name *Sarras* may not likewise be a form of the Welsh *Gwanas*, more distorted than in the case of *Ganys*. The *rr* cannot create any difficulty, and it is frequently far from easy to distinguish between small *s* and *g* in our manuscripts. Be that as it may, we here append an attempt to translate the verses alluded to in the text as referring to Gwanas. They are so obscure, however, that we only do it in the hope of obtaining help from others to make out the sense. The following is the reading of Evans' *Aut. Facsimile*, p. 33 [b], except the —, which we insert :—

> ' Bet gurgi gvẏchit a guindodit—lev.
>   a bet llaur llu ouit.
>   ẏg guarthaw guanas guẏr ẏssit.'

> *The grave of Gwrgi, lion of Gwyneď's braves,*
>   *The grave of lLawr, leader of hosts :*
> *On Gwanas' top in Gwyr are they.*

> ' E beteu hir ẏg guanas
>   nẏ chauas ae dioes.
>   pvẏ vẏnt vẏ pvẏ eu neges.'

The long graves in Gwanas—
He who —— them has not found,
Whose they are, what their business.

' Teulu oeth ac anoeth—a dẏuu
ẏ/noeth ẏeu gur ẏeu guas.
ae ceisso vẏ clated guanas.'

Oeth's are they and Anoeth's Household's, that came
There younger men, younger youths :
Whoso seeks them should Gwanas dig.

In spite of the uncertainty attaching to the interpretation of
these verses, it is clear that Gwanas was one of the most remarkable burial-places known to Welsh tradition. On the other hand,
the importance of Sarras is very manifest in the pages of
Malory, who speaks of it as the City of Sarras possessed of a
' spyrytual place,' wherein were buried Galahad, together with
Perceval and his sister: see xvii. 11, 20-23. It appears as
the Spiritual City in Tennyson's *Holy Grail*, where he makes
Perceval say :—

' Then in a moment when they blazed again
Opening, I saw the least of little stars
Down on the waste, and straight beyond the star
I saw the spiritual city and all her spires
And gateways in a glory like one pearl—
No larger, tho' the goal of all the saints—
Strike from the sea ; and from the star there shot
A rose-red sparkle to the city, and there
Dwelt, and I knew it was the Holy Grail,
Which never eyes on earth again shall see.'

INDEX.

— ✦✦ —

THE END.

SELECT LIST OF STANDARD WORKS

PRINTED AT

The Clarendon Press, Oxford.

———◆◆———

———◆◆———

1. DICTIONARIES.

A New English Dictionary on Historical Principles, founded mainly on the materials collected by the Philological Society. Imperial 4to. In Parts, price 12s. 6d. each.

    Vol. I (**A** and **B**), half morocco, 2l. 12s. 6d.

    Part IV, Section 2, **C—CASS**, beginning Vol. II, price 5s.

    Part V, **CAST—CLIVY**, price 12s. 6d.

      Edited by James A. H. Murray, LL.D.

    Vol. III (**E**, **F**, and **G**), Part I, edited by Henry Bradley. *In the Press.*

An Etymological Dictionary of the English Language, arranged on an Historical Basis. By W. W. Skeat, Litt. D. *Second Edition.* 4to. 2l. 4s.

A Middle-English Dictionary, containing Words used by English Writers from the Twelfth to the Fifteenth Century. By Francis Henry Stratmann. A new edition, re-arranged, revised, and enlarged by Henry Bradley. 4to, half-bound, 1l. 11s. 6d.

An Anglo-Saxon Dictionary, based on the MS. collections of the late Joseph Bosworth, D.D. Edited and enlarged by Prof. T. N. Toller, M.A., Owens College, Manchester. Parts I–III. A–SAR. 4to, stiff covers. 15s. each. Part IV (completing the Work) *in the Press.*

An Icelandic-English Dictionary, based on the MS. collections of the late Richard Cleasby. Enlarged and completed by G. Vigfússon, M.A. With an Introduction, and Life of Richard Cleasby, by G. Webbe Dasent, D.C.L. 4to. 3l. 7s.

A Greek-English Lexicon, by H. G. Liddell, D.D., and Robert Scott, D.D. *Seventh Edition, Revised and Augmented throughout.* 4to, 1l. 16s.

Oxford: Clarendon Press. London: HENRY FROWDE, Amen Corner, E.C.

An Intermediate Greek-English Lexicon, abridged from the above. Small 4to. 12s. 6d.

A Latin Dictionary, founded on Andrews' edition of Freund's Latin Dictionary, revised, enlarged, and in great part rewritten by Charlton T. Lewis, Ph.D., and Charles Short, LL.D. 4to. 1l. 5s.

A School Latin Dictionary. By Charlton T. Lewis, Ph.D. Small 4to. 18s.

A Sanskrit-English Dictionary. Etymologically and Philologically arranged, with special reference to Greek, Latin, German, Anglo-Saxon, English, and other cognate Indo-European Languages. By Sir M. Monier-Williams, D.C.L. 4to. 4l. 14s. 6d.

Thesaurus Syriacus : collegerunt Quatremère, Bernstein, Lorsbach, Arnoldi, Agrell, Field, Roediger : edidit R. Payne Smith, S.T.P. Vol. I, containing Fasc. I-V, sm. fol. 5l. 5s.

    Fasc. VI. 1l. 1s.   Fasc. VII. 1l. 11s. 6d.   Fasc. VIII. 1l. 16s.

---

2. LAW.

Anson. *Principles of the English Law of Contract, and of Agency in its Relation to Contract.* By Sir W. R. Anson, D.C.L. *Fifth Edition.* 8vo. 10s. 6d.

—— *Law and Custom of the Constitution.* Part I. Parliament. 8vo. 10s. 6d.

Bentham. *An Introduction to the Principles of Morals and Legislation.* By Jeremy Bentham. Crown 8vo. 6s. 6d.

Digby. *An Introduction to the History of the Law of Real Property.* By Kenelm E. Digby, M.A. *Third Edition.* 8vo. 10s. 6d.

Grueber. *Lex Aquilia.* The Roman Law of Damage to Property : being a Commentary on the Title of the Digest 'Ad Legem Aquiliam' (ix. 2). With an Introduction to the Study of the Corpus Iuris Civilis. By Erwin Grueber, Dr. Jur., M.A. 8vo. 10s. 6d.

Hall. *International Law.* By W. E. Hall, M.A. *Third Edition.* 8vo. 22s. 6d.

Holland. *Elements of Jurisprudence.* By T. E. Holland, D.C.L. *Fifth Edition.* 8vo. 10s. 6d.

—— *The European Concert in the Eastern Question ;* a Collection of Treaties and other Public Acts. Edited, with Introductions and Notes, by T. E. Holland, D.C.L. 8vo. 12s. 6d.

Holland. *Gentilis, Alberici, De Iure Belli Libri Tres.* Edidit T. E. Holland, I.C.D. Small 4to. half morocco, 21s.

Holland. *The Institutes of Justinian,* edited as a recension of the Institutes of Gaius, by T. E. Holland, D.C.L. *Second Edition.* Extra fcap. 8vo. 5s.

Holland and Shadwell. *Select Titles from the Digest of Justinian.* By T. E. Holland, D.C.L., and C. L. Shadwell, B.C.L. 8vo. 14*s.*

Also sold in Parts, in paper covers, as follows :—

    Part I. Introductory Titles. 2*s*.6*d*.

    Part II. Family Law. 1*s*.

    Part III. Property Law. 2*s*. 6*d*.

    Part IV. Law of Obligations (No. 1). 3*s*. 6*d*.

    Part IV. Law of Obligations (No. 2). 4*s*. 6*d*.

Markby. *Elements of Law considered with reference to Principles of General Jurisprudence.* By Sir William Markby, D.C.L. *Fourth Edition.* 8vo. 12*s*. 6*d*.

Moyle. *Imperatoris Iustiniani Institutionum Libri Quattuor;* with Introductions, Commentary, Excursus and Translation. By J. B. Moyle, D.C.L. *Second Edition.* 2 vols. 8vo. Vol. I. 16*s*. Vol. II. 6*s*.

Pollock and Wright. *An Essay on Possession in the Common Law.* By Sir F. Pollock, M.A., and R. S. Wright, B.C.L. 8vo. 8*s*. 6*d*.

Poste. *Gaii Institutionum Juris Civilis Commentarii Quattuor;* or, Elements of Roman Law by Gaius. With a Translation and Commentary by Edward Poste, M.A. *Third Edition.* 8vo. 18*s*.

Raleigh. *An Outline of the Law of Property.* By Thos. Raleigh, M.A. 8vo. 7*s*. 6*d*.

Stokes. *The Anglo-Indian Codes.* By Whitley Stokes, LL.D.

    Vol. I. Substantive Law. 8vo. 30*s*.

    Vol. II. Adjective Law. 8vo. 35*s*.

    A Supplement to the above, 1887–1888. Stiff covers, 2*s*. 6*d*.

Twiss. *The Law of Nations considered as Independent Political Communities.* By Sir Travers Twiss, D.C.L.

    Part I. On the Rights and Duties of Nations in time of Peace. New Edition. 8vo. 15*s*.

    Part II. On the Rights and Duties of Nations in time of War. Second Edition. 8vo. 21*s*.

---

3. HISTORY, BIOGRAPHY, ETC.

Baker's Chronicle. *Chronicon Galfridi le Baker de Swynebroke.* Edited with Notes by Edward Maunde Thompson, Hon. LL.D. St. Andrews ; Hon. D.C.L. Durham ; F.S.A. ; Principal Librarian of the British Museum. Small 4to, stiff covers, 18*s*. ; cloth, gilt top, 21*s*.

Bentham. *A Fragment on Government.* By Jeremy Bentham.

Edited with an Introduction by F. C. Montague, M.A. 8vo, 7*s*. 6*d*.

Bluntschli. *The Theory of the State.* By J. K. Bluntschli. Translated from the Sixth German Edition. 8vo, half bound, 12*s*. 6*d*.

Boswell's *Life of Samuel Johnson, LL.D.* Edited by G. Birkbeck Hill, D.C.L. In six volumes, medium 8vo. With Portraits and Facsimiles. Half bound, 3*l*. 3*s*.

Calendar *of the Clarendon* State Papers, preserved in the Bodleian Library. In three volumes. 1869-76.

Vol. I. From 1523 to January 1649. 8vo. 18s.

Vol. II. From 1649 to 1654. 16s.

Vol. III. From 1655 to 1657. 14s.

Calendar *of Charters and Rolls* preserved in the Bodleian Library. 8vo. 1l. 11s. 6d.

Carte's *Life of James Duke of Ormond.* 6 vols. 8vo. 1l. 5s.

Clarendon's *History of the Rebellion and Civil Wars in England.* Re-edited from a fresh collation of the original MS. in the Bodleian Library, with marginal dates and occasional notes, by W. Dunn Macray, M.A., F.S.A. 6 vols. Crown 8vo. 2l. 5s.

—— *History of the Rebellion and Civil Wars in England.* To which are subjoined the Notes of Bishop Warburton. 7 vols. medium 8vo. 2l. 10s.

—— *History of the Rebellion and Civil Wars in England.* Also his Life, written by himself, in which is included a Continuation of his History of the Grand Rebellion. Royal 8vo. 1l. 2s.

—— *Life, including a Continuation of his History.* 2 vols. medium 8vo. 1l. 2s.

Earle. *Handbook to the Land-Charters, and other Saxonic Documents.* By John Earle, M.A., Professor of Anglo-Saxon in the University of Oxford. Crown 8vo. 16s.

Finlay. *A History of Greece from its Conquest by the Romans to the present time,* B. C. 146 to A. D. 1864. By George Finlay, LL.D. A new Edition, revised throughout, and in part re-written, with considerable additions, by the Author, and edited by H. F. Tozer, M.A. 7 vols. 8vo. 3l. 10s.

Fortescue. *The Governance of England :* otherwise called The Difference between an Absolute and a Limited Monarchy. By Sir John Fortescue, Kt. A Revised Text. Edited, Notes, with Introduction, etc., by Charles Plummer, M.A. 8vo, half bound, 12s. 6d.

Freeman. *History of the Norman Conquest of England; its Causes and Results.* By E. A. Freeman, D.C.L. In Six Volumes. 8vo. 5l. 9s. 6d.

—— *The Reign of William Rufus and the Accession of Henry the First.* 2 vols. 8vo. 1l. 16s.

—— *A Short History of the Norman Conquest of England.* Second Edition. Extra fcap. 8vo. 2s. 6d.

Gardiner. *The Constitutional Documents of the Puritan Revolution,* 1628-1660. Selected and Edited by Samuel Rawson Gardiner, M.A. Crown 8vo. 9s.

Gascoigne's *Theological Dictionary* ('*Liber Veritatum*') : Selected Passages, illustrating the Condition of Church and State, 1403-1458. With an Introduction by James E. Thorold Rogers, M.A. 4to, 10s. 6d.

George. *Genealogical Tables illustrative of Modern History.* By H. B. George, M.A. *Third Edition.* Small 4to. 12s.

Greswell. *History of the* Dominion of Canada. By W. PARR GRESWELL, M.A. Under the auspices of the Royal Colonial Institute. Crown 8vo. With Eleven Maps. 7s. 6d.

—— *Geography of the Do-* minion of Canada and Newfoundland. By the same Author. Crown 8vo. With Ten Maps. 6s.

Gross. *The Gild Merchant;* a Contribution to British Municipal History. By Charles Gross, PH.D. Instructor in History, Harvard University. 2 vols. 8vo. Half-bound, 24s.

Hodgkin. *Italy and her In-* vaders. With Plates and Maps. By T. Hodgkin, D.C.L. Vols. I–IV, A.D. 376–553. 8vo. 3l. 8s.

—— *The Dynasty of Theo-* dosius; or, Seventy Years' Struggle with the Barbarians. By the same Author. Crown 8vo. 6s.

Hume. *Letters of David Hume* to William Strahan. Edited with Notes, Index, etc., by G. Birkbeck Hill, D.C.L. 8vo. 12s. 6d.

Kitchin. *A History of France.* With Numerous Maps, Plans, and Tables. By G. W. Kitchin, D.D. In three Volumes. *Second Edition.* Crown 8vo, each 10s. 6d.

Vol. I. to 1453. Vol. II. 1453–1624. Vol. III. 1624–1793.

Luttrell's *(Narcissus) Diary.* A Brief Historical Relation of State Affairs, 1678–1714. 6 vols. 8vo. 1l. 4s.

Lucas. *Introduction to a* Historical Geography of the British Colonies. By C. P. Lucas, B.A. With Eight Maps. Crown 8vo. 4s. 6d.

Lucas. *Historical Geography* of the British Colonies:

Vol. I. The Mediterranean and Eastern Colonies (exclusive of India). With Eleven Maps. Crown 8vo. 5s.

Vol. II. The West Indian Colonies. With Twelve Maps. Crown 8vo. 7s. 6d.

Magna Carta, *a careful Re-* print. Edited by W. Stubbs, D.D., Bishop of Oxford. 4to, stitched, 1s.

Metcalfe. *Passio et Miracula* Beati Olaui. Edited from a Twelfth-Century MS. by F. Metcalfe, M.A. Small 4to. 6s.

Ranke. *A History of Eng-* land, principally in the Seventeenth Century. By L. von Ranke. Translated under the superintendence of G. W. Kitchin, D.D., and C. W. Boase, M.A. 6 vols. 8vo. 3l. 3s.

Rawlinson. *A Manual of* Ancient History. By George Rawlinson M.A. *Second Edition.* 8vo. 14s.

Ricardo. *Letters of David* Ricardo to T. R. Malthus (1810–1823). Edited by James Bonar, M.A. 8vo. 10s. 6d.

Rogers. *History of Agricul-* ture and Prices in England, A.D. 1259–1702. By James E. Thorold Rogers, M.A. 6 vols., 8vo. 7l. 2s.

—— *First Nine Years of the* Bank of England. 8vo. 8s. 6d.

—— *Protests of the Lords, in-* cluding those which have been expunged, from 1624 to 1874; with Historical Introductions. In three volumes. 8vo. 2l. 2s.

Smith's *Wealth of Nations.* With Notes, by J. E. Thorold Rogers, M.A. 2 vols. 8vo. 21s.

London: HENRY FROWDE, Amen Corner, E.C.

Sprigg's *England's Recovery;* being the History of the Army under Sir Thomas Fairfax. 8vo. 6s.

Stubbs. *Select Charters and other Illustrations of English Constitutional History, from the Earliest Times to the Reign of Edward I.* Arranged and edited by W. Stubbs, D.D., Lord Bishop of Oxford. *Fifth Edition.* Crown 8vo. 8s. 6d.

—— *The Constitutional History of England, in its Origin and Development. Library Edition.* 3 vols. Demy 8vo. 2l. 8s.

Also in 3 vols. crown 8vo. price 12s. each.

—— *Seventeen Lectures on the Study of Medieval and Modern History, delivered at Oxford* 1867–1884. Crown 8vo. 8s. 6d.

Stubbs. *Registrum Sacrum Anglicanum.* An attempt to exhibit the course of Episcopal Succession in England. By W. Stubbs, D.D. Small 4to. 8s. 6d.

Wellesley. *A Selection from the Despatches, Treaties, and other Papers of the Marquess Wellesley, K.G., during his Government of India.* Edited by S. J. Owen, M.A. 8vo. 1l. 4s.

Wellington. *A Selection from the Despatches, Treaties, and other Papers relating to India of Field-Marshal the Duke of Wellington, K.G.* Edited by S. J. Owen, M.A. 8vo. 1l. 4s.

Whitelock's *Memorials of English Affairs from* 1625 *to* 1660. 4 vols. 8vo. 1l. 10s.

4. PHILOSOPHY, LOGIC, ETC.

Bacon. *The Essays.* With Introduction and Illustrative Notes. By S. H. REYNOLDS, M.A. 8vo. half bound. 12s. 6d.

—— *Novum Organum.* Edited, with Introduction, Notes, &c., by T. Fowler, D.D. *Second Edition.* 8vo. 15s.

—— *Novum Organum.* Edited, with English Notes, by G. W. Kitchin, D.D. 8vo. 9s. 6d.

—— *Novum Organum.* Translated by G. W. Kitchin, D.D. 8vo. 9s. 6d.

Berkeley. *The Works of George Berkeley, D.D., formerly Bishop of Cloyne; including many of his writings hitherto unpublished.* With Prefaces, Annotations, and an Account of his Life and Philosophy, by Alexander Campbell Fraser, LL.D. 4 vols. 8vo. 2l. 18s.

The Life, Letters, &c., separately, 16s.

Bosanquet. *Logic; or, the Morphology of Knowledge.* By B. Bosanquet, M.A. 8vo. 21s.

Butler's *Works, with Index to the Analogy.* 2 vols. 8vo. 11s.

Fowler. *The Elements of Deductive Logic, designed mainly for the use of Junior Students in the Universities.* By T. Fowler, D.D. *Ninth Edition,* with a Collection of Examples. Extra fcap. 8vo. 3s. 6d.

—— *The Elements of Inductive Logic, designed mainly for the use of Students in the Universities.* By the same Author. *Fifth Edition.* Extra fcap. 8vo. 6s.

Fowler. *The Principles of Morals.* (Introductory Chapters. By T. Fowler, D.D., and J. M. Wilson. B.D. 8vo, boards, 3s. 6d.

—— *The Principles of Morals.* Part II. By T. Fowler, D.D. 8vo. 10s. 6d.

Green. *Prolegomena to Ethics.* By T. H. Green. M.A. Edited by A. C. Bradley. M.A. 8vo. 12s. 6d.

Hegel. *The Logic of Hegel ;* translated from the Encyclopaedia of the Philosophical Sciences. With Prolegomena by William Wallace, M.A. 8vo. 14s.

Hume's *Treatise of Human Nature.* Edited, with Analytical Index, by L. A. Selby-Bigge, M.A. Crown 8vo. 9s.

Locke's *Conduct of the Understanding.* Edited by T. Fowler, D.D. *Third Edition.* Extra fcap. 8vo. 2s. 6d.

Lotze's *Logic,* in Three Books ; of Thought, of Investigation, and of Knowledge. English Translation ; Edited by B. Bosanquet, M.A. *Second Edition.* 2 vols. Cr. 8vo. 12s.

—— *Metaphysic,* in Three Books ; Ontology, Cosmology, and Psychology. English Translation ; Edited by B. Bosanquet, M.A. *Second Edition.* 2 vols. Cr. 8vo. 12s.

Martineau. *Types of Ethical Theory.* By James Martineau, D.D. *Third Edition.* 2 vols. Cr. 8vo. 15s.

—— *A Study of Religion :* its Sources and Contents. Second Edition. 2 vols. Cr. 8vo. 15s.

5. PHYSICAL SCIENCE.

Aplin. *The Birds of Oxfordshire.* By O. V. Aplin. 8vo. 10s. 6d.

Chambers. *A Handbook of Descriptive and Practical Astronomy.* By G. F. Chambers, F.R.A.S. *Fourth Edition,* in 3 vols. Demy 8vo.
- Vol. I. The Sun, Planets, and Comets. 21s.
- Vol. II. Instruments and Practical Astronomy. 21s.
- Vol. III. The Starry Heavens. 14s.

De Bary. *Comparative Anatomy of the Vegetative Organs of the Phanerogams and Ferns.* By Dr. A. De Bary. Translated and Annotated by F. O. Bower, M.A., F.L.S., and D. H. Scott, M.A., Ph.D., F.L.S. Royal 8vo, half morocco, 1l. 2s. 6d.

—— *Comparative Morphology and Biology of Fungi, Mycetozoa and Bacteria.* By Dr. A. De Bary. Translated by H. E. F. Garnsey, M.A. Revised by Isaac Bayley Balfour, M.A., M.D., F.R.S. Royal 8vo, half morocco, 1l. 2s. 6d.

De Bary. *Lectures on Bacteria.* By Dr. A. De Bary. *Second Improved Edition.* Translated by H. E. F. Garnsey, M.A. Revised by Isaac Bayley Balfour, M.A., M.D., F.R.S. Crown 8vo, 6s.

Fisher. *A Class Book of Elementary Chemistry.* By W. W. Fisher, M.A., F.C.S. Crown 8vo. 4s. 6d.

Goebel. *Outlines of Classification and Special Morphology of Plants.* A new Edition of Sachs' Text-Book of Botany, Book II. By Dr. K. Goebel. Translated by H. E. F. Garnsey, M.A. Revised by Isaac Bayley Balfour, M.A., M.D., F.R.S. Royal 8vo, half morocco, 1l. 1s.

Sachs. *Lectures on the Phy-siology of Plants.* By Julius von Sachs. Translated by H. Marshall Ward, M.A., F.L.S. Royal 8vo, half morocco, 1*l.* 11*s.* 6*d.*

—— *A History of Botany.* Translated by H. E. F. Garnsey, M.A. Edited by I. Bayley Balfour, M.A., M.D., F.R.S. Crown 8vo. 10*s.*

Solms-Laubach. *Introduction to Fossil Botany.* By Count H. von Solms-Laubach. Authorised English Translation, by H. E. F. Garnsey, M.A. Edited by Isaac Bayley Balfour, M.A., M.D., F.R.S. *In the Press.*

Annals of Botany. Edited by Isaac Bayley Balfour, M.A., M.D., F.R.S., Sydney H. Vines, D.Sc., F.R.S., and W. G. Farlow, M.D.

  Vol. I. Parts I–IV. Royal 8vo, half morocco, gilt top, 1*l.* 16*s.*
  Vol. II. Parts V–VIII. 2*l.* 2*s.*
  Vol. III. Part IX. 11*s.* 6*d.* ; X. 13*s.* 6*d.* ; XI. 18*s.* ; XII. *in the Press.*
  Vol. IV. Part XIII. 12*s.* 6*d.* ; XIV. 13*s.* 6*d.* ; XV. 10*s.* 6*d.* ; XVI. *in the Press.*
  Vol. V. Part XVII. 10*s.* 6*d.*

Biological Series. *(Translations of Foreign Biological Memoirs.)*

  I. *The Physiology of Nerve, of Muscle, and of the Electrical Organ.* Edited by J. Burdon-Sanderson, M.D., F.R.SS. L. & E. Medium 8vo. 1*l.* 1*s.*

  II. *be Anatomy of the Frog.* By Dr. Alexander Ecker, Professor in the University of Freiburg. Translated, with numerous Annotations and Additions, by G. Haslam, M.D. Med. 8vo, 21*s.*

  III. *Contributions to the History of the Physiology of the Nervous System.* By Professor Conrad Eckhard. Translated by Miss Edith Prance. *In Preparation.*

  IV. *Essays upon Heredity and Kindred Biological Problems.* By Dr. August Weismann. Translated and Edited by E. B. Poulton, M.A., Selmar Schönland, Ph.D., and Arthur E. Shipley, M.A. Medium 8vo, 16*s.*

Prestwich. *Geology, Chemical, Physical, and Stratigraphical.* By Joseph Prestwich, M.A., F.R.S. In two Volumes.

  Vol. I. Chemical and Physical. Royal 8vo. 1*l.* 5*s.*
  Vol. II. Stratigraphical and Physical. With a new Geological Map of Europe. Royal 8vo. 1*l.* 16*s.*
  New Geological Map of Europe. In case or on roller. 5*s.*

Rolleston and Jackson. *Forms of Animal Life.* A Manual of Comparative Anatomy, with descriptions of selected types. By George Rolleston, M.D., F.R.S. *Second Edition.* Revised and Enlarged by W. Hatchett Jackson, M.A. Medium 8vo. 1*l.* 16*s.*

Oxford
AT THE CLARENDON PRESS
LONDON : HENRY FROWDE
OXFORD UNIVERSITY PRESS WAREHOUSE, AMEN CORNER, E.C.

Printed in Great Britain
by Amazon

83446599R00244